Institutions and Policies of the European Community

Institutions and Policies of the European Community

Edited by
Juliet Lodge

St. Martin's Press, New York

All rights reserved. For information write:
St. Martin's Press, Inc., 175 Fifth Avenue, New York, N.Y. 10010
Printed in Great Britain
First Published in the United States of America in 1983

ISBN 0-312-41887-6

Library of Congress Cataloging in Publication Data

Institutions and Policies of the European Community.

   Includes Index.
   1. European Economic Community.   I. Lodge
Juliet.
HC241.2.15935   1982   341.24'22   81-23271
ISBN 0-312-41887-6   ACR2

To
Arthur and Lenore

Contents

PART III   EUROPEAN COMMUNITY EXTERNAL RELATIONS

Abbreviations

ACP	Africa, the Caribbean and the Pacific
ASEAN	Association of South East Asian Nations
BCC	Business Cooperation Centre
CAP	Common Agricultural Policy
CBI	Confederation of British Industry
CCP	Chinese Communist Party (Chapter 21)
CCP	Common Commercial Policy
CCR	Central Commission for the Navigation of the Rhine
CDU	Christlich-Demokratische Union
CEA	European Insurance Committee
CET	Common External Tariff
CFM	Conference of Foreign Ministers
CFP	Common Fisheries Policy
CIEC	Conference on International Economic Cooperation
CMEA	Council for Mutual Economic Assistance
COGECA	General Committee of Agricultural Cooperation in the EC
COMECON	Council for Mutual Economic Assistance
COMITEXTIL	Coordination Committee for the Textile Industries in the EC
COPA	Committee of Professional Agricultural Organizations in the EC
COREPER	Committee of Permanent Representatives
CSCE	Conference on Security and Cooperation in Europe
CSP	Confederation of Socialist Parties of the EC
CSU	Christlich-Soziale Union
CVP	Christelijke Volkspartij
DC	Democrazia Cristiana
DG	Directorate-General
DIFE	Defence of the Interests of France in Europe
DKP	Danmarks Kommunistiske Parti
EAGGF	European Agricultural Guidance and Guarantee Fund
EC	European Community
ECHR	European Convention on Human Rights
ECJ	European Court of Justice
ECOSOC	Economic and Social Council
ECSC	European Coal and Steel Community
ECU	European Currency Unit
EDC	European Defence Community
EDF	European Development Fund
EEC	European Economic Community
EFTA	European Free Trade Area
EIB	European Investment Bank
ELD	Federation of European Liberals and Democrats
EMS	European Monetary System

EMU	Economic and Monetary Union
EP	European Parliament
EPC	European Political Cooperation
EPP	European People's Party
ERDF	European Regional Development Fund
ESC	Economic and Social Committee of the EC
ESF	European Social Fund
ETUC	European Trade Union Confederation
EUA	European Unit of Account
EURATOM	European Atomic Energy Authority
FDP	Freie Demokratische Partei Deutschlands
FIRA	Foreign Investment Review Act
FRG	Federal Republic of Germany
GATT	General Agreement on Tariffs and Trade
GCECEE	Savings Bank Group of the EC
GDP	Gross Domestic Product
GNP	Gross National Product
GSP	Generalized System of Preferences
HA	High Authority (ECSC)
IAEA	International Atomic Energy Agency
IBRD	International Bank for Reconstruction and Development (World Bank)
ICES	International Council for the Exploration of the Seas
IEA	International Energy Agency
ILO	International Labour Organization
IMF	International Monetary Fund
JCC	Joint Cooperation Committee
LDC	Less Developed Country
MAFF	Ministry of Agriculture, Fisheries and Food
MEP	Member of the European Parliament
MFA	Multi-fibre Agreement
MP	Member of Parliament
MRC	Market Relations Committee
MRG	Mouvement des Radicaux de Gauche
MTN	Multilateral Trade Negotiation
NATO	North Atlantic Treaty Organization
NEAFC	North Atlantic Fisheries Commission
NIC	Newly Industrializing Country
NIEO	New International Economic Order
NTB	Non-tariff Barrier
OAS	Organization of American States
OAU	Organization of African Unity
ODA	Official Development Assistance
ODI	Overseas Development Institute
OECD	Organization for Economic Cooperation and Development
OEEC	Organization for European Economic Cooperation
OPEC	Organization of Petroleum Exporting Countries
PAC	Political Affairs Committee in the EP
PCF	Parti Communiste Français
PRL	Parti des Reformes et de la Liberté
PS	Parti Socialiste (France)

PS	Walloon Socialist Party (Belgium)
PSC	Parti Social Chrétien
PVV	Partij voor Vrijheid en Vooruitgang
RIA	Regional Impact Assessment
RPR	Rassemblement pour la République
SALT	Strategic Arms Limitation Talks
SAP	Social Action Programme
SF	Socialistisk Folkeparti
SGCI	Secrétariat Général du Comité Interministériel
SP	Flemish Socialist Party (Belgium)
SPD	Sozialdemokratische Partei Deutschlands
STABEX	System for stabilizing export earnings
TAC	Total Allowable Catch
TCG	Group for the Technical Coordination and Defence of Independent Groups and Members in the EP
The Nine	Members of the EC after the first enlargement (Six plus Denmark, Ireland and United Kingdom)
The Seven	Members of EFTA (Britain, Switzerland, Austria, Sweden, Denmark, Norway and Portugal)
The Six	Members of the EC before enlargement (France, Italy, FRG, Belgium, Netherlands and Luxembourg)
The Ten	Members of the EC after the second enlargement (Nine plus Greece)
u.a.	unit of account
UK	United Kingdom
UN	United Nations
UNCLOS	United Nations Conference on the Law of the Sea
UNCTAD	United Nations Conference on Trade and Development
UNEP	United Nations Environment Programme
UNICE	Union of Industries in the EC
USA	United States of America
USSR	Union of Soviet Socialist Republics
VAT	Value Added Tax
VER	Voluntary Export Restraint
VS	Venstre Socialisterne
WEU	Western European Union

Introduction

JULIET LODGE

It often seems in Britain that people are exasperated with the European Community (EC). Questions are asked constantly about the EC's apparent failure to 'do something' about all manner of problems, many of which it could not address for want of political will on the part of national governments, for want of finance, and for want of the requisite authority. The EC is not omnicompetent. Nor is the much reviled EC Commission in a position to pass legislation to combat pressing problems. It may wish to see certain policies enacted. It may suggest that action be taken but its best intentions often fall foul of national politics. The Commission, like the EC generally, and increasingly the European Parliament (EP) are easy scapegoats on whom blame can be apportioned when 'things go wrong'. However, as should become apparent from this book, things in the EC are a good deal more complicated than they appear to be, and it is more often than not the national governments who prevent agreement or action on Commission proposals designed to make but a necessarily limited attempt to confront pressing problems. It is essential that, in seeking to understand how the EC works and what powers have been conferred on it by the treaties to carry out policies in a limited range of policy areas, the power of national governments to promote or frustrate agreement be realized. Moreover, it must be remembered that a Commission proposal is subjected to extensive and sometimes extremely lengthy scrutiny (occasionally lasting several years) before it is adopted by the EC Council of Ministers. In the intervening period, the constellation of political forces in individual national governments and national governing coalitions may have changed a number of times; and any intervening national level (general) elections are likely to have resulted in the deferral of a decision by the individual representatives to the Council of Ministers.

Furthermore, the EP is an institution whose limited powers have been commonly derided. Its ability to influence EC decision-making has been seen as negligible. However, since the EP's first direct election in 1979, it has been augmenting its substantive influence over EC decision-making and is agitating for the accretion of the powers that the Rome Treaty confers on it. In addition, the EP has launched a drive to reform the EC, both in terms of the policy areas it confronts and the distribution of power among the EC's various institutions. The aim is to create a European Union in which policy-makers are responsive to public needs and in which the institutions themselves are, therefore, capable of acting swiftly and effectively. In other words, the EC is an adaptable Community in which resistance to change emanates from national governments who, paradoxically, also want to see the EC's efficiency improved but who, in the name of preserving national sovereignty, are loathe to sanction the appropriate measures to fulfil such a goal. In their defence, it must be said that the notion of a European Union remains rather imprecise and that there remains widespread misunderstanding and confusion over what purpose lies behind European integration.

After the Second World War, a prime aim was clearly to intertwine West European economies in such a way as to make them interdependent and to make each country unable secretly to arm itself and wage war against one of its partners in the European Communities. At the same time, it was hoped that there would be economic prosperity and that the working and living conditions of people would improve appreciably. As should become apparent from the chapters in Part II of this book, this has not remained an altogether pious hope. But the economic recession of the last decade has made the attainment of such a goal elusive. Moreover, commitment to the principle of a common policy for a given area, no matter how high-minded the inspiration behind it, does not automatically ensure that any policy or, more accurately perhaps, any measures taken to further such a policy will result in an optimum policy which maximizes the common good. On the contrary, there are so many constraints—institutional, national, ideological, political, economic and social—that an optimum outcome is unlikely. Compromise is the order of the day, and compromise that, in the short term, may seem inimical to the common good.

Whereas the EC's jurisdiction over aspects of domestic policy is rather limited and whereas originally the EC was deliberately excluded from what were termed the 'high politics' of foreign affairs (being restricted instead to the 'low politics' of trade), increasingly security matters are being raised and action sought on issues formerly regarded as the preserve of foreign office diplomats. This eradication of the false distinction between and compartmentalization of what are clearly inseparable considerations in external relations poses acute difficulties for the EC's actors. This is because, if such issues are to be confronted effectively, the EC's institutions must be given the requisite authority *and also* be subject to effective political control. As shown in Part I of this book, this means that the EC's competence must be expanded. Inevitably, in turn, this means that more and more issues that were formerly the sole prerogative of national governments require at least discussion in the supranational arena: the aim being to promote at a minimum consultation and at maximum cooperation, and ultimately a common policy. However, there are manifold difficulties in this since any question of expanding the competence of EC institutions immediately revives the spectre of federalism. This is an extremely ill-understood concept but it is commonly taken to imply a severe curtailment of member states' autonomy and sovereignty. Witness, for example, in Britain the reiterated argument that by joining the EC and by staying in it, the powers and sovereignty of the Parliament of the United Kingdom (and notably the powers of the House of Commons) have been irremediably eroded. This is because much EC legislation is directly applicable and effective in every EC member state without further action by national parliaments. Yet, this is something that all member governments on acceding to the EC knew. Furthermore, these arguments, when viewed alongside the quest by the EP for greater powers, are seen as vindicating opposition to further European integration and European Union in order to safeguard national autonomy.

However, it is erroneous to believe that national parliaments' powers over EC matters are being cumulatively eroded. It is true that national parliaments, for the most part, have marginal and minimal influence over the content of EC draft legislation. It is equally true that the EP's powers are restricted. The battle for parliamentary control of the executive in the EC is one that has to be fought for vigorously since accession to the EC has meant a substantial increase in the power of national *governments*. Small wonder that national governments should fear majority voting *de rigueur* in the Council, and shy away from plans to promote

European Union along lines that would increase the EP's influence—something that connotes federalism and institutional reforms reducing national governments' autonomy and the Council of Ministers' lack of accountability. Moreover, as the national governments' activities within the European Council and Conference of Foreign Ministers (CFM) become increasingly institutionalized and part of the EC's decision-making procedures, the idea that the EC is nothing more than a trading bloc will be revealed for the illusion it always was. Only if one understands how the EC works, what it tries to do, why it fails and how it succeeds, can one hope to appraise it and possibly influence it. It is hoped that this book will make a small contribution towards developing knowledge and understanding about the EC.

The book has been written primarily with an undergraduate readership and the general public in mind. The aim is to provide an introduction to each of the topics covered, and hopefully to stimulate further research and inquiry. Part I examines decision-making and institutions in the EC. Part II considers a number of EC internal policies, such as the Common Agricultural Policy (CAP) and social policy. Part III is concerned with the EC in the international system and examines aspects of its external relations. Given the importance of the CAP and trade, sections of Part II and Part III should not be considered in isolation from one another. Space limitations make more detailed scrutiny of all EC policies and of the less influential —politically speaking—institutions impossible. Nevertheless, it is hoped that the book will interest also those who have some knowledge of the EC already. The authors of the individual chapters have not followed any common model, but as specialists in their respective areas have discussed those aspects of the topic they deem most vital to an appreciation of the issues raised. All contributors have tried to outline also the main features and developments of given policies or institutions and, where appropriate, to outline contemporary controversies.

PART I   DECISION-MAKING AND INSTITUTIONS IN THE EUROPEAN COMMUNITY

1   European Community Decision-Making: The National Dimension

JOHN FITZMAURICE

The aim of this chapter is to look at an aspect of the European Community's (EC) decision-making process which is often overlooked, or simply ignored. Mostly, the EC is regarded as a relatively closed political system in which decisions are taken. Naturally, there is an awareness that the Council of Ministers is a forum in which national interests are represented and have to be reconciled. Indeed, considerable attention has been paid to this aspect of the EC's institutional structure, with the concomitant demands for the correct application of majority voting in the Council.

However, most analysis is EC-centric; it concentrates on how the institutions of the EC operate; it concentrates on how member states' governments evolve their positions in the Council or how pressure groups influence these positions. These aspects are the subject of some of the other chapters in this book. Here, we shall, so to speak, attempt to look through the telescope from the other end. We shall look at how national politics affect the EC.

It is important to underline here that for governments there is no distinction between one type of 'politics', which is national politics, and another type which is EC politics. Governments simply see problems or issues which they wish to resolve in a particular way, having regard to their national interests and political ideology. For them there is only 'politics'. Certainly, the national forum, or the EC or wider international forums offer different instruments and impose different constraints, but are not sharply differentiated from each other. As a result, it is reasonable to expect the political considerations which impinge on national policy-making to impinge likewise upon EC decision-making, at least to a certain degree depending on the saliency of the issue.

We shall seek to argue that this is indeed the case, with the added complication that, although domestic political conflict may be attenuated in the EC, in the belief that—as in other international forums—such conflict weakens the national position, the EC's development into a hybrid political system has led to the break-down of this convention and the creation of new cleavages at the interface of the ten national political systems.

Given space limitations, our aim will be to awaken sensitivity to this theme and to illustrate it by setting the context and by some examples, rather than to provide exhaustive coverage. The approach is therefore eclectic, being that of an essay into the subject. The reader should be left with the sense of a different dimension, a different perspective on the EC's decision-making process.

The issues dealt with, by or in the EC framework differ significantly from the type of issues dealt with in traditional international organizations, in that they are matters of direct concern to citizens, groups of citizens, organized interest groups and companies. In short, just like domestic political issues, they are often questions of distribution between competing interests. The EC decision-making process, like the national decision-making processes, must then arbitrate between competing interests, as well as between the more obvious national interest conflicts, which are the stuff of press headlines. However, in many cases, the reality behind the concept of 'national interest' may be that of a sectoral interest.[1]

This characteristic of EC decision-making means that important political decisions, which would in any case be posed at the national level, also now have to be considered either almost exclusively at the EC-level (agricultural prices, for example) or at both levels. A considerable number of matters which have been considered on the national level and which involve conflicts of interest, or specific distribution problems, are now dealt with at least partially by the EC. A number of (certainly not limitative) examples can be cited such as agricultural prices, budget contributions, fisheries quotas, the responsibility of a producer for a defective product, and equal pay and equal treatment of women at work. All these issues have one point in common: they are of particular interest to a particular group *within* any given member state and may be opposed to the interests of another group within the *same* member state. In this way such issues are much closer to domestic policy-making even when treated at the EC-level than the issues dealt with by classic intergovernmental organizations. It is probably true therefore to say that the EC's decision-making procedures are a hybrid of domestic and classic intergovernmental-type procedures.[2] Not surprisingly, therefore, domestic politics in the member states have direct repercussions on the resolution (or non-resolution) of issues and on the functioning of the EC's institutions themselves.

Our concern here will be to look at examples of how the internal developments in the member states affect the efficacy of the EC's decision-making process. However, at the outset, one general point should be made which is often overlooked by observers of the EC's political scene. The EC's political system is in fact made up of ten individual political systems which interface in the EC institutions. This means that the whole system can only be as effective and stable as its weakest link. A serious political crisis in one member state, or prolonged electoral uncertainty, can block the EC mechanism as a whole. The cycles of crises, of weak governments and elections are not synchronized between the ten member states, which means that the periods of relative political calm and stability, in which all ten member governments are in a sufficiently strong position to make bold and perhaps unpopular decisions which the situation may require, are few and brief.

By way of example, it is worth looking at the record over the last three full years. Of the three years, only 1980 was relatively calm, with only one election (Federal Republic of Germany (FRG)), which did not result in any change of government. In 1979, there were four elections, of which two (United Kingdom and Luxembourg) led to changes of government. The year 1981 was a dramatic one, with elections in six of the ten member states, with the historic victories for the Socialists in France and Greece, and changes of coalition in Ireland and the Netherlands. There was no country which did not hold an election in this period. Only two Prime Ministers held office uninterrupted throughout the period (Mr Schmidt and Mr Jørgensen). If one were to look for a politically calm period, then the only possibility would be the early months of 1980, before the German election campaign got under way.

As for the EC's more long-term and ambitious goals which are defined by the summit conferences (known since 1974 as the European Councils), the same problems of continuity may be observed. Within two years of the 1972 'enlargement summit', at which a whole range of new EC policies were set out and the goal of 'European Union' declared,[3] not one of the prime actors (Pompidou,

Table 1.   Elections in the Ten 1979–81

	1979	1980	1981
Belgium			x
Denmark	x		x
France			x
FRG		x	
Greece			x
Ireland			x
Italy	x		
Luxembourg	x		
Netherlands			x
United Kingdom	x		

x indicates an election was held in the year in question.
Source: Keesing's Contemporary Archives, 1979–81.

Heath and Brandt) was in power and even most of the other leaders were no longer in office.

Another aspect which impinges closely on the EC is the structure and organization of national governments. In France, the constitutional structure and practice of the Fifth Republic ensure that the President of the Republic is directly involved in all major foreign policy and EC decisions. As a result, the foreign minister and other ministers may have little margin for manoeuvre, given that the final decision will lie with the President.[4] Over a year after the electoral victory of François Mitterrand on 10 May 1981, there has been no discernible change in this pattern; the regime is as presidential as it ever was.

In other countries, the realities of coalition politics or the role of parliament may impinge on the EC's decision-making process. Almost all governments in the EC other than the British Government are coalitions.[5] This may weaken governments, although the British image of weak and unstable coalition governments is largely a myth. It is, however, a fact that coalition governments often find it difficult to take a given decision which may affect the interests of the coalition partners unequally.

In both the FRG and France, the politics of their respective coalitions have greatly influenced attitudes towards reform of the Common Agricultural Policy (CAP) in general and the annual price fixing exercise in particular. At times, no doubt, President Giscard d'Estaing would have preferred to be more conciliatory on agricultural prices, but faced the prospect of severe competitive outbidding by his Rassemblement pour la République (RPR) 'allies' under Jacques Chirac. In the FRG, until 1982, a Social Democrat (SPD)–Liberal (FDP) coalition remained in power. The small FDP is a vital swing faction in German politics, having held office almost continuously since the FRG's foundation in 1949, except for short interruptions in the early 1960s and during the 'Grand Coalition' from 1966–9. Within the FDP, agricultural interests—especially those of its Bavarian electorate—are of vital importance to a party constantly concerned about its ability to secure more than 5 per cent of the vote without which, under German electoral law, it would fail (as other small parties have done) to gain seats in the Bundestag. In practice, its ability to muster between 5.8 per cent and 12.1 per cent of the vote at federal elections, coupled with the inability of the major parties—the SPD and the Christian Democrats (CDU) and their Bavarian sister-party, the CSU—to win more than half the seats, has resulted in the FDP holding the balance of power. As a rule, both the SPD and the CDU/CSU have to court FDP support if they are to form a government. Consequently, in coalition, the FDP has disproportionate power relative to its share of the vote. Indeed, FDP spokesman Josef Ertl, the Agriculture Minister, is a figure of very considerable power. Furthermore, he was one of the few members of the SPD/FDP coalition to have held office, and indeed the same office, since 1969. This has meant that the SPD/FDP coalition has been unable to formulate any line on the reform of the CAP which did not take into account the position of Herr Ertl. It has established in practice also the virtual autonomy of the Agriculture Minister from his colleagues.[6]

Coalition politics in Belgium have over the last three years greatly influenced the reaction of the Belgian Government to EC policy on the steel industry and, in particular, on state aids in that sector. The coalitions which held office before the November 1981 election all included the Walloon Socialist Party (PS), and the responsible minister was a Socialist, albeit from the Flemish Socialist Party (SP). These governments resisted attempts to limit, beyond a certain degree, state investment in the ailing steel companies in Liège and Charleroi, whereas the present Christelijke Volkspartij (CVP)/Parti Social Chrétien (PSC)–Parti des Reformes et de la Liberté (PRL)/Partij voor Vrijheid en Vooruitgang (PVV) coalition is prepared to limit aid to firms in difficulties to a much greater extent. Indeed, it could be argued that three EC actions—the question of state aid to the steel sector, the Commission Recommendation to Belgium of July 1980 which suggested both a heavy compression of public expenditure beyond what had been planned already and the automatic indexation of wages to inflation (a long-standing Belgian practice) should be ended or at least severely limited—were contributory factors in the fall of the Government in October 1981.[7]

Denmark presents yet another variation. Apart from the period from December 1973 until early 1975, and 1978, since joining the EC in 1973, Denmark has been governed by minority social democratic governments. These have, by and large, sought their support from the small parties of the centre and centre-right. Thus, in theory, a parliamentary majority has always existed for a more positive policy towards many EC issues on which the Danish Government has in fact exercised a brake—direct elections to the European Parliament (EP); education policy; use of Article 235 of the Rome Treaty; certain matters relating to harmonization and recognition of qualifications are obvious examples. However, the Government has preferred to adopt a prudent and pragmatic posture. This may be explained by the fact that an important minority of the Social Democratic Party (including about twelve MPs) are what it is now usual in Denmark to call 'EC sceptics' and at the same time the party is under pressure from the three far left anti-EC parties (Socialistisk Folkeparti (SF), Venstre Socialisterne (VS) and the Communists (DKP)) which also support the People's Movement against the EC, the vocal and active umbrella-organization which won four out of sixteen seats in the EP elections of 1979. Thus, whatever the parliamentary arithmetic, anti-EC sentiment is a factor that the Government cannot ignore, especially since it may wish to cooperate, admittedly only on an *ad hoc* issue-to-issue basis, with at least one of the far left parties in order to carry through some aspects of its domestic policy. There would seem to be a very subtle, indirect and certainly unstated trade-off.[8]

We have looked at how different types of coalition constraints can affect the positions of governments. A final example from Britain will show how the role of an individual can have the same effect because of his position in the governing party. In the last Labour Government, the Minister of Agriculture, Mr John Silkin, was able to exercise an influence out of all proportion to the apparently modest office of state that he held. He became, because of the central role of the CAP in Labour's attack on the EC, in a certain sense the leading spokesman of the main-stream Labour anti-marketeers.

The factors so far examined reflect political constraints or elements which have to be taken into account by governments in their behaviour in the EC's Council of Ministers. There are also, in some member states, institutional factors to be taken into account. These may lie in the realm of the organization and coordination of EC policy inside the government machine or in the parliamentary procedures which may act as a constraint upon the government. Parliaments are not, in most member states, significant elements in EC policy-making, which is not to say that they have no influence at all. However, rarely do they have an institutionalized role enabling them to exercise *prior* influence on EC policy in a *specific* direction. Most member states' parliaments tend to regard EC policy-making as essentially within the domain of the executive, as is the generality of foreign policy, except where major policy options have to be chosen. Some national parliaments even tend to prefer to remain outside the process, in the belief that the control of EC decision-making should be the responsibility of the EP. Most observers have concluded that, with the exception of the Danish Parliament, to which we shall return, national parlia-ments have been largely either unable or unwilling to play a significant role in the EC's decision-making process.[9] The sole exception to this is the Danish Parliament —the Folketing. However, there has recently been some 'revisionist' thinking about the Folketing's role in EC policy, tending to the view that the effectiveness and importance of its Market Relations Committee (MRC) has declined. Even so, the MRC retains an important role in Danish EC policy-making. The Government must consult with the MRC on all matters which are up for decision in the EC Council of Ministers. The MRC is a political committee, not a technical committee. Its members are senior figures from the various political parties—party leaders, former ministers. Apart from sometimes seeking an opinion from the competent specialist committees, the MRC undertakes no investigations or hearings. It meets weekly at least to hear reports from ministers on their intended negotiating man-date on matters that are to come before the Council. Ministers do not present their 'mandate' on a take it or leave it basis. They give an initial statement of the intended negotiating position and then hear the MRC's reaction which may lead to positions being revised. Of course, the minister's initial position may well reflect what he/she knows of the likely consensus in the MRC.

The MRC exercises delegated powers from the Folketing. It does not report back to the Folketing, nor pass resolutions. Indeed, its proceedings are not subject to debate in the whole House, and may be declared confidential at the request of the Government or by the Chairperson. The MRC does not vote. The Chair-person takes the 'sense of the meeting' by taking into account the weight repre-sented on the floor of the House by the different party spokespersons. He then sums up the discussion. The originality of the procedure lies in the fact that it is a 'negative clearing' procedure. The Government does not need to obtain an active majority *for* its position; it may negotiate on the basis of the mandate proposed, provided that the Chairperson can declare that there is no majority *against* the mandate. This clearly gives the Government some extra room for manoeuvre, but respects the basic parliamentary principle current in Denmark that a govern-ment (and with frequent minority governments the matter is far from theoretical) may remain in office as long as there is no majority against it in Parliament.[10]

It is argued often—though less in the last few years—that such procedures, especially other detailed refinements practised in the MRC such as emergency sessions during EC Council meetings to discuss new Commission compromise proposals, not only inhibit decision-making in the Council, but are also contrary to the spirit, if not the letter, of the EC method. The contrary view is forcefully argued in Denmark, namely that, with minority governments the rule, such a system gives more solidity to the EC positions of Danish governments, in that once they have obtained the MRC's backing they are safe from parliamentary 'accidents'. Irrespective of the merits of the two views, it seems evident that, ironically, the view which is critical of the MRC procedure as 'anti-communautaire', in effect—perhaps without seeking to do so—reduces the EC process to an 'international relations process' at arms-length from domestic political forces. The emergence of a system of parliamentary control of this type is rather a recognition that the EC forms an organic part of the political processes of the member states in which the political forces of the nation should be involved. These special Danish arrangements have of course arisen out of the political situation in Denmark, where the EC, its role and indeed specific policies such as reform of the CAP, harmonization, the European Monetary System (EMS) and all moves towards greater political, cultural (*vide* Danish opposition to an EC education policy) and economic integration are controversial and where governments must negotiate their support from issue to issue. As we have intimated already, in other member states this 'negotiating process' takes place in the cabinet between the wings of the government party or between coalition partners. Not surprisingly, therefore, it is often suggested in Denmark that a majority government would decrease the MRC's influence.

Approaches to the question of national control over EC decision-making vary greatly between member states. Some insist on very careful coordination between departments via a myriad of official and ministerial coordinating committees, which ensure that government policy is always consistent and always shows a united front towards the other member states and EC institutions. Other member states operate on a much looser rein, with individual ministries virtually pursuing independent policies. It is perhaps worth looking at a few varying examples of practices. France is possibly the most extreme example in the first direction. The main orientations of policy are set by the President of the Republic. The key instrument of coordination is the Secrétariat Général du Comité Interministériel (SGCI), which is a small, highly qualified unit, under the Prime Minister, which was set up in the 1950s to serve a cabinet committee, and which has long since atrophied. It has no theoretical powers of decision, these being exercised by the Minister of External Relations and by other technical ministers, who directly coordinate their positions on major issues. However, in practice the SGCI exercises a very real influence on policy and on day-to-day negotiations and instructions to officials. Above all, it serves to ensure that the French position is coherent and watertight. Under the new Socialist Government, the procedures and concepts remain the same, but it is too early to tell whether the presence of such a large number of 'ex-Europeans' in key posts (M. Cheysson, M. Mauroy, M. Delors and Mme Cresson) and the appointment of a Minister of European Affairs (M. Chandernagor) will breach this carefully constructed system. The betting must be that it will not. The nature of the regime and the effective dominance of one party, albeit in a theoretical Parti Socialiste (PS)–Parti Communiste Français (PCF)–Mouvement des Radicaux de Gauche (MRG) coalition, will no doubt ensure that the highly centralized and well coordinated system, closer to the classic foreign policy-making schema survives.[11]

Italy and the FRG, though in very different forms and for similar but distinct reasons, are at the other extreme. The political constraints as well as the nature (though quite different) of their government systems, have led to a much lower level of coordination than in France. In Italy, neither structures based on a special Minister of State Secretary for EC matters, nor the Coordinating Committee set up in 1967 have been able to prevent divergences between ministries blocking decision-making and even appearing externally, though the Permanent Representation in Brussels has attenuated this aspect.[12] Our point here is not that greater coordination is not desired, nor that it is impossible—indeed, on the official level, it is often by no means unattainable—but that the nature of the cross-cutting checks and balances imposed by not only coalition dynamics, but factional divergences within the Democrazia Cristiana (DC) makes such coordination impossible.

In the FRG, basic coordination is undertaken by the competent Department of the Economics Ministry, but a complicated structure, which has varied over time, of official European Affairs Groups, a 'State Secretaries' Committee, a Cabinet Committee, a Special Minister and more frequent discussions in full Cabinet, has emerged. It is the tradition of relative independence of the various competent ministries and the political fact of the nature of the party composition of successive SPD–FDP cabinets that has left the main 'EC' Departments—Foreign Affairs (Scheel then Genscher), Agriculture (Ertl) and Economics (Lambsdorff), but not Finance—in the hands of the smaller FDP partner, and that has necessitated a very complex and rather top-heavy structure of checks and balances.[13]

Our conclusion must be that in a sense 'countries get the approach to the EC that they deserve'. The government structure, the domestic decision-making process on EC matters depends largely on the internal political necessities. Internal politics have a much greater influence on member states' EC policy than is usually realized, which makes itself felt through coalition politics and weak governments. One might go so far as to say that it is illusory to expect a better decision-making process at the EC level than the sum of the national situations in the member states which compose the EC system. The interlocking political realities—coalitions, weak governments, domestic political controversy about the EC—in the member states condition the situation and cannot be ignored as if they did not exist, or as if they were irrelevant, as they may often seem, as seen from Brussels. The modest aim of this essay has been to bring a certain corrective analysis to a 'Brussels-centred' approach to the working of the EC. No claim to completeness is made; the aim is rather to suggest a dimension that is often ignored.

Notes

1. The issue is well dealt with in Wallace, H., Wallace, W. and Webb, C. (eds), *Policy Making in the European Communities* (Chichester, Wiley, 1977).
2. Coombes, D., *The Future of the European Parliament* (London, Policy Studies Institute, 1979), pp. 38–65.
3. Communiqué published in *Bull. EC*, 10 (1972), pp. 15 ff.
4. The institutional and political presidentialism of the Fifth Republic is covered by Frears, J. R. in his *Political Parties and the Elections in France* (London, Hurst, 1977), pp. 28–31 and pp. 208–20. On the question of European policy-making, see Sasse, C., *Regierungen, Parlamente, Ministerrat* (Bonn, Europa Union, 1975), pp. 19–25.
5. See Henig, S., 'Conclusions' in Henig, S. (ed.), *Political Parties in the European Community* (London, Allen & Unwin, 1979).
6. On the role of the FDP, see Burkett, T., 'The Federal Republic of Germany' in Henig, S. (ed.), op. cit., pp. 103–12.
7. Fitzmaurice, J., *Politics in Belgium* (London, Hurst, 1983); especially Chapter VIII, 'Foreign and Security Policy', and Chapter II, 'Economy and Society'.
8. Fitzmaurice, J., *Politics in Denmark* (London, Hurst, 1981), pp. 23–5 and pp. 149–53.

9. For an overview of this problem, see Sasse, C., op. cit., pp. 76–114 and Fitzmaurice, J., *The European Parliament* (Farnborough, Saxon House, 1978), pp. 27–50.
10. On the Danish case, see Fitzmaurice, J., 'National Parliaments and Community Policy Making: The Case of Denmark', *Parliamentary Affairs*, 29 (1976), 281–92. See also, Fitzmaurice, *Politics in Denmark*, pp. 137–45.
11. Sasse, C., op. cit., pp. 20–4.
12. Sasse, C., ibid., pp. 39–42.
13. Sasse, C., ibid., pp. 25–38.

2 The European Community's Bicephalous Political Authority: Council of Ministers–Commission Relations

STANLEY HENIG

Political authority in the EC is essentially the preserve of two institutions—the Commission and the Council of Ministers. One classic view of political systems makes an analytical distinction between different branches of government and notably between executive and legislative powers. The founders of the EC reflected this approach in their vision of the likely evolution of the institutions. The Commission would be the basis of a European executive, whilst the Council—the place where decisions would be formally taken and legitimated—would become essentially a legislative body. In fact, the Council would only be a part of the ultimate legislature of a United Europe: like the Senate in the USA it would represent the states, whilst the Assembly or Parliament (EP) would represent the peoples. It is an interesting, if now slightly curious, historical fact that in original drafts of the European Coal and Steel Community (ECSC) there was no Council. It appeared almost as an afterthought at the behest of the smaller countries who saw in it protection from the likely dominance by the larger countries of the High Authority.[1]

The course of EC and institutional evolution has actually been considerably different, reflecting the decline of the 'European' idea and also the success of nation states—aided by the achievements of the EC—in making a political and economic comeback. In the circumstances, the power relationship between the Commission which embodies the 'European' ideal and the Council which effectively represents national interests in the EC has undergone profound changes. The earlier vision seemed to imply that the Commission would be the 'motor' for EC development whilst the Council would be very much more passive. In historical perspective this was to an extent the case up to the mid-1960s, but subsequently the partnership has been very much more even. Developments since the mid-1960s have depended as much on positive decision and leadership from the Council as from the Commission. The Council itself has developed from being an inter-ministerial gathering into an EC and European organ, albeit as will be shown one in which the negotiating principle is more important than rules about voting rights. Over the last few years the balance between Council and Commission has changed further. The development of European Political Cooperation (EPC),[2] initially outside the formal context of the EC but now increasingly a part of the whole complex of relations between the Ten, has further increased the power and authority of Council at the expense of the Commission.

This chapter focuses on the relationship between Commission and Council and examines the way in which they embody and administer the power which they share. The first part of the chapter describes the structure and functions of each, as well as examining various subsidiary bodies and adjuncts. The second part concentrates on working styles and attempts a portrait of the EC at work, taking decisions and potentially promoting cooperation and integration. Finally, there is an attempt to assess the likely future development of the relationship.

The basic structure of the Commission is defined in Articles 9–18 of the 'merger' treaty[3] as subsequently amended by enlargement. It consists of fourteen members appointed by the member governments for a four-year period of office. Every member state is entitled to one Commissioner: it is understood but not specifically stated in the treaty that the 'big four'—France, the FRG, Italy and the United Kingdom—will have two. Whilst formally the governments act collectively in designating the Commission, in practice each country nominates its own Commissioner(s). Whilst no clear procedure is laid down for the appointment of a President for the Commission, in practice this is effectively in the hands of the member governments and it rotates between member states and informally between categories of members, such as new/old and large/small. The term of office of the President is two years, but the current norm is to give one renewal making a total of four years. No less than five of the other Commissioners are given the title Vice-President, but it is hard to attach much significance to this. Commissioners once appointed are to be strictly independent of their national governments, but in practice behaviour can be influenced by possible desire for a further period of office.

The Commission operates as a College and the President is intended to be no more than first among equals. Decisions are to be made by majority vote. Collective responsibility applies in so far as all Commissioners are responsible for all actions of the Commission, but this does not always ensure uniformity of expressed views. Commissioners come from all ten member states and usually many political tendencies are represented. Just as member states cannot recall a Commissioner within the term of four years, so the President has no power of dismissal. The coherence and effectiveness of the Commission depends greatly on the personal prestige and authority of the President and his power of leadership. Collectively the Commission as a whole is responsible to the EP which by a two-thirds majority can dismiss it. Even the EP, though, has no formal sanction against individual Commissioners.

It follows from the above that there can be no individual Commissioner responsibility to parallel the formal ministerial responsibility which characterizes many national systems. None the less, the work of the Commission has to be divided and in an administrative rather than legal sense different Commissioners have a responsibility for particular fields. At the beginning of each Commission portfolios are distributed between the members of the College by agreement between them. A good deal of lobbying by member states is occasioned by this process,[4] and this is an early test for the President.

The Commission's internal structure has been considerably modified and streamlined following the Spierenburg report,[5] which commented adversely on the allegedly excessive number of operating divisions and sections. Theoretically the broad structure has always been easy enough to comprehend. The Commission is divided into twenty Directorates-General (DGs) which cover all aspects of the EC's activities and there are also a number of organically separate common specialized services.[6] As there are fourteen Commissioners, many are in control of more than one DG. Further complexities arise when an area of activity becomes specially important or when Commissioners are competing for sensitive or politically significant portfolios. One DG is currently responsible for all external relations other than overseas development, although this has not always been the case. None the less, at the time of writing (mid-1982), Commissioner Natali has responsibility for

Mediterranean policy and the question of enlargement, both falling within the general purlieu of DG1 which is otherwise the province of Commissioner Hafer-kamp. DGs are divided into Directorates, usually around three or four although some have as few as two and others as many as eight. In turn the Directorates are sub-divided into Divisions, again usually three or four but in one case as many as twelve. The Division is the basic administrative unit and its head (graded A3) is the lowest official with a definable responsibility for a specific area of policy or activity.

The Commission employs about 11,000 people but of these practically one-quarter are in the nuclear research establishments. Theoretically there is apportion-ment between the different member states but this only has significance for grade A personnel—equivalent to the old administrative class in the British civil service. In fact a disproportionate share of the overall total goes to those member states which house the different parts of the Commission.[7] Competition between member states to ensure distribution in accordance with the key which reflects national weighting in the EC operates at grade A and becomes almost obsessional where posts at A3 level and above are concerned. Vacancies are an issue for resolution at Commission level rather than by the DG for personnel and there is a tendency for posts to become reserved for particular nationalities. This can be easily explained by reference to, for example, the very small number of A1 posts—about two dozen in all. Mostly these are Directors-General or their equivalent. If a vacancy is filled by somebody of another nationality then the country which has lost out is going to look for compensation elsewhere. The words are carefully chosen. Commissioners may claim to be above national considerations, but they are usually at great pains to ensure that fellow nationals receive their share of available posts at this level. Moreover, member governments themselves may well become involved in manoeuvring for positions, even depriving the Commission of autonomy over its own staff. It is significant that when the EC was enlarged it was the member governments who decided to limit Commission staff to existing levels: to make way for the newcomers some existing employees had to leave albeit on generous terms.

An immediate result of the effective politicization of promotion above A4 level is akin to the position of Principal in the British civil service in that career prospects are limited. This relates to a wider issue as to the nature of a European civil service. An early view particularly associated with Hallstein, first President of the EC Commission, favoured the creation of a European *corps d'élite* to pilot the cause of European integration. The French and subsequently the British Government have favoured the possibility of national civil servants undertaking terms of duty with the Commission in Brussels. The second view may imply further restriction on Commission autonomy, but it does mean that over the years the number of national civil servants with firsthand experience of the workings of the EC will increase—a positive development in the context of any belief that member states rather than the Commission are now the more likely 'motor' for any further integration.

There is one other significant tier in the Commission's internal structure. Each Commissioner is assisted by a personal Cabinet. The notion of the Cabinet which goes well beyond the British ministerial private office is based primarily on French experience, although the technique has been used successfully elsewhere. A Cabinet consists of a group of people serving, directly responsible to, and themselves depen-dent upon a Minister, or in this case a Commissioner. Since Cabinets are personally appointed, their members are not necessarily established Commission officials.

They act as eyes and ears of the Commissioner, in particular keeping him informed about general developments—important in the context of the collegial responsibility discussed above. More controversially, and this was criticized in the Spierenburg report,[8] the Cabinet may act as a buffer between Commissioner and DG officials. The development of the power of the head or Chef de Cabinet has undoubtedly meant that Directors-General lack some of the authority normally associated with civil servants operating at that level. The Chefs have become almost deputies to their Commissioners. As will be shown later, horizontal articulation in the Commission is weak. Much coordination between DGs is carried out through contact between the Chefs either at their regular weekly meeting prior to the meeting of the Commission or informally.

The functions of the Commission are based on statute and custom. Statutes are for the most part the foundation treaties, whilst custom relates to working practices within the EC. The first function is one traditionally associated with international secretariats. The Commission oversees the implementation of commitments made by member states both in the original treaties and in subsequent EC legislation. The Commission itself is not normally the agent of implementation: this is the task and preserve of national administrative machinery. The role of the Commission is concerned with supervision of this essentially national implementation: a kind of watchdog function which may well involve the Commission in seeking to cajole dilatory member states and in the ultimate taking possible cases of non-implementation to the Court of Justice.

The number of precise commitments entered into by member states by virtue of the foundation treaties is limited. The greater part of EC endeavour is featured in the treaties by agreement to agree, and the facilitation of these introduces the second and in some ways most characteristic function of the Commission. It is the institution which tables initial proposals for EC action or legislation. The near standard treaty rubric runs: 'on a proposal of the Commission . . . the Council will decide'. In a strictly judicial and formal sense this delineates the relationship: the Commission proposes, the Council disposes.

If it were as simple as that, this chapter would be very much shorter! However, whatever complications arise in practice in the implementation of this implied dyarchy of relations, it remains that the Commission does have the function of proposer and this necessitates it keeping under review the entire work and progress of the EC.

The two remaining functions arise from the previous, although in a sense they move in different directions. Because the Commission both supervises implementation and in making proposals reviews the entire work of the EC, there is a sense in which it can regard itself as the epitome of Europe. The Commission represents the EC whilst each member state working in the Council represents itself. This third function of the Commission, of which it tends to be acutely conscious when discussing the future political evolution of the EC,[9] implies the elevation of national sectional interests to a higher plane and it is countered by the final major function. Proposals are made to the Council and they may well reflect the Commission's European view. Politics, though, is the art of the possible and the Commission also has the task of working with the member states in the Council to harmonize national differences and seek to win some agreement, however far removed from the original proposal. This mediating function may well be little more than a traditional lowest common denominator approach to international agreement.

The basic structure of the Council is established in the first eight articles of the merger treaty,[10] but constitutional lore owes even more to practice and established precedent than in the case of the Commission. Lessened overall commitment to integration has necessarily increased the salience of the most inter-governmental of the major institutions, but slightly paradoxically this has helped the Council to become a genuine European organ in its own right. In this respect it is significant that the merger treaty gives the first official mention to the Committee of Permanent Representatives (COREPER), the most important of the Council's subsidiary bodies. Another major source for the constitution of the Council lies in agreements between the member states on EPC. These are examined elsewhere in this book,[11] but although the EPC agreements are legally separate from the Communities their impact on how the Council works has been profound.

Formally the Council consists of ministerial representatives from each member state. They are accompanied inevitably by officials and sometimes by junior ministers and the Commission attends meetings as of right. Each member state designates its own representative but their level at any one meeting is likely to be similar for all member states. The practice has developed of holding various series of Council meetings with different, but for each individual series regular, attenders. The most frequent and regular meetings are those attended by Foreign Ministers and Ministers of Agriculture and these account for around half of all Council sessions, but many other sectoral ministers are also involved. In total, Council sessions use up about one hundred working days per year. Very roughly, each national Minister of Agriculture and each Foreign Minister can expect to spend at least twenty-five working days per year in Council. The next heaviest involvement is on the part of second-string Ministers of Finance who are concerned with the EC budget.[12]

The Council is not normally considered to be a Cabinet or even a College, although amongst some ministerial groupings such as agriculture there is a considerable sense of 'community'. The post of President of the Council rotates on a six-month basis. The Presidency involves the member state in question presiding over all meetings under the aegis of the Council and is a considerable administrative burden. As the work of the EC has grown in complexity, so the role of the Presidency has necessarily increased. The Council has its own administrative back-up in the form of a Secretariat which has grown and developed despite some opposition from the Commission which saw in it a possible rival. The Secretariat has desk officers to watch over policy developments in different areas. In contrast to their opposite numbers in the Commission, their main function tends to be that of collective memory rather than policy formulation. The major administrative task of the Secretariat is to process the decision-making of the Council in the sense of making available EC legislation—directives, regulations etc.—in all official languages. A majority of the staff are jurists or linguists of some kind.

It has been suggested that the Council of Foreign Ministers is superior to other 'sectoral' Councils. There is no strict legal basis for this assertion. Any set of ministers meeting as the Council possess the same official rights and powers, although the biggest and broadest political issues are normally handled by the Foreign Ministers. It was argued by some that the decision of the Agriculture Ministers to override a British 'veto'[13] on increased farm prices in spring 1982 was somehow a usurpation of the rights of the Foreign Ministers' Council. Quite apart from the intrinsic unlikelihood that the national Foreign Ministers were uninformed and totally uninvolved in the decision-taking process in question, there is simply no basis for the claim that the Agriculture Council lacks any of the legal attributes of the Council of Ministers. The truth is that the Foreign Ministers' Council is only differentiated from the others in that they fulfil a coordinating role and their alleged failure to do this adequately attracted a good deal of adverse criticism in the Report of the Three[14] in 1979.

The development of the EC during the 1960s necessitated occasional meetings of the heads of government. Strictly outside the context of the Council these summits offered an opportunity to review progress, lay down goals and solve outstanding problems. With enlargement and the disappearance of the old consensus on European integration, the number of problems left to the summit tended to increase with a consequent debilitating effect on normal decision-making processes. More positively the development of the parallel EPC machinery also seemed to point to a need for more regular meetings at the highest level.[15] It is now established that the heads of government meet three times a year—once in the country of each President and once in Brussels—as the European Council. The European Council brings together at their apex the EC institutions and the EPC machinery: to all intents and purposes it should be considered as the Council of Ministers in its highest manifestation.[16]

As well, then, as spreading itself along a horizontally articulated axis through all the sectoral Councils, the Council of Ministers has extended itself vertically—upwards to the European Council and downwards to COREPER. There is no reference to this body in the three foundation treaties, but so important had it become by the mid-1960s that it earned a reference in the merger treaty. According to Article 4, it is composed of the Permanent Representatives of the member states (accredited to the EC) and it is responsible for preparing the work of the Council and for carrying out tasks assigned by the latter. This modest statement gives less than full credit to the crucial role of COREPER in the decision-making process, but it is important to recognize that it does not have any formal decision-making competence. Much of the critical work in the decision-making process is undertaken by COREPER as will be shown, but the legal act remains the province of the Council. There is no sense in which COREPER is the Council.

The sheer weight of EC business has actually forced COREPER to operate at two levels, although the split is horizontal rather than vertical. COREPER II is the Permanent Representatives themselves, whilst COREPER I is their Deputies. The former deals with external questions and any matters with significant political considerations, whilst the latter tends to focus on internal EC issues. The vertical axis extending downwards from the Council goes through COREPER to a whole range of specialist and *ad hoc* committees. The special significance of COREPER is that it and not the Council supervises the lower level groups. In all of them the principle of representation is the same—member states are represented by officials who may be based in the national capitals or in the Permanent Representations and the Commission at the appropriate level participates as of right.

So far the essentially structural-functional analysis contained in this chapter has given a static picture of the respective roles of Commission and Council.

In considering the way in which the decision-making process works, it is useful to return for a moment to the notion that the Commission could evolve into a European executive with the Council becoming all or a major part of a European legislature. En route to this long-term objective, the founding fathers of the EC assumed that the Commission would be the 'motor' of the EC. It would promote proposals aimed at producing those detailed agreements which the member states had undertaken in general terms to try to reach. As guardian of the European conscience the Commission would also keep an overview of the state of integration and would gear its initiatives towards the longer-term goals of economic and political unification. In this model the Commission is essentially a political rather than a technocratic body and this perception of its role and style seems to be strengthened by the detailed treaty provisions for Council decision-taking. After the end of the second phase of the transitional period Council decisions on most questions were to be made by qualified majority vote. The original provisions which have been subsequently modified by the admission of four new members gave four votes each to France, the FRG and Italy, two each to Belgium and the Netherlands and one to Luxembourg. The qualified majority was to be twelve out of the total seventeen. If, however, the decision was not being taken on the basis of a Commission proposal, then the winning majority had to include the votes of four countries. For many reasons which will shortly be elaborated, the Council has never operated in this way, but the Commission has long claimed insight into the implications of its own role. It would have brought forward proposals as required by the treaties, discussed them with member states, sought general agreement and finally have determined the point at which to go for a political majority. Decisions would be taken: the 'motor' would operate.

This last view offers a fascinating and idealized type of decision-making, but it does not bear too much resemblance to actuality. During 1965, with the end of the second phase of the transitional period in sight and the imminent prospect of a considerable extension of majority voting, the Commission took a major initiative aimed at producing progress on a number of separate but important outstanding questions. The Commission was producing a package on issues apparently unlinked—a well-tried EC method which brought about progress by giving something to everybody. For various reasons the French Government took strong exception to the Commission tactics and ended up by walking out of the institutions for a number of months. At least one French motivation was concern that the Commission was overdoing its political role. The French boycott was ended after the Foreign Ministers met at Luxembourg and issued an agreed statement which has subsequently been much cited but little read. Its crucial paragraphs ran as follows:

1. Where, in the case of decisions which may be taken by majority vote on a proposal of the Commission, very important interests of one or more partners are at stake, the Members of the Council will endeavour, within a reasonable time, to reach solutions which can be adopted by all the Members of the Council while respecting their mutual interests and those of the Community, in accordance with Article 2 of the Treaty.
2. With regard to the foregoing paragraph, the French delegation considers that where very important interests are at stake the discussion must be continued until unanimous agreement is reached.
3. The six delegations note that there is a divergence of views on what should be done in the event of a failure to reach complete agreement.
4. The six delegations nevertheless consider that this divergence does not prevent the Community's work being resumed in accordance with the normal procedure.

For some time after 1966 it was the custom to refer to the above as the Luxembourg agreement, even though the only agreement was to disagree! Later it became known as the 'Luxembourg compromise', but the text as quoted offers no accommodation between the opposed concepts of veto and majority vote. The only compromise was to resume work despite the disagreement and the failure to register a position acceptable to all six member states!

It is easy enough to perpetuate myths about the past and this certainly applies to developments in the EC prior to the French boycott—the period sometimes

known as the 'golden age of integration'. The 1950s had certainly been characterized by agreement between the Six on the long-term goals of the EC and the
impetus given by the foundation treaties spilled over to produce agreements in
many of the areas designated for joint endeavour. Even so the Commission had
progressively found itself facing difficulties when making proposals in the face of
six, often differently conceived, national interests. Increasingly it had developed
the practice of linking sometimes very different issues in complex package deals
which it brought to the Council in the hope that by offering something to all it
could ensure progress. Before 1966 majority voting was not an important element
in the decision-taking structure. Its use had hitherto been sufficiently restricted
by the treaties to ensure this, but the style and method operating within the EC
already militated somewhat against it for the future. France raised the crucial
issue of the capacity of the EC to take the institutional strain of majority voting
with its consequence of out-voted minorities who were themselves independent
and sovereign nation states. Despite the disagreement of all the other five, there is
not really that much in their record within the EC before or after 1966 to suggest
that they genuinely visualized majority voting becoming the *deus ex machina* for
decision-taking. This is a good note on which to turn to the way in which the EC
actually operates and the existing relationship between the Commission and Council.

The flow of business through the decision-making machinery of the EC is heavily
influenced by what almost amount to 'taps'. The first, as foreseen in the treaties,
is the Commission which constantly promotes proposals—to fulfil the specific
objectives laid down by the treaties, to further the cause of integration in general,
to respond to immediate economic and social problems and pressures, and in
response to requests made from time to time by member states usually through the
Council. Normally Commission policy is evolved with the appropriate DG. Articulation within the Commission goes along vertical lines to almost the highest level
and there is little horizontal communication between different DGs. Coordination
becomes the responsibility of the Chefs de Cabinet who meet in advance of the
weekly Commission meeting. The Chefs have the task of undertaking a preliminary
look at matters requiring Commission decision and isolating potential problems.
Once policies are adopted by the Commission in the form of proposals, they are
transmitted to the Council Secretariat whence they are normally sent for discussion
by the EP. Only after the latter has given its opinion does the work of the Council
really commence.

The work of proposer tends to be carried on by the Commission in the full glare
of publicity. Making a proposal is a political act and this implies a similarity between
the Commission and a national cabinet. However, work at earlier stages and lower
levels tends also to be semi-public. This is perhaps inevitable given the involvement
of so many different nationalities and the frequency with which outside interests
are consulted in the policy planning stage. It does have the disadvantage that the
Commission may be publicly identified with apparent policies based only on
rudimentary ideas and which never become formal proposals.

Initially, the Council is unlikely to do more than take cognizance of a Commission proposal before sending it to COREPER for detailed study. COREPER
is really the second tap controlling the work of the decision-taking machinery.
It determines whether all or part of the proposals can go straight back to the
Ministers, by seeking to isolate the major problems and disagreements and instituting studies by various of the working groups which operate under its aegis. The
Commission participates at the appropriate level in all these deliberations, but as
they proceed the original proposal tends to be blurred. Formal treaty rubric does

lay down voting requirements for the Council to amend Commission proposals, but these are even less operative than other clauses relating to votes. The Commission works towards consensus or at any rate tacit agreement between the member states. When this is in sight it can formally change its proposal itself so as to conform to the legalities.

It has long been observed that the Commission is far better at bringing about agreements in Council than it is at steering through its own initial proposals.[17] The Commission inevitably sees this too as a product of the failure to operate the rules on voting. If the Council did take decisions by majority vote then the Commission would seek a political majority for its original proposal and would only need to change its position when this turned out to be impossible. So significant though is the mediating task that the Commission now has a partner in the process. The third control or tap on the flow of decision-making and the only one with some pretence at being able also to adjust the speed is the Presidency. This plays an ever more important role in the building of consensus in the Council as a prerequisite for agreeing decisions.[18]

The concept of voting is actually irrelevant to the actual taking of EC decisions, but it would not be true to say that all members are, or even need to be, happy with all decisions reached. Consensus and tacit agreement imply the absence of majority voting, but they are not the same as unanimity. Some observers have concluded that because there is no majority voting, progress is determined by unanimous agreement and that there is a veto. It is worth returning for a moment to the Luxembourg statement. Five countries then argued that the Treaty provisions should be implemented while one wanted a national veto. In so far as there was a compromise, it was that neither were to have their way as the style of decision-making post-1966 developed.

A crucial aspect of the contemporary decision-making process in the EC has been the evolution of the Council. It is no longer a peripatetic and changing collection of Ministers: the Council is now a permanent European organ even if its external appearance undergoes frequent change. As already stated the Council of Ministers and the European Council meet for more than one hundred days per year, whilst COREPER is in session for another hundred. On a majority of working days the Council or COREPER is in session, to say nothing of the plethora of committees and working groups. Foreign and Agriculture Ministers come to know each other—professionally and socially—reasonably well, whilst the Permanent Representatives and their Deputies are in constant communication. In promoting cohesiveness within the EC the Permanent Representatives may well be more important even than the Commission. Not only do they meet in COREPER, but they also are in attendance at Council and have a major responsibility for briefing their own respective Ministers. The extent and range of all these contacts has an important behavioural effect. International organizations invariably offer nation states another forum within which they can legitimately assert their own national interests. Such assertion must inevitably be a threat to the cohesiveness and achievement of the organization, but in the EC it has always been muted. In the beginning this was occasioned by shared perception of long-term goals concerned with integration and unification, and latterly there has been general agreement on the value of the EC as a European instrument for carrying out essential inter-state business. This latter consideration can be translated into mechanical terms.

Essential inter-state business in the EC has grown to the point where the member governments find themselves continually working and operating together in the Council and COREPER and this forces them to moderate the assertion and promotion of national goals. One may hypothesize a meeting within the Council framework on a Monday. Country A would like to block something which countries B and C would particularly wish to promote. Crucial in the decision of country A is the fact that on Wednesday there will be another meeting in the Council framework on another issue on which it has a positive view and on which it is going to need the support of countries B and C. In the 1960s issue linkage and package deals were a Commission technique for promoting agreement and progress. Sponsored by the Commission or not, they are inevitably endemic to the EC. The non-specificity of many of the behind-the-scenes arrangements which are made to reconcile differing national interests has helped promote the role of the Presidency as a potential mediator alongside, perhaps even in rivalry with, the Commission.

Rules of the game are crucial in the operation of the decision-taking machinery and not legalistic voting requirements, although there is an extent to which both approaches must reflect the realities of political power.[19] In the Ten, one or two member states cannot and do not indefinitely hold up all progress on a proposal which is being positively and purposefully pushed by eight or nine member states. Equally groups of member states seek the consent of individual member states opposed on particular questions and seek to avoid forcing them into submission. The size and weight of the member states within the EC is reflected in the decision-making process and some have considerably more influence than others. If France, the FRG and the UK are agreed, they are likely to have their way. It is worth considering in the light of the above the 'crisis' in May 1982 when the UK sought to 'veto' a rise in farm prices and the other nine member states used the majority voting procedure against her. The UK claimed this was against the 'Luxembourg compromise', but the truth was slightly different. Cries of woe that the EC system had been overturned were as wide of the mark as the short-lived excitement in some 'European' circles that majority voting would at last be introduced. The UK had found herself on her own in seeking to prevent a rise in farm prices which the other nine member states and the Commission had all accepted and which was generally regarded as a matter of considerable urgency. At the same time the UK was also on her own on certain other issues. Normal inter-EC 'messages' with regard to linkage, packages and compromise were either lost or ignored. The UK went outside the rules of the game in seeking to cast a national veto and the others stayed outside by publicly and humiliatingly overruling her. It could be argued that this was a stark and public edition of the more diplomatic, discrete approach enshrined in the rules of the game, but reactions afterwards on the part of France and the FRG to the effect that nothing had changed were broadly correct. The post-Luxembourg system, correctly analysed, remains the key to the operation of the decision-taking process.

There are four major typologies for future institutional development in the EC decision-making process. One suggests a revolutionary re-write of the constitution of Europe. This implies a sharp disjunction with the current process of evolution and presupposes a 'federator'—internal or external. The theory is that for some reason the member governments operating outside the day-to-day context of the EC determine on a great leap forward to political unification or some kind of federation. The present constellation of political forces within Western Europe makes any development of this kind for internal reasons seem extraordinarily improbable. It has been argued that an external shock was far more likely to bring about such a quantum leap than any internal European developments and this certainly reflects the idea that the Cold War and Suez were more instrumental than most events in bringing about the establishment of the three Communities. However, contemporary European reactions to extraneous events have not tended to go in this direction. Perhaps the last major external shock was the oil supply crisis of 1973. The initial EC reaction was total confusion and failure to produce any agreed line. The second much slower reaction was gradually to build up the EPC machinery—devised as a corollary to the balance of institutional power within the EC and securely based on the primacy of the member governments.

Other typologies are evolutionary. The Commission still cherishes its old blue-print as shown when it gave evidence to Tindemans for his report on European Union.[20] The Commission visualized a 'governmental organ [which] would be a collegiate body whose members would be independent of the national govern-ments' and which 'would naturally absorb all the executive functions of the Council and the executive and administrative functions of the present Commission'. Legisla-tive power would be epitomized by a Chamber of States and a Chamber of Peoples. The problem which impedes this vision is that virtually every institutional develop-ment for two decades has been in the opposite direction! Idealism certainly has a role in politics, but its adoption requires that it be harnessed to realistic ends. This happened with the Schuman plan and the later Spaak report which led respec-tively to the ECSC and the EEC. Unfortunately such a coincidence of idealism and realism does not figure at present in the constellation of European politics.

The third typology suggests that the Council in all its manifestations might evolve into a European government. Certainly political authority has progressively been assumed by the Council and this is demonstrated formally by recent institu-tional developments, particularly the establishment of EPC. It is not altogether fanciful to imagine the Commission as a kind of eleventh member of such a govern-ment or authority. Ten members would represent the nation states and the Com-mission would embody the collective endeavour. There is a sense in which this notion reflects the kind of role already fulfilled by the Commission within the Council-dominated structure of the EC.

In practice, of course, the ten member governments will not decide formally or systematically that even this third type of evolution is to be the EC future. It has long been argued that the institutions are facing a crisis and that major reforms are necessary. Concentrating on the preserve of this chapter it is argued that the Council is a bottleneck which slows down the whole process of decision-making; that the absence of majority voting, which already caused problems when there were only six EC member states, is making the EC virtually inoperable with ten member states and will be quite impossible after further enlargement. It is an old argument, but it has produced few changes. The most recent EC-inspired examina-tion of its own institutions by the Committee of Three[21] shied away from pro-posing major constitutional changes, although it was suggested that member governments might be willing to accept voting on questions not deemed to be of national importance. In effect this would preserve the post-Luxembourg system but would require member governments clearly in a minority to give way at an earlier stage. For the rest the Committee saw responses to current problems in a greater coherence to the decision-making process, the Foreign Ministers re-acquiring their coordinating role and the Presidency being strengthened. In effect this is the fourth typology or, more accurately, scenario for the future and it implies that the present pattern of decision-making processes within the EC despite their problems are likely to remain for the foreseeable future.

Notes

1. The High Authority was the equivalent of the Commission in the ECSC. It became part of the unified Commission as a result of the merger treaty of 1965, see 3 below.
2. See Part III.
3. 'Treaty establishing a Single Council and a Single Commission of the European Communities.'
4. The Prime Minister of Britain, Mrs Margaret Thatcher, actually telephoned Commission President Thorn during discussion on the distribution of portfolios in January 1981.
5. 'Proposals for Reform of the Commission of the European Communities and its Services' (Brussels, Commission of the European Communities, 1979). The five-man team responsible for the preparation of this report met under the Chairmanship of Dirk Spierenburg, a former Dutch Permanent Representative.
6. There are Directorates-General for External Relations; Economic and Financial Affairs; Internal Market and Industrial Affairs; Competition; Employment, Social Affairs and Education; Agriculture; Transport; Development; Personnel and Administration; Information; Environment, Consumer Protection and Nuclear Safety; Science, Research and Development; Information Market and Innovation; Fisheries; Financial Institutions and Taxation; Regional Policy; Energy; Credits and Investment; Budgets; Financial Control. Apart from the Office of the Secretary-General there are also the following services: Legal; Statistical; Interpreting and Conferences; Customs Union.
7. For a more detailed discussion, see Henig, S., *Power and Decision in Europe: The Political Institutions of the European Community* (London, Europotentials, 1980).
8. 'Proposals for the Reform of the Commission of the European Communities and its Services', op. cit.
9. As for example in the Commission's presentation of evidence to Spierenburg when he was preparing his report on European Union, see below.
10. 'Treaty establishing a Single Council and a Single Commission of the European Communities', op. cit.
11. See Part III.
12. Again for a more detailed discussion, see Henig, op. cit.
13. See below.
14. 'Report on the European Institutions', Brussels, Council of Ministers, 1979. The Committee preparing the report was composed of Berent Bieshuvel, Edmund Dell and Robert Marjolin (respectively a Dutch diplomat, a former British Minister and a former French Commissioner).
15. See Morgan, A., *From Summit to Council: Evolution in the EEC* (London, Chatham House/PEP, 1976).
16. Although from a strictly legal point of view it is not the Council and does not have formal treaty powers—an interesting contrast with the argument that purely legally all actual Councils of Ministers are equal!
17. This notion was developed in some of the supporting papers which were incorporated into 'The Institutional Structure of the European Communities', published as part of 'The Federal Trust Papers' in the *Journal of Common Market Studies*.
18. See Edwards, G. and Wallace, H., *The Council of Ministers of the European Community and the President-in-Office* (London, Federal Trust, 1977).
19. Although downplayed here, the voting arrangements for the Ten as outlined in the amended treaties should perhaps be given: France, the FRG, Italy and the UK each have ten votes; Belgium and The Netherlands five; Denmark, Greece and Ireland three; and Luxembourg two. The qualified majority is forty-five and if there is no proposal from the Commission involved then six member states must be in favour.
20. Published as 'European Union: Report to the European Council' (Brussels, Council of Ministers, 1975). This was a one-man report team. Mr Leo Tindemans was at the time Prime Minister of Belgium.
21. 'Report on the European Institutions', op. cit.

3 Pressure Groups and Policy-Making in the European Community

ALAN BUTT PHILIP

The institutions of the EC provide a large number of opportunities, often spanning several years, for pressures to be brought to bear on policy-makers. The EC decision-making process is conducted at the Brussels level initially with much openness, but in its final and often critical stages with great secrecy. At the same time as EC institutions are preparing their plans and positions, member governments have to start gathering together domestic reactions and pursuing their individual strategies in regard to particular EC proposals.[1] Thus the process provides a rich field for interest group activity at several levels of government.

The formation of policy in the EC will normally begin with the preparation of proposals by one of the Directorates-General of the EC Commission. The Commission is not merely the civil service arm of the EC but has the important Treaty-based right of initiative in policy matters. After collecting advice and information from interested parties, the Commission must then decide on the nature and scope of any proposals it promotes and submit these for comments by the EP and the ESC. Once the 'opinions' of these two bodies have been received and any resulting amendments have been made to the proposals, the Council of Ministers will then take on the lengthy task of scrutinizing the proposals line by line. This will be the role allotted to a working group of officials from each member state, with specialist knowledge, and which will occupy the working group intermittently for a period of about two to three years. A great deal of new material can be introduced at this stage of the discussions—which are held in camera—and the search for compromises and trade-offs which all member states can accept is begun in earnest. It is only the most politically or technically difficult issues that will normally be passed up the line for resolution by diplomats at ambassador level meeting in COREPER or an equivalent specialist committee. They will then try to dispose of as many of these points as they can so that only the most politically important or sensitive issues are passed for settlement by government ministers meeting as the full Council of Ministers. Policies thus decided will often call for new or amending legislation at the national level and in most cases will be administered by national governmental authorities.

There are estimated to be around 500 Europe-wide pressure groups which direct their attentions to decision-making in the EC: of these some 150 are specifically agricultural interest groups. Most Euro-pressure groups are based in Brussels, although some are to be found in London and Paris, and a few elsewhere. The Commission occasionally publishes a register of those pressure groups with whom it is officially in contact and has over the last two decades encouraged their development.[2] Some national pressure groups and industrial corporations have also appointed several representatives or agents in Brussels circulating among the diplomatic, bureaucratic and representational circles which surround the Charlemagne and Berlaymont buildings.[3]

The function of these individuals and organizations is to find out and report back to national organizations what is in the minds of Commission officials and those who take part in debates within the Council of Ministers, and to influence their decisions wherever possible. They are listening posts and liaison groups. They provide an important means by which interest groups can react to policy development in the EC.

But it is only in comparatively few cases that the leadership of a Europe-wide pressure group plays a major role in laying down policy. Most of these Euro-pressure groups have an extremely loose structure: they meet occasionally and have a very small secretariat to service their organizational needs. Only five Euro-pressure groups have a central secretariat numbering ten or more: these are COPA/COGECA (agriculture), UNICE (industry), CEA (insurance), ETUC (trade unions) and the GCECEE (savings banks). The membership of such groups is typically allocated places on their executives on a nation state basis, with the presidency rotating between states perhaps every two years. The Euro-pressure group provides a forum where various national interest groups can get together to discuss matters of mutual interest. Such matters are frequently then passed to standing sub-committees or *ad hoc* working parties to resolve in detail, with the initiative also lying in the hands of one or two executive members wearing a European hat rather than with the European secretariat or a permanently established leader.[4]

A few of the most significant Euro-pressure groups will not conform to this model, mainly because their workload is continuously heavy owing to the wide scope of their interests and the existing significant involvement of the EC—and in particular the Commission—in their concerns. This élite of the pressure groups has tended to evolve a more centralized organization and leadership and is likely to be in daily contact with the Commission.

The most important of the Euro-pressure groups are the Committee of Professional Agricultural Organizations of the EC (COPA), the Union of Industries of the EC (UNICE), and the European Trade Union Confederation (ETUC). But smaller groups can also make their presence felt such as COMITEXTIL (textile manufacturers), the Savings Bank group of the EC (GCECEE), the European Consumers' Bureau and the European Environmental Bureau. Their extensive lobbying activities are not confined to legislative proposals emanating from the Commission but include also the way policies are administered from Brussels. They may also be able to influence other international lobby groups and organizations in policy areas where the EC does not have an exclusive field of competence. Export or ship-building credit terms, for example, are discussed at OECD level as well as EC level. Working conditions are settled at the International Labour Organization in Geneva as well as in Brussels. Economic and trade questions affecting the whole EC are covered by GATT and the United Nations' Economic Commission for Europe. This blurring of boundaries is reflected too in the fact that many Euro-pressure groups draw some of their clientele from non-EC countries either as full members (for example, ETUC or the Comité Européen des Assurances) or as associate members (for example, UNICE).

Euro-pressure groups, large and small, frequently find that they have to contend with significant constitutional problems which affect both their membership and their performance. These problems of structure and composition can be summarized as arising from overlapping memberships, wider geographical coverage than the EC, insufficient membership, insufficient geographical spread, conflicts of interest within the membership, and membership imbalance. Such problems provide much of the explanation of the reluctance of their component members to equip such Euro-groups with independent negotiating powers or the means by which they could develop into centralizing, disciplined and integrated bodies. The vast majority of these Europe-wide pressure groups are facilitators of contacts with the EC, permitting 'national' interests to acquire a more acceptable 'Community' hat before going to talk to Commission officials. Where matters of substance arise, the Euro-groups provide a framework within which a collective position may be evolved by a whole family of interest groups. To the extent that this occurs the objectives of the Commission in encouraging the formation of such Euro-groups would appear to be met: namely, that the Commission is able to receive and react to a coordinated set of views from an EC-wide set of interests; and that the ideal of European integration is shown to be working in relevant and practical ways for a variety of interests spread throughout the member states.

However, the theory of the integrative effects of Euro-groups is greatly weakened by the fact that many such Euro-groups find that on important issues they are unable to reach an agreed position among themselves. The views they then express to the EC then suffer either from ambiguity or from insufficiency: this greatly devalues the utility of such positions from the Commission's viewpoint, and ultimately causes separate national pressure group representations to be made to or requested by Commission officials.

Given the balance of power within the EC institutions and the dominant role of national governments acting within the Council of Ministers, the most important task for pressure groups with an interest in EC policy is to secure access for themselves to the Commission in Brussels and other EC institutions, to relevant Europe-wide pressure groups, and to officials of their national governments in Brussels (serving on COREPER) and their home capitals. Such access should ensure in the first place that interest groups know the changing state of play in the 'game' they form part of and, secondly, that they have the chance to persuade officials to take their ideas or representations seriously. The lobbyist can offer the official relevant information, which may otherwise be difficult to obtain, while the official can tell the lobbyist what stage the game has reached. The more technical the subject matter, the more officials will seek briefings from outside interests and the less likely it is that governments will have an independent point of view.

A second factor which usually operates in EC decision-making is the need to make representations at several different levels, sometimes simultaneously. The master-lobbyist like the chess-master must be able to play several games at once at different tables, as far afield as Strasbourg, Luxembourg, Brussels as well as in his national capital. This physical separation of the centres of power severely limits effective lobbying to those that have the financial resources, the time and the persistence to see an EC proposal through to the end. In the case of the introduction of a common value added tax this took fourteen years, yet long timescales for implementation are often the very essence of delicate EC compromises.

Despite the rapid growth in the numbers of European pressure groups clustered around the EC's activities, few such pressure groups have developed into very effective powerful forces in their own right—COPA being the most obvious exception. This is largely a reflection of the lack of development of common policies for the EC (as is the case with regional policy), but it is also a result of the reluctance of many national interest groups to allow much discretion to any Euro-secretariat representing their interests. If bureaucracy has been kept to a minimum, so has the extent of any genuine integration of interests and attitudes among pressure groups. To a large extent, it is the weaker organized groups at national level (for example, savings banks or environmentalists) that are keen on maintaining a strong federal Europe-wide organization, unless as in COPA's case EC policy is already wide-ranging and well developed. In this respect the national pressure groups often echo strikingly the attitudes of their national governments.

Furthermore, the weaknesses of the European pressure groups described above led the Commission in the mid-1970s very much to relax its rule of only discussing proposals with European rather than national pressure groups. The Commission is frequently highly dependent on information supplied by non-governmental sources and has found that vital information was simply not getting through if only Euro-groups were consulted, either because of disagreements or ambiguities of view or because of the Euro-group's lack of detailed knowledge of conditions in a particular member state. The more the Commission has ceded its right of initiative to member states in the formulation of policy proposals, which can be very substantial in the Council of Ministers working groups, the more interest groups must rely on making representations at national government level through national, rather than Euro-pressure groups. It has even been known for the French Patronat, having failed to influence its own Government, to contact the British CBI with a view to persuading (successfully) the British Government of its point of view.[5]

Policy-making in the EC should not be thought of simply in terms of the pre-paration and agreement of legislative proposals. There are also two other key areas of decision where interest groups can have a crucial impact. The implementation of policies provides a rich field for influence, especially where management com-mittees and advisory committees have been set up to oversee the day-to-day admini-stration of existing policies (especially the CAP) and/or to provide advice to the Commission on the development of future policy. Policy implementation at the national level, where a government is required to make its national laws consistent with EC directives, also offers opportunities for interest groups to make their weight felt. In addition, there are areas where the Commission enjoys substantial delegated powers as in the administration of the competition policy and the negotia-tion of trade agreements with third countries on behalf of the EC. Here too are crucial concerns for industrial interests where lobbying is frequent and influential.

The EC lobbyist may well find that the obstacle to his plans comes from a par-ticular national government which is out of step with other member governments and with its own domestic pressure groups. There is frequently an administrative interest at work within government which may be unwilling to share control of an area of policy (such as regional policy) despite what domestic interest groups think. Governments may also be reluctant to accept the inconvenience of having to change legislation in order to conform to EC standards. In such circumstances, governments can find themselves isolated in the Council of Ministers, if most other member states wish to push forward with a proposal. More often than not a govern-ment in this position will be forced to yield ground in return for deferred applica-tion of the policy (for example, the 1977 banking law harmonization directive). But where several governments share a similar interest in keeping the EC dimension at bay, they may be able so to frame a regulation or directive (during the Council of Ministers stage) that most of its administration remains securely in national officials' hands. In these circumstances, which apply for example to the ERDF, attempts by prospective beneficiaries to lobby EC institutions become pointless. In addition, it is an observable fact that national governments seek to place their own nationals of like mind in key posts of the Commission in pursuit of their own policy goals: this applies not only at Commissioner level but also to Director-General and Director level appointments.

Yet it is by no means always the case that national governments completely dominate when the EC makes its decisions. In some areas of policy—such as transport and social policy—the social partners have a statutory role to play in policy formation and implementation. Occasionally, national governments are shocked to discover the long-term implications of legislation they have agreed to, even though national interest groups may have seen the implications and welcomed them. It must also be emphasized that the Commission formally possesses the sole right of initiative in most policy matters in the EC. The Commission's Directorates-General are not all so heavily committed with work nor so well endowed with future projects that they would not welcome an approach from an interest group suggesting a feasible and worthwhile field of policy where EC intervention would be legitimate and welcomed by interested parties.

While it would not be accurate to suggest that national governments do not dominate the EC's decision-making process, there are some scenarios in which the Commission and pressure groups would appear to wield comparable influence. The banking law harmonization directive mentioned earlier pointed to the difficulty national governments can face in the Council of Ministers when their views are not in line with their own pressure groups. It matters greatly whether or not the subject matter for negotiation is of 'high' political interest, that is, in those areas national governments commonly insist on their political demands being met. Yet a great deal of the work of the EC is taken up with technical or specialist problems, where the argument is usually over details. In such circumstances, government representatives are often acting in the Council of Ministers mainly to protect the interests of definable interest groups. The sponsoring department at home in all probability worked out a collective view and an agreed negotiating position with affected domestic parties before setting off for meetings in Brussels. On occasions, it may also be possible for interest groups to work successfully with the Commission to produce a common policy for the EC: this was the strategy adopted by Commissioner Mansholt in agriculture in the 1960s and by Commissioner Davignon in regard to steel in the late 1970s and 1980s. The incorporation of interest groups into the process of policy initiation took on a new character with the setting up of the advisory committee on banking law, where the interests represented rather than the Commission were given the right to chair the proceedings.

The Council of Ministers itself is not immune from criticism about its internal workings or from the pressure of outside events. The first enlargement of the EC certainly changed the orientation of the banking law directive; the second enlargement is likely to alter the character of many policies, including the workings of the ERDF. On the more technical matters for negotiation, the Council working groups of experts are often heavily dependent on the information and advice supplied by interest groups. All too often the clash of national traditions leads to an impasse in the Council working group, on legislation, which then has to be rescued by COREPER diplomats who trade off technical obstacles in order to achieve a political result. Even so, the implications of proposals can still fail to be appreciated by governments and even when they are realized, they may still prove difficult to resist.

The EC's decision-making process is complex and protracted, and it requires specialist knowledge to influence it. The length of time taken to make decisions allows for interests to organize themselves where necessary but makes for uncertainty over a period of years. Yet, the policy decisions taken by the EC in many fields often seem predictable to those who know the EC well and who have a wide knowledge of all the competing interests. Changes in policy and practice are rarely agreed suddenly, and ample time for adjustment is usually provided before a policy comes fully into effect. Thus, despite the obstacles in the way of effective pressure group activity at the EC level, it is possible for most economic and other interests to get a hearing in the EC's institutions and, not uncommonly, to find that certain national governments have become their spokesmen on a particular issue.

Notes

1. Among the many books and articles on EC decision-making, Wallace, H., Wallace, W. and Webb, C. (eds), *Policy-Making in the European Communities* (Chichester, Wiley, 1977) and Rosenthal, G. G., *The Men Behind the Decisions* (Lexington, D. C. Heath, 1975) are recommended.
2. Comparatively little has been written in general terms on the subject of Euro-pressure groups. The principal sources are Meynaud, J. and Sidjanski, D., *Les Groupes de Pression dans la Communauté Européenne 1958-1968* (Brussels, Institute de Sociologie, U.L.B., 1971); Sidjanski, D., 'Pressure Groups and the European Economic Community', *Government and Opposition*, 2 (1967), 397–416; Sidjanski, D. and Ayberk, U., 'Bilan des Groupes et du processus de Décision dans la Communauté des Six', *Res Publica*, 16 (1974), 33–61; Sidjanski, D., 'Les Groupes de Pression dans la Communauté', *L'Europe en Formation*, Bulletin of the European Federalists, 207 (June 1977); Kirchner, E., 'Interest Group Behaviour at Community Level' in Horowitz, L. (ed.), *Contemporary Perspectives of European Integration* (Westport, Connecticut, Greenwood, 1980); Kirchner, E. and Schwaiger, K., *The Role of Interest Groups in the European Community* (Farnborough, Gower, 1981); and Butt Philip, A., *Pressure Groups in the European Community* (London, Allen & Unwin, 1982).
3. The Berlaymont building in Brussels is the main office of the Commission, while the Charlemagne building houses the secretariat of the Council of Ministers.
4. The most recent information on leading European pressure groups can be found in *European Interest Groups and their Relationships with the Economic and Social Committee* (Farnborough, Gower, 1980).
5. This occurred during the negotiation of legislation requiring the international advertisement of large public procurement contracts open to tender.

4 The European Parliament

JULIET LODGE

The European Parliament (EP) is the EC's institution most associated with the pressures to reform the EC's institutional balance and to advance European Union through supranational-level parliamentary democracy. It is the institution agitating for greater accountability by the Council of Ministers and the Commission in EC decision-making; for itself to be given greater power and influence over the content and nature of the legislative process; and for progress to be made towards both creating a sense of European identity for EC citizens and realizing European Union, however that may be defined.[1] The attainment of all these objectives, it is argued, would be enhanced were the EC's key decision-making institutions to be accorded a single seat and place of operation. The Members of the European Parliament (MEPs) are especially keen to acquire a permanent seat in Brussels.[2] This would assist efficiency by abolishing the present need (in default of member governments' agreeing to fix a seat for the EP) to travel between Brussels and Strasbourg, and occasionally Luxembourg, where once all and now part of the EP's Secretariat is located. It would also provide a visible focus of identity for the public.

While it may seem that the EP's visibility and the extent of its powers are separate issues, they are closely linked in MEPs' minds. Certainly, since shortly after the first direct election of MEPs in 1979 (who formerly had been nominated to serve in the EP from among the members of national parliaments), MEPs have tried to increase their role in EC decision-making and to make sure that the public, who elected them, is sufficiently aware of their existence and activities to turn out to vote in the 1984 direct elections.[3] They hope to convince the public that their work is relevant and important and that they perform the representative function generally associated with members of parliaments in the EC's national parliaments. Moreover, given the national parliaments' negligible ability to influence and effectively control EC decision-making, the EP must assume such powers that will enable it to meet the consequent democratic deficit. This chapter will, therefore, concentrate on the EP's quest for greater authority. However, first, a brief comment on the EP's composition and organization is warranted.

Composition and organization

In 1979, 410 MEPs were elected (twenty-four Greek MEPs joined upon Greece's accession to the EC in 1981). There are eighty-one MEPs from each of France, the FRG, Italy and the UK. Luxembourg has six MEPs, Denmark has sixteen MEPs, Ireland has fifteen MEPs, Belgium has twenty-four and the Netherlands has twenty-five MEPs. The majority of MEPs are members of the main supranational political party groups: the Socialist Group, the European People's Party (EPP), the European Democratic Group, the Communist and Allies Group, the Liberal and Democratic Group and the Group of European Progressive Democrats.

Apart from independent MEPs not attached to any group, there is a group of MEPs known as the Group for the Technical Coordination and Defence of Independent Groups and Members (TCG). Its eleven members formed this group under the EP's old Rules of Procedure. Their aim was to secure parliamentary privileges and powers reserved for official party groups. The new Rules of Procedure increased the number of MEPs needed for a group to attain official status but the TCG managed to preserve their status. The requirement is twenty-one MEPs (if of one nationality), fifteen MEPs (if from two or more member states) and ten MEPs (if from three or more member states). The groups' leaders, as members of the EP's Enlarged Bureau, draft plenary agenda and plan the EP's work, allocate committee chairpersonships, rapporteurships and so on, and group spokesmen have priority in debates over other MEPs.[4] The groups themselves have internal party organizations and some are linked to the transnational parties (the EPP, the Confederation of Socialist Parties (CSP) and the Federation of European Liberals and Democrats (ELD)) that helped mobilize voters in the 1979 elections.[5]

While MEPs sit in political party groups, the cohesiveness of each group varies. Although inter-party competition and rivalry are intensifying, cross-party voting is common, especially where issues of national interest unite MEPs from a given state regardless of their EP party affiliation. National party considerations do intrude into EP party politics for both political and technical reasons (such as the filling of vacant seats according to the provisions of the member states' different direct election laws, and the 'tourniquet' discussed below). However, the EP's parties are becoming increasingly important and guard jealously their independence from sister national parties. They play a major role in the highly political business of electing the EP's officers, allocating resources and organizing the EP's work. Intense political bargaining between the parties typifies the nomination and election of MEPs for key EP posts such as the EP Presidency or chairpersonship of one of the eighteen scrutiny committees. These deal with areas of EC activities and many, not surprisingly, reflect the Commission Directorate–Generals' responsibilities. Their work is crucial to enabling the EP to play an effective role in the EC's legislative process as they scrutinize draft legislation and their views are often adopted by the plenary as a motion for resolution constituting the EP's Opinion on draft proposals.

Party considerations influence the appointment of MEPs to serve on particular committees and as rapporteurs for given issues before the committees. MEPs wishing to sit on a given committee indicate their preferences to their party chairperson and party bureau (which mirrors the national make-up of the EP party group). Specialist expertise as well as political considerations will affect their chances of gaining a seat on their preferred committee (which may in any case seek outside expert advice, draw on the EP's own research facilities, send MEPs on fact-finding exercises in and outside the EC, hold public hearings and set up sub-committees as necessary).

The EP's officials consist of a President whom MEPs elect, if necessary in several ballots, to serve for half of the EP's fixed five-year term. Inter-party bargains are often struck at this stage. The President delegates duties to the twelve Vice-Presidents (who reflect the EP's party composition). These officers constitute the EP's Bureau which meets as the enlarged Bureau when the EP parties' chairpersons or deputies attend. There is also a College of Quaestors that deals with MEPs' working conditions, etc.

The quest for power

MEPs' dissatisfaction with the scope of their powers antecedes the 1979 elections. In fact, shortly after the Rome Treaty had entered into force, pressure to improve the EP's role and to secure its election by direct universal suffrage began to build up. Not until 1974 did MEPs manage to persuade member governments to honour Article 138 of the Rome Treaty and approve direct elections. Even then, a less than perfect decision on elections was taken and the problem of ensuring their representativeness and fairness still has to be solved[6] by member governments approving a draft common electoral procedure drawn up by the EP. As late as 1982, the EP's own draft of a common electoral procedure was such a compromise that it left member governments with a great deal of freedom of manoeuvre and did not even commit the British Government to proportional representation. Errors in the draft, discovered after their eventual approval by the EP, had to be 'corrected' later—that is, before the Council met to approve the electoral procedure in 1983.

The first election of the EP occupies an important psychological position in the EP's quest for greater powers as it meant that the traditional 'chicken-and-egg' arguments over the sagacity of electing the EP before its powers had been increased or vice versa were solved in the former's favour. This helps to account for MEPs' subsequent concentration on their powers. However, MEPs' self-respect and self-interest may also motivate them in this; and arguably their quest is just an extension of the continuing battle between the EC's parliament and executive over the distribution of legislative powers. Over the years, the EP has managed to increase its authority, notably in budgetary matters during the 1970s, but the fact that it is denied some key legislative powers possessed by its national counterparts has led it to seek them in the name of democracy and its own credibility as a mature parliamentary institution—something that is still publicly contested.

The EC itself, anxious about its evolution and the need for policy and institutional reforms, began a thorough reappraisal of them in the 1970s. In 1972 the Vedel Report appeared, followed in 1975 by the Tindemans Report on European Union, the Spierenburg Report (1979), the Report of the Committee of Three (known as the Report of the Three Wise Men) (1979), the Commission's 30 May Mandate (1980), the various reports of the EP (1981), the Genscher–Colombo initiative for a draft European Act (1981) and the subsequent responses by the EP in 1982. The EP, spurred into action by the 'Crocodile Club' (founded by former Commissioner and Communist MEP Altiero Spinelli, and Felice Ippolito), took up the Club's recommendation to set up a committee committed to investigating institutional matters and amendments to the Rome Treaty. MEPs who felt that simply an *ad hoc* working group would suffice found themselves in a minority, and on 9 July 1981 MEPs voted for such a committee. It first met in January 1982. On 6 July 1982, an absolute majority of MEPs voted in favour of new guidelines for further work by this committee. The importance MEPs attach to it is illustrated not just by the fact that the vote was 258 in favour, 37 against and 21 abstentions, but by the unusually high turnout for the vote (72.8 per cent of all MEPs) in a parliament where sometimes much more than a quorum is hard to muster. Furthermore, all the major political parties approve the move (only the Danes had a majority against it). The idea of a new Messina has also begun to find adherents outside EP circles.

In practical terms, MEPs have adopted two main approaches to the problem of increasing their power. The first involves a direct assault (guided by the new committee) on the actual powers the treaties confer on the institutions by seeking appropriate treaty amendments or a new treaty. The second involves an indirect expansion of the EP's powers by exploiting its advisory and supervisory powers under Article 137 of the Rome Treaty, and by capitalizing on its right to devise its own Rules of Procedure and interpreting them expansively without actually altering treaty provisions (something precluded by Article 4 of the Rome Treaty). The year 1981 saw the first results of MEPs' deliberations on improving the EP's role in EC decision-making.

Two areas of particular weakness concern the EP's exclusion from the processes of initiating and passing EC legislation (ignoring for a moment its role in drafting a common electoral procedure and approving the annual EC budget). These two functions are reserved exclusively for the Commission and Council, even though in the member states parliaments have the legislative powers (denied the EP) and the scrutiny and control powers that the EP exercises with some and increasing effect.

The EP's quest for legislative powers relates to its existing scrutiny and control powers.[7] It is incumbent on it to supervise and scrutinize Commission legislative proposals and to control the Commission (if necessary by censuring it), and to approve the draft annual EC budget over which it may (and did in December 1979) use its veto.[8] However, the EP lacks any power to make binding amendments to draft legislation and much of its pressure to reform its legislative role (or lack of an influential one) focuses on ways of enabling it to ensure that either its views become incorporated into draft legislation (something attainable without revision of the Rome Treaty), or that draft legislation it opposes not be passed by the Council. Necessarily, then, MEPs have concentrated on altering their relationship with the Commission and Council. How is this to be achieved?

EP–Commission relations

As the EP alone has the power to censure and force the resignation of the whole Commission (whose members are appointed by accord of the member governments), MEPs argue that they have a correlative right to influence the Commission's composition to ensure that it enjoys their confidence. Consequently, they have argued for a right to be consulted over the appointment of the Commission President at the start of the Commission's four-year term of office, and for a right to hold an investiture and confidence debate on the new Commission:[9] an idea with which Italian Foreign Minister Colombo (co-drafter of the Genscher–Colombo initiative for a draft 'European Act') sympathized.

However, MEPs' ambitions *vis-à-vis* the EP's far from constructive relations with the Commission go beyond having some role in the Commission's appointment. In 1980, MEPs argued that from their right to censure the Commission stems not only the desirability of the EP holding a public debate in the presence of the new Commission President and ending with a vote ratifying his appointment, but also a further power for the EP over the content of the Commission's legislative programme. To this end, they proposed wide-ranging consultations between the EP and the Commission and called on the Commission to consult the EP on all preliminary draft decisions; to defer their presentation in definitive form to the Council pending agreement on their content with the EP; and, significantly, 'to make more correct use of the powers assigned to it by Article 149 of the EEC Treaty'.[10] Article 149 permits the Commission to amend its draft proposal at any time in the legislative process providing the Council has not taken a decision on it. This would allow the Commission to amend proposals to accord with MEPs' wishes.

By 1981, MEPs had made several additional proposals, including the following. They demanded that the Council take no decision on Commission proposals before the Commission has either submitted an amended proposal conforming to the EP's Opinion, or has given the EP an explanation of the reasons for not doing so. MEPs requested the Commission to discuss its annual programme with appropriate committees whenever the EP decided the programme was deficient; and to agree to explain the nature and content of every new draft legislative proposal to the EP's relevant committee before submitting it to the Council: the aim being to enable the Commission promptly to incorporate EP suggestions at the drafting stage.

Much of the impetus behind the quest for the MEPs' greater influence over the content of legislative proposals lay with the deficiencies of the existing decision-making procedures. Thus, while MEPs were and are able, via their scrutiny committees (whose meetings may be attended by officials from the Commission and Council secretariat), to exercise a scrutiny function effectively, that scrutiny had little impact on legislative outcomes. This was because any proposals for a motion for a resolution to form the basis of the EP's Opinion on the legislative item at hand lacked any binding force. In view of the fact that the Council and Commission could ignore the EP's Opinions, MEPs had to find alternative ways of inducing them to respond to the content of these Opinions. A major symbolic success was recorded in October 1980 when the European Court of Justice (ECJ) annulled the isoglucose regulation, as the Council had passed it before receiving the EP's Opinion. The Court had thereby confirmed the EP's right to intervene in a case where it felt its institutional rights were being infringed (a point contested in some member states), and by the fact that, in all cases where the EP has a right to be consulted, the Council may not decide on and pass a Commission proposal before receiving the EP's Opinion. This reinforced the EP's right to be heard and endorsed the importance of its consultative and scrutiny functions. It was also politically significant as it meant that the EP had a means of delaying the passage of legislation of which it either disapproved or which it felt was lacking in certain respects. Not surprisingly, therefore, its amended Rules of Procedure that came into force in May 1981 built on this.

Specifically, Rules 35 and 36 are designed to complement the EP's rather negative power of delay by enabling the EP to put constructive ideas for amending proposals to the Council, and to encourage the Commission to incorporate MEPs' views in any new proposal it may draft. The EP President may request the Commission to withdraw a proposal before the EP votes on its motion for a resolution if the proposal lacks majority support. If the Commission refuses to withdraw it, MEPs may delay issuing their Opinion and refer the matter back to the appropriate EP scrutiny committee. Rule 36 also allows the EP to postpone emission of its Opinion until the Commission states its views on any amendments MEPs have proposed.[11] It is a moot point whether the Council could argue that delay in the emission of the EP's Opinion, if deliberate, means that it is not obliged to await the Opinion before acting; that it has fulfilled its obligations towards the EP simply by consulting it. Mindful of such a possibility, the EP's new Rules of Procedure indicate the need for a resolution for a motion to constitute the basis of the EP's Opinion to be re-presented to the EP within a month (or shorter period) of its referral back to committee. MEPs could then argue that any delay was not wilful (that is, politically inspired) but born of reservations over the content of the disputed piece of legislation. Moreover, referral back to committee is not forbidden, and is clearly preferable—in terms of influencing the content of legislation—to rejecting the proposal as rejection would be tantamount to an Opinion. The Council could then simply pass the legislation 'rejected' by the EP.

It is clear that procedural innovations affect EP–Commission relations and have a two-fold purpose: (i) to increase Commission accountability and responsiveness to the EP for the content of EC legislation; and (ii) to augment the relevance and substantive influence of the EP's deliberations in the consultative and scrutiny processes. However, they have an important political and symbolic value *vis-à-vis* the Council. Just as the motion of censure has been used symbolically against the Council, so the aim of the procedural changes is to help the EP to influence and shape legislation passed by the Council. Indeed, Rule 39 permits the EP periodically to review Council decisions that deviate significantly from the EP's Opinion on matters of particular importance and not already subject to EP–Council conciliation under Rule 38.

MEPs have adopted additional practices to enable them to influence the direction and content of Commission proposals. The EP can draft 'own initiative' reports on matters of concern to the EC and pass resolutions asking the Commission to introduce appropriate legislative proposals and to agree, by means of a joint declaration with the EP, to submit policy proposals to the Council embodying MEPs' 'own initiative' reports within a time-limit fixed by the EP.[12] Both the Committee of Three[13] and the EP advocated the Commission explaining any failure to do so. What MEPs are trying to do here is to translate their political right to make policy proposals into EC legislation by inserting their voice into the Commission's formal legal right of initiative. The 'own initiative' reports have been likened to British private members' bills,[14] and clearly they are a means for MEPs to press for and acquire some indirect power of initiative. Similarly, provisions for scrutinizing Commission and Council responses to EP views are designed to further MEPs' desires to influence EC decision-making.

However, the 'weapons' for achieving this at MEPs' disposal are weak: MEPs cannot exert any effective 'control' over the Commission and Council via Question Time, important as Question Time is as a symbol of openness and democratic accountability to the EC's elected institution. While Commission replies to MEPs' questions are generally informative, the Council's are lamentably evasive. Nor does the EP's right to hold a debate on the Commission's annual *General Report* materially affect the nature of the EP's influence on EC activities. Indeed, so meaningless has this exercise become (as the debate is on what has happened already) that a debate now takes place on the Commission's intended programme. As indicated, there is growing pressure for the Commission to detail its programme before the EP on a six-monthly basis, and to attend an EP debate on major items of proposed legislation to facilitate the incorporation of the EP's majority views into the draft legislation at the pre-legislative stage. Certainly, such a practice would give Commission proposals submitted to the Council added legitimacy. It might also be interpreted as a challenge to the Council's supremacy as any Council prevarication could become politically charged and used by MEPs to 'embarrass' recalcitrant Council members. These examples show how alterations to, or refinements of, EP–Commission inter-institutional procedures have ramifications that inevitably imply the possibility, though not the inevitability, of confrontation with the Council.

Furthermore, the Commission is anxious generally to avert confrontation with the Council. Indeed, MEPs have accused it of being far too malleable in this respect; and of becoming as cavalier in disregarding EP views as the Council. For example, the Commission's provision of information to the EP (by way of replies to questions[15] and, more importantly, by way of its statements at the start of the EP's plenary sessions) has been praised as something the Council should emulate. But this display of Commission responsiveness and accountability to the EP masked the sometimes vacuous nature of such statements. They have been castigated as devoid of policy implications for the actual content of Commission proposals. In March 1982, British MEPs rebuked the Commission for the uninformative nature of its written statement on action taken on EP resolutions which is circulated before the start of EP sessions.[16] The cause of advancing Council accountability to the EP by adopting the same practices is thus nullified.[17] Nevertheless, the EP is inventive in exploiting any means given it to supervise EC decision-making, and so to enhance its legislative role.

EP–Council relations

From the above, it is obvious that the question of ensuring Commission and Council accountability to the EP for their legislative outputs is imperfect (and non-existent outside the budget in the Council's case). It is also highly problematic and politically explosive. Not until 1982 did the EP venture to invoke Article 175 of the Rome Treaty against the Council for failure to act (on transport policy). Given a feeling that direct confrontations with the Council could be counterproductive and thwart the EP's aims, concentrating on steps to enhance the EP's ability to influence the content of legislative proposals, rather than simply inadequately 'control' their passage, seems justified. Indeed, many procedural reforms advocated by MEPs rest on the premiss that the EP has a moral and political obligation to EC voters to represent their interests by affecting, if not drafting and alone determining, the content of EC legislation. This spurs them to further action.

MEPs have shrunk neither from calling on the Council to adopt majority voting, nor from capitalizing on the Council's readiness to reply to parliamentary questions even though it is not obliged to do so by the Rome Treaty. While in the name of democratic openness it may have seemed for the Council politically expedient to accede to Question Time, this has been expanded since 1975 to cover questions put to the Chairman of the Conference of Foreign Ministers (CFM) meeting in European Political Cooperation (EPC).[18] The Council President, or his/her representative, does participate in special EP debates, and Council members occasionally attend EP committee meetings to exchange views. Council members also become involved in extensive consultation with MEPs when the 'conciliation procedure' is invoked to resolve disagreements over the budget,[19] and over any conflict having financial implications. MEPs want this extended to cover any important matters over which the EP and Council disagree, and the 'conciliation procedure' has been seen as a way for the EP to participate in the exercise of legislative power.[20] MEPs have been trying to capitalize on each of these practices with the aim of augmenting both the Council's accountability to the EP, and their own legislative role and powers.

The case for the EP achieving both the above goals can, moreover, be justified on the grounds of national parliaments' negligible ability either to influence the content of EC legislation or to control Council members. The deficiencies of the British system of parliamentary scrutiny are legion compared to Danish practice.[21] Yet, even the German Bundestag fails miserably on both counts. Between January 1978 and June 1980, only 106 documents (5.8 per cent) about Council regulations, directives and decisions were brought to a plenary sitting in the form of an original document with a recommendation for a decision from the appropriate committee. Over half (sixty-four) had entered into force *before* the committee or Bundestag could discuss them.[22] As this situation is typical, a strong case for supranational parliamentary control can be made.

As unimpeachable as the rationale behind the EP's moves is, how does the EP propose exerting influence over the Council and, more especially, over its legislative output? As in the Commission's case, changes to current practice regarding the provision of information to the EP could help. For example, the content and speed with which Council replies to EP questions are issued could be improved. In September 1982, the Council told the EP that it was prepared to attend important EP debates and Question Time on Wednesdays. The Council stressed that the EP would have to give it adequate notice of the agenda and of when it wanted Council attendance. Furthermore, EP–Council relations could be improved in the budgetary sector, at least in respect of the Council's consultation and partial acceptance of EP views.[23] (Divergencies over allocations to given sectors (with over 60 per cent going on the CAP and compulsory spending exempt from EP control) are likely to persist and be aggravated as the EP insists that more should be spent on tackling unemployment and other recession-related issues.)

The EP, as part of the EC's budgetary authority, could be given access to the minutes of Council and COREPER meetings at which budgetary issues are discussed. It might also be represented at Council deliberations on the budget, although the EP does not want the right generally to attend and speak at Council meetings. Moreover, there are regular fierce political EP–Council disputes over budgetary matters. These centre on determination of the 'maximum rate' and its consequent effect on the extent of EP control over EC expenditure (confined as it is to 'non-obligatory' spending).[24] The disputes also focus on the diametrically opposed views of the Council and the EP on the correct application of Article 205 and the Commission's exclusive powers to adopt individual financing decisions. The EP is adamant that the Commission's power should not be infringed by any committee procedure which infringes Commission autonomy and results in the implementing decision diverging from what was intended when the EP and Council passed the budget. The problem inheres in the fact that the EP—a full participant in the EC's budgetary authority—sees both its budgetary powers and its political priorities reflected in budgetary decisions, subsequently 'undermined by Council using legislative brakes'.[25] Robert Jackson (MEP) cites the example of the EP voting significant sums for industrial policy ventures such as shipbuilding and aerospace that, in view of subsequent Council intransigence over the attendant Commission draft regulations, resulted in but a few studies sponsored by the Commission which itself felt unable to go ahead and spend the funds as intended.[26]

Various advisory and/or management committees help the Commission implement the budget. Jackson has isolated four main types of committee procedure. First, there are purely advisory, consultative committees (like that of the European Social Fund (ESF)) that offer advice that the Commission may either accept or reject before taking the final decision itself on whether or not to fund individual projects 'within the context of an overall Community regulation'.[27] Secondly, there are committees (like the Regional Fund committee) exercising suspensive vetoes: if they disagree with a Commission proposal, the Council can overrule the Commission if it acts within a limited period (usually two months). Thirdly, there are committees 'in which unanimity must be achieved to support a Commission proposal, prior to Council arbitration, where unanimity is not attained' (for example, on energy issues). Fourthly, there is the procedure whereby Council unanimity is the precondition to action: the Commission submits proposals directly to Council for individual projects. The Council has to take a unanimous decision. Failure to do so means that funds voted in the budget may not be spent. Council disagreements over Commission proposals under the non-quota section of the Regional Fund (ERDF) have led to no spending on the very area desired by the EP. The EP used its right to raise non-compulsory expenditure to vote sums for the ERDF's non-quota section to make it more flexible than the main ERDF. Council inaction eroded the EP's budgetary power over non-compulsory expenditure. According to Jackson, the Council thereby acquired administrative and executive authority and excessive powers over the implementation of the budget.[28] Clearly, attempts in 1982 to resolve inter-institutional problems over the budget must clarify the EP's and Council's roles and strengthen the conciliation procedure. If the EP's role is not to be nullified, it is crucial that it have useful informative links with the Commission and Council. Difficulties over communications with the Council are not limited to the budgetary sector as the EP recognizes.

On taking office, the Council President-in-Office makes a speech to the EP detailing the aims of his Presidency, and the EP can give an Opinion on it. To facilitate more effective exchanges, the EP wants to receive the statement in writing in advance to enable it to hold a well-prepared debate on it. MEPs have called also for regular formal contacts between parliamentary committees and the appropriate Councils for confidential talks: to build, therefore, on the practice of some EP committees of inviting the Council President periodically to attend a committee session and answer specific questions. Such contacts could be extended to enable the EP regularly to impress its more detailed views on those responsible for passing and seeking further compromises and amendments to proposals to facilitate their adoption. This would neither require revision of the Rome Treaty nor legally alter the balance of power among the EC's institutions. However, it would entrench the EP's political right of legislative influence. This in turn would be used to justify subsequent moves to codify the EP's role in the EC's legislative process, and to make the Council's consultations with the EP significant in terms of policy content. Clearly, the key to increasing the EP's ability to influence EC policy lies in the amount and usefulness of information available to it from the Commission and Council, as well as from its own sources (including interest group links) and from the Economic and Social Committee of the European Communities (ESC). Indeed, not only could the ESC improve its image by regularly transmitting information and opinions to the EP, but the latter could use its expertise.[29]

It is in the sphere of foreign affairs that the EP is acutely aware of its negligible role and of the democratic deficit at the supranational level. EPC is formally outside the EC but it is widely argued that it should come within it. Furthermore, the EP does exercise, as indicated above, some scrutiny over the work of EC Foreign Ministers. However, if it is to exercise both its *advisory* and its supervisory powers more effectively over both EPC and external relations in accordance with treaty provisions it needs to be consulted more regularly and at a pre-decisional phase in the decision-making process. Under the Treaty, the EP must be consulted only on a selective basis on external relations' agreements. Under Article 228, it must be consulted after the signing, but before the conclusion, of agreements in cases specified by the Treaty (excluding trade agreements pursuant to Article 113, agreements on the EC's enlargement under Article 237, or agreements pursuant to the EURATOM and ECSC treaties). In this sphere, it is difficult for the EP to increase its role without treaty revision. Certainly, its demand to be involved in matters of the EC's enlargement cannot be realized without treaty amendment.

More problematic is the dilemma posed by the question of determining at what point in the process of concluding treaties with third countries consultation with the EP can be said to be completed. In 1962, the Council argued that, provided the EP was consulted before an agreement (in this case the association agreement with Greece) was concluded, Article 238's requirements on consulting the EP had been met. The EP contended that *ex post facto* consultation precluded it from influencing the agreement's content, infringed the Treaty, and constituted grounds for action under Article 175: a threat it did not act upon as the Council agreed to submit the details of future proposed agreements to the appropriate EP committee for scrutiny before the text was finalized. This is known as the 'Luns–Westerterp' procedure. Dissatisfied with the scope of consultation under this and Article 228, the EP wants consultation to be extended to all agreements concluded on the basis of EC treaties before they are signed, as both new agreements and the extension or renewal of old ones involve political considerations. Additionally, given the EP's network of bilateral contacts with parliaments around the world, MEPs may have important insights on matters covered by the agreements. However, they may also complicate their conclusion by linking political demands (for example, on providing havens or landing-places for terrorists) to trade agreements with developing countries. This involves very sensitive matters of international diplomacy. Given the European Council's general pronouncements on foreign affairs and its role in EPC, and given the EP's hope to make both subject to supranational parliamentary control—despite their formal position outside the EC—it is not surprising that MEPs have tried to capitalize on the EP's role in EPC.

The EP's role in EPC is neither strictly advisory nor supervisory although parallels are clear between its role in EC decision-making in other areas. Moreover, MEPs have increasingly focused and taken stands on topical international matters like human rights, apartheid, hunger, racism and so on, as well as on security matters. The EP holds an annual debate on EPC, following the submission of the Foreign Ministers' annual report. The Council replies to MEPs' questions on EPC (often evasively as it claims that it is difficult to reflect the Ten's views more precisely). The EP's Political Affairs Committee (PAC) holds quarterly colloquies with the Chairperson of the CFM to examine progress in EPC. To improve the usefulness of such contacts and to augment the EP's role in EPC, several suggestions have been made. Since a decision in October 1981, instead of very broad discussions in the colloquies, a few issues are selected for scrutiny. The EP also wants the CFM chairperson or deputy to attend and reply to EP debates held under the urgency procedure and to brief the PAC on most recent EPC discussions held either 'en marge du Conseil' or at Schloss Gymnich type informal meetings. More importantly, too, notwithstanding national parliaments' negligible role in formulating foreign policy, the EP wants to be apprised of policy developments; to influence them, and to ensure a measure of ministerial accountability not least over major shifts in the Ten's policies. The EP has also advanced important suggestions for improving the administration of EPC.[30] So far, the EP's involvement in foreign affairs has not resulted in inter-institutional clashes although this is a field in which there is scope for the EP increasing its role.

There is a further way by which the EP can attempt to augment its influence over the EC and that is by exploiting Article 235 of the Rome Treaty. This provides for the EP to be consulted by the Council on Commission proposals on EC goals where the Treaty does not provide the requisite powers. Clearly, if the EP manages to extend its influence over the Commission at the pre-legislative stage of EC decision-making, it may use this provision to stimulate EC action in areas relevant to EC publics and which it, in accordance with Article 235's provisions, deems 'necessary to attain, in the course of the operation of the common market, one of the objectives of the Community'. The EP's claims for consultative and control powers *vis-à-vis* EPC and the European Council's decisions expanding EC activities can also be vindicated with reference to this Article.

So far, we have stressed the constitutional and procedural devices the EP employs to extend its opportunities for increasing its influence over the content of EC legislation. Clearly, the scope for inter-institutional confrontation is vast. Much conflict is hidden from the public eye. Generally, the EP's own activities receive little public attention and often only emotional or potentially scandalous issues gain wide media coverage (in the UK, at least). The annual Council–EP wranglings over the budget are an exception to this but the sheer technicalities of the budget deter detailed coverage by the media. Nevertheless, if the EP is to play the 'grand forum' role attributed to parliaments, it must not only hold debates on major issues but be seen to be doing so. Interestingly, MEPs have backed the idea of a European television channel, and they see the media playing an important role in creating a sense of European identity.[31] Media coverage of the EP's work is crucial. Without it the EP's relevance will be lost on voters and EP President Piet Dankert is particularly keen to impress the EP's relevance on the public mind lest ignorance and apathy deter turnout and so erode the second elected EP's claims to democratic legitimacy and increased powers.

The EP's public image has to be cultivated not least because of its lack of authority in the legislative sphere that is seen as the essence of parliament's being deprives the EP's members of a chance of campaigning on their record as legislators or members of government. It is, certainly, no excuse either to argue that the EP's original nomenclature—'assembly'—denotes that its role is not supposed to be anything more than a consultative chamber. Some French constitutionalists may be satisfied with such a limited role for the EP but that does not accord with the EP's self-image or aspirations.[32] Nor should MEPs desist from agitating for the removal of additional barriers, such as the 'revolving list' or 'tourniquet' system introduced by the French Gaullist Rassemblement pour la République (RPR), and the absence of a single seat for the EP.

The legality of the tourniquet has been doubted. The tourniquet forces RPR MEPs (who were elected on the 'Defence of the Interests of France in Europe' (DIFE) list) to resign after one year in the EP to allow others on the RPR's list for the 1979 Euro-elections to have a spell in the EP. It is seen as a way of inhibiting the socializing effects which EP membership has on MEPs and some DIFE MEPs have refused to comply and complained that they have been compelled to sign almost identical letters of resignation in advance. Other MEPs have taken the whole issue up with the EP's Committees on the Verification of Credentials and on the Rules of Procedure and Petitions.[33]

Far more serious is the failure to fix the EP's seat in a single place. This is the one step that would make a major contribution to European Union, the EC's and EP's public image, and to the enhancement of MEPs' efficiency. Member governments are empowered under the Rome Treaty to determine the EP's seat, and to fix a single working place for the EC's decision-making bodies. In theory, they could opt for any place in the EC since the EC's location policy has been based on the rental of buildings, at great and increasingly greater cost to the EC's over-extended budget. In practice, it would be quite logical to fix Brussels (where EP committees meet) as the EP's seat. The EP would then be close to the Council and the Commission, neither of which is likely to move from Brussels. Recently, key sections of the EP's Secretariat have been moved from Luxembourg to Brussels and the Val d'Or project on new EP buildings in Brussels has also provoked speculation of relocation.[34] Easy and rapid communication between the EP, Council and Commission would improve and expedite EC decision-making, increase efficiency and reduce the travel and subsistence costs incurred by the expanding, peripatetic EP. In 1983, expenditure on buildings is expected to be £14,476,274. The overall cost of running the EP is to rise by 8.7 per cent to £118,948,510. Of that, £52,978,070 will be spent on staff, £19,930,134 on MEPs, £4,197,075 on travel, and £6,800,000 on the political groups (half of whose funds are earmarked for expenditure relating to the 1984 direct elections campaign).

From being in 1965 a 142-strong non-elected body of MEPs having a back-up staff of 492, the EP has grown into an elected body of 434 MEPs (likely to grow with the accession of Spain and Portugal to the EC) with a staff, including inter-preters and translators, and that of the political groups, of nearly 3,000. The extra cost of staff travelling to part-sessions of the EP (that is, plenary meetings) at Strasbourg per annum has been estimated at 4.5 million EUA; and travel time at 124,800 hours for Strasbourg, and 46,000 hours for Brussels. If the packing, unpacking and repacking of documents is included, the time becomes 187,200 hours and 57,500 hours for Strasbourg and Brussels respectively. The total of 244,700 hours annually has been calculated as equal to 142 'man years' of 215 days each, to which is added the annual administrative costs of organizing the EP's work in three different places of twelve 'man years'.[35] Then there are the expenses of staff and MEPs needing telex and telephone facilities, office equipment and accommodation in three places, duplicate copies of various documents, vehicles, incidental expenses for auxiliary staff and canteen staff, postage and security. Furthermore, officials and members of other institutions, notably the Commission and Council, incur extra expense by having to travel to attend parliamentary meetings. Depriving the EP of a single seat is wasteful, illogical and to be compared to dividing the United Kingdom Parliament's work between London, Edinburgh and Cardiff. However, even MEPs themselves disagree over a permanent site for the EP. Voting on the issue in 1980 and 1981, they divided over Brussels and Stras-bourg, with northern MEPs predominantly favouring Brussels, and southern MEPs Strasbourg. By contrast, many EP officials prefer Luxembourg which is the seat of the ECJ, European Investment Bank (EIB) and the increasingly politically impor-tant Court of Auditors.

Reporting in 1979 on the accommodation policies of the EC's institutions, the Court of Auditors criticized the lack of permanent sites, forward planning, and inter-institutional consultation on accommodation requirements. It noted also how costly the diffusion of meeting places was, and how unfavourable rental agreements were. Although the EC institutions are exempt from all national or local taxes, under certain rental agreements they pay indirect property tax or value-added tax to the Belgian and Luxembourg Governments. Since the Court of Auditor's report, an inter-institutional group on accommodation policy has been established. It has made a number of recommendations and suggested that in future EC institutions should be built or purchased rather than rented. In addition, a standard document on rental agreements has been prepared and representations made to the Belgian Government for exemption from or refund of, the indirect payment of property tax.[36]

The whole question of a permanent site for the EP and for other EC institutions has been scrutinized by the EP's Committee on Budgetary Control. The EP first authorized the Committee to report on the EC's institutions' accommodation policy (or lack thereof) on 15 September 1980, since when it has met and reported on several occasions. Not until April 1982 was it able on the basis of an interim report[37] to adopt a motion for resolution on the matter. This endorsed the Court of Auditors' views and advocated investigating the practicality of the institutions having compatible needs sharing facilities and accommodation, especially that which was only used for part of the month. It requested the inter-institutional group on accommodation policy to prepare a five-year rolling plan for the EC's institutional bases, and asked the Commission to report on this to the EP within six months, to present the five-year rolling plan promptly and to report annually on accommodation policies and any changes to the plan.

Expeditious and efficient decision-making in the EC clearly demands that the key institutions be located in one city. Deciding the EC's 'capital' has always been a politically contentious matter. This is why the member governments have repeatedly procrastinated over determining the EP's seat and condemned it to a peripatetic existence. While it is plain that different governments—notably those of France, Belgium and Luxembourg—have competing claims to host the EC's institutions, settling the matter is not simply a question of political niceties. Rather, it would be a step towards European Union in the sense that the EC would have an identifiable capital, a seat of 'government'. This might make it more of a reality to EC publics. Moreover, as it is obvious that locating, for example, the Commission, Council and EP in Brussels would ameliorate decision-making, there can be little doubt that improved and easier contact between the EP, Council and Commission would spur MEPs to press for greater legislative powers to be entrusted to the EP. They would certainly confront the Commission and Council in the event of difficulty and would encounter few obstacles to securing media and public attention to the issue in view of the presence of the press corps in Brussels. At the moment, it is easy to criticize the EP for profligate expenditure on its three meeting places, but as it asserts its desire to see this situation ended in the name of greater decision-making efficiency and the freeing of funds (including those in reserve, or unspent on policies for which they were earmarked originally) for expenditure on other items (such as under-financed EC policies salient to the EC's publics), prevaricating member governments will come under increasing pressure to act. European Union, whether it takes a federal or confederal form, will then prove ineluctable.

Neither major constitutional reforms nor minor constitutional revisions along either the maximalist lines advocated by Spinelli, the Crocodile Club and many MEPs, or the minimalist lines adumbrated by Genscher and Colombo will be realized in a political vacuum.[38] There is certainly broad-based support for Spinelli's report on guidelines for reform of the treaties and the completion of European Union. This was demonstrated in July 1982 when the EP endorsed by 257 votes to 37 votes with 21 abstentions the conclusions of the Committee on Institutional Affairs[39] that defines European Union according to the basic principle of subsidiarity. This calls on the EC to act only where goals can be best achieved more effectively in common than by member governments individually; but it permits the EC to act in all domestic economic, international and security matters. The resolution also endorsed strengthening the EP's political role to allow it to exercise legislative power jointly with the Council: a bicameral legislature may not be so fanciful an idea in a European Union as some have suggested.[40]

Given MEPs' career aspirations and interests in increasing the EP's power (and irrespective of whether this shared goal is related to electoral considerations or not), cross-party support for strengthening the EP's role in the context of European Union is perhaps not surprising. However, party political considerations will become increasingly important as stimuli to both reforms beneficial to the EP, and to influencing legislative proposals in accordance with party political preferences. (Indeed, considerations of party strength have given rise to MEPs abusing electronic voting devices in the EP to vote more than once on motions.) The EP's influence will increase as its politicization progresses. It is not without reason that MEPs, anxious about the distortion in relative party strengths in the first elected EP that were occasioned by the different electoral systems used in the Nine in 1979, should be keen to draft a common electoral law to redress the balance. Indeed, this is one area reserved for the EP to exercise the legal right of legislative initiative.

Nevertheless, the EP's draft uniform electoral procedure submitted in March 1982 to the Council for adoption and to the member states for ratification represents but a modest attempt to harmonize electoral procedures for the 1984 elections. It was heavily criticized in the EP. Ninety-five amendments to it were voted on before it was adopted by 158 votes to 76 votes with 27 abstentions. The accompanying resolution was passed by 138 votes to 77 votes with 24 abstentions.[41] The EP's draft does not confront and alter the inequalities arising out of the ratio of seats to population[42] among the four big member states, for example. However, it does give the vote to all EC nationals regardless of their place of residence.[43] (Thus British officials working for the EC in Brussels or Luxembourg should—if the procedure is adopted and implemented—have a vote in 1984 whereas British electoral law deprived them of it in 1979.) The draft also provides for proportional representation with member states divided into multi-member constituencies in which a minimum of three and a maximum of fifteen MEPs would be elected. Whether or not a more or less common electoral procedure will be adopted in time for the 1984 elections remains to be seen. In the meantime, MEPs will continue to try and submit decision-making practices escaping EP control (for example, in COREPER) to parliamentary scrutiny and control. MEPs will also continue attempting to arouse public awareness of their work to stimulate a good turnout in the elections, and to vindicate their claims for more extensive powers.

Notes

1. Lodge, J., 'The European Parliament After Direct Elections: Talking-Shop or Putative Legislature', *Journal of European Integration*, 5 (1982), 259–84.
2. See the *Report on the seat of the institutions of the European Communities and in particular of the European Parliament* (Zagari Report), Luxembourg, European Parliament, Doc. 1–333/81.
3. See Piet Dankert's inaugural address as the new President of the EP (January 1982).
4. See Palmer, M., *The European Parliament* (Oxford, Pergamon, 1981) for details.
5. See Pridham, G. and Pridham, P., *Transnational Party Co-operation and European Integration* (London, Allen & Unwin, 1981).
6. See Lodge, J. and Herman, V., *Direct Elections to the European Parliament: A Community Perspective* (London and New Haven, N.J., Macmillan and Humanities Press, 1982).
7. See Herman, V. and Lodge, J., *The European Parliament and the European Community* (London and New York, Macmillan and St Martin's Press, 1978); and Palmer, M. op. cit. See also Marquand, D., *Parliament for Europe* (London, Cape, 1979).
8. On the budget, see Strasser, D., *The Finances of Europe* (Luxembourg, Office for Official Publications of the European Communities, 1981). See also Shaw, M., *The European Parliament and the Community Budget* (London, European Conservative Group, 1978).
9. See *Report on the relations between the European Parliament and the Commission of the Community with a view to the forthcoming appointment of a new Commission* (Rey Report), Luxembourg, European Parliament, Doc. 1–71/80.
10. Ibid., p. 7.
11. See Lodge, J., op. cit.
12. See *Report on the right of legislative initiative and the role of the European Parliament in*

the legislative process of the Community (Van Miert Report), Luxembourg, European Parliament, Doc. 1-207/81.

13. See Committee of Three, *Report on the European Institutions* (Three Wise Men's Report), presented to the European Council, October 1979, p. 79.

14. See Palmer, M., op. cit., p. 60.

15. Schwed, J. J., 'Les questions écrites du Parlement européen à la Commission', *Revue du Marché Commun*, 135 (1970), 365-8; see also Cohen, L., 'The Development of Question Time in the European Parliament', *Common Market Law Review*, 16 (1979), 41-59.

16. *EP News*, March 1982, p. 4.

17. See Lodge, J., op. cit., p. 272.

18. See *Report on European Political Cooperation and the role of the European Parliament* (Elles Report), Luxembourg, European Parliament, Doc. 1-335/81.

19. On the budget, see Strasser, D., op. cit., pp. 11 and 363-72.

20. See *Report on relations between the European Parliament and the Council of the Community* (Hänsch Report), Luxembourg, European Parliament, Doc. 1-216/81, pp. 9-11.

21. The House of Lords' scrutiny is admirable and efficient but the effects of it limited. The Commons' scrutiny has minimal influence and is not as effective as that of the Lords. See, too, Herman, V. and Schendelen, R. van (eds), *The European Parliament and the National Parliaments* (Farnborough, Saxon House, 1979).

22. See Hänsch Report, op. cit., pp. 9-11.

23. See Ehlermann, C-D., 'Article 205 of the EEC Treaty', paper presented to the Ninth FIDE Congress, September 1980.

24. See *Report drawn up on behalf of the Committee on Budgets on the joint declaration by the European Parliament, the Council and the Commission on various measures to improve the budgetary procedure*, Luxembourg, European Parliament, Doc. 1-450/82. See, also, *The Times*, 24 July 1982 and the *Report on the preliminary draft budget in the light of the Parliament's resolutions on guidelines for the 1983 budget*, Luxembourg, European Parliament, 1-410/82.

25. See remarks by Robert Jackson (MEP) in the reports of the Ninth Congress on 25-7 September 1980 of the FIDE, 3 (1980), p. 5.2.

26. Ibid.

27. Ibid., p. 5.3. These committees are presided over by the Commission and members are drawn from the member states.

28. Ibid., pp. 5.3-5.4.

29. See *Report on the relations between the European Parliament and the Economic and Social Committee* (Baduel Glorioso Report), Luxembourg, European Parliament, Doc. 1-226/81. Note also that the Economic and Social Committee's role in EC decision-making is minimal. For a discussion of its weakness, see Lodge, J. and Herman, V., 'The Economic and Social Committee in EEC decision making', *International Organization*, 34 (1980), 265-84; also Bernard, N., Laval, C. and Nys, A., *Le Comité Economique et Social* (Brussels, Brussels University Press, 1972) and ESC General Secretariat, *Community Advisory Committees for the Representation of Socio-Economic Interests* (Farnborough, Saxon House, 1980).

30. See Elles Report, op. cit.

31. See *EP Briefing*, 8-12 March 1982, pp. 9-10. See also the chapters on the role of the media in Lodge, J. and Herman, V., 1982, op. cit., and Herman, V. and Lodge, J., 1978, op. cit. Also on the media and direct elections, see Blumler, J. G. and Fox, A. D., *The European Voter: Popular Responses to the first Community Elections* (London, PSI, 1982).

32. See Inglehart, R., Rabier, J-R., Gordon, I. and Lehmann Sørensen, C., 'Broader powers for the European Parliament', *European Journal of Political Research*, 8 (1980), 113-32.

33. See *Report on disputes concerning the validity of appointments in connection with the 'tourniquet system'*, Luxembourg, European Parliament, Doc. 1-398/82.

34. A new building in Strasbourg was built for the directly elected EP; and a Conference Centre in Luxembourg was also designed to house the new EP but not built under EC auspices.

35. See the *Interim Report on the Accommodation Policy of the Community Institutions* (Price Report), Luxembourg, European Parliament, Doc. 1-104/82, p. 21. See, too, the Zagari Report, op. cit.

36. See Price Report, op. cit.

37. Ibid.

38. See *Crocodile*, 7, 12/1981 and 8, 5/1982. Also see Jonker, S., *Draft Treaty Establishing European Union* (Luxembourg, European Parliament, 1981).

39. This was established by EP decision of 9 July 1981. It began work in February 1982.

40. See, e.g., *Report of the Working Party examining the problem of the enlargement of the powers of the European Parliament* (Vedel Report), *Bulletin of the European Communities*, Supplement 4/1972; the election manifestos of the EPP and ELD; and Herman, V. and Lodge, J., 1978, op. cit., Chapter 9.

41. See *Bulletin of the European Communities*, March 1982, pts. 2.4.2 and 2.4.5.

42. On the electoral systems and for a breakdown of the election results, see Lodge, J. and Herman, V., 1982, op. cit. See also *European Journal of Political Research*, Special Issue (April 1980) and Herman, V. and Hagger, M. (eds), *The Legislation of Direct Elections to the European Parliament* (Farnborough, Gower, 1980).

43. See *Report drawn up on behalf of the Political Affairs Committee on a draft uniform electoral procedure for the election of Members of the European Parliament* (Seitlinger Report), Luxembourg, European Parliament, Doc. 1-988/81/A and B/C. See, too, Hand, G., Georgel, J. and Sasse, C. (eds), *European Electoral Systems Handbook* (London, Butterworths, 1979).

5 The European Court of Justice

DAVID FREESTONE

On Luxembourg's Plateau du Kirchberg, at an apparently seemly distance from the buildings housing some of the EC's political institutions, stands the European Court of Justice (ECJ). The somewhat reserved position that it occupies may well reflect a popular prejudice about the detached, unworldly nature of judicial institutions. In fact, the very modern court building houses an institution which has played a central role in the process of European integration—a role some would argue more significant than any other institution, including the Commission.[1] As the EC's only judicial tribunal, the ECJ is charged with ensuring that 'in the interpretation and application of [the EC] Treaty the law is observed' (Article 164). Its constitutional position is very different from that of the judiciary in, for example, the United Kingdom. Brown and Jacobs have pointed out that 'while a decision of even the highest court in the United Kingdom can be reversed by Act of Parliament, even with retroactive effect, the decisions of the Court of Justice cannot be reversed by any Act of Council; on the contrary, any measure of the Council having legal effect can be annulled by the Court if contrary to the Treaties.'[2] Indeed in the recent *Isoglucose cases* (1980)[3] the ECJ found that the failure of the Council to consult the European Parliament on the text of a draft regulation, as required by Article 43 of the Rome Treaty, was grounds for declaring the resulting Council regulation void. This case highlights particularly the fact that the ECJ, unlike other EC institutions, is not answerable to any other body for its decisions; its independence from any form of political pressure (either from member states or within the EC) is crucial to the task it performs.

The members of the Court—its judges and advocates general—are chosen for six-year renewable terms by common accord of the member governments from persons 'whose independence is beyond doubt' and 'who possess the qualifications required for appointment to the highest judicial office in their respective countries or who are jurisconsults of recognized competence.'[4] Impartiality is written into both the Treaty and the basic rules of procedure contained in the Statutes of the Court—protocols to the founding Treaties.[5] Changes in the rules of procedure require the unanimous approval of the Council (Article 188). Judgments are collegiate; individual judges are not permitted separate or dissenting opinions, thereby avoiding any basis for political pressure on members of the Court. Judicial solidarity is further maintained by the oath each judge swears, 'to preserve the secrecy of the deliberations of the Court'. The resulting decisions can take a long time to reach and are on occasions frustratingly short. A 'laconic unanimity' may be preserved in such cases, but for the detailed argument which is the distinctive feature of the judgments of the highest national courts, the lawyer must turn instead to the often wide-ranging and scholarly submissions of the advocate general (whose task is to advise the court on the directions that its decision might take)[6] without always being aware of the extent to which the judges have accepted his arguments. Significantly it has been the experience of the International Court of Justice at The Hague, where dissenting and separate opinions are permitted, that national judges are continually reluctant to vote against their own states. Despite the disadvantages therefore, the integration of national interests has clearly not yet reached the stage that the collegiate judgment could be abandoned without risk.

The ECJ's powers derive from the Treaty (principally Articles 164–88) and the tasks with which it is entrusted are very wide-ranging. It is, for example, called upon to act as an international court (in disputes between member states, Article 170, and/or between the Commission and member states, Article 169); as an administrative court (to hear allegations of illegal action or inaction by EC organs, Articles 173–6, 178, 184); as an industrial tribunal (for complaints by EC employees, Article 179); and as a transnational constitutional court (ruling on the interpretation of the Treaty and the interpretation or validity of EC legislation at the request of national courts, Article 177). For an analysis of the total case-load of the ECJ up to December 1981 see Tables 1 and 2. Its task may perhaps be summarized as the building of a new legal system applied throughout the EC, grafted on to the existing national systems. EC law does not extend into all areas of national law, but its extent is wider than earlier envisaged; for example, although it was suggested that national criminal law would be unaffected, the ECJ has had to deal with a number of criminal issues involving notably the deportation of criminals and the importation of pornography.[7] That such a 'new legal order' could be developed at all is no minor achievement; that it has provided one of the most dynamic areas of EC activity when, as Dashwood has commented, 'lawyers... are generally regarded as nature's conservatives',[8] suggests that the work of the ECJ merits close attention by all students of European integration.

The Treaty provides the ECJ with its powers and, like a written constitution, outlines the aims and objectives of the EC in general terms (for example, Articles 2–8) and in the detailed programmes of the substantive provisions. Just as the framework of the Treaty requires supplementation by legislation, so the provisions of the Treaty and the supplementary legislation require interpretation and application. Application is the preserve of the national legal systems, but interpretation is the work of the ECJ. Drawing the dividing line between the two tasks is difficult and highly controversial:[9] but it is in the crucial work of interpretation that the ECJ's distinctive style can be found. Its policy-oriented or teleological approach to interpretation based on the declared policies of the Treaty[10] has meant that many of the problems encountered in developing, for example, the EC's fundamental freedoms have been solved by what is effectively judicial law-making. In a number of key decisions, the ECJ has eliminated potential obstructions to free movement, so that the integration process has continued without having to wait, perhaps indefinitely, for the Council to take a political decision. For example, in the *Reyners* case,[11] the ECJ held that all the national restrictions on individuals' freedom to provide services in other member states were automatically abolished at the end of the transitional period, notwithstanding the fact that many states had still to act to meet the obligations of Article 59. A more recent example can be seen in the *Cassis de Dijon* case discussed in Chapter 11.

In formulating a 'Community' approach to its task, the ECJ has faced some formidable obstacles. Originally six and now ten different legal systems, some with widely differing legal traditions, are represented on the bench. The linguistic problems of working with seven official languages take on a new significance when each of the official versions of the Treaty is authoritative. (Note, for example, A. G. Warner's consideration of the various texts of Article 119 in the recent equal

Table 1   Activities of the Court in figures
Cases analysed by subject-matter[1]
Situation at 31 December 1981

	ECSC				EEC									Eura-tom	Privi-leges and immu-nities	Pro-ceed-ings by staff of insti-tutions	Total
	Scrap com-pensa-tion	Trans-port	Com-peti-tion	Other[2]	Free move-ment of goods and cus-toms union	Right of estab-lish-ment and free-dom to supply services	Taxa-tion	Com-peti-tion	Social secur-ity and free move-ment of workers	Agri-cul-ture	Trans-port	Article 220 Con-ven-tions	Other[3]				
Actions brought	169	36	63	74 (33)	300 (53)	37 (12)	79 (20)	201 (7)	211 (26)	606 (55)	15	32 (5)	59 (18)	4	8	1,898 (94)	3,800[4] (323)
Cases not resulting in a judgment	22	6	22	19 (10)	40 (10)	5 (3)	7	16 (3)	12 (4)	40 (7)	2	1	4	1	1	116 (9)	322[4] (46)
Cases decided	147	30	41	32 (4)	200 (31)	24 (3)	52 (8)	175 (8)	167 (10)	488 (26)	13	27 (5)	37 (8)	3	7	493 (46)	1,936 (149)
Cases pending	–	–	–	23	60	8	20	10	32	78	–	4	18	–	–	1,289	1,542

The figures in brackets represent the cases dealt with by the Court in 1981.
[1] Cases concerning more than one subject are classified under the most important heading.
[2] Levies, investment declarations, tax charges, miners' bonuses, production quotas.
[3] Contentious proceedings, Staff Regulations, Community terminology, Lomé Convention, short-term economic policy, commercial policy, relations between Community law and national law and environment.
[4] Including seven cases in which no service was effected and the cases were removed forthwith from the register, and one case in which legal aid was granted; these cases are not included elsewhere in the table.
Source: 15th General Report of the Activities of the EC in 1981. (Luxembourg: Office for Official Publications of the EC, 1982.)

Table 2   Cases analysed by type (EEC Treaty)[1]
Situation at 31 December 1981

| | Proceedings brought under | | | | | | | | | | | | |
	Art. 169, 93 and 171	Art. 170	Art. 173 By governments	By individuals	By Community institutions	Total	Art. 175	Art. 177 Validity	Interpretation	Total	Art. 215	Protocols to Art. 220 Conventions	Grand total[2]
Actions brought	165	2	35	229	4	268	16	124	841	906	160	32	1,540[6]
Cases not resulting in a judgment	41	1	6	22	—	28	1	5	41	44	16	1	132[6]
Cases decided	79	1	24	179	3	206	12[5]	103	693	746	124	27	1,186
In favour of applicant[3]	22	1	4	33	1	38	—				17		
Dismissed on the merits[4]	1	—	19	105	2	126	1				96		
Rejected as inadmissible	—	—	1	41	1	42	10				11		
Cases pending	45	—	5	28	—	34	3	16	107	116	20	4	219

[1] Excluding proceedings by staff and cases concerning the interpretation of the Protocol on Privileges and Immunities and of the Staff Regulations (see Table 1).

[2] Totals may be smaller than the sum of individual items because some cases are based on more than one Treaty article.

[3] In respect of at least one of the applicant's main claims.

[4] This also covers proceedings rejected partly as inadmissible and partly on the merits.

[5] Including one non-suit.

[6] Including five cases in which no service was effected and the cases were removed forthwith from the register.

Source: 15th General Report of the Activities of the EC in 1981. (Luxembourg: Office for Official Publications of the EC, 1982.)

pay case of *Jenkins* v *Kingsgate (Clothing Productions) Ltd.*)[12] Nevertheless, in those areas of the Treaty where it has the scope, the ECJ has been able to utilize the strengths of the national legal traditions and incorporate concepts of national law into 'general principles of Community law'.[13] In reviewing the legality of EC acts various principles of national law have been relied upon; for example, the principle of German law that action should be proportionate to the end it seeks to achieve (Verhältnismässigkeit). Similarly, the principle of English law that both sides to a dispute be heard before judgment is given (*audi alteram partem*) was used to strike down a Commission decision in the *Trans Ocean Marine Paint Association* case,[14] where the Commission, having initially decided that an agreement between certain paint producers did not conflict with the competition rules, later altered its decision without allowing the producers to present their arguments. The ECJ has also recognized fundamental human rights entrenched in some national constitutions and protected by international treaty—particularly the European Convention on Human Rights (ECHR)—as rights which EC law ought to recognize.[15] In *Prais* v *Council*[16] it accepted that the institutions had an obligation to respect the right of religious freedom contained in Article 9 of the ECHR. This eclectic approach to the task of judicial review provides the basis of a new and truly European system of administrative law.

Arguably the ECJ's most important achievement, however, has been the development of the concept of direct effect (or enforceability) of EC law. It originated in the now famous *Van Gend en Loos* case (1963).[17] In a dispute before the Dutch courts, Van Gend en Loos, importers of ureaformaldehyde argued that a duty imposed by the Dutch authorities constituted a 'new customs duty' prohibited by Article 12 of the Rome Treaty. The Dutch court referred the issue to the ECJ for a preliminary ruling under Article 177, asking *inter alia* whether Van Gend en Loos could indeed rely upon Article 12 before the Dutch courts, or whether that Article represented a purely international obligation on the Dutch Government which could not be invoked in domestic proceedings. It is worth noting here that under international law treaties do not usually create rights and obligations directly for individuals,[18] but only for entities with international personality (for example, states and international organizations). Whether the provisions of a treaty can be relied upon before a national court is therefore a concern of national constitutional law alone. International law is only concerned that states honour their treaty obligations. (Consequently, a state cannot plead the defects of its own legal system as a defence to a breach of a treaty obligation: in the recent *Tyrer* case before the European Court of Human Rights in Strasbourg, the UK was held responsible for a breach of the ECHR by allowing birching on the Isle of Man, even though constitutionally the Westminster Parliament has no power to prevent it.)[19]

It is against this background that the following well-known passage from the ECJ's judgment in *Van Gend en Loos* should be read:

> The Community constitutes a new legal order of international law for the benefit of which the states have limited their sovereign rights, albeit within limited fields, and the subjects of which comprise not only member states but also their nationals. Independently of the legislation of member states, Community law not only imposes obligations upon individuals but is also intended to confer upon them rights which become part of their legal heritage. These rights arise not only where they are expressly granted by the Treaty, but also by reason of obligations which the Treaty imposes in a clearly defined way upon individuals as well as upon the member states and upon the institutions of the Community.[20]

Because the blanket prohibition on new customs duties in Article 12 was felt to be such a 'clearly defined' obligation, it conferred directly enforceable rights which could be used before national courts. The 'constitutional' significance of this case therefore, which Stein has called the 'corner stone' of the courts' 'transnational constitution',[21] is that the ECJ in interpreting the Treaty has also prescribed the Treaty's *effects* on national legal systems, thereby claiming for itself a role more closely akin to a federal court than an international court, for a federal court not merely interprets federal law but also lays down the respective areas of competence of federal and state law. Federal systems, however, must have some means for deciding conflicts between federal and state law. The Rome Treaty does not provide for the supremacy of EC law over national law, but such supremacy is the logical corollary to direct effect, if these new-found rights are not simply to be overridden by state law. In so far as this issue was left unresolved in *Van Gend en Loos*, it was faced squarely a year later.[22] In *Costa* v *ENEL* (1964)[23] the applicant had refused to pay his electricity bill (of 1,950 lire—then just over £1) on the ground that the Italian statute nationalizing the electricity industry contravened the Rome Treaty. The Italian court asked whether the relevant Treaty provisions supported Costa's contention—which the ECJ ruled they did not—and whether a directly effective provision of EC law did in fact prevail over conflicting national law. The unequivocal answer (recently reasserted in the *Simmenthal* case, 1978),[24] that in cases of conflict EC law was supreme, meant that the ECJ had provided that 'supremacy clause'[25] omitted from the Treaty. Since *Costa*, national courts have accepted this with remarkably few problems.[26]

Since those early decisions, a large number of other Treaty provisions have been found to confer direct effects upon individuals, provided that like Article 12 they are 'clearly defined' or 'complete and legally perfect', that is as long as their obligations are unconditional, unqualified and require no further implementation by national or EC legislation.[27] While a simple prohibition is the clearest of such provisions, the ECJ subsequently held that a positive obligation upon member states, such as the obligation to act by a certain date, could become directly effective once that date was reached. Thus, a large number of provisions became directly enforceable at the end of the transitional period. A further important step was taken when the ECJ decided that certain Treaty provisions may be enforced not only against the state, or its organs (that is, vertically), but also against other individuals (that is, horizontally). For example, in *Defrenne* v *Sabena*,[28] Gabrielle Defrenne, an air hostess, claimed that as the conditions in her contract were different from those of male stewards they violated the equal pay provisions of Article 119. The Belgian courts asked the ECJ if this Article was directly effective and if it could indeed be relied upon in domestic proceedings between individuals (that is, Mlle Defrenne and the airline). The UK and Irish Governments intervened in the proceedings to argue that such a finding would cause economic hardship as it would have retrospective effect and result in considerable sums of back pay being owed to women workers. The policy-oriented nature of these decisions emerges clearly here,[29] for in a bold and controversial move the ECJ ruled that Article 119 was directly effective horizontally, *but* only from the date of its judgment (with the limited exception of cases currently pending).

In addition to the Treaty provisions and those of other treaties entered into by the EC, the concept of direct effect has been extended to legislation, notably directives. Article 189, in defining the effects of directives, specifically provides that 'a directive shall be binding as to the result to be achieved upon each member state to which it is addressed, but shall leave to the national authorities the choice of form and method'. The directive also indicates the time within which it must be implemented. Thus, obligations imposed on states by directives are similar to those imposed by the Treaty. If Treaty provisions can confer direct effects, then why not provisions of directives—provided that they are 'complete and legally perfect' which, depending on the wording, they might well become once the implementation period has expired. It is on this basis that the ECJ has ruled that where a state acts in breach of such clear obligations in a directive, individuals may rely on the direct effects of the directive in order to challenge state action. So, in *Van Duyn* v *Home Office*,[30] Yvonne Van Duyn, a Dutch scientologist, was given the right to rely upon provisions of Directive 64/221 in her attempts to challenge her exclusion from the UK on the grounds of 'public policy'. In addition, if a state fails to implement a directive, an individual may still use that directive as a defence to an action in the national courts, for example, in *Pubblico Ministero* v *Ratti*,[31] where Ratti, a producer in Italy of paint and solvents, chose to comply with a directive setting common EC labelling standards, which had not been implemented by the Italian Government, and he was then prosecuted in the Italian courts for a consequent breach of existing Italian law. In other words, the ECJ accepts that certain directives have vertical direct effects. It has not as yet accepted their horizontal effects.

Many[32] feel that this is as far as the ECJ will, or should, go without eliminating the important distinction between the two main forms of EC legislation—directives and regulations—the latter being in any event 'directly applicable' as they become automatically part of national law without the need for national implementation.[33] More fundamentally it is argued that it is one thing to allow a directive to be used against a government (which is after all responsible for implementing it) but quite another to permit an individual to rely on a directive—which has not been implemented or has been implemented incorrectly—in proceedings against another individual, who in regulating his or her affairs may have been careful to comply with national law without appreciating that national law may conflict with that directive's obligations.

To take a hypothetical example, if the sex discrimination directives[34] were to be held to be horizontally directly effective, then employees could rely on the rights they gave, even where those rights had not been properly implemented, and thus protected, by national sex discrimination laws. Employers would therefore need to meet the standards imposed both by national law and by the directives. If these standards were to vary, or even conflict through faulty state implementation, then confusion and uncertainty might result. Of course, problems would arise even if these directives were only to be directly effective vertically in that public employees could therefore rely upon them against their employer, while private firms' employees could not.

This may appear a somewhat technical debate—perhaps it is the inevitable result of piecemeal development of the law by judicial activism: after all, judges can only decide the issues that are referred to them. Nevertheless the wider significance of direct effectiveness and its extension should not be ignored. It means that individuals can rely on principles of EC law at all levels of the national legal systems. They can utilize EC law to attack conflicting national law. Direct effect thus provides an efficient method of ensuring that member states comply with their EC obligations or risk being impugned before their own courts. This in turn accustoms those courts to the idea of a superior legal order and incidentally ensures the ECJ a consistent flow of work—for when presented with such a case any national judge may use Article 177 to seek the ECJ's interpretative assistance. Under Article 177,[35] any national court or tribunal presented with an issue of EC law on which a decision is necessary to enable it to give judgment may (and if it is a final court, must) request the ECJ to rule on the interpretation of the Treaty, or on the validity or interpretation of any act of an EC institution. It is not an appeal. The national court suspends the case while awaiting answers to specific questions. When the ruling is given, the national court applies it. Thus Article 177 provides the constitutional mechanism for linking the national and the EC legal systems. Table 2 shows that the ECJ's success can be judged in numerical terms alone, for it depends on the cooperation of the national courts in actually referring questions to it.[36]

The development of direct effect, linked with Article 177, has therefore provided an opportunity for individuals to gain access to the ECJ through their national courts. In limited circumstances the Treaty (Article 173) permits individuals direct access to the court to challenge EC acts, but paradoxically the ECJ has consistently interpreted these limited rights in a most restrictive way[37] (see Table 2). The ECJ takes a similar restrictive view of its power to award damages (under Article 215) in cases where individuals seek redress from the EC for losses suffered as a result of EC actions.[38]

This remarkable contrast between the ECJ's expansive approach to Article 177 cases and its restrictive approach to direct actions should be seen in the context of other legal systems. It is rare (and, in the UK prior to accession to the EC, impossible) for individuals to have the power to apply to a national court to strike down national legislation,[39] it is equally rare for them to be able to seek redress for damage suffered as a result of legislation. Where national legislation can be challenged (as in the FRG) it is only on the grounds of unconstitutionality. It is perhaps understandable that the ECJ is not keen to encourage such actions from too many quarters, and thus raise uncertainty as to the binding effect of all EC legislation. Even so the ECJ does seem to be deliberately restricting the time-consuming 'fact finding' role it has to play in direct actions,[40] and expanding its jurisdiction under Article 177 where it has an 'appellate' type of jurisdiction—dealing only with questions of law, with the issues of fact left to the national tribunal. It is certainly no secret that the ECJ has for many years been trying to rid itself of its exclusive and increasingly onerous direct jurisdiction over staff disputes between the EC and its employees.[41]

It is clear that the ECJ in a purely 'appellate' role would resemble more closely the federal model of, for example, the US Supreme Court. But even without such a change of emphasis, the ECJ has already advanced a long way down the federal road. Stein[42] stresses the contribution of the ECJ itself to the forging of a 'transnational constitution', for its decisions in a number of 'key' cases demonstrate an independence from the arguments of the Commission, the member states and even its own advocates-general. Nevertheless, the establishment of a system of directly effective EC law superior to national law, ultimately depends on national courts accepting it.[43] Given that virtually all the ECJ's decisions are declaratory in that there are no sanctions available to enforce them, the degree of acceptance of all its rulings is remarkable. There have been few direct challenges to its authority. Of all the cases (see Table 2) initiated by the Commission against member states for a breach of EC law, only once has a state specifically refused to comply with a judgment: in 1979 when the ECJ found the French ban on the import of lamb from the UK illegal. There have naturally enough been constitutional difficulties, some of which continue,[44] over the precise relationship between national courts and the ECJ, but the precept of the 'new legal order' which is the basis of the EC legal system is now beyond dispute. It may indeed seem ironical, in Dashwood's words, 'that lawyers, who are generally regarded as nature's conservatives, should have so readily taken the hard, though necessary, decisions on which progress to European Union depends.'[45]

Notes

1. Schermers, H. G., 'The European Court of Justice: Promoter of European Integration', *American Journal of Comparative Law*, 22 (1974), 444–64.
2. Brown, L. N. and Jacobs, F. G., *The Court of Justice of the European Communities* (London, Sweet and Maxwell, 1977), p. 3. For further more detailed works on the jurisdiction and case-law of the ECJ see Hartley, T. C., *The Foundations of European Community Law* (Oxford, Oxford University Press, 1981); Schermers, H. G., *Judicial Protection in the European Communities* (Deventer, Kluwer, 2nd ed., 1979); Toth, A., *Legal Protection of Individuals in the European Community* (Amsterdam, North Holland, 1978).
3. Cases 138/79 and 139/79, *Roquette* v *Council* and *Maizena* v *Council* [1980] European Court Reports (E.C.R.) 3333.
4. Article 167 of the EEC Treaty. Under the original ECSC Treaty, now amended, this latter legal qualification was not necessary. Of the earliest judges, one, Joseph Serrarens, was a politician, and another, Jacques Rueff, an expert in finance and banking.
5. See Article 166 of the EEC Treaty and, e.g., Articles 4 and 16 of the Court Statute. For the text of the Statute of the Court see, e.g., Rudden, B. and Wyatt, D., *Basic Community Laws* (Oxford, Oxford University Press, 1980), pp. 102–9. Future references will be to the EEC Treaty only.
6. On the role of the advocate general see Warner, J. P., 'Some Aspects of the European Court of Justice', *The Journal of the Society of Public Teachers of Law* (New Series), 14 (1976), 15–30, and now Dashwood, A. A., 'The Advocate General in the Court of Justice of the European Communities', *Legal Studies*, 2 (1982), 202–16.
7. See further Hartley, T. C., 'The Impact of European Community Law on the Criminal Process', *Criminal Law Review* (1981), 75–85.
8. Dashwood, A., 'The Principles of Direct Effect in European Community Law', *Journal of Common Market Studies*, 16 (1978), 229–45, p. 245.
9. See Hampson, C. J., in Reports of *Judicial and Academic Conference* (Luxembourg, Court of Justice, 1976), p. 15.
10. On the ECJ's interpretative style see Brown and Jacobs, op. cit., Chapter 12; see further *Judicial and Academic Conference*, op. cit.
11. Case 2/74, *Reyners* v *Belgium* [1974] E.C.R. 631; [1974] Common Market Law Reports (C.M.L.R.) 305.
12. *Jenkins* v *Kingsgate (Clothing Productions) Ltd.* [1981] E.C.R. 911; [1981] 2 C.M.L.R. 24.
13. On general principles of law, see Brown and Jacobs, op. cit., Chapter 13, and further Usher, J. A., 'The Influence of National Concepts on Decisions of the European Court', *European Law Review*, 1 (1975–6), 359–74.
14. Case 17/74, *Transocean Marine Paint Association* v *Commission* [1974] E.C.R. 1063; [1974] 2 C.M.L.R. 459.
15. See, e.g., Edeson, W. R. and Wooldridge, F., 'European Community Law and Fundamental Human Rights', *Legal Issues of European Integration* (1976), No. 1, 1–54.
16. Case 130/75, *Prais* v *Council* [1976] E.C.R. 1589; [1976] 2 C.M.L.R. 708.
17. Case 26/62 *Van Gend en Loos* v *Nederlanse Administratie der Belastingen* [1963] E.C.R. 1; [1963] C.M.L.R. 105.
18. For example, in the *Finnish Ships Arbitration* (1932) the British Government argued 'International law is a law regulating the rights and duties of States *inter se* and creating no rights and imposing no duties on individuals . . .'. But in its Advisory Opinion on the *Jurisdiction of the Court of Danzig* (1928), the Permanent Court of International Justice (predecessor of the International Court of Justice) accepted (P.C.I.J. Reports, Series B, No. 15) that if there was a clear intention on the part of the signatories of a treaty to give individuals enforceable rights, this would be respected. See Stein, E., 'Lawyers, Judges, and the Making of a Transnational Constitution', *American Journal of International Law*, 75 (1981), 1–27, p. 9, where he argues this creates a presumption *against* direct effect in general international law. Where the Treaty expressly gives directly enforceable rights, as, for example, under Article 25 of the European Convention on Human Rights 1955, then this presumption will be rebutted.

19. *Tyrer* v *United Kingdom*, European Court of Human Rights, Judgment of 25 April 1978, Series A.
20. [1963] E.C.R., p. 12.
21. See Stein, op. cit., p. 3.
22. Ibid., p. 10.
23. Case 6/64, *Flaminio Costa* v *E.N.E.L.* [1964] E.C.R. 565; [1964] C.M.L.R. 425.
24. Case 106/77, *Amministrazione delle Finanze dello Stato* v *Simmenthal SpA.* [1978] E.C.R. 629; [1978] 3 C.M.L.R. 263; and see Freestone, D., 'The Supremacy of Community Law in National Courts', *Modern Law Review* 42 (1979), 220–3.
25. See Stein, op. cit., p. 10.
26. See, e.g., Bebr, G., 'How Supreme is Community Law in National Courts?', *Common Market Law Review*, 11 (1974), 3–37, and for a national case study Judge M. Simon, 'Enforcement by French Courts of European Community Law', *Law Quarterly Review*, 90 (1974), 467–85; Part II, 2 (1976), 85–92; and Dowrick, F., on the controversial *Cohn-Bendit* decision of the Conseil D'État, 95 (1979), 376–85.
27. For a list of Treaty articles found to be directly effective see Collins, L., *European Community Law in the United Kingdom* (London, Butterworths, 2nd ed., 1980), p. 73.
28. Case 43/75, *Gabrielle Defrenne* v *Société Anonyme Belge de Navigation Aérienne* (SABENA) judgment of 8 April 1976 [1976] E.C.R. 455; [1976] 2 C.M.L.R. 98.
29. For criticism see Hampson, op. cit., p. 10 ff.
30. Case 41/74, *Yvonne van Duyn* v *Home Office* [1974] E.C.R. 1337; [1975] 1 C.M.L.R. 1.
31. Case 148/78, *Pubblico Ministero* v *Ratti*, [1979] E.C.R. 1629; [1980] 1 C.M.L.R. 96.
32. See, e.g., Wyatt, D., 'The Direct Applicability of Regulations and Directives', *Cambridge Law Journal* (1977), 216–19, and Usher, J. A., *European Community Law and National Law. The Irreversible Transfer?* (London, U.A.C.E.S. and Allen and Unwin, 1981). See *contra*, Easson, A. J., 'The "Direct Effect" of EEC Directives', *International and Comparative Law Quarterly*, 28 (1979), 319–53.
33. For a development of the distinction, see Winter, J. A., 'Direct Applicability and Direct Effect: Two distinct different concepts in Community Law', *Common Market Law Review*, 9 (1972), 425–38.
34. Council Directive of 10 February 1975 on the approximation of laws of the member states relating to the application of the principle of equal pay for men and women (75/117) *OJ*, 1975, L45/19; Council Directive of 9 February 1976, on the implementation of the principles of equal treatment for men and women as regards access to employment, vocational training and promotion, and working conditions (76/207) *OJ*, 1976, L39/40; Council Directive of 19 December 1978, on the progressive implementation of the principles of equal treatment for men and women in matters of social security (79/7) *OJ*, 1979, L6/24. Despite repeated requests from UK courts, the ECJ has to date declined to rule on the direct effects of these directives. See Freestone, D., 'Equal Pay in the European Court', *Modern Law Review*, 45 (1982), 81–8.
35. On the preliminary reference procedure see, e.g., Jacobs, F. G., 'When to refer to the European Court', *Law Quarterly Review*, 90 (1974), 485–93; Schermers, H. G., 'The Law as it stands on Preliminary Rulings', *Legal Issues of European Integration* (1974), No. 1, 93–112.
36. See Bebr, G., 'Article 177 of the EEC Treaty in the practice of National Courts', *International and Comparative Law Quarterly*, 26 (1977), 241–82.
37. For comment see Stein, E. and Vining, G. J., 'Citizen Access to Judicial Review of Administrative Action in a Transnational and federal context', *American Journal of International Law*, 70 (1976), 219–41; Harding, C. S. P., 'Decisions addressed to member states and Article 173 of the Treaty of Rome', *International and Comparative Law Quarterly*, 25 (1976), 15–34; Rasmussen, H., 'Why is Article 173 interpreted against Private Plaintiffs?', *European Law Review*, 5 (1980), 112–27. For a reply to Rasmussen, see Harding, C., 'The Private interest in Challenging Community Action', *European Law Review*, 5 (1980), 354–61.
38. See, e.g., Hartley, T., 'Compensation for loss caused by illegal regulations', *European Law Review*, 4 (1979), 265–8.
39. For example, see the report that I.C.I. has begun an action against the UK Government for violating Article 92 of the EEC Treaty, by subsidizing its competitors under the Finance Act. (*The Guardian*, 3 July 1982.) Prior to accession to the EC, no form of challenge of legislation was possible, see Jaconelli, J., 'Constitutional Review and Section 2(4) of the European Communities Act, 1972', *International and Comparative Law Quarterly*, 28 (1979), 65–71.

40. Rasmussen, op. cit.
41. See, e.g., Memorandum of the European Court of Justice to the Council of Ministers, 1978, quoted in Rasmussen, ibid.
42. Stein, E., 'Lawyers, Judges and the Making of a Transnational Constitution', op. cit.
43. See, e.g., Warner, J. P., 'The relationship between European Community Law and the National Laws of Member States', *Law Quarterly Review*, 93 (1977), 349–66.
44. For example, in the recent case, 104/79, *Foglia* v *Novello* [1980] E.C.R. 745, [1981] 1 C.M.L.R. 45, the ECJ refused to give a response to an Italian court's request for a reference as it was an abuse of procedure. For criticism see Barav, A., 'Preliminary Censorship?', *European Law Review*, 5 (1980), 443–68. See *contra*, Wyatt, D., 'Following up Foglia: Why the Court is right to stick to its guns', *European Law Review*, 6 (1981), 447–51.
45. Dashwood, 'The Principle of Direct Effect in European Community Law', op. cit., p. 245.

PART II   EUROPEAN COMMUNITY INTERNAL POLICIES

6   The Common Agricultural Policy

JOHN S. MARSH and PAMELA J. SWANNEY

This chapter seeks to answer four questions about the Common Agricultural Policy (CAP): why it exists; how it is organized; what effects it has had and what options now exist for its development. One theme dominates the discussion. This is the need to evolve policies against a changing political and economic framework. One of the greatest dangers to the EC is that its response to change is so slow that its credibility as a means of providing a framework of government within which Europeans can cooperate is threatened. Since the CAP represents so central a part of total EC activity, it merits attention even by those whose concerns lie outside agriculture.

Why a Common Agricultural Policy exists

Policies exist because governments believe that they change circumstances in preferred directions. Many of the agricultural problems which faced early societies remain.

Amongst these, one of the most important is the assurance of a secure supply of food. Since food production is subject to the vagaries of weather and to biological hazard, there is always a risk that insufficient will be produced in any one season. Various tactics may be deployed to minimize this risk. For example, governments may stimulate a greater level of production than markets alone warrant. Alternatively, a government may ensure security of supplies by safeguarding access to imported foodstuffs, both through defence policy and by making sure that there are sufficient funds to pay for imports even when their prices rise. A third approach is to accumulate and hold contingency stocks on a scale which ensures that no serious shortages are likely to occur. In Europe awareness of the need for food security was greatly strengthened by the experience of the Second World War. Governments of the countries now in the EC sought to stimulate their agriculture in ways that would increase the security of food supplies.

A second important reason why European governments intervene in agriculture is price instability. In the short run the quantity of food bought is relatively unresponsive to changes in price. Many agricultural products are, in a formal sense, price-inelastic. Thus, increases in the quantity placed on the market will, unless governments take action, result in a reduction in the aggregate revenue to producers. At the same time supply, in the short run, is also inflexible. Once produced, the costs of storing output or processing it into more durable forms are considerable. Thus, increases in output are likely to reach markets reluctant to absorb additional supplies.

There are several reasons why governments should be concerned about such fluctuations. The industry itself is essentially competitively organized. Uncertainty about price movements may lead farmers into a series of inappropriate investment decisions. These, if they lead to a cycle of events such as that described in 'the cobweb theorem', represent a substantial wastage of resources and loss of real wealth for the country as a whole. Second, wide movements in agricultural price lead to substantial changes in the real incomes of consumers, particularly the poor who spend a large proportion of their income on foodstuffs. Such movements in real income may, according to some theories, give rise to inflation. If governments believe that a food price instability contributes to inflation, they are likely to find this a good reason for intervention. Finally, instability matters in terms of the political and economic context of agriculture. Wide variations in farm incomes generate dissatisfaction, at least in low income years, amongst farmers. There are secondary effects. Farmers' spending on machinery and buildings is likely to fluctuate with their own incomes. Rural communities as a result have substantially differing cash flows according to ups and downs in farm incomes. Such instability represents a political hazard.

A third reason for intervention in agriculture has been the pursuit of economic efficiency. Given the atomistic character of farming, the development of research and its application has depended to a large extent upon public investment. In some European countries, this has been undertaken by farmer organizations such as cooperatives. However, governments too have recognized that, by providing advice as well as supporting research, they may stimulate efficiency within the agricultural industry. Very substantial increases in productivity have taken place in all EC countries since 1968 (Table 1). Improvements in productivity benefit not simply those engaged in agriculture but also consumers. The same concern for efficiency has justified public investments in infra-structural facilities such as roads, power systems and water supplies. These facilities benefit the public as a whole and should not be charged wholly against the accounts of farmers.

Table 1 Annual percentage growth in the productivity of labour in agriculture[a]

	1968–73	1973–9
FRG	7.9	4.1
France	7.7	3.1
Italy	4.9	4.0
Netherlands	–	8.3
Belgium	8.5	3.2
Luxembourg	2.5	2.8
UK	–	3.4
Ireland	4.9	4.5
Denmark	3.7	1.5
EUR 9	7.2	3.6
Greece	–	3.4
EUR 10	–	3.5

Note: [a]Calculated on the basis of gross value added.
Source: EC Commission, The Agricultural Situation in the Community 1981 Report.

One of the most pressing reasons for agricultural policy in Europe has been the persistence of low farm incomes. Much academic work has gone into explaining why farm incomes tend to be chronically low. A number of characteristics help to explain why the income problem in agriculture is endemic. First, agricultural products generally have low income elasticities of demand. Nutritional require-ments are satisfied at a relatively low income level. Additional spending on food tends to concentrate on improving its quality and its variety.

If no state intervention took place, farmers as a whole would experience slower growth in total revenues than other sectors. Costs, which farmers have to meet in competition with the rest of the economy, tend to rise at prices broadly proportional to the growth of incomes in the economy as a whole. Thus, taken in aggregate, farm incomes are likely to decline relatively and even absolutely. Some individual farmers, by reason of their excellence, may increase their own personal incomes, but for the industry as a whole the picture remains gloomy.

A second reason why farm incomes tend to be relatively unsatisfactory stems from technology. New methods use more capital but less labour. In the context of a market unable to absorb rapid increases in output, such a shift in relative productivities inevitably means that the value of labour (the basis of its income) is falling.

Low farm incomes tend to persist because of the relative fixity of many farm resources and the poor opportunities which exist for farm people in other occupations. The resources committed to agriculture have relatively low second-hand values. Alternative employment opportunities are generally limited by the geographical location of farms. This is particularly true of farmers who work in less favoured areas of Europe. Movement to a new job usually demands fundamental changes in their way of life as well as in the place in which they live. These reasons for low incomes in agriculture in Europe have led governments to intervene to maintain incomes and ease adjustment. In a period of downward adjustment, the salvage value of the fixed assets is so low that it will often pay farmers to continue to use them even though prices have fallen to a level which would not justify their replacement by new equipment. Since some of these resources are long lived, any contraction in agricultural production in relation to market requirements can be protracted. Throughout this time incomes will be depressed.

Government involvement in agriculture may also try to give weight to the social costs and benefits of agricultural activity where these are inadequately reflected in the private accounts of farmers. Some elements of this have already been foreshadowed. For example, the threat of depopulation of the least favoured areas may justify support for farming. Without such aid, not only may farming decline but the unit costs of facilities such as schools, hospitals, shops and transport rise. In such a case the residual population is likely to consist of the very old and the very young; a situation which is often judged to be socially undesirable. Similarly, government action may seek to protect the environment. As new technology changes the face of the countryside, as powerful pesticides can transform the ecological balance of whole areas and as some farm chemicals create risks of pollution and danger to health, governments must take these elements into account in devising agricultural policy. Although the countryside is, from the farmers' point of view, a place of work, its value to the community exceeds the product of agriculture.

Finally, agricultural policy may form part of an overall economic policy. Two examples demonstrate this. In the UK in the post-war period, there was much debate about the extent to which support for agriculture would improve the balance of payments. In France, in addition to seeking to expand agriculture as a means of increasing export revenues, successive plans saw agriculture as an important contributor to national economic growth.

All this helps to explain why, when the EC came into existence, each of the six member states had its own agricultural policy. The EC faced a dilemma in relation to such policies. On the one hand, free movement of agricultural goods was essential if the common market were to extend to agriculture. On the other hand, free movement of agricultural goods among EC countries would undermine the agricultural support systems of many member countries. Agriculture was too important to leave out and too vulnerable to be exposed to free market competition. It was thus decided that the EC should have a common policy to replace but give effect to the goals of national policies. Articles 38–45 of the Rome Treaty embody this intention. Article 38 states that the common market shall extend to agriculture and trade in agricultural products. It permits the development of specific rules in the form of a Common Agricultural Policy (CAP), which will exempt agricultural goods from some of the requirements for competition specified elsewhere in the Treaty. Article 39 outlines the CAP's main goals. These include (1) an improvement in agricultural productivity; (2) as a result, an improvement in the standard of living of the agricultural population; (3) market stabilization; (4) guarantee of regular supplies; and (5) reasonable prices to consumers. The Treaty indicates that the CAP must take into account the social and structural characteristics of agriculture and the natural disparities between the various agricultural regions. Adjustments were to be gradual and made within the context of the economy of the member states as a whole. In recent years greater attention has been given to the need to preserve a regional balance within the EC and to maintain employment in agriculture. The Treaty, whilst setting out general objectives and principles for a CAP, is unspecific concerning the mechanisms and instruments to be used.

How the Community gave effect to the Treaty

Inevitably the CAP reflects the previous experience of the EC's founding members. In contrast with the UK, where policy had permitted relatively low food prices and free imports from the rest of the world, the emphasis was upon ensuring that market prices gave satisfactory returns to farmers. The CAP has two aspects, the first a set of 'regimes' for particular products, the second a series of 'structural' measures. Full details of these arrangements are beyond the scope of this chapter, but it is possible to illustrate their character.

The earliest regime was for cereals. It represented a critical decision because cereals occupy a central role in the agriculture of northern Europe. Not only do they compete with other enterprises for resources, they also form the basic ingredient for feedingstuffs, the largest single cost element in the production of intensive livestock. Thus a decision about the cereals regime had implications for many other products. Cereals were also critical because of the past differences among the member countries. Cereal prices had been relatively high in Germany and Italy and relatively low in Holland and France. What emerged was a compromise which raised prices to most farmers. The regime hinges upon the determination of 'target' prices for particular cereals. These target prices are fixed by the Council of Ministers to represent prices which they feel would be appropriate in wholesale markets within the EC. Two other prices are fixed in relation to them. The first, the threshold price, represents the price at which goods can enter the EC from outside without undermining the target price. The second, an intervention price, is the price at which the EC stands prepared to buy the commodity.

The threshold price is the basis of the relationship between the EC and the rest of the world. Once it is fixed, a variable levy is calculated representing the difference between the lowest world price offer for a substantial delivery and the threshold price. Provided the system works as intended, once this variable levy has been paid it should be impossible for goods produced outside the EC to compete below the target price with EC output.

The intervention price represents the EC's intention to support internal markets even when EC output is above current requirements. Intervention leads to the possibility of the accumulation of stocks, 'mountains' or 'lakes'. These can be disposed of by sale abroad or by utilization at home. Sale abroad is only possible with the aid of a subsidy, 'an export restitution', which bridges the gap between the domestic and the world prices. Such a subsidy might be thought of as a step down to the 'world price', equivalent to the step up imposed via the variable import levy. In practice it has been used to undercut world market prices. Disposal within the EC may require a subsidy, to allow a product to be used as animal feed or to enable some specified group, pensioners or children, to buy at lower prices.

This brief sketch of the cereals regime indicates the characteristic instruments of many CAP regimes: export restitution, variable import levy, intervention purchase, the setting of target prices and, if necessary, the accumulation of stores. Critical in assessing the effects of such regimes is the level of the target price. Political factors meant that in 1962 when the cereals policy was given effect, prices were fixed nearer the high German level than the lower levels prevailing elsewhere within the EC. The results of this and its implications for the EC as a whole are discussed later.

The Community went on to devise policies for each of the main product areas. These are shown in Table 2.

In addition to its price policies, the EC has sought to contribute to agriculture's development through structural policy. Initially it supported national initiatives which seemed to be in the interest of the EC as a whole. However, from the late 1960s onward there was a more formal EC approach.

The earliest attempt in this direction dates from the late 1960s when the Commission drew up its Memorandum on the Reform of Agriculture in the EC. From this plan stemmed a series of policies designed to promote the movement of agricultural resources into a more economic conformation. The plan contemplated a reduction of 5 million in the labour force and a reduction in the land area engaged in agriculture of 5 million hectares. To assist this process it sought to encourage the modernization of farming, the enlargement of farms, the movement of people from agriculture into other industries and the early retirement of some farmers. After much discussion, the principles which lay behind this policy were given partial effect in the series of structural Directives 159–161 of 1972.

The group of policies of 1972 sought to assist agriculture to respond to continuing economic changes. More recently, structural policy has been more concerned with resisting or modifying the operation of autonomous economic forces. This can be seen in directives of the later 1970s concerned with less favoured areas. These gave particular assistance to farmers in essentially high cost areas. This contradictory approach to structural policy reflects both political reality and the EC's changing fortunes. In the late 1960s and early 1970s, it seemed plausible to expect people displaced from agriculture to find work in other sectors. By the 1980s, such assumptions were ill-founded. A major aim of policy became to maintain employment. Politically, the need to intervene in the less favoured areas was strengthened as their population fell and other industries, also vulnerable because of their regional isolation, came under pressure. Thus the justification of structural policy switched from economic to social criteria during the 1970s. The instruments chosen included the provision of both capital at low interest rates and capital

Table 2 Measures used in the major commodity regimes

Commodity	Desired Price	Intervention Price	Deficiency Payment	Threshold Price	Sluicegate Price	Variable Levy	Supplementary Levy	Customs Duty	Export Refund
Cereals	Target	x		x		x			x
Sugar	Target	x		x		x			x
Milk products	Target (milk)	x		x		x			x
Beef and veal	Guide	x				x		x	x
Pigmeat	Basic	x			x		x		x
Poultrymeat					x		x		x
Sheepmeat	Basic	x	x			x			
Fruit and vegetables	Basic	x						x	x
Olive oil	Target	x	x	x		x			x
Oilseeds	Target	x	x					x	x
Wine	Guide	x						x	
Tobacco	Norm	x	x						x

grants, assistance in retraining programmes, investment in facilities to improve the marketing of agricultural products, etc.

The effects of the Common Agricultural Policy

The measurement of any policy's performance must be made in terms of the goals it seeks to achieve. In an area as complex as agriculture in which several differing goals are simultaneously pursued, it is frequently difficult to measure success overall. To do so implies some weighting of the various goals. However, since such weights imply an expression of political judgement, it is not possible to devise a wholly satisfactory, objective means by which the CAP's success can be determined.

(a) *Is agriculture in 'a common market'?*

The CAP's first intention was to 'provide a framework within which the common market could apply to agriculture'. It is not entirely clear what this means. In other sectors it appears to imply that separate national arrangements should be substituted by common arrangements which would ensure a degree of protection against third-country suppliers and free trade within the EC. Within such a common market the forces of competition would tend to squeeze out relatively high cost producers. For agriculture, however, the test of 'being within the common market' seems to exclude the possibility of competitive forces eliminating high cost producers. Instead, the degree to which they survive is dependent not upon the market within the EC but upon the Council of Ministers' readiness to finance intervention and export restitutions. Thus it seems proper to interpret the concept of 'common market' as it is applied to agriculture as meaning only that the goods are free to move and not that there is competitive free trade within the EC.

Table 3 shows that both in the Six and in the Nine there has been a substantial expansion of trade. This trade has grown more rapidly within the EC than with the rest of the world and, in the most recent period, exports have expanded more rapidly than imports. Judged on this criterion the CAP may be regarded as a success. It seems highly unlikely that, in the absence of such a common policy, individual member states would have been prepared to admit into their own markets other member countries' more costly produce rather than cheaper goods of equal quality available from the rest of the world.

Economists would assess this change in trade in terms of its effects on trade creation and trade distortion. Trade-creating effects emerge where lower cost production displaces higher cost production. Trade distortion arises when high cost producers are enabled to displace lower cost producers. Thus the economic interpretation of this increased flow of intra-EC trade cannot be separated from the question about the relative prices at which products from the world market might have been available to the EC in the absence of the CAP or with a policy which operated at a lower degree of protection. There is much argument about the degree to which world prices would be changed had the EC pursued a more liberal policy. Table 4 shows that, except in the unusual circumstances of 1973/4, world prices have consistently been well below EC prices. Thus, it seems that the CAP's trade distorting effects exceed its trade creating impact. If this is so, the overall level of Community GNP must have been reduced. Arguments about what the world price would be if the EC pursued a more liberal policy cannot be satisfactorily resolved. However, it seems unlikely that world prices would, in the long term, have risen to the EC level to a degree which eliminated the protection the CAP affords EC

Table 3   The development of trade in agricultural and food products

A. EC6—Trade in agricultural products

	1958 million ECU	1972 million ECU	1972 as % 1958
Total imports	9,683	23,425	242
Imports from EC6	1,243	9,425	758
Imports from non-EC	7,440	14,000	188
Total exports	3,139	14,116	450
Exports to EC6	1,213	9,434	777
Exports to non-EC	1,926	4,682	243

Source: Yearbook of Agricultural Statistics 1974 Eurostat.

B. EC9—Trade in agricultural and food products

	1973 million ECU	1980 million ECU	1980 as % 1973
Total imports	39,857	78,552	197
Imports from EC9	15,486	36,342	235
Imports from non-EC	24,371	42,210	173
Total exports	22,620	55,792	247
Exports to EC9	15,242	36,271	238
Exports to non-EC	7,378	19,521	265

Source: EC Commission, The Agricultural Situation in the Community 1976 and 1981 Reports.

agriculture. If this is so, the argument that the CAP has made the EC poorer holds true.

(b) *Has the policy made supplies secure?*

The CAP took responsibility for ensuring a secure supply of food for EC citizens. It has had considerable success in this. EC production has grown substantially throughout its existence (Table 5). The EC has become increasingly self-sufficient in foodstuffs and as a result could regard itself as more secure. Such an argument needs two qualifications. First, the increased domestic production of EC agriculture is itself dependent upon sustained imports of inputs, e.g. fuel, feedingstuffs and chemicals. Should these supplies be cut, EC production would fall. Thus, the judgement as to whether the EC is more secure at this higher level of output depends in part upon whether these inputs are more secure in their delivery than food imports themselves. Secondly, the increase in production to a large extent reflects not any particular agricultural policy but changes in agricultural technology. Outside the EC in countries with different types of policies output has also risen (Table 6). Thus, it is perfectly proper to ask whether an equivalent increase in output could have been achieved at lower resource cost in the EC. If so, then the EC would have been more secure with an alternative policy. This would have left it with the same volume of food and with more resources to spend to meet any deficits in either inputs or food by purchases from abroad.

Table 4   Prices of certain agricultural products

Product	Year	EC 'entry price' ECU/100 kg	Third country offer (normally lowest available) ECU/100 kg	EC entry price as % of world market price
Common wheat	1968/9	13.24	6.78	195
	1973/4	14.34	18.06	79
	1977/8	19.72	9.14	216
	1979/80	20.72	12.69	163
Barley	1968/9	11.53	5.86	197
	1973/4	12.91	13.44	96
	1977/8	18.12	8.78	206
	1979/80	18.86	11.71	161
White sugar	1968/9	27.02	7.60	355
	1973/4	29.98	45.36	66
	1977/8	41.78	16.38	255
	1979/80	43.26	33.11	131
Beef and veal	1968/9	82.21	48.65	169
	1973/4	103.04	93.71	110
	1977/8	148.58	75.86	196
	1979/80	154.58	75.63	204
Pigmeat	1968/9	89.40	66.50	134
	1973/4	103.75	79.30	131
	1977/8	134.04	97.88	137
	1979/80	139.07	91.36	152
Butter	1968/9	230.83	45.82	504
	1973/4	232.52	72.63	320
	1977/8	303.91	78.42	388
	1979/80	309.90	75.39	411
Skimmed milk	1968/9	61.63	16.86	365
	1973/4	93.80	60.11	156
	1977/8	133.13	26.92	494
	1979/80	135.54	35.77	379
Olive oil	1968/9	139.33	80.75	173
	1973/4	165.83	172.30	96
	1977/8	227.02	107.48	211
	1979/80	235.04	121.74	193

Note: The figures in column 4 represent the annual average of, normally, the lowest third country offer price used for the purposes of managing the agricultural markets. They do not necessarily represent the prices at which the EC could purchase on the world market if it had to buy substantially more of its supplies from third countries. Further, it is to be noted that world market prices are often residual prices and are not the prices at which a large part of agricultural produce is traded internationally.

Source: EC Commission, The Agricultural Situation in the Community 1980 Report.

(c) *Stability and the CAP*

Table 7 compares the movements in internal EC prices from 1969 to 1980 with movements in the price level of imports and prices in countries outside the EC. It can be seen that, although prices within the EC have varied substantially for some agricultural products, the CAP has provided a high degree of price stability. The value of such stability is subject to both political and economic analysis. In political terms, governments may be very embarrassed by shortages or sharp rises

Table 5   Increases in the production of major commodities in the EC
('000 tonnes)

	1960 EUR 6	% increase 1960–72	1972 EUR 6	1973 EUR 9	1980 EUR 9	EUR 10	% increase 1973–80
Total cereals	52,687	50.4	79,246	105,726	119,163	124,261	12.7
Sugar	6,902	17.4	8,103	9,010	12,086	12,260	34.1
Milk	64,172	9.0	69,966	92,984	106,094	107,788	14.1
Beef and veal	3,284	20.9	3,970	5,403	7,075	7,176	30.9
Pigmeat	3,527	77.4	6,258	8,166	10,003	10,147	22.5
Poultrymeat	414	416.9	2,140	3,125	3,901	4,021	24.8
Sheepmeat	203	4.4	212	480	593	713	23.5
Fruit	–	–	12,777	15,128	18,541	20,551	22.6
Vegetables	–	–	22,077	26,529	28,659	32,086	8.0

Sources: Food and Agriculture Organisation Production Yearbooks, 1961, 1974 and 1981.
Eurostate Review 1971–80.

Table 6   Production of major agricultural products, 1960 and 1981
('000 tonnes)

	1960	1981
Cereals		
USA	191,897	333,748
Canada	25,870	50,257
South America	34,410	74,725
Australia	10,804	23,242
New Zealand	349	915
USSR	130,408	167,306
Beef and veal		
USA	7,183	10,330
Canada	629	1,020
South America	2,369	7,124
Australia	643	1,481
New Zealand	240	498
USSR	3,200	6,690
Pigmeat		
USA	5,264	7,220
Canada	469	860
South America	264	1,762
Australia	110	234
New Zealand	41	35
USSR	3,300	5,250
Milk		
USA	55,702	60,161
Canada	8,393	8,025
South America	15,000	23,462
Australia	6,592	5,324
New Zealand	5,335	6,500
USSR	60,800	88,000

Source: Food and Agriculture Organisation, Production Yearbooks, 1961 and 1981.

Table 7   Variability in agricultural commodity prices 1969-80[1]

	Common wheat	Barley[2]	Fat cattle	Pigmeat	Butter[3]	Skimmed[3] milk powder
FRG	9.8	9.3	7.6	11.7	10.4	11.8
France	9.3	9.6	7.8	16.1	10.4	10.0
Italy	5.2	8.5	9.3	28.4	9.2	–
Netherlands	16.3	13.5	14.0	7.9	17.1	7.3
Belgium/Lux.	11.5	11.3	11.0	10.0	15.9	7.5
UK	13.0	13.8	10.7	18.0	15.1	28.3
Ireland	13.6	14.3	14.5	18.6	–	–
Denmark	6.5	9.6	10.7	15.5	6.3	–
USA	26.3	31.8	16.2	21.9	8.0	4.4
Imports[4]	40.3	31.8	22.3	20.8	21.8	56.5

Notes: [1] As measured by the coefficient of variation. Prices have been deflated using the retail price index for each country. Prices are those received by producers unless otherwise stated. For precise definition of prices, see sources of data.
[2] USA barley price is a wholesale price.
[3] Butter and skimmed milk powder prices are wholesale prices.
[4] The series used is the lowest Third Country offer price to the EC.

Sources: Eurostat, Agricultural Price Statistics, 1969-80. EC Commission, Agricultural Markets, Special Number, 1978. EC Commission, The Agricultural Situation in the Community 1980 Report. United States Department of Agriculture, Agricultural Outlook, various issues 1976-82.

in product prices. Since the CAP has helped to moderate such movements it is undoubtedly of political value. In economic terms, stability has been achieved around the higher end of the spectrum of world price movements. As a result, consumers have, in normal years, paid more for their food in order to avoid facing considerable price increases in the occasional years of shortage. Discounting the benefits of such risk-avoiding expenses is complex. Simple calculations showing the net cost to consumers over a period may not themselves reveal that the appropriate degree of stability has been achieved. A more critical issue may be that the same degree of price stability could have been attained at lower cost. For example, a different price policy might have allowed lower consumer prices whilst providing the EC with resources either to build up stocks or financial reserves. At a time of shortage either actual commodities or price subsidies could then have provided a measure of stability. It is not necessarily the case that the CAP's approach to agricultural price stability is the most cost-effective.

(d) *The CAP: contribution to agricultural productivity*

Table 5 shows the development of agricultural output and Table 1 the development of agricultural productivity in the EC since 1968. Both measures show considerable improvement over this period. The EC now enjoys a larger supply of food at lower unit resource cost than was the case in 1958. This suggests that the CAP has been a considerable success. However, it is hard to prove that additional productivity is directly attributable to it. On the one hand, the CAP may have encouraged a larger number of people to remain in agriculture than would have been the case given a different policy stance. That by itself might both reduce the rate of increase in labour productivity and allow output to continue to grow. On the other hand, and equally significant, however, is the fact that the mix of EC output since 1960 is largely a result of the relative prices for different commodities fixed under the

CAP. Administered prices have sustained production at costs covered by prices which consumers are not prepared to pay. As a result, surpluses have emerged, most importantly for milk, sugar, cereals and wine. These may have been more tolerable than equivalent shortages; however, it is proper to ask whether alternative policies might have provided, at lower resource cost, a pattern of output as well as a level of output more attuned to the EC's needs.

(e) *Regional implications of the CAP*

The EC consists not only of ten separate member countries but of regions within them that vary considerably. Thus, the circumstances of production and agriculture in the south of Italy differ markedly from those in the north. Such differences led to increasing concern with the CAP's regional impact which can be assessed in two ways. In the EC it is usually discussed in terms of the impact upon regional agriculture. It can be shown that, since the policy is a price support policy, it benefits most substantially those whose output is greatest. The bulk of the EC's output is produced in the more favoured areas where incomes already tend to be higher and where there often exist numerous alternative occupations. In the remote areas, because little is sold and because some of the products which are sold, store stock, etc., have no direct support system, the benefits derived from the CAP may be much lower. A recent EC study demonstrated this clearly.[1] It indicated the importance of such special schemes as the hill compensatory allowances in achieving a better balance of benefit.

The other approach examines the CAP's impact on the regional economies of the EC as a whole, including its effect not only upon agriculture but upon other industries and upon consumers. The picture which emerges may be very different from that shown in a purely agricultural context. Table 8 shows the distribution of spending per head on agriculture among the EC's member states. It is clear that expenditure per capita varies considerably among EC states. Evidence suggests that within each country the lower income groups spend a higher than average proportion of their income on food. Given that the poor regions within countries usually have few alternative job opportunities, and that many of these regions also have relatively poor agricultures, the net effect of the CAP in terms of the welfare of most citizens of these regions seems to be negative.

Table 8   Per capita expenditure on food among EC member countries 1979

	FRG	FR	It	NL	Belgium/ Lux.	UK	Irl	Dk
Total expenditure in million ECU	72,441	43,363	41,969	10,802	9,830	30,562	1,467	4,961
Population 000	61,315	53,499	56,888	13,986	10,199	55,883	3,365	5,118
Per capita ECU	1,181	810	737	772	964	546	435	969

Sources: Food expenditure as data from Organisation for Economic Co-operation and Development, National Accounts. Population data from Milk Marketing Board, EEC Dairy Facts and Figures 1980.

(f) *The CAP and farm incomes*

Throughout its existence one of the principal arguments in favour of the CAP has been the need to defend, maintain and improve the level of personal earnings in agriculture. The main instrument used has been to raise prices above their market equilibrium level and to sustain them by subsidizing exports and intervention purchase. Such an approach, however, is consistent with the structure of the agriculture sector. Essentially, the agricultural industry is organized in a competitive form. It may not match all the criteria of perfect competition, but in the sense that individual farmers are unable to affect either the price at which they buy or the price at which they sell, it approximates to that model.

If we take as our starting-point the conventional diagrams of equilibrium in perfect competition in the long term, it is clear why raising prices can produce only short-term benefits whilst at the same time increasing output. Diagram A shows long-run equilibrium output and cost levels for a firm in perfect competition under two differing price assumptions. At p_1 the output level produced is q_1 and the profits the firm receives are normal. In this context, normal may be taken to mean sufficient to keep resources in their present uses but not to attract additional resources. If price is increased to p_{11}, the profits made by a firm operating at its optimum level, where MC_1 crosses p_{11}, become 'supernormal'. At that level additional resources will be drawn into the enterprise in order to expand its output to q_2. However, since p_{11} is not a private price to the individual business but shared by all producers, resources in other industries which are receiving only normal profits will be attracted into this type of production. As they enter the business the costs of acquiring appropriate resources are likely to increase. There are two elements in this rising cost, one the actual availability of suitable resources such as land, the other changes in quality as labour and land and capital of less suitable types are drawn into production. However, expansion will continue until a condition is reached in which, once again, the average total cost is tangential to the price received, in this case p_{11}. The profits will simply be 'normal' once again and the benefits which farmers initially received will have been eroded. To restore their position farmers would require a further increase in price beyond p_{11}. In fact, as production is expanded the proportion of costs to the value of output is likely to rise and the level of prices needed to sustain farm incomes at a given amount

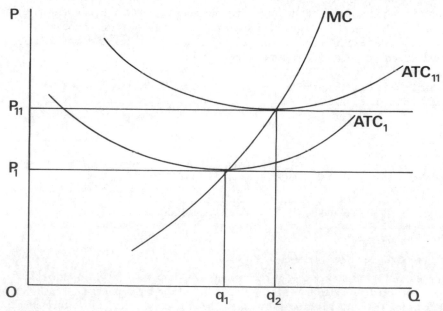

Diagram A   Equilibrium of firm in conditions of perfect competition.

above the equilibrium level will itself have to rise, with consequential effects on the level of output.

Diagram B illustrates the significance of this from the point of view of the industry as a whole. Initially, the industry is in rough equilibrium at p_1 with quantity of output q_1. By administrative process the price is increased to p_{11}. At such a price less will be purchased, q_{c11}. However, the output of the industry, the results of adjustments amongst farmers, seeking to capitalise on 'supernormal' profits, will rise in this case to q_{s11}. p_{11} can only be sustained as a market price if the quantity represented by the difference between Oq_{c11} and Oq_{s11} is removed from the market. In the context of the Community, removal from the market requires either intervention purchase or export subsidies or both. This characteristic of the operation of price policy within a competitive market seems to have been overlooked when, in the determination of prices, farmers and Ministers have argued that higher prices are necessary to sustain farm incomes. In practical terms, farm incomes can only be increased if more farmers leave the industry because of the improved opportunities elsewhere in the economy. In effect they will be improved if the concept of what is a 'normal profit' is itself enhanced.

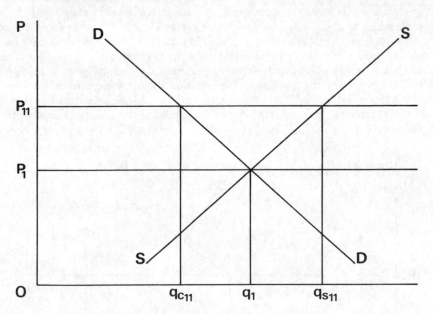

Diagram B   Implications of administered price increase at the level of the industry.

Apart from this quite fundamental flaw in the CAP as an instrument of income maintenance, the EC's policy suffers because, by paying higher prices for output, it benefits most those who produce most. A considerable proportion of all EC output comes from large producers. Thus even in the short run there is an unintended and undesirable distributional element in the income effects of a price policy which does little to help the poorest farmers.

A third important defect of the CAP as an income-raising policy is the fact that it discriminates in the degree of protection it affords to different types of output. Thus prices have been more protected for the northern products, cereals and milk, than they have for the products of southern agriculture, fruit, vegetables and wine. However, in general terms there is a higher proportion of very poor farmers in the south than in the north of the EC. Viewed, therefore, in terms of the EC's geography, the CAP's income effects seem misguided.

(g) *Consumers and the CAP*

It is especially difficult to assess how the CAP has affected consumers. Diagram C outlines in an abstract form their predicament. The CAP's effect is to add to world prices a variable levy, here indicated by $(WP + L) - WP$. The difference between the prices which would be open to consumers without the CAP and the prices they actually pay is represented by the gap between p_1 and p_{11}. In this situation, consumers lose the whole of the consumer surplus represented by the area ABCD. Part of their loss is simply a transfer to others; A to farmers in terms of increased producer surplus and C to the state in terms of increased taxes. The area B represents the costs to the economy of the misallocation of resources induced by raising prices from p_1 to p_{11}. Area D, however, is lost by consumers but benefits no-one else. Clearly the extent of consumer loss depends both upon the gap between p_1 and p_{11} and the slope, the elasticity, of the demand curve for the product concerned. Neither issue is unequivocally clear. Whilst the EC may, as Table 4 showed, have been able to import at considerably lower prices than it actually paid to its own farmers, the effect upon the world market of substantial increases in EC purchases which might result from lower prices to EC producers is complex. In the short run, if the EC's demand for imports rose substantially, higher world prices would result. However, in the longer run, the supply price for imports should be equivalent to the costs of production plus transport from the lowest cost producers. It seems likely that these prices would be below those currently paid to EC farmers. An important element in assessing the effect on import prices is the degree to which EC output would fall were prices lowered. Again it is

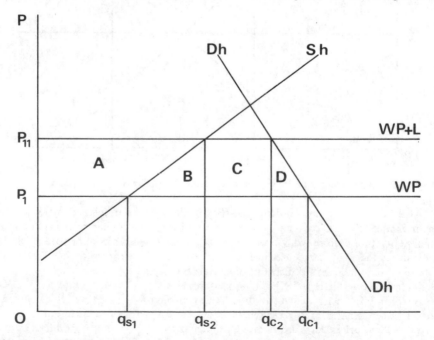

Diagram C   The impact on consumers of an import levy.

important to distinguish between catastrophic price collapses which would bankrupt many farmers and a more gentle process of price squeeze. In the first case, dislocation of agriculture might cause calamitous reductions in EC output. However, it is not clear that, given a more gradual change, output would fall. Fixed costs are an important element in the situation of many farmers. So long as variable costs are covered by current prices it will pay farmers to continue in production until their fixed assets need renewal. A gentle squeeze on margins may stimulate efficient farmers to exploit new technology more energetically. It they do so, and are able to secure assets from less efficient farmers at lower prices because the output for agriculture in general is regarded less favourably, the output of the transferred assets will rise. Thus, in the long run the EC's production could rise or fall in response to a gentle pressure on prices.

A further element in assessing the CAP's effect on consumers is the elasticity of demand for assumed products subject to price policy. Calculations of consumer response are based on past experience but within the EC market substantial economic and social changes are occurring. These may have profound long-run implications for demand. Figures published in the United Kingdom by MAFF give some guidance about prices and consumer reaction.[2] It is, however, dangerous to take such evidence and project on the wider geographical basis of the EC or for a substantial period ahead. At the most it provides an indication of the probable characteristics of demand.

Adequate measurements of the CAP's effect on consumers are difficult and contentious. However, it seems likely that consumers could have enjoyed an adequate supply of food at a lower price and this would have benefited most those who were poorest. In this sense the question of the 'reasonableness' of price is political rather than economic. Consumers may feel that food price rises no greater than those in the general price level are reasonable. Such a historical perception of reasonableness has certainly influenced policy-makers. Another popular approach is that a reasonable price level must provide adequate incomes for farmers. Although such an argument is misleading this may not prevent it being used to persuade consumers that prices are 'reasonable'.

(h) *The impact of the CAP on the EC's economies*

The most critical single dimension in which the CAP is assessed is in terms of its cost. There are several aspects to the CAP's so-called 'cost'. They include:

(1) the cost of resource misallocation;
(2) transfers from consumers to the agricultural sector;
(3) transfers which take place between member states as a result of higher prices within the EC than in world markets and net budget flows between the member states and the EC; and
(4) the expenditures from the EC's budget on the CAP.

The costs of resource misallocation occur when resources are drawn into or retained in agriculture which would have a higher value were they employed in other EC sectors. Such costs have both an immediate static character and, because they influence the rate at which the EC's economy may grow, can have important dynamic effects. It is difficult to come to satisfactory estimates of the degree to which the CAP has shifted resources between industries. If its only effect had been to keep in production resources which would otherwise have been wholly idle, then it must have had a positive effect on GDP. However, in so far as it has attracted resources from uses in which the market value of their products was higher than in agriculture, its effect on economic output must have been negative. Probably the balance of advantage has shifted somewhat over time. In its early years when the EC's economy was growing resources 'trapped' in agriculture must have tended to reduce both output and economic growth. Since 1974, however, stagnation and growing unemployment has made this effect less important.

Transfers from consumers arise because the price of food is higher than it would be in a market in which imports were freely available. The size of these transfers depends upon the discrepancy between world market and EC prices were barriers to imports removed. Yet, as shown, a transfer of resources achieved by raising food prices imposes a higher proportional burden on the poor than an equivalent transfer financed from taxation.[3] Consumer lobbies in the EC have been relatively ineffective. Although concern about prices is expressed by such organizations as The Bureau of European Consumer Organisations, this has been ineffective compared with the claims of the agricultural pressure groups.

The CAP's net cost to member states comprises two elements; via trade and via the EC budget. Net importing countries pay higher prices for their imports because of CAP levies which increase internal prices and are additional charges on imports from the rest of the world. The second element results from net transactions via the EC budget. Some 60 to 70 per cent of the budget (see Table 9)

Table 9   EAGGF expenditure on CAP
        (million ECU)

	Guarantee	Guidance	% of total budget
1967/8	1,313.0	285.0	93.2
1970	3,149.5	243.8	92.9
1972	2,732.4	202.3	82.8
1973	4,165.7	229.2	80.3
1978	8,672.7	323.6	74.1
1981	11,570.5	730.6	67.0

Sources: MAFF, Agricultural and Food Statistics, 1974. EC Commission, The Agricultural Situation in the Community 1981 Report.

is used to support agricultural prices which tends to occur in net exporting member countries. The EC's budget revenue derives, in addition to receipts from customs unions and levies, from the equivalent of up to 1 per cent value added tax. Thus, countries with relatively large agricultural populations gain most from the EC's budget whilst those who are net importers or who have a relatively high propensity to consume, contribute a disproportionate share to budget revenues. Various calculations have been made of the CAP's net budgetary effects. These are subject to variations stemming from changes in the EC market balance and in the world prices. The example given in Table 10 illustrates the nature of these flows.

Anxiety about the budget cost of the CAP stems in part from fears that it may run out of funds. Table 9 showed expenditure on the CAP from 1968 to 1981. This has risen almost continuously. Since surpluses seem likely to grow and world prices may fall, the costs of price support are likely to grow. Price support is given priority over other EC expenditure. Whilst it would be unrealistic to predict a date when funds will run out there is a danger that low world prices and high quantities produced in the Community could exhaust available resources. At that stage either additional money would have to be found to finance the budget or alternatively the price level supported by the Community would fall.

Table 10   Net contributions and receipts in respect of the Community budget (million ECU)

	1980	1981
FRG	−1,540	−1,647
France	423	624
Italy	735	619
Netherlands	441	223
Belgium	255	388
Luxembourg	232	282
UK	−1,521	−1,505
Ireland	644	591
Denmark	331	302
Greece	−	123

Note: These figures are Commission estimates for 1980 and 1981 Community budgets.
Source: HM Government, Statement on the 1982 Community Budget, Cmnd 8513.

Where to now?—future directions for agricultural policy in Europe

In this section some of the alternatives for the development of the CAP are explored. There are four main distinct approaches to improving the CAP. These cover changes in administered prices, introducing more quantitative controls, imposing regional discrimination and finally applying direct income supports.

Price adjustments do not produce easily predictable results. Attempts to contain surpluses by gradually reducing prices may eventually become effective but not in the short term. If cuts are pushed to a point at which production falls immediately, the market could well be short of supplies. This would result in politically embarrassing instability. The difficulty of manipulating short-run agricultural output by price policy reflects uncertainties of weather and the need to take account of the relative prices of other agricultural products which might compete for the same resources. Such complications make the process of fixing prices to achieve a level of agricultural output difficult and inexact.

Further difficulties arise because of political repercussions. Lower agricultural prices inevitably mean lower farm revenues. In the long term as some farmers leave the industry costs will adjust and profits return to normal. In the time scale in which politicians have to survive this recovery is so remote as to be unimportant. Reductions in price affect both farm incomes and the capital value of farm assets. A collapse in the capital value of assets would push farmers who were heavily borrowed into insolvency. Thus rapid adjustment by price alone would result in political and social distress as well as economic wastage.

One difficulty in adjusting common prices is the continuing but differing rates of inflation in member countries. If no action were taken, the real prices available to farmers would fall at different rates in member countries. Such a process would not necessarily lead to the elimination of the highest cost farmers judged in European terms. The fortunes of farmers would depend more upon the macro-economic policies of member countries than their own efforts.

Clearly, as it stands, the CAP's price policy is at an impasse. Real prices cannot be raised because increased output would be too costly for the budget. Prices cannot even be held constant, given a tendency for technology to increase output more rapidly than consumption. However, if even as a result of inflation real prices fall, the political consequences are intolerable. Yet, price policy remains necessary to ensure a degree of preference for EC producers, to maintain internal price stability and to enable the EC to achieve the volume of output it prefers. To permit it to be used for those purposes, agricultural prices must be raised and lowered according to changing needs and opportunities. At present problems are more likely to be connected with the need to allow prices to fall. Thus the successful use of price policy depends upon the invention of additional policies which cope with the undesired effects of lower prices.

Structural policy has sometimes been claimed to enable farmers to cope with lower prices. This logic depends upon the assumption that there exist opportunities to use resources released from agriculture. However, since 1974, the energy crisis, the world recession and inflation have dampened optimism on this score and the emphasis of policy has changed.

The new approach tries to improve the situation of some of the most hard-pressed farmers without raising prices. However, it complicates rather than relieves the general problems of price policy. By enabling such farmers to produce more, the total volume reaching the EC market is increased and the pressure on prices intensified. There is a conflict here that may be explicable in political terms but which destroys structural policy as a means of easing the problems of price policy. In practice the scale of structural expenditure has been so small that its effects are likely to have been almost negligible.

The failure of price policy to check the growth of surpluses has encouraged interest in quantitative controls. A variety of such controls can be considered. Popular among some farmers but not among those who seek to promote a single EC economy are regional quotas for production or sales. Such quotas, if they worked, would freeze the pattern of production and regulate the volume of output on that particular key. The consequences would be a lack of dynamism in the EC and increasing but hidden real costs as the potential for a more efficient agriculture grew but was frustrated by the quantitative restrictions. In fact such developments are unlikely to take place. All governments seem to expect to increase their own agricultural output and indeed, although this is clearly unworkable, their share of the EC market. Given such expectations they are unlikely to accept quantitative restrictions.

An alternative approach is to set a total quantity which the EC is prepared to support. A number of alternative ways of achieving this can be considered. The one that has received most attention in the EC is the imposition of 'co-responsibility levies'. These levies come into play when the volume produced exceeds the level thought appropriate by the EC. They represent a tax imposed between the consumer and the producer, reducing the price producers receive without cutting the amount paid by consumers. They accumulate funds which become the EC's property and help to defray the costs of maintaining the policy as it stands. However, a policy of 'co-responsibility' applied to balance the books when output rises will mean lower and lower residual returns to farmers. If this is not the case, then output will have to be supported from EC funds. If it is the case, then the problems of cutting price will occur even if in a somewhat disguised form and the political odium which that entails will again surface.

Another approach to the quantitative manipulation of the whole market would be to indicate a 'standard quantity' which the EC stood prepared to underwrite through intervention or export restitution. Such a quantity might be determined on an annual basis but the eligible amounts tied to particular months. On products seeking support through intervention or export restitution, an initial payment of only part of the full amount would be paid. If more than the standard quantity was produced, then the final topping-up payment would be diluted so as to contain the overall commitment of budgetary resources by the EC to the predetermined level. Farmers and others would have to visualize the effect of bumper crops upon this buffered price. Should it seem likely that the final intervention price would be lower than that originally intended by the Council of Ministers, they would have the option of accepting at once a lower than 'intervention' price on the open market of the EC. The effect of such an approach would be to share the benefits of increasing production to a greater degree among the EC's consumers. However, it would clearly allow prices to farmers to fall in years of over-production. How far they fell would depend upon political decisions about the degree of support the EC was prepared to provide. However, this policy, too, means that the problems of lower prices have to be faced.

A third approach to the quantitative regulation of production is through intervention on the individual farm. Such intervention has precedent in Europe. Various patterns exist. In the UK farmers who want to grow potatoes must obtain a quota area. An alternative approach limits the quantity individuals may sell in any time period. Disposal of surplus production on his farm then becomes the farmer's responsibility. In the USA, set-aside programmes, which require farmers to cut the area planted, have been used to combat surpluses. It would be simplistic to neglect the difficulties which individual quota arrangements involve. They imply a degree of rigidity in the distribution of production through the EC. This becomes increasingly expensive as technology changes the competitive position of different farmers. They impose considerable administrative requirements on agricultural policy. Someone has to decide how the quotas are to be allocated, and then to police them.

One important CAP reform proposal made by Pisani advocates the use of 'quantums'. In essence this implies the division of the quantities which farmers sold of particular products into successive layers. The earliest small quantities would receive relatively high prices. As the quantity sold rose the prices attaching to successive amounts would fall. Eventually it would be possible for very large farmers to find themselves producing at a price which represented the value of marginal output to the EC. Such a scheme has much to commend it in terms of elegance. It represents one way of using a price mechanism to distribute income in favour of the relatively poor producer. It does, however, present severe problems in an EC context. First of all, the distribution of farm sizes varies considerably. Thus the benefits to individual member states of such an approach would also vary. Secondly, considerable administrative difficulties would emerge if large farms split their units up into small blocks farmed by individual members of the family. Such farms presumably would then qualify for a large number of high priced units. More generally, the idea of discriminating in favour of small producers when economies of scale seem to be of growing significance in farming runs counter to the Treaty's goal of efficiency.

It would be dangerous to exclude the possibility of some form of quantitative control. However, there are important practical reasons to doubt whether it can have a very substantial role. The experience the EC has of quantitative controls relates to the sugar regime. There it proved incapable of limiting the production of sugar despite a situation in which the EC had guaranteed to purchase sugar from ACP countries and at the same time finds itself requiring to subsidize exports to the rest of the world.

This review of some of the most commonly discussed alternatives for the CAP, co-responsibility, standard quantities and various types of quantitative restriction indicates that none of them frees the EC from the political embarrassments implicit in cutting prices to prevent surpluses. The social and political consequences of lower prices are such that only by using a much more sensitive instrument is the Community likely to become free to regulate farm output in relation to its needs. This suggests that attention must be directed towards forms of direct income support. Direct income aids have some clear-cut advantages. First, they can discriminate in terms of the situation of different people throughout the EC. This is important on both social and political grounds. On social grounds the justification for transfers from the rest of the EC can be related to the actual poverty of those involved. Direct income aids are also attractive on political grounds. Within the EC standards of living vary. Levels of income support which seem socially necessary in West Germany would prove excessively generous in such relatively poorer countries as Greece, Portugal or Italy. A further political attraction of direct income aids is that it links the social dimension of the EC's approach to agriculture to social policies which apply to the majority of its citizens. This is likely both to achieve goals of equity within member countries and to facilitate approaches to agricultural adaptation which integrate developments in that sector with progress elsewhere in the economy. Since there is no long-run prospect of increases in agricultural employment it seems sensible that such an approach should dominate the long-run attitudes of the EC towards its agricultural industry.

Direct income aids are not without difficulty. First, the very fact of discrimination causes considerable anxiety within the EC. It appears to be a departure from the 'commonness' of agricultural policy as it stands. As we have seen, such a 'commonness' is a façade rather than a reality so long as the EC consists of differing economies with different tax and social security systems and with different real levels of prices resulting in part from the existence of several monetary systems within the EC.

Direct income aids would result in a substantial visible transfer of funds to a particular group of people. Although in real resource terms the cost of direct income supports is lower than the cost of supporting incomes to an equivalent extent through raising prices, payments to individuals have to be financed via a budget whereas payments via prices can be extracted from consumers. As a result there is considerable alarm at the budgetary implications of direct income supports.

One response to this alarm is to suggest that direct income supports should be financed by member countries instead of via the CAP. Various possibilities exist. Some would require a Community contribution to all direct income supports, others might simply use the EC's contribution to top up expenditure in those countries where incomes were relatively low and the financial burden of direct income supports greatest. Another approach would use EC money to compensate net exporters who, if they had to subsidize their low income farmers from their own budgetary sources, would cease to derive so much benefit from membership of the EC. All these alternatives exist and combinations of them are feasible. However, it is feared that individual governments would deliberately, or unintentionally, favour their own farmers so as to distort competition in the EC and damage farmers in those countries where governments were less generous. To avoid such problems of inequity, direct income supports would need to be administered on the basis of a common set of guidelines and supervised at an EC level.

A further area of anxiety about direct income supports is their psychological effect on the recipients. It is argued that farmers resent suggestions that they are recipients of public charity and prefer to be rewarded in terms of the work they carry out. Price policy, it is argued, does this, direct income aids do not. It would be disingenuous to ignore such strong feelings. Even though it can be demonstrated that artificially maintained prices are just as much an act of public charity as direct income aids, they do not have this appearance and farmers therefore cannot be expected to welcome such a change. One possible alternative would be to pay farmers for specific tasks of public importance in addition to the market price they receive for their products. For example, in areas where conservation is of great importance and landscapes appear to be threatened, farmers might be paid to maintain hedges, walls, drainage, numbers of livestock, etc., in order to protect the environment. Such an approach would give flexibility in adjusting rural employment and an instrument whereby concerns for the environment were recognized and handled. Priorities in this area will vary considerably among member countries. At a purely Community level, it would be difficult to finance more than minimal conservation and environmental payments. To do so more generously would mean taxing some poor EC members to subsidize the environment of some who are rich. However, an approach which allowed national initiatives, coordinated and policed by the EC, could escape some of these snags whilst enabling a positive response to be made to growing concern about ecology and the environment.

The use of such amenity aids might ease some problems concerned with direct income aids. It shares with direct income aids, however, the need to conceive of a satisfactory institutional framework for its implementation.

The institutional arrangements of the CAP have been highly centralized. Decisions and the execution of the policy in relation to prices have been wholly controlled from Brussels and a very substantial control exercised over structural policy. Both income and amenity aids produce the need for great sensitivity to local requirements and a great deal of decision-making best taken within the local framework. To manage this wholly from Brussels would involve enormous bureaucratic resources and considerable wastage. Thus, a new role for the Commission in relation to these parts of the CAP may need to be forged. In essence the Commission's role would be to draw up guidelines of compatibility for these policies in relation to the needs of the EC as a whole and to police policies to ensure that EC interests were not damaged.

This framework of responsibility only becomes effective if some sanctions can be exercised against offending parties. The Treaty is relatively weak in such matters. It may be an extension of the concept of the EC to strengthen it. One possibility would be to establish, within the framework of the European Court, a section particularly responsible for reviewing infringements of EC guidelines on agricultural policy. Cases could be brought either by the Commission itself, by individual member countries, or by individuals who felt they were adversely affected through the activities of governments in their own or other member countries. The Court would adjudicate on each case and find in favour of the complainant or the accused member government. Should a member government be found at fault, it could then be given an option either to compensate the aggrieved party or to desist from the particular aid complained against. Calculations of compensation would be complicated but they need not be more so than those faced by many courts dealing with claims of negligence under the existing legal framework. A body of expertise would need to be developed in these matters and precedent would become important.

An institutional structure of this type would avoid facing governments with ultimatums which might clash with their own political priorities. If the Community continues to do this, the likelihood is that it will either be defied, with resulting loss of credibility, or that the governments will collude with one another in a series of trade-offs and so change the rules in ways incompatible with the needs of the Community as a whole. Thus a development along these lines could be a positive move forward for the Community. It would make it more possible to accommodate the political diversity of an EC of Ten and possibly Twelve members.

Notes

1. Commission of the European Communities, *Study of the Regional Impact of the CAP* (Brussels, Commission of the European Communities, 1981).
2. Ministry of Agriculture, Fisheries and Food, *National Food Survey.*
3. Josling, T. E. and Hamway, D., 'Income Transfer Effects of the Common Agricultural Policy' in Davey, B., Josling, T. E. and McFarquhar, A. (eds), *Agriculture and the State* (London, Macmillan, 1976), pp. 180–205.

7   The Common Fisheries Policy

DAVID FREESTONE with ANNA FLEISCH

The protracted negotiations over the Common Fisheries Policy (CFP) have probably provoked more controversy than any other single EC policy.[1] Fisheries have
dominated Council and Summit meetings.[2] They were the direct reason for Norwegian public opinion rejecting EC membership, and have been the continued
cause for calls for United Kingdom (UK) withdrawal from the EC. They have
also prompted the first inter-state dispute to go to the European Court of Justice
(ECJ).[3] Yet in none of the member states does fishing account for more than 1 per
cent of the work-force. Why then has the conclusion of a comprehensive EC fisheries
policy proved so intractable a problem? In part the difficulty may be intrinsic to all
international fishery management schemes. It may also lie partly in the radical
changes of the international regime of the seas, which has coincided with the EC's
assumption of responsibility for fisheries, and partly in the problems of reconciling
the diverse interests of the EC national fishing industries.[4]

Problems of fisheries management in the area

Growing awareness of the dangers of over-exploiting fish stocks led to the establishment of multilateral arrangements governing the North Atlantic and North Sea
area even before the Rome Treaty was signed.[5] The 1946 Overfishing Convention
was replaced shortly after coming into force in 1954 by the conclusion of the
North East Atlantic Fisheries Convention (NEAFC). This has a permanent Commission, empowered to regulate the sizes of net meshes used, and of fish caught,
by signatory states. The Convention also contemplated the control of fishing gear,
the establishment of closed seasons and areas, and, most importantly, so as to maintain yields from fish stocks, the fixing of catch quotas—total allowable catches
(TACs) determined on the basis of findings of scientists working under the auspices
of the International Council for the Exploration of the Seas (ICES)—a non-
governmental body. Membership of NEAFC was however voluntary, for fishing
took place on the high seas outside coastal jurisdiction, and consequently NEAFC
possessed inadequate powers of compulsion on its members. Conservation measures
could be defeated by the objection of one member, with the result that for political
reasons TACs were consistently set at levels higher than scientists thought advisable.
Once TACs were set, each member state was responsible for policing its own
fishing vessels (thus, flag state jurisdiction obtained). Even the Joint Enforcement
Scheme set up in 1972 only provided for mutual *inspection*, prosecution of detected
breaches of NEAFC regulations being again left to the discretion of the flag state.

   As a result of the handicaps under which it operated, the NEAFC was unable
to prevent consistent overfishing of certain species—particularly the North Sea
herring, which by the 1970s had reached critical levels. Some white fish species too,
such as sole, were seriously depleted. Against this background the introduction of

the EC, with its power to pass acts legally binding on its members, into the sphere of fisheries management and conservation should have been an important initiative. Unfortunately the EC has itself faced many of the same problems.

The original Common Fisheries Policy

The EC Commission first presented proposals to the Council for a CFP on 6 June 1966. Two draft regulations were presented in 1968, but it was not until 30 June 1970—the day that negotiations with the new member states began—that the first fisheries regulations 2141/70 and 2142/70 were accepted by the Council. The two facets of the CFP are reflected by the two regulations: 2141/70[6] provided a common structural policy for the fishing industry regulating access to, and management of, fishery resources, while 2142/70[7] set up a common organization of the market in fishery products. Article 38(1) of the Rome Treaty includes within the Common Agricultural Policy (CAP) 'agriculture and trade in agricultural products', and defines the latter to include 'fisheries and the products of first stage processing (of such) products'. The marketing policy of regulation 2142/70 extends CAP principles to these products.[8] It provides for a system of guide and intervention prices, common rules on competition, an external tariff and a management committee, and funds for the partial reimbursement of state aids to producers' organizations to help them adapt to the new system. These arrangements remained in force until they were reviewed in 1981. CFP disputes, however, have centred around the structural regulation 2141/70, which raises problems in relation both to its legal basis and territorial scope and, more seriously, to the adaptation of its regime to the requirements of the new EC members.

There is in fact no clear legal basis in the Rome Treaty for a *structural* fisheries policy. The preamble to regulation 2141/70 states that 'the establishment of a common organization of the market in products of the fishing industry must be complemented by the establishment of a common structural policy for the fishing industry.' It does not say why. If the structural policy is based upon Article 38(4) of the Rome Treaty, then the aims of the policy should fall within the objectives of the CAP set out in Article 39. The linchpin of the structural regulation is the principle of 'equal access' for all EC fishermen to the maritime waters of member states (Article 2(1)). But Churchill[9] points out that this principle does not fall within Article 39, arguing poignantly that there is no equal access to agricultural products of other member states. Others[10] argue that the liberalization of the trade in fish should be accompanied by a liberalization of access to fishing grounds. Olmi[11] even goes so far as to argue that without the principle of freedom of access there can be no genuine common market in fish. Critics[12] maintain that a more satisfactory basis for a structural policy would be freedom of establishment for fishermen of all member states at the ports of other member states. Such establishment would have to be on some form of permanent basis, presumably sailing under the flag of the coastal state.

In fact the reason for the use of the CAP as the basis for the structural policy may simply be pragmatic: the CAP provisions permit actions to be taken by directly applicable regulation, whereas freedom of establishment can only be achieved by directive.[13] Nevertheless these difficulties appear to be recognized by the fact that regulation 2141/70 is not only based on Articles 42 and 43 (agriculture), but also on Article 7 (non-discrimination) and, as if to recognize the inadequacy of these, on Article 235 (which allows action to be taken to achieve the EC's aims when the Treaty does not provide the necessary powers). It might also be noted that

Article 235 provides for action only by unanimous vote, whereas the CAP provisions, were it not for the 'Luxembourg compromise', permit action by majority vote.[14]

The scope of the principle of 'equal access' is also unclear, for Article 2(1) of the regulation applies it to 'fishing in the maritime waters coming under its sovereignty or within its jurisdiction'. 'Maritime waters' has no precise legal meaning.[15] In so far as the Rome Treaty applies to the territory of the member states (Article 227), it must also apply to those maritime zones which are under their direct sovereignty, such as territorial waters. But controversy has long existed over how far sovereignty and jurisdiction may extend beyond the coastal baseline. Neither the First United Nations Conference on the Law of the Sea (UNCLOS I) in 1958, nor the Second (UNCLOS II) in 1960 could agree a uniform width for territorial waters. In 1964 the majority of North European States signed the London Fishing Convention which settled a six-mile exclusive fishing zone for coastal states (in which fishing was restricted to the coastal states), followed by an outer six-mile zone where fishing was open to fishermen of the coastal state and of those states 'which had habitually fished there between January 1953 and December 1962'. These zones were not territorial waters (in which full coastal sovereignty and jurisdiction is exercisable) and hence not prima facie state territory for the purpose of Article 227. However, in so far as the coastal state does exercise a degree of jurisdiction, they appear to come within the terms of Article 2(1) and are thus subject to the principle of equal access. Of course these uncertainties were exacerbated once fishing zones were extended in the 1970s to 200 miles. Regulation 2141/70 did, however, permit a five-year derogation from its principles in certain three-mile zones where local fishermen were heavily dependent upon fishing for their livelihood (Article 4).

The Act of Accession

Serious problems with the 1970 structural policy only became apparent, however, with the first accession in 1973. All the four original applicants had important fishing interests. Norway and the UK both had major distant water fleets as well as large offshore fisheries, while Denmark had a major industrial, though localized, fleet. Irish fishing was virtually entirely offshore. By contrast, the original six were net importers of fish, and of those with North Sea and North Atlantic seaboards (all except Italy and Luxembourg) only the FRG and France had fishing industries comparable in size to the applicants. The West German fishing industry was virtually exclusively a distant water fleet. The French, with a longer coastline, had a distant water fleet, but the majority of its fishing effort was like that of Belgium and the Netherlands, localized mainly in waters off the shores of the applicant states. These latter interests in the waters of the applicants do provide an explanation for the conclusion of the CFP so soon before accession, although it seems unlikely that the longer implications of equal access (with the extensions of fishing limits) were foreseen in 1970. Certainly the CFP was probably the major reason that Norwegian public opinion rejected the EC in the pre-accession referendum.

The 1972 Act of Accession did, however, make a number of concessions to the new members. Article 100 permitted member states to restrict, until 1982, fishing in a six-mile zone measured from its coastal baseline to vessels which fish traditionally in those waters and which operate from ports in that geographical coastal area.[16] In certain areas, specified in Article 101, member states were permitted to extend these zones to twelve miles—which for the UK included areas from which 95 per cent of its inshore catch was taken.

Article 102 also obliged the Council, by 1978, to 'determine conditions for fishing with a view to ensuring protection of the fishing grounds and conservation of the biological resources of the sea.' This phrase appears to justify virtually 'any regulatory measure relating to fishing',[17] and indeed its wide scope was confirmed by the ECJ's ruling in the case of *Kramer et al.* (1976)[18] that, pending such action by the Council, member states retained the right to regulate national fisheries both in their own territorial waters and on the high seas. This confirmation of the EC's competence to act outside territorial waters (and arguably the ambit of Article 227) is in line with the ECJ's established view that where the EC acquires the power to regulate an internal policy area, it acquires *ipso facto* external competence. In fact, Birnie[19] argues that it was the *Kramer* decision that encouraged the EC to apply to join the NEAFC as a Community, so that the consequent withdrawal of EC states' individual membership, together with the refusal of Eastern bloc states to recognize the separate personality of the EC, led to the virtual collapse of the NEAFC.

Given the ten-year derogation from the equal access principle envisaged by Articles 100 and 101, the Act of Accession also requires the Commission, by the end of 1982, to present a report to the Council on the 'economic and social development of the coastal areas of the member states and the state of stocks'. In the light of this report and the CFP's objectives, the Council must examine the provisions which could follow the derogations in force until 31 December 1982.

No sooner were the accession negotiations completed than the whole character of the CFP debates was altered by developments in the international regime of the seas. This was because the EC's 1973 enlargement coincided with the first session of the Third United Nations Conference on the Law of the Sea (UNCLOS III).[20] It soon became clear that there was at least considerable agreement among the states at UNCLOS on the future regime for fisheries. The early negotiating texts[21] envisaged exclusive economic zones of 200 miles from the coastal baselines in which coastal states would have sovereignty over fishery and other resources. Even the UK, which had hotly disputed Iceland's unilateral extension of fishing limits (first to 50 and then 200 miles), soon recognized that it could not afford to exclude itself from such a development.

However, a regime based on 200-mile coastal zones would have had a drastic effect upon the fishing industries of those states in the EC, particularly the UK and the FRG, which caught a large proportion of their fish from waters soon to be within the 200-mile zones of third states. The EC member states themselves could claim 200-mile limits, but depleted North Sea stocks would be unable to sustain the level of catches which the highly sophisticated distant water fleets needed for economic viability. The British fishing industry was particularly aggrieved that, having suffered this setback, the stocks within the UK 200-mile zone (which together with the Irish zone represented the majority of EC stocks) would, under the principle of equal access, be open to all EC fishermen. These stocks would also have to support quotas for any reciprocal fishing arrangements which could be negotiated with non-EC states.

However, in default of formal agreement the member states concluded a binding gentlemen's agreement: The Hague Resolution. This provided that in any future agreement the rights of certain areas (notably the North and South-West of England, Scotland and Ireland) would be recognized, that member states would restrict their 1977 catches to 1976 levels and that (in Annexe VI) member states could, pending the promulgation of Community measures, adopt 'as an interim measure and in a form which avoids discrimination, appropriate measures to ensure protection of the resources situated in the fishing zones off their coasts.' Such measures, however, should not prejudice the success of future EC measures and should, prior to adoption, be submitted for approval to the Commission, which should be consulted at all stages.

The Commission quickly recognized the new role that it could play in managing such an increased 'pond' of resources, and in February 1976 put forward proposals to revise the CFP. After discussion these were amended for The Hague Council in October. By this time, however, Britain was pressing (under threat of unilateral action) for a simultaneous extension of EC states' fishing limits to 200 miles, and with strong Irish support was also insisting upon exclusive national zones of fifty miles. The simultaneous extensions to 200 miles of fishing limits on the North Sea and North Atlantic seaboards were agreed at The Hague meeting, as was the proposal that the EC assume responsibility for the negotiation of reciprocal fishing agreements with third states. However, the ambitious programme of conservation and management for these zones put forward by the Commission was rejected. The October proposals included the following: a twelve-mile fishing zone under national control (to continue beyond 1982) but with member states obliged to recognize the historic rights of fishermen from other EC states; the establishment of a yearly total allowable catch (TAC) for each species to be allocated among member states on the basis of their catch over a reference period (at that point unspecified); the establishment of a Scientific and Technical Committee for Fisheries and a Management Committee for Fishery Resources; a licensing system for commercial fishing, linked to sanctions for breach of regulations; financial assistance for economic dislocation caused by the rundown of certain fisheries and to encourage investment in new species, areas and techniques. However, the obligation to recognize historic rights, added to the February proposals at the insistence of France and Holland, was unacceptable to the UK and Ireland.[22]

Agreements with third states

Since The Hague, the Commission, as the negotiator of EC agreements, has been relatively successful in establishing itself as a fisheries negotiator with third states. Framework agreements[23] have been entered into with states that were able to offer reciprocal access—Sweden, the Faroes and Norway—as well as with states with surplus capacity—the USA, Canada[24] (which demanded tariff concessions in return)—and with the Third World states of Senegal and Guinea–Bissau (for whom financial compensation was agreed). Those states which fished in EC waters, but were unable to offer any reciprocity, were either expelled, as with Bulgaria, Romania and the USSR, or offered reduced access—as is the case of Spain and Portugal in the light of the accession negotiations. The difficulty remains, however, that until the EC states have agreed to a system of allocation of resources between themselves, the surplus capacity of EC waters can neither be accurately determined, nor quotas for third states fixed.

Towards revision of the CFP

Since The Hague, and notwithstanding the passing of the 1978 deadline, the CFP negotiations have continued. British demands for exclusive zones of up to fifty miles were moderated into more 'communautaire' terminology of 'dominant preference' in specified areas. The Commission had made a number of attempts to move towards the British position, but attitudes in the British fishing industry have hardened. Because of the concentration of the distant water fleets in certain ports—notably Hull, Grimsby and Fleetwood—the rundown which has followed the closing of traditional fishing grounds has had disproportionate effects upon those regions and therefore directly on UK political life. Having witnessed a radical reduction of distant water fishing, and given that the UK 200-mile zone constitutes nearly 60 per cent of EC waters and fish stocks, the protection of national interests has become a highly charged issue. The British Government has thus felt unable to compromise its claim for a proportionate allocation of the total EC catch. Hence a Commission proposal that all EC fishing be regulated by fishing plans (under which the EC could regulate fishing in areas where the UK was claiming 'dominant preference') was opposed by the British fishing industry because of uncertainty about the plans after 1982.

Disagreement about the allocation of quotas has also held up the conclusion of a comprehensive conservation and management scheme. Certain short-term conservation measures have been taken by the EC,[25] and also by member states under the terms of Annexe VI of The Hague resolution. But the exact scope of such 'interim measures' has caused some legal problems: the ECJ has had to rule on the extent of national powers to enact conservation measures in the continued absence of EC action. In two cases[26] involving an Irish measure of February 1977 (banning vessels over 33 metres and 1,000 hp—of which there were only two in the Irish fleet), the ECJ held that national measures must not discriminate either directly (that is, in form) or indirectly (that is, in content). The UK too has been held to have acted illegally[27] by instituting a number of measures without prior consultation and collaboration with the Commission as required by Annexe VI of The (non-binding) Hague Resolution.

In addition to these measures, in 1979 a Scientific and Technical Committee for Fisheries was set up with a mandate to prepare an annual report on fish stocks and their conservation, and in 1980 the Council was able to agree TACs for species and zones, as well as a system of catch regulation (by the keeping of catch registers) and vessel inspection. As yet, however, there is no move towards coastal, as opposed to flag, state policing of catches, so there is a great deal of mutual suspicion about national enforcement even within harmonized standards of inspection. Even this, however, is a considerable improvement on the NEAFC regime. But the lack of basic agreement between the UK and the rest of the EC, with the consequent bitterness and suspicion, has continued to threaten both fish stocks and the EC's general well-being. The Commission has to an extent recognized the justice of the British arguments by increasing its proposed allocations. For example, its 1980 proposals for the UK catch were increased from 288,602 tonnes in July to 309,034 tonnes in October. But there is also justice in other national arguments—the FRG distant water fleet too has been hard hit[28]—and the resources on offer are finite.

As the end of 1982 and the ten-year derogation period approaches, despite national posturing, some accommodation appears to be inevitable. However, it is clear that there will have to be a substantial, perhaps permanent, compromise of the principle of 'equal access' contained in the structural regulation. It is clear also from the 1.25 million tonnes of fish which the Commission has on offer for 1982[29] that, despite its insistence that its quotas are based upon scientific advice, it is encountering the same difficulties as the NEAFC, which was consistently forced for political reasons to set quotas higher than scientists recommended. Already the Commission has been accused of allocating 'paper' fish which can never be caught. The CFP still has great potential as an international—or supranational —fisheries conservation and management regime. Whether the economic recession (making redeployment of fishermen more difficult, but increasing pressure for restructuring monies) and the prospect of the accession of two major fishing nations (Spain and Portugal) make long-term agreement more or less likely must still be an open question.

Notes

1. The best detailed study of the negotiations problems of negotiating the CFP is still Driscoll, D. J. and McKellar, N., 'The Changing Regime of North Sea Fisheries' in Mason, C. M. (ed.), *The Effective Management of Resources* (London, Frances Pinter, 1979), pp. 125–39. See also (with a legal bias) Birnie, P., 'The History of the Common Fisheries Policy of the European Community' in Fifth Report of the Expenditure Committee, *The Fishing Industry*, vol. 1, H.C. (1977–8) 356, pp. 92–118; Churchill, R., 'Revision of the EEC's Common Fisheries Policy', *European Law Review*, 5 (1980), 3–37 and 95–111; Yandais, D., 'La Communauté et la Pêche', *Cahiers de Droit Européen* (1978), 158–201 and (1979), 185–244. On policy-making aspects see Allen, R., 'Fishing for a Common Policy', *Journal of Common Market Studies*, 19 (1980), 123–39 and Shackleton, M., 'The Common Fisheries Policy' in Wallace, H., Wallace, W. and Webb, C. (eds), *Policy Making in the European Communities* (Chichester, Wiley, 1977).
2. See also, e.g., Volle, A. and Wallace, W., 'How Common a Fisheries Policy?' *The World Today*, 33 (1977), 62–72.
3. Case 141/78 *French Republic* v *United Kingdom* [1979] E.C.R. 2923; [1980] 1 Common Market Law Reports (C.M.L.R.) 6. For comment see Churchill, R., 'Scope of national fishery measures', *European Law Review*, 5 (1980), 71–3.
4. For a brief review of the EC national fishing industries see Fishery Economic Research Unit, *Fisheries of the European Community* (Edinburgh, White Fish Authority, 1977).
5. See, e.g., Koers, A. W., 'Freedom of Fishing in Decline: The case of the North East Atlantic' in Churchill, R. *et al.* (eds), *New Directions in the Law of the Sea* (London and New York, British Institute of International and Comparative Law and Oceana, Vol. III, 1973), pp. 19–35; and by the same author *The International Regulation of Marine Fisheries* (London, Fishing Books, 1973). See also Driver, P., 'International Fisheries' in Barston, R. P. and Birnie, P. (eds), *The Maritime Dimension* (London, Allen & Unwin, 1980), pp. 27–53.
6. Council Regulation (EEC) No. 2141/70 of 20 October 1970, laying down a common structural policy for the fishing industry, *OJ*, No. L236 (27 October 1970), p. 1. Amended by Council Regulation (EEC) No. 101/76 of 19 January 1976, *OJ*, No. L20 (28 January 1976), p. 19.
7. Council Regulation (EEC) No. 2142/70 of 20 October 1970, on the common organization of the market in fishery products, *OJ*, No. L236 (27 October 1970), p. 5. Amended by Council Regulation (EEC) No. 100/76 of 19 January 1976, *OJ*, No. L20 (28 January 1976), p. 1, and now by Council Regulation (EEC) No. 3796/81 of 29 December 1981, *OJ*, L379 (31 December 1981), p. 1.
8. For an extended discussion see Garron, R., *Le Marché Commun De La Pêche Maritime* (Paris, Librarie Techniques, 1971), No. VIII, Collection de droit maritime et des transports, Part III. And for a detailed criticism from the perspective of the British fishing industry see Laing, A., 'The Common Fisheries Policy of the Six', *Fish Industry Review*, 1 (1971), 8–18.
9. Churchill, R., 'The EEC Fisheries Policy—towards a revision', *Marine Policy*, 1 (1977), 26–36, p. 36.
10. Garron, op. cit., p. 73.
11. Olmi, G., 'Agriculture and Fisheries in the Accession Treaty', *Common Market Law Review*, 9 (1972), 293–321, p. 313.
12. Churchill, op. cit.
13. See Article 54, EEC Treaty. Winkel, K., 'Equal Access of Community Fishermen to Member States Fishing Grounds', *Common Market Law Review*, 14 (1977), 329–37, argues that equal access could be within the scope of Articles 59–66 governing the provision of services.
14. In May 1982 on the issue of the increase of CAP farm prices, the Luxembourg Compromise

was departed from and the United Kingdom out-voted in the Council of Ministers and although France maintained afterwards that the compromise (and thus the veto) still stood, its future must be uncertain.

15. For a detailed analysis of the regulation and its international law background see Brown, E. D., 'British Fisheries and the Common Market', *Current Legal Problems* 25 (1972), 37–73, and Mensbrugghe, V. van der, 'The Common Fisheries Policy and the Law of the Sea', *Netherland Yearbook of International Law*, 6 (1975), 199–225.

16. For analysis of the difficulties to which this imprecise phrase gives rise see Brown, op. cit. and Mensbrugghe, op. cit.

17. Churchill, R., 'Revision of the EEC's Common Fisheries Policy—Part I', *European Law Review*, 5 (1980), 3–37, p. 14.

18. *Public Prosecutor of Arrondissementsrechtbank, Zwolle v Kramer et al.*, joined cases 3, 4 and 6/76, [1976] E.C.R. 1279; [1976] 2 C.M.L.R. 440.

19. Birnie, P., 'Contemporary Maritime Legal Problems' in Barston and Birnie, op. cit., pp. 169–89, at p. 176.

20. See, e.g., Barston, R. P., 'The Law of the Sea Conference: The Search for New Regimes' in Barston and Birnie, ibid., pp. 154–68.

21. *United Nations Third Conference on the Law of the Sea, Informal Single Negotiating Text* (ISNT), A/CONF/62/A/CONF/62/WP8/Pt 11, 7 May 1975 reprinted in *International Legal Materials*, 14 (1975), 682–761. Revised Single Negotiating Text, A/CONF/62/WP8/ Rev 1/Pt 11, 6 May 1976, text in Churchill *et al.*, op. cit., Vol. VI, pp. 582–673.

22. See Driscoll and McKellar, op. cit., pp. 144 ff.

23. On the various negotiations see Churchill, R., 'Revision of the EEC's Common Fisheries Policy—Part II', *European Law Review*, 5 (1980), 95–111. For a list of fishery agreements in force as of January 1981 see Parry and Hardy, *EEC Law* (London, Sweet & Maxwell, 2nd ed. by Parry, A. and Dinnage, J., 1981), Appendix III.

24. For a detailed examination of the Canadian agreement see Swords, C., 'External Competence of the EEC in relation to International Fisheries Agreements', *Legal Issues of European Integration* (1979/2), pp. 31–64.

25. For a detailed survey of such measures see Churchill, op. cit., pp. 27 ff.

26. Case 61/77, *Commission v Ireland* [1978] E.C.R. 417; [1978] 2 C.M.L.R. 466 and case 88/77, *Minister of Fisheries* v *Schonenberg* [1978] E.C.R. 473; [1978] 2 C.M.L.R. 519.

27. For example, case 141/78, above; case 32/79 *Commission* v *United Kingdom* [1980] E.C.R. 2403; [1981] 1 C.M.L.R. 219; and case 804/79, *Commission* v *United Kingdom* (not yet reported).

28. For further discussion see Shackleton, op. cit.

29. See *Europe 82*.

8 Regional Policy

STEPHEN GEORGE

The problem

In the EC common policies have to be justified by reference to problems, which they are designed to solve. An EC regional policy is needed because of the existence of a regional problem in the EC. The problem is that there are considerable disparities in income and employment levels between different regions in the EC, and these disparities hinder the achievement of the objectives of the EC, form an obstacle to its further advance, and even threaten its continued cohesion.

The existence of the disparities is not disputed by anyone. It has been statistically established in several EC documents, and in particular in two Commission reports on the regions of Europe.[1] Measured in terms of Gross Domestic Product (GDP) per head, the gap in income between the richest and poorest regions of the EC in 1970 was in the ratio of 2.9:1. This represented a considerable narrowing of the gap from the mid-1960s, when it had stood at nearer to 4:1, but this narrowing was based on a high level of labour migration from the poor to the rich regions, and when the recession of the 1970s led to a decline in migration, and even some reverse migration as job opportunities in the richer regions became scarcer, so the disparity in GDP per head widened once more, reaching the 4:1 ratio again by 1977, and widening to 5:1 with the accession of Greece to the EC.

In 1970 Hamburg, the richest region in the EC, had a GDP per head which was 197.5 per cent of the EC average: the poorest region, Calabria in Italy, had only 39.4 per cent of the EC average. By 1977 the figure for Hamburg, still the richest region, was 224.6 per cent: that for Calabria, still the poorest, was 34.6 per cent.

Regions with less than the average GDP per head in 1977 included the whole of Ireland, almost all regions in Italy and the UK, West and South West France and the Massif Central, some regions in Belgium, the Netherlands and the FRG, and the whole of Greenland. Several regions had less than 75 per cent of the EC average, including all regions in the UK other than the South East, the whole of Ireland, Greenland and the Italian southern regions which are known collectively as the Mezzorgiorno.

The poor regions tend to fall into one of two categories: they are either areas with a traditional dependence on small-scale agriculture which have never developed the infrastructure for industrial development, or they are regions which have been heavily dependent on traditional industries, such as steel, textiles, or shipbuilding, that have been in decline in post-war Europe. Their difficulty is in attracting investment in modern, productive industrial activities. For the first group, their lack of infrastructure (roads, communications networks, social facilities) is a serious handicap. For the second group there is an infrastructure, but it is often in poor condition to meet the requirements of new industries. Also, the work-force will tend to possess inappropriate skills. There is, in addition, a distinct likelihood that the poorer region will be situated on the geographical periphery of the EC, at a distance from the centre of the market, which acts as a further disadvantage.

Policies to correct these deficiencies in their poorer regions have been adopted by all the member states of the EC individually at various times since the last war. There has been a general recognition that the existence of major disparities in the distribution of economic activity within a state produces an inefficient use of resources. Not only are there factors of production lying idle in the poorer regions, but the concentration of economic activity in a central core area puts strain upon the infrastructure of that area and damages the environment. These national considerations apply equally at the EC level. In addition, there are particular reasons why regional disparities present a problem to the EC.

First, the Rome Treaty states that the objective of the EEC is 'a continuous and balanced expansion'[2] in economic activity. It can be argued that the persistence of regional imbalances works against both of these objectives. It obviously means that there is not a balanced expansion. But in so far as resources are being used inefficiently, and in so far as the poverty of the weak regions limits the potential market for the products of the strong regions, it also works against continuous expansion.

Secondly, the existence of such wide disparities may weaken the commitment to the EC felt by the inhabitants of the weak regions. This point was well put in the Thomson Report:

> No community could maintain itself nor have a meaning for the peoples which belong to it so long as some have very different standards of living and have cause to doubt the common will of all to help each Member to better the conditions of its people.[3]

Thirdly, the commitment of the member states of the EC to the achievement of EMU makes the regional question much more urgent. Such a union would involve member states surrendering control over the rate of exchange of their national currencies. Manipulation of exchange rates is one of the few means still left open to member states to protect their economies against the full effects of the existence of a common market. If they are to be asked to surrender this last instrument for alleviating economic hardship, they must first be sure that the EC is serious about helping those parts of their national territory which might find themselves in particular difficulties. Similar considerations apply, with only slightly less force, to the formulation of common policies in other fields, such as transport and energy.

Finally, on a more specific note, at the time when the Commission made its first proposals for an EC regional policy in the late 1960s, it was particularly concerned that regional disparities were being used as an excuse by the member states for offering investment incentives to industry, and that competition was developing to see which state could offer the most favourable terms to attract multinational capital. This was seriously jeopardizing EC objectives on fair competition.

Approaches to a policy

It was on this issue of member states using regional aid schemes in a way which distorted competition that the first effective agreement was reached in the construction of a common regional policy in 1971. In an effort to tackle this problem the six original member states agreed to set a ceiling of 20 per cent on the amount of government assistance for investment projects in the more prosperous regions of the EC. Following enlargement of the EC, the system of ceilings was extended in

1975. The regions were divided into four groups. In the first group were the richer regions, for which the 20 per cent ceiling continued to apply. In recognition of their special problems in attracting investment, West Berlin and the eastern frontier regions of the FRG were allowed an increase in their investment ceiling to 25 per cent: this formed the second group. The third group comprised those regions of the UK mainland which were classified by the British Government as Assisted Areas, their French equivalents, and some Italian regions. This group had a 30 per cent ceiling. Finally, the poorest regions formed a group for which there was no ceiling, although the Commission was permitted to scrutinize projects for which government aid exceeded 35 per cent, to ensure that EC principles were not being breached. In this group were placed the Italian Mezzorgiorno, Ireland, Northern Ireland, and Greenland.[4]

Although an important step, this agreement was purely concerned with the negative aspect of regional policy. It was not possible even to lay the foundation of a positive policy until 1975, although the Commission had recognized the need for such a policy from an early stage. Regional problems were mentioned in both the First and Second *General Reports of the Commission*. In 1961 a Conference on Regional Economies was convened by the Commission, and it set up three working groups, which reported in mid-1964.[5] Although the reports left several important technical questions unanswered, such as the definition of problem regions, the exercise succeeded in creating an atmosphere in which regional policy was placed on the agenda of EC concerns. Perhaps a sign of this success was the decision of the Council in 1964 to include regional policy in the remit of the Medium Term Economic Policy Committee which was set up in that year. The momentum was maintained in 1965 when the Commission produced its first memorandum on regional policy, based on the reports of the groups of experts.[6]

But the next major step towards a positive regional policy came with the merger of the executives of the three Communities in 1967, after which regional policy had a Directorate-General (DG XVI) of its own within the enlarged Commission. Following the creation of DG XVI, the Commission made its first set of proposals for the creation of a regional policy in 1969. It proposed to the Council that provision be made for the coordination of national regional policies and of EC policies with a regional impact, and that a European Regional Development Fund (ERDF) be set up. The initiative was not well received by the member states, with the exception of Italy, which stood to gain most from the ERDF. Progress had to await the first enlargement of the EC, which brought in two new members with serious regional problems—the UK and Ireland.

Both these states made the creation of a regional fund a priority issue. The British Government in particular saw such a fund as a means of allaying growing anti-EC sentiment in the UK. It would provide receipts that would offset some of the large contribution which the UK would have to make to the 'own resources' section of the EC budget, and it would provide immediate and tangible benefits to the regions, which could be turned into political capital.

The pressure exerted by the UK and Ireland coincided with an awareness by the original six member states that regional disparities might be a barrier to the achievement of economic and monetary union (EMU) by 1980, which was a commitment made at the 1969 Hague summit and which was a high priority for the Government of the FRG. Together these two factors produced a decision at the October 1972 Paris summit to set up an ERDF by the end of 1973. But there was no agreement on the size of the Fund.

On the one hand, Ireland, Italy and the UK wanted a large fund. On the other hand, the German Government was thinking in much more modest terms. Concern was growing in the FRG at the size of its contribution to the EC budget, and there was a strong desire on the part of the Government to avoid any further open ended commitments, such as that to the Common Agricultural Policy (CAP). As the richest member state, the FRG was becoming the paymaster of the EC, and stood to become the largest net contributor to any regional fund. Its agreement to the principle of the ERDF at the Paris summit was probably based on two considerations: a desire to smooth the accession of the three new member states, enlargement being in the interest of German exporters, and the need to avoid obstacles in the way of progress to EMU. Yet events outside the EC were soon to harden the German attitude.

The Arab–Israeli war of October 1973 led to the disruption of Middle East oil supplies to Europe. It was followed by the decision of OPEC to increase substantially the price of oil. The cumulative effect of these two events was to divert attention in the EC away from regional matters towards energy, and to cause a distinct cooling of relations between the UK and the FRG. The Germans wanted emergency action to formulate an EC energy programme. The British, much more favourably endowed than their partners with indigenous energy resources, were resistant. Following established EC principles of linking issues together in order to arrive at package deals, the Germans attempted to negotiate the energy question *in tandem* with the regional fund. But the British would not accept this linkage, and continued to be difficult on energy. The German response was to become much more difficult on the regional fund, a line which the FRG found easier to follow, since the recession caused by the oil price rises had made the objective of economic and monetary union by 1980 unrealistic anyway.

It proved impossible to reach agreement on an ERDF by the end of 1973. Then in March 1974 a general election in the UK led to the return of a Labour Government committed to total renegotiation of the terms of British entry to the EC. This meant the removal of British pressure for progress on the regional fund, which was much less central to the concerns of the new British Government.

Faced with this weakening of the front which had championed the regional fund, the Italian and Irish Governments, for whom it was still a central concern, resorted to desperate measures. They threatened to boycott the summit in Paris in December 1974 unless they were promised progress on the creation of the ERDF. Paradoxically, the removal of the British from the pro-fund coalition may have made it easier for the FRG to agree to this demand, and the summit reached decisions on both the size and the distribution of the ERDF. Without British backing, the alliance of the Commission, Italy and Ireland was not able to overcome German parsimony, with the result that the ERDF was created smaller as well as later than had been hoped. But at last there was a regional fund in existence, and the biggest step yet had been made towards an EC regional policy.[7]

Policy instruments

It is important not to confuse the EC's regional policy with the ERDF. Although the ERDF is central to the policy, there are other policy instruments with regional significance. Funds for retraining of workers and restructuring of regional economies are available under European Coal and Steel Community (ECSC) auspices; the European Investment Bank (EIB) makes loans for regional development purposes; and the European Social Fund (ESF) also has a regional impact. EC policies in other areas, particularly agriculture, have regional implications. And to the financial instruments we must add the Regional Policy Committee.

The most relevant section of the Treaty of Paris, which created the ECSC, is Article 56, which allows ECSC funds to be used for purposes of readaptation and reconversion in regions where the existence of the common market in coal and steel has had an adverse effect on the structure of the local economy. The funds have been used to finance studies on the re-employment of redundant workers, to assist schemes for the creation of new employment and for investment in infrastructure improvement. But the retraining and re-employment measures apply only to redundant coal and steel workers, the investment only to regions where problems have been caused by a dependence on these two declining industries. In fact, it would be incorrect to suggest that there was a positive ECSC regional policy prior to the creation of the EEC: the old ECSC High Authority sought only to offset the adverse effects of the common market.

In the Rome Treaty, the only institution catering explicitly for regional problems is the EIB. At the time when the Treaty was drawn up, only Italy of the six original member states had a national regional policy, and that only for the Mezzorgiorno. It was largely to satisfy Italy that the EIB was included in the Treaty: the prevailing assumption at the time was that regional problems would be solved by the general economic growth which the EEC would facilitate.

The EIB is charged by the Treaty to contribute to the balanced and steady development of the common market. To this end it is empowered to make loans and guarantees to projects for developing less developed regions, and to projects for the modernization or conversion of undertakings where this is called for by the impact on them of the common market. But it may not initiate projects, nor advance more than 50 per cent of the total cost of a project. Neither can it finance ventures unless they are of such a size and nature that they cannot be entirely financed by the various means available in the individual member states. Its loans are to be offered at commercial rates of interest, not subsidized, although by borrowing internationally, always in the cheapest capital market within the EC, it does often undercut prevailing interest rates in any individual state. There is a minimum size to the projects which are eligible for EIB assistance, which puts it beyond the reach of most small and medium-sized private concerns. There are also tight controls on the type of project which may be funded, with the emphasis on directly productive investment rather than infrastructure projects. Overall this means that the EIB is rather a weak instrument of regional policy, in addition to which it operates independently of the Commission, so that its interventions are not necessarily coordinated with the overall EC approach to regional problems.

The ESF provides money for the retraining and relocation of workers in all industries, rather than just in specific industries as is the case with ECSC funds. Although there is no requirement that ESF expenditure be directed to problem regions, it is in such regions that the largest proportion of redundancies occurs, and so the bulk of ESF money is devoted to projects which have a regional policy dimension. The Commission is concerned that ESF expenditure should be coordinated with its general regional policy, and this is true for other common policies too.

The other major policy with a regional impact is the CAP. The guidance section of the European Agricultural Guidance and Guarantee Fund (EAGGF) is in theory another of the regional policy instruments available to the Commission. But despite ambitious proposals made in 1968 (the Mansholt Plan), there has never been any vigorous attempt to use the guidance fund to reduce disparities in farm efficiency and in farming incomes. The blame for this must rest not with the Commission, but with the Council of Ministers, and the main considerations against such a policy are largely political. The result is that the guidance section of the EAGGF tends to have an adverse regional effect, widening rather than reducing disparities. This is because the Fund receives far more proposals for modernization and rationalization projects from the rich farming areas, which tend to be situated in the more prosperous regions of Europe, than from the poor areas, which largely coincide with the poor regions.

The guarantee section of the EAGGF also has a perverse regional effect. Although it has been instrumental in increasing agricultural incomes in poor regions, it increases the incomes of efficient farmers much more. This is because prices are set at the level necessary to maintain the least efficient farmer in business (for political reasons again) and this allows efficient farmers, with lower production costs, to make very large profits. The support price system is also more developed and more generous for the products typical of the richer regions (cereals, sugar, milk) than for those of the poor, and particularly the products of Mediterranean regions (fruit, vegetables, wine). The overall effect of the EAGGF therefore works against the objectives of the regional policy.

It will be seen below that the coordination of EC policies with regional implications is one of the primary aims of the Commission in the field of regional policy.[8] Another is the coordination of national regional policies, and it is here that the Regional Policy Committee, which was set up in 1975, has a role to play. This Committee must not be confused with the Regional Fund Committee, which assists the Commission in the allocation of ERDF money to the various development projects, although like the Fund Committee the Policy Committee consists of representatives of the member states and of the Commission. Its objective is to contribute to the coordination of national regional policies, both with one another and with the EC regional policy. It pursues this aim by undertaking studies on the regional question, drafting model regional development plans, and generally contributing to the availability of information and advice necessary to effective coordination. It also comments on the initial draft of the report on the regions which is presented to the Council of Ministers every second year. Thus it is an institution which facilitates policy coordination, but which has no planning powers to push coordination forward where the will is lacking. It is another useful, but ultimately weak instrument of regional policy.

At the centre of the regional policy stands the ERDF. As indicated above, this is administered by the Commission in conjunction with the Regional Fund Committee. The Fund Committee follows the management committee pattern which was originally established for the regulation of markets for agricultural products.[9] It consists of officials from the member states plus the Commission, and unlike the Social Fund Committee, there is no input from interest groups. The whole management committee procedure may be viewed as a device, inspired by the French, to avoid having to delegate decision-making power to the Commission alone. Yet it is a system which works very smoothly most of the time, and may even have extended the influence of the Commission, because had the management committee procedure not existed the Council of Ministers might have hesitated to allow the Commission any role in administering common policies.

What is disappointing is the size of the fund which the Committee helps to administer. The political considerations determining the size of the ERDF have been touched on above. Commissioner Thomson's original proposal was for a fund of 3 billion units of account (u.a.) (approximately £1,260 million), which was reduced to 2.4 billion u.a. before the proposal even left the Commission. Already this was a 'political' figure, designed to get Council approval, rather than a realistic figure for the task in view. Eventually agreement was reached by the Council on a fund of only 1,300 million u.a. (approximately £540 million) for the three years 1975 to 1977 inclusive. When the Fund came up for renewal it was calculated in the new European Unit of Account (EUA). The sum was set at 1,850 million EUA for 1978–80 inclusive, which was roughly equivalent to £1,234 million. The size of the Fund was thus doubled, but still only reached approximately the size originally proposed by Commissioner Thomson some five years earlier.

Since the ERDF is now classified as non-compulsory budget expenditure, it is likely that the EP will increase its size each year by the maximum amount permissible. This maximum is calculated according to a complex formula and applies to the whole category of non-compulsory expenditure rather than to just the ERDF, but it at present limits the increase to single figure percentage points. In addition, the budget as a whole is in danger of reaching an absolute financial ceiling when the limit is reached of the EC's own resources. This check to the growth of the ERDF can only be avoided if either the member states agree to increase the ceiling, or some progress is made in restructuring the budget to allocate less to agriculture and more to other policy areas, including regional policy. This is an issue which is returned to below.[10]

Another limitation on the effectiveness of the ERDF is that the bulk of it is allocated to be spent on specific member states according to a quota system. Originally the whole fund was allotted in this way. In 1977 the Commission proposed that a non-quota section be created which would be used to offset the effects of integration wherever they might arise. At first the Council rejected this idea, but in 1979 it was agreed that 5 per cent of the total be reserved for the non-quota section. In its latest proposals the Commission has suggested that this be increased to 20 per cent.

The quota section has been redivided since the accession of Greece to full EC membership. It now takes the form shown in Table 1.

Table 1   Distribution of the Quota Section of the European Regional
             Development Fund

Luxembourg	0.07%
Denmark	1.06%
Belgium	1.11%
Netherlands	1.24%
FRG	4.65%
Ireland	5.94%
Greece	13.00%
France	13.64%
Britain	23.80%
Italy	35.49%

Source: Sixth Annual Report of the European Regional Development Fund, COM(81) 370 final.

This is not a distribution with which the Commission is happy. Its latest proposals suggest that the quota section should be concentrated in the regions suffering particularly serious structural problems.[11] On the basis of per capita GDP and long-term unemployment figures, the proposal is that the whole quota section be

Table 2   Commission Proposal for the Redistribution of the Quota Section of the European Regional Development Fund

1. Ireland	7.31%
2. Northern Ireland, parts of Scotland, of Wales and of the North and North West of England	29.28%
3. The Italian Mezzorgiorno	43.67%
4. Greece, except Athens and Thessalonika	15.97%
5. Greenland	1.30%
6. French Overseas Departments	2.47%

Source: Bulletin of the European Communities Commission, vol. 14, no. 10, 1981.

allocated as in Table 2. These proposals must be seen in the light of the new regional policy guidelines which have been laid down by the Commission.

Policy guidelines and priorities

On two occasions, in 1977 and again in 1981, the Commission has produced new guidelines for regional policy.[12] These have aimed to make regional policy more effective, and have concentrated on identifying areas where procedures need changing, and outlining the type of projects which should receive priority funding.

The 1977 guidelines saw a new and comprehensive system of analysis of regional trends as being a priority. This would indicate how disparities were developing, pinpoint regions with problems on the horizon, and allow assessment of the effectiveness of national and EC regional policies. It was an objective which required the compilation of better statistics, and it should tend to the production of regular reports on the regional situation every two years. The first of these reports was scheduled for 1979, but actually appeared in December 1980.[13]

A second objective, upon which the Commission placed a great deal of emphasis, was the application of Regional Impact Assessment (RIA) when other common policies were being prepared. This would allow the Commission and Council to see the regional implications of all policies, rather than treating the regional question as though it were separable from other policy areas. In the new 1981 guidelines this point is reiterated, and the Commission calls for any adverse regional effects of common policies to be offset either by measures which form part of the policy itself or by the use of parallel measures drawing on the resources of the non-quota section of the ERDF.

Coordination of national policies is also singled out for mention in both sets of guidelines. In the 1977 guidelines the Commission stressed the need for member states to be more precise in stating the aims and priorities of the regional development programmes which they presented to the Commission. This would facilitate assessment of their effectiveness, but would also make it easier to coordinate measures across national borders. One area where this would be important, for example, is infrastructure development in frontier regions, where complementary measures taken on each side of the border would greatly increase their effectiveness.

Attention was also drawn, in the 1977 guidelines, to the need to coordinate disincentive measures, which are designed to deter firms from investing in already congested regions. If such measures were not coordinated, a firm deterred from investing in a congested region in one state might easily switch the investment to an equally congested region in another state.

That coordination of national policies, positive or negative, has not proved easy is indicated by the return to the theme in the 1981 guidelines. But there is hope for improvement in the area of coordinating EC and national policies, and in the introduction of a new scheme of joint financing for regional development programmes. In future the member states will be required to prepare development programmes which contain a package of measures with specific EC-aided projects incorporated in them. This should help to make the programmes more precise. It will also make a major contribution to solving the problem of ensuring that ERDF monies really are additional to the amount which member states would have spent on regional development anyway, rather than being substituted for national funds.

Ensuring the additionality of ERDF aid should increase the total amount of money spent on regional projects. Even so, the 1981 guidelines note gloomily that the various regional policy instruments have inadequate resources available to them. It is a constant theme of Commission pronouncements on regional policy. But, in realistic vein, the 1977 guidelines accepted that there was no prospect of a major increase in the size of the ERDF given 'budget constraints'. This makes it imperative that the limited resources which are available should be concentrated on the regions with the greatest need, which are identified in the 1981 guidelines as those with serious problems of structural under-development. To ensure that this can be done, the Commission would like to see a larger proportion than the original 5 per cent of the ERDF allocated to the non-quota section, which is not earmarked to be spent in any particular member state.

It is also important, in the light of the paucity of funds, that EC regional aid be concentrated on the most effective projects. The 1981 guidelines point to the reduction in labour mobility consequent on the recession and argue from this that priority should be given to investment in labour intensive activities in regions of high unemployment. However, the Commission hopes that these labour intensive activities will be based on new technologies, which to some eyes might appear curious, since new technologies are generally instrumental in reducing the labour component of both manufacturing and service activities.

Prospects

This issue of new technology is very important. At present the whole of the capitalist world is in recession. When recovery from that recession comes, it will be based on the restructuring of industrial production to utilize new labour saving technologies. This means that the scale of investment which will be needed to create a given number of new jobs will be much greater than in the past. Indeed, some see the prospect of an economic expansion which does not involve anything like a return to full employment in the West. It may be that we shall have to face the fact of continuing high levels of unemployment in the EC, with the emergence of a new class system—those who have jobs and those who do not. If this is so, it is likely that the distribution of employment prospects will have a distinct spatial pattern, and it is not difficult to guess where the highest rates of unemployment will probably be.

Equally important is what the Commission calls 'the new international division of labour'. The main facet of this is the tendency for multinational corporations to direct their investment in labour intensive activities towards cheap labour countries in the developing world, such as South Korea, Taiwan, the Philippines, Mexico and Brazil. There has even been some direction of such investment to the Soviet bloc countries of Eastern Europe. Proponents of free market economics have to accept that this is the logic of the labour market, and will presumably welcome the development. But politicians in the EC will find that they come under increasing political pressure to combat it in the only way possible short of driving down wage rates to unacceptably low levels—by protectionist measures, restrictions on free trade. This goes against the spirit of the Rome Treaty, but it has already been forced on the EC to some extent, as with the multi-fibre agreements (MFAs) which restrict imports of textiles from the developing countries into the EC. Demands already exist for more derogations from the principle of international free trade, and they are likely to grow in the future. If the demands are not met at the EC level, there is a risk that the member states which are suffering the most from such competition from abroad will break ranks with the EC and impose protectionist measures unilaterally.

Within the EC, the main opponent of import controls will be the FRG. But its Government is in a very difficult position. Since its foundation in 1949 the FRG has had an export-oriented economy; this is why it has benefitted so much from the lowering of tariffs within the EC. The EC is economically dominated by the FRG, which has now long since reached the stage where it wishes to spread out from its secure EC market base to export to the rest of the world. But it still needs to keep that EC base intact, and indeed wishes to extend it (through enlargement of the EC) and deepen the level of EC integration (through EMU). So the Government of the FRG faces a dilemma: if it accepts protection of the EC market it risks the imposition of retaliatory restrictions against EC exports, including German exports, by the rest of the world; yet if it resists protection it risks the breakup of the EC as other member states resort to national protectionist measures.

There is one other possible option open to the FRG: to promote EC policies which will allow the EC as a whole to attract new investment and become more profitable. This could mean an overall industrial policy, but at the very least it will mean an effective regional policy. It is in particular regions of the EC that the pressure of competition from low-cost industries in the developing world is most intense. The run-down of industries such as textiles or steel expresses itself in the form of worsening regional disparities. And the competition from developing countries for scarce investment capital affects these regions plus agricultural regions which are striving to diversify their range of economic activity and improve their output and living standards. So the problem is legitimately within the sphere of EC regional policy. But if the EC regional policy is to make any impression on the problem, it needs more resources devoting to it.

The first section of this chapter demonstrated that the initial regional problem of the EC has not been solved by the present inadequate policy instruments. The accession of Greece has made the problem worse. The future accession of Spain and Portugal will make it worse again. The inescapable conclusion is that the FRG could only hope to escape from its dilemma on protection if it were prepared to see an ERDF vastly larger than at present exists. But this would involve German net contributions to the EC budget rising to levels which would be politically unacceptable within the FRG.

There may be other ways of finding some extra money for regional development programmes. The Commission made it clear in its response to the Council mandate of 30 May 1980, which asked it to examine ways of restructuring the budget, that it hopes for agreement on a reform of the CAP to release funds for the Regional and Social Funds, which in 1981 stood at 3 billion ECUs (£1.76 billion), a figure that 'leaves little room for flexibility in attaining the objectives of the Funds'.[14] But even leaving aside the difficulty in getting agreement to reform the CAP, which for some member states is the holy cow of the EC, it is not self-evident that this reform would leave more for the ERDF and the Social Fund. The FRG is not the only member state which is concerned with limiting the size of its contribution to the EC budget nowadays. Any saving on the CAP might be treated as simply a way of reducing the overall size of the budget. In particular, the present UK Government is ideologically opposed to high levels of public sector expenditure, whether by the national Government or the EC, and is also presumably well aware of the fact that the accession of Spain and Portugal to full EC membership will lead to a redistribution of ERDF priorities which could even make Britain a net contributor to the Fund.

Until such time as the size of the ERDF is increased, the Commission is doing the best that it can to make the maximum impact on regional problems using the existing policy instruments. To that end it is proposing greater geographical concentration of the money available, and promoting the growth of small and medium-sized firms in the problem regions, encouraging the development of rural tourism, and even supporting the activities of artisans and craftsmen.[15] Yet these can be seen as little more than minor ameliorative measures in the face of the economic forces making for regional divergence.

It was stated at the outset of this chapter that the existence of severe and widening regional disparities within the EC threatens not only its progress to further integration, but its cohesion and continued existence. It is perhaps the most important problem facing the EC today, yet there seems to be an absence of the political will necessary to solve it. The prospects for an effective EC regional policy therefore look bleak. And that could mean that the prospects for the future of the EC are equally bleak.

Notes

1. *Report on the Regional Problems in the Enlarged Community* (known as the Thomson Report) (Brussels, COM (73) 550, 5 May 1973); *The Regions of Europe* (Brussels, COM (80) 816, December 1980).
2. *Treaty Establishing the European Economic Community* (Rome, 25 March 1957), Article 2.
3. *Report on the Regional Problems of the Enlarged Community*, op. cit., para. 12.
4. Although the principles have remained the same, the details have changed somewhat since 1975. There is now a 75 per cent ceiling for regions which were in the last group, with the exception of Greenland for which there is still no ceiling. West Berlin has now been reclassified to join the 75 per cent ceiling group, to which have also been added the French Overseas Departments.
5. *Documents de la Conférence sur les Economies Régionales* (Brussels, 1961), 2 vols; *Rapports des groupes d'experts sur la politique régionale dans la CEE* (Brussels, 1964), 3 vols; *Community Topics 24—Regional Policy in the European Community* (European Community Information Service, December 1966) (contains the reports of the groups of experts).
6. *Première Communication de la Commission sur la politique régionale dans la Communauté*, 1170 final (Brussels, May 1965).
7. On the politics of negotiating the ERDF, see Talbot, R. B., *The European Community's Regional Fund* (Oxford, Pergamon, 1977) and Wallace, H., 'The Establishment of the Regional Development Fund: Common Policy or Pork Barrel?', Chapter 6 in Wallace, H., Wallace, W. and Webb, C. (eds), *Policy Making in the European Communities* (Chichester, Wiley, 1977).
8. See section of this chapter on 'Guidelines and Priorities'.
9. Bertram, C., 'Decision-Making in the EEC: The Management Committee Procedure', *Common Market Law Review*, 5 (1967), 246–64.
10. On the budgetary position, see Wallace, H., *Budgetary Politics: The Finances of the European Communities* (London, Allen & Unwin, 1980); the issue of restructuring the budget is returned to in the last section of this chapter, 'Prospects'.

11. *Bull. EC*, 10–1981, points 1.2.1–1.2.9, pp. 8–10.
12. *Bull. EC*, Supp 2/77, *Community Regional Policy: New Guidelines* and *New Regional Policy Guidelines and Priorities*, Brussels, COM(81) 152 Final, August 1981.
13. *The Regions of Europe*, op. cit.
14. *Bull. EC*, Supp 1/81, *Report from the Commission of the European Communities to the Council pursuant to the mandate of 30 May 1980*.
15. *Bull. EC*, 10–1981, point 1.2.4, p. 9.

9 Social Policy

DOREEN COLLINS

First thinking on social policy

Social policy in the EC is generally held to be somewhat immature and there is some truth in this. Nevertheless, in practice, its range is surprisingly varied. It includes specific commitments, formulated in regulations and directives, which are often detailed, complex and technical and also embraces a constant discussion of current social issues as well as research and study programmes of a collaborative nature. In so far as this work is leading to a shared culture about the appropriate lines of social progress which can supply a general framework for national action, it can be suggested that social policy is moving into harmony over the years, stimulated by the precise obligations which states undertake. It is fair to say, however, that it is still less developed than the policies carried out by members and it will probably be a long time before it reaches such a level.

It is worth devoting a little attention to the meaning that was attached to the term 'social policy' when the EC was created, since it has given rise to misunderstanding and it needs to be contrasted with widespread assumptions as to what is contained in the phrase. Today, at least in the industrial world, social policy is commonly held to imply a state commitment to ensure adequate provision in social security coverage, health, housing and welfare and often education as well, although its boundaries are ill-defined. EC social policy is primarily concerned with employment matters. In part, this represents a particular tradition that social policy is essentially concerned with the totality of relations between employers and workers in industrial society, the 'social partners' of EC discussion, but the logic of the EC also demanded this particular focus. It does not imply, of course, no overlap with the first approach to social policy: social security systems, the financing of health and welfare, the relationship of educational provision to manpower needs, are all obvious examples of this and a great deal of *ad hoc* development has always occurred in EC social policy, for there is nothing to prevent it moving into any fields that the members find necessary. The formal treaty structures have thus become overlain by later activities but they remain as the foundation for social policy and interact with the changing nature of the EC to determine its scope and development.

The three original treaties, creating ECSC, EEC and EURATOM respectively, all contain a general dedication to the improvement of living conditions in the EC area. The first two specifically refer to improved working conditions as well, EURATOM confining itself to health and safety matters resulting from the development of nuclear energy. Since this latter treaty is quite specific that basic standards of health care shall be laid down in the EC area, there will be no further discussion of this particular responsibility which can be subsumed for discussion purposes in the function of improved health and safety standards at work. What the treaties do *not* do is to give the EC a fully developed capacity to redistribute wealth in order to ensure such improvement although they do provide particular obligations.

The underlying assumption is that the main contribution of the EC to enhanced well-being is an indirect one, stemming from the increased wealth that its existence makes possible, and that it is for member states to ensure the appropriate amount of redistribution. The clearest example of this is to be found in the Rome Treaty (Article 117) which refers to the agreement of member states, not the duty of the EC, to promote improvements in living and working conditions so that workers share in the general progress.

The main reason for this arrangement was, of course, that the Rome Treaty was a preliminary document dealing with the first stages of creating a customs union and common market and was not the constitution of a new state. The negotiations were undertaken in great haste and the treaty therefore dealt with those social issues deemed relevant to the immediate tasks. In any case, to have gone further would not have been politically acceptable at that time for each member prided itself on its advanced welfare system, its union traditions, its dedication to social progress, and to have asked them to dismantle their cherished edifices would have met with no response.[1] When the Spaak Report came to consider the question of welfare in relation to the introduction of a general common market, it simply concluded that what states did about providing cash benefit systems, hospitals and schools was irrelevant to the immediate purpose.[2] Attention was therefore directed to specific issues which, whether for economic imperatives or for reasons of political acceptability, were necessary to get the new organization established. Here it is helpful to look at the Communities separately for a moment for, although in many ways similar, there are differences between them from the point of view of social responsibility.

The ECSC, as the first organization of the three, inevitably set the stage for later developments to some degree. Its creation was viewed with mixed feelings in union circles for fear that the cost of the new competitive system would be borne by those working in the industries[3] and it was thus essential to insert safeguards into the treaty. The High Authority (HA) itself was informally intended to have at least one member acceptable to the international trade-union movement[4] and the consultative committee, with union members, was brought close to decision-taking mechanisms. Specific powers included the right of the HA to consult employers and workers, to obtain information from firms and the right of such persons and groups to submit information to it. These powers extended into the area of living and working standards (Treaty of Paris, Articles 46–8) and formed the basis of many social investigations. Whilst domestic wage and social security levels were not to be included in the competence of the new structure, it did have power to prevent members using reductions therein as a means of maintaining a competitive position (Article 68). The treaty also gave positive powers to the HA to promote social well-being and these did much to establish its credibility, and thus to encourage the development of the EEC. They included the possibility of grant-aid to help with the re-deployment of excess labour in coal and steel whether in these industries or elsewhere (Article 56) and the promotion of research into occupational safety (Article 55). Since it also had the capacity to invest and grant loans (Articles 51, 54), these provisions came to be applied in the social field also, notably in housing schemes. The ECSC was able to use these provisions in a very active way. It was not just that it was helped by its right to impose a levy on coal and steel firms and to raise loans but that it seized the challenge presented by the run-down of the coal, and later steel, industries to provide grants for retraining and resettlement of workers on a large scale and to encourage plans for the redevelopment of the old, industrial areas of Western Europe at a very early stage before states had really come to grips with these issues.[5] When, therefore, the same six states came to set up the EEC they could look to the type of social activity which had proved effective as an example to be followed in the wider organization.

Major social themes

As far as the Rome Treaty is concerned, there became two themes in social policy. The first one was the necessity to deal with certain issues relating to the field of employment and this must be interpreted in a broad sense to include industrial relations, social security and labour mobility. Within this category fall the particular concerns of certain states. The two most important were the Italian requirement for the free movement of labour and the French worry about the high social costs her employers covered, which she feared might render her firms uncompetitive in the single market. Certain provisions of the Rome Treaty (for example, Articles 48, 119) resulted from such necessities. The economic analysis of the time also suggested that some attention might need to be given to special problems such as equal pay.[6]

The second theme is less clear cut. Although the general fears about the effect of a common market on living and working conditions had largely gone, it was necessary to ensure some commitment from member states, and the EC itself, that ordinary people, and not just business, would benefit from the increased wealth which was expected to result from the creation of the EC. It was not possible, however, to lay down overall social policy standards since it was obvious that member states were in different positions concerning the development of welfare services, wage levels and social protection. Whilst it was not unreasonable that the less well-off should hope to be pulled up to higher levels in the new arrangements, the imposition of overall standards in some form of global social policy was not seen as the way to achieve this and any such aim in social policy has never been accepted.[7] Such ideas led to a general commitment by members to continue to work for improved living and working conditions and to the recognition that the effect of a common market and of the adaptation of national provisions necessary to make it work would gradually have the effect of bringing social provisions more closely together. The treaty also laid the duty on the Commission to ensure close collaboration between members and between them and itself on a wide range of matters such as working conditions, labour law, occupational health and safety, since further study was required in order to determine whether the existing differences were really significant from the point of view of integration or not and to ensure that member states did not pigeon-hole their commitment to promote social progress. All in all, the treaty provided rather a patchy blueprint for social policy and, although very considerable developments have occurred, the edifice still suffers from the lack of clear driving impulse in the social field. This, in turn, has allowed states to retain their autonomy. From the viewpoint of the EC, the result is that social policy is a particularly difficult field in which to pursue integration.

Worker mobility

Although it is not formally classified as social policy in the treaty, the undertaking that people should be able to move freely within the EC to take work is clearly a very basic social right and in fact underlies many other social provisions. In 1957, the principle was looked at in a much more limited way than would be acceptable today. Labour was considered primarily as an economic resource and rules concerning equality of treatment at work were laid down and gradually implemented. These relate, in particular, to non-discriminatory treatment of Community nationals regarding the obtaining of jobs, pay and conditions of work generally so that workers can look for jobs, use employment services, stay on in a country after retirement, have their families with them and the like. Many of these provisions were conceived as a necessary protection for the indigenous labour force as much as an extension of rights for the migrants. Allied to this policy are two supporting buttresses, each of great complexity in its own right. The first is the need to ensure that national employment services are effectively linked so that vacancies and available workers are matched. Computerization has helped a great deal to make this a reality, but years of work have been needed to obtain proper standardized job specifications and to ensure reasonably effective understanding of skill levels and qualifications obtained in different parts of the EC. It cannot even yet be claimed that a basic requirement for labour mobility, that is to say knowledge of opportunities, of the formalities and of basic social conditions really exists. The main channel of movement within the EC has always been between the FRG and Italy and the formal system is supported by exchange schemes amongst employment service officials.[8] The second is the arrangement whereby social security entitlements are preserved on moving. In order to achieve this, four guiding principles have been evolved; namely, to ensure the equal treatment of migrants by social security schemes, the continuity of coverage by assimilating periods together even though the rules of entitlement in schemes may be different, the principle that the rules of the country of employment must take priority in cases of conflict, and the payment of benefits freely throughout the EC. The application of these rules is imperfect and their interpretation is a large task for the European Court of Justice. It will, undoubtedly, take many years before they are uniformly applied everywhere and there are still certain gaps. One example is that there has been a considerable growth in occupational welfare schemes, notably pensions, in the last twenty years and these lie outside the existing rules. It should also be noted that this is not a policy for aligning social security itself on any uniform basis throughout the EC (see above). Nevertheless, both the free movement and the social security regulations represent technical achievements for which the EC deserves considerable credit.

The implementation of these rules had been achieved in essentials by the late 1960s when the policy was carried along by prosperity and the continuing demand in Western Europe for unskilled labour. Thus the free movement objective worked particularly to the benefit of Italy whose un- and under-employed workers were absorbed elsewhere, notably in the booming German factories, and she was further helped by mobility grants from the European Social Fund (ESF) during this period (see below). The weaknesses in the policy are threefold. It began to be increasingly questioned whether the process whereby labour migrated into the cities should not be modified, if not reversed, by stronger EC efforts to create employment in the home areas and although there are certain EC instruments, such as the European Investment Bank (EIB) and the European Regional Development Fund (ERDF), which can be used for this, the EC still lacks a regional policy as such. Secondly, the treaty had not considered issues of social integration at all so that the principle of equality of treatment appeared to be somewhat hollow once questions pertaining to the work contract had been largely surmounted. Housing difficulties meant migrants in practice had lower living standards than other people and they often prevented family reunion or allowed it in extremely adverse circumstances.

Unfamiliarity with language and social customs meant migrants remained un-assimilated and this was particularly so for non-working wives and for children. As the children of migrants grew up and presented themselves on the labour market the previous unresponsiveness of educational systems to their needs was manifest.

Finally, the rules were limited to EC nationals, but in number they were soon overtaken by the large immigration from outside the EC frontiers of people who, culturally, were more diverse and often noticeably different from EC nationals themselves. Protection of employment rights remained a matter for bilateral agreement and welfare promotion a national responsibility. By now, however, to be effective an EC policy could not be limited to the original concepts but required extension to control the degree to which the area should rely on migrant labour and to close gaps in existing policy especially in the family and social fields. To such extensions states have noticeably failed to agree. In 1976, the EC published a new policy for migrants[9] which enunciated particular areas where work is required. This refers to such matters as improving existing work in employment services over the field of social security provisions and recognizes the existence of social, educational and health difficulties of migrants. The question of civic and political rights is touched upon. States have, however, made it plain that desirable policy consists in the long run of the creation of better opportunities at home and that, in the provision of services in the meantime, EC nationals must come first. As far as migrants from third countries are concerned, states did no more than aspire to aim at their equal treatment, to consult each other on migration policy and to strengthen the campaign against illegal immigration.

A directive has been passed on the education of migrants' children[10] and migrants form a special group for whom application may be made to the ESF. Logically, the rules are less comprehensive in relation to schemes to aid 'third-country migrants' and their continued existence as second-class migrants is a serious blot on the EC's claims of social responsibility. It is believed that many such workers, in recent years, have lost their jobs because of high unemployment rates and have remained in the EC illegally. They are, therefore, very exploitable by any new, unscrupulous employer, and by landlords, children are at risk of truancy and income levels likely to fall.

The free movement policy is not limited to wage-earning employment but covers the self-employed and professional people. At first, most attention was given to business activity by formulating rules to ensure access to necessary facilities such as bank loans, trading licences and premises and to enable specialized services to be sought and provided across state frontiers. It was assumed that rules concerning professional people might prove more difficult because of the need to ensure that qualifications are truly comparable and that the public is adequately protected, but in fact ways have been found to overcome these hesitations even in fields such as medicine[11] and legal practice.[12] The rules are careful, nevertheless, and have not led to significant labour movements for it is usually only in rather special circumstances that individuals feel it is worth their while to overcome the language and social barriers which inhibit successful practice elsewhere.

There are still gaps and reserve powers in these arrangements. States have power to refuse admission and stay on grounds of public policy, security and health and considerable discretion in how to interpret these concepts. Neither employment in public services nor professional posts in which the holder can act in an official capacity need be included. It is not, however, the formal limitations which have been the weakness up till now, rather the lack of development of a more comprehensive policy to ensure a realistic rather than a formal interpretation of the concept of equality of treatment. States show no sign at present of allowing this to occur.

Young people

The treaty had made a special mention of the intention to encourage the exchange of young workers, a policy which derived from the need to modify the attitude of a rising generation towards a sense of European identity. Only modest programmes have been conducted since expanding job opportunities in the earlier years, tourism, student jobs and travel rather superseded the original thinking. More recently there have been signs that the EC is expressing its interest in young people in rather different ways. There has been a serious start on cooperation under the auspices of the Ministers of Education. Educational initiatives have been taken to encourage teaching in schools relating to Western Europe, including language teaching, to make it possible for university students to sample each others' higher education and to set up a European University at Florence for higher study.

The realization that young people form a group amongst whom unemployment is particularly high has directed Commission interest to their lack of vocational guidance and to the unfortunate gap that often exists between the educational and vocational worlds.[13] Young people are a special group for aid under the ESF (see below) and approximately 39 per cent of Fund grants are currently directed to them.[14] It is here that the Fund has been particularly innovative in supporting work experience and job creation schemes in addition to more orthodox training.

Industrial training

The Spaak Report had not been confined to the need for labour movement in the physical sense and, indeed, thought that as job opportunities increased everywhere people would probably prefer to stay at home. It was also concerned with qualitative improvement so that workers would be able to take more skilled posts. It therefore recommended the creation of a Fund which would assist both geographical and occupational mobility. As the EIB would help get projects going and thus create more jobs, so the ESF would play its part in the creation of a more effective labour force and here one sees a direct influence from the grant aid provisions of the ECSC which had proved so successful. During the 1960s, the ESF primarily functioned by shouldering part of the cost of physical movement and the simple induction of unskilled workers into factory work. Very significant reforms carried out in 1971, supplemented in 1977, changed the function of the Fund in interesting ways.[15] Up till then it had worked as a reimbursement system so that states obtained grants for approved schemes automatically. Thus the EC had no real influence over the Fund and could not encourage developments it considered desirable. As disenchantment with migration grew, and Third World competition in certain industries became more apparent, the interest in labour training to meet new industrial challenges increased. The opening of the Common Market stage of development in 1970 suggested that integration would deepen and that the Fund should be able to encourage this process whilst the introduction of an EC budget brought the question of the financing of ESF under wider scrutiny. Both the Council of Ministers and the EP became more interested in the work of the Fund for this reason alone and as employment difficulties increased all states have been anxious to get what they can from the Fund and to influence its objectives in ways which will suit them best. A very significant influence on the work of the Fund after 1971 came from the first enlargement of the EC. Since the Irish, from the start, were very anxious to utilize the Fund in view of their relative lack of industrial training they have always made enthusiastic use of it and in Ireland the grants now have an important influence.[16] The British entry made its impact in a different way for the UK posed the problem of the relative decline of older industrial regions on a far vaster scale than the Fund had had to face hitherto.

The 1971 reform gave the Commission a part to play in the selection of schemes put up by governments for grant aid and also made it possible for private firms and organizations to receive ESF grants provided they were backed by public authorities. It also defined the areas in which the ESF can help on the basis of a compromise between the views of the Commission and the Council of Ministers. Specific groups, such as workers in textiles or agriculture, women and young people became eligible for grant aid but approximately half the budget must be spent in the less developed regions where its function is more to support the employment schemes of individual states. With the growth of unemployment in recent years, which is much higher in such regions, the Commission has given preference to schemes to help special groups living in the regions so that in practice the bulk of the Fund money flows to those areas. The Fund is an interesting example of the real independence of the Commission to act on its own initiative although within defined limits and this role is supported by a small budget for pilot schemes and studies.

Unlike the ERDF, the ESF has no national quotas and this again suggests that a real degree of decision-making was transferred to the EC in 1971. It must be said, however, that the figures suggest that the Commission is careful to try to keep national shares on an even keel.

There have been two outstanding weaknesses in the reformed ESF. The first, which now shows welcome signs of being overcome, is a complex of managerial, administrative and financial issues which together have created a system cumbersome to operate, slow to decide and to pay out and which operational bodies find very hard to understand. Because of the problems, in practice the Commission relies very heavily on national administrations, but this has the further consequence that the latter largely determine the destination of the monies, thus clouding the independent initiatives which are so important if the ESF is to be used to further EC objectives and the integrative process. The second is, if anything, even more important. The rigidities of the EC budget have prevented the expansion of the Fund to match the rapid increase in the number of the unemployed and, indeed, to reflect the industrial rather than the agricultural base of the EC. Thus the review of the tasks of the ESF which the EC is bound to undertake in 1982 is a critical occasion. The Fund has, in addition, to accommodate the entry of Greece which, being relatively ill developed and with a high percentage of its labour force in agriculture and textiles,[17] can be expected to make heavy demands of a sort which can only be increased by the entry of Spain and Portugal. Since Greece, at least, does not have sufficient infrastructure to provide retraining schemes, *extra* resources are in truth required to enable her to make best use of what the ESF can currently offer.

A strong case can be made out for the argument that the best role for the ESF at the present time is to help keep people in jobs. This would mean increasing its aid to schemes such as work opportunities and preparation for young people, wage subsidies to make people re-employable or to prevent workers losing their jobs in the first place as opposed to traditional training for skills programmes. The ESF is already interested in such activities and states with high unemployment

Table 1   National shares of ESF %age

	Belgium	Denmark	FRG	France	Ireland	Italy	Luxembourg	Netherlands	UK
1973	3.9	2.8	10.9	17.7	5.4	24.0	0.1	3.7	31.5
1974	2.6	4.7	10.9	19.6	6.6	28.4	0.1	2.6	24.5
1975	2.2	2.4	11.2	19.8	6.1	27.7	0.1	2.9	29.6
1976	1.8	2.4	10.2	17.5	7.2	33.3	0.1	2.9	24.4
1977/8	0.7	0.2	5.9	18.6	7.3	57.5	0.1	–	9.7
1977	1.5	2.3	9.6	20.4	7.6	19.5	–	2.0	37.1
1978	2.0	2.5	10.1	15.2	7.8	41.0	–	1.7	19.7
1979	2.1	1.9	6.8	17.4	7.5	36.3	0.1	2.5	25.4
1980	2.9	1.9	10.6	19.2	7.9	32.3	0.1	1.8	23.3

Source: Commission of the European Communities, *9th Report on the Activities of the European Social Fund*, op. cit., p. 69. The supplementary entry for 1977/8 resulted from the use of the new monetary unit and cannot be equated with other years.

rates are clearly attracted by such a possibility. However, one of the strengths of the ESF as it exists at the moment is the way in which it can identify the employment problems of a particular group such as young people, the handicapped, migrant and women workers and it would be unfortunate if the stimulus to training and job search, which the grants provide, were to be swallowed up in work which is essentially support to the activities of the national employment services. It is difficult to see that, with government expenditure being curtailed everywhere, there would be an end result other than the EC shouldering costs which would otherwise have been borne internally. Experience suggests that one of the valuable functions of the ESF is its ability to act as a catalyst through such schemes and through the support of pilot schemes and studies. It is here that its independent role appears most clearly. If this were to be lost, then the ESF would no longer be in a position to turn attention to the newer problems of the West European labour force such as increased leisure time, the problems of partial retirement and job-sharing, all of which face workers and employers with the need for re-thinking their traditional methods and beliefs. Underlying all such possibilities, however, is the stark fact that the ESF budget bears little relation to need, whatever criterion is adopted to define this elusive concept.

The very existence of the ESF is bound to raise questions about the proper role of the EC in related matters such as training standards, employment policies and labour market policies, not to mention the allied questions of the costs of unemployment benefits, retraining services and retirement policies. The only issue that the Rome Treaty seriously considered was that of occupational training (Article 128), where it seemed to assume that a move towards a degree of alignment of standards would be a necessary part of the creation of a common market. In fact developments in such a direction have been very slow and early steps were not followed up. EC policy at present rests on the acceptance by members of general guidelines[18] and the work of the European Centre for the Development of Vocational Training which operates from West Berlin as a study centre. By virtue of the interest in the twin issues of the difficulties of special groups of workers and of the need for all workers to have satisfying jobs, the EC proceeds also by encouragement and advice to states. Vocational guidance and the 'humanization of work' are two particular interests. A number of studies have been completed such as that on shift work, there has been a recommendation from the Commission on the adoption of a forty-hour week and four-weeks' paid holiday,[19] whilst an active policy on safety, hygiene and health protection at work is conducted for which directives are frequently used.[20] The Commission is particularly active in setting standards and undertaking research work in the coal and steel industries where it has precise responsibilities and can directly commit resources.

The women's policy

In the discussions leading up to the Rome Treaty much attention had been given to the question of whether the differential social costs carried by employers would impede the development of the economic unit, and France, in particular, was anxious to ensure that her policy of equal pay, relatively generous holiday and overtime rates and of high social security costs would not impede her industry from successful operation.[21] The treaty provided an interesting gradation of commitment in regard to these three matters. A firm obligation was undertaken in relation to equal pay for men and women, member states agreed to endeavour to maintain the existing equivalence of paid holiday schemes whilst social security was to be a subject on which there should be close collaboration, studies and consultation (apart from the need to make arrangements for migrants as already discussed). This reflected the real ignorance about the effect of such cost differences and, indeed, little comparative knowledge existed about such costs, social security coverage and the importance of occupational benefits. Studies of such matters continue to be an important contribution to social understanding made by the Commission so that the publication of comparative material relating to social issues and industrial relations generally, both statistical and otherwise, is a significant area of EC social policy.

It was not until the 1960s that the equal pay policy began to be taken seriously. In part, this was a reflection of the growing interest in the place of women in society, the realization that women had become a significant part of the paid labour force but suffered particular difficulties at work and the recognition of the changing pattern of family life and child-rearing responsibilities. National societies were adapting to these factors with changes in divorce and family planning laws, and in employment regulations, in the attempt to remove some of the differential disadvantages experienced by the working woman. The EC was not immune to these pressures and 1975 and 1976 were particularly critical years. An Irish application to delay the implementation of the equal pay policy was refused, whilst a Court judgment stated that Article 119 had both economic and social aims. It should thus be seen as part of the process of improving living and working conditions to which the treaty was dedicated.[22] The question of equal pay was also taken up again by the Commission much more forcibly than in the past and a directive in 1975 established a wider definition of equal pay, compelled members to repeal legislative acts incompatible with the policy, to refuse to acknowledge collective agreements which did not accept equal pay and to provide proper information to working women on their rights together with a formal claims procedure.[23]

This policy has been strengthened with two directives which show the capacity of the EC to go beyond the Rome Treaty when the political will exists to strengthen social policy. Since the principle of equal pay is of limited value if women's employment opportunities are restricted, a directive to ensure that men and women have equal access to employment, training and promotion was accepted in 1976,[24] and a special 'women's group' has been opened in the ESF. This directs grants to courses specifically designed to help women with work preparation as well as training and which are directed to help women move into jobs where men usually predominate.[25] Finally, a directive of 1979[26] requires the progressive implementation of equality of men and women in social security schemes which, traditionally, have been built round the notion of the man as breadwinner and have been slow to adapt to the large number of women now at work, the increase in the number of married women at work and the growing incidence of divorce. In the main, the implications of these directives are to improve the position of women but equality works both ways. Men must be allowed access to jobs traditionally held by women whilst the lower retirement age generally available to women under social security legislation has become illogical.

To support policies, whether at national or EC level, designed to improve the position of women, the Directorate-General for Social Affairs now includes a small women's bureau which is largely promotional in scope. It seems, therefore, that in a totally unforeseen way, the EC has not only become involved in a social issue undefined at the time of the creation of the EC but has found it possible to extend the scope of its interest far beyond the immediate demands of a common market.

The alignment of social policies

Much of the EC's work in the social field falls under the heading of harmonization and collaboration, notions which are rather diffuse and processes whose effects are long term, often expressing themselves in changing attitudes and approaches to social issues rather than affecting them directly. The commitment to improve well-being and to collaborate over social questions is now considered to express a willingness to work together and to align national policies when changes become necessary but there is still no question of the imposition of a single pattern of social welfare. There seems little point in trying to impose an artificial uniformity on widely variable structures of social services when there is no obvious reason for it and when these structures have evolved over long periods to accommodate national requirements. There remain very considerable differences of living standards, family patterns and employment conditions within the EC and social protection has to fit into the context such factors create. It will evolve in the same direction to the extent that these underlying conditions do so. There is, therefore, no policy of trying to urge the same level of cash benefits throughout the EC or to standardize the organization of health care. It has from time to time, however, been queried[27] whether there is a case for the EC to take over the costs of unemployment benefit and vocational training since employment problems must be very much its concern and any move towards EMU must increasingly remove the capacity of member governments to influence employment levels directly themselves.

It is, therefore, through the study, research and experimental programmes that the Commission is likely to influence a move towards the harmonization of social systems, and the importance attached to such work is symbolized by the creation of two separate study foundations created to promote work in vocational training and in improving living and working conditions. It remains true, however, that much of the more traditional work on the study of social security and on labour law has proved equally valuable in improving the level of knowledge in fields where comparative studies are still lacking. An interesting development has been to produce a European Social Budget. This is not concerned with EC social spending but the collation of national data relating to demographic trends, national social expenditure and social security costs in order to assess the likely trend of social security expenditure as an integral part of economic projections.[28] Quite a different type of initiative developed in 1975 when the EC began to finance a small anti-poverty programme to support both cross-national studies and grass roots projects whose experience could be utilized elsewhere. One criterion for support in the latter case was that schemes should involve the participation of the participants in their operation.

In fact, this particular principle is integral to EC thinking on social policy. The notion of involvement and participation runs through the institutional structure from the days of the ECSC onwards. It exists in the formal, and the *ad hoc*, committee structure and constituted a major theme of the Social Action Programme (SAP) of 1974.[29]

A standing committee on employment, drawing representatives of the social partners into discussion, meets at least once a year and from time to time the Tripartite Conference brings Ministers of Social Affairs and Finance together with such representatives to discuss the social issues of the day. The Commission is also trying to encourage forms of industrial democracy in the national settings and this has an important relationship to the statute for a European Company and the approximation of national company law. Both issues require a solution to the question of employee participation in decision-making in firms, upon which national practices are very variable.[30]

During the 1970s, the EC was looking forward to a positive future. The transitional period had been completed, successful negotiations had enlarged the membership and new policies were required to move towards further integration. It appeared time to take a new initiative in social policy and not just because the options for national social policy would steadily close if more decisions were henceforth to be taken at EC level. The previous period had seen considerable debate about the values of a materialistic society, the uses to which the new economic wealth was being put and the plight of many disadvantaged groups whose well-being was not well promoted. Thus the Paris summit conference of 1972 appeared to herald a new dawn for social policy. It committed the EC to the belief that social policy was of equal importance to the drive for EMU. One of the important commitments was that there should be 'concrete measures and the corresponding resources' and this seemingly strong social statement was widely interpreted as a recognition that the EC had neglected social policy in the past and that henceforward it would require to be considerably more purposeful. Subsequently, the Commission produced the SAP, accepted by the Council of Ministers on 1 January 1974. This was a wide-ranging document which set out a package of measures to be undertaken, ranked in priority order and grouped under three main headings. These were the achievement of full and better employment, improved living and working conditions and the increased participation of employers and workers in EC decisions. Much of the more modern work referred to in this chapter has stemmed from the programme.

This impetus did not last long for many of the measures required expenditure which states were unwilling to permit after the onset of the oil crisis and the recession. But this argument simply highlights, although in a different form, the central weakness of EC social policy, for it is surely contrary to common sense to create an organization whose social commitment is only operative in good times. States may feel that an EC social policy is at present a luxury they cannot afford, suggesting that it is still considered a peripheral activity. It is difficult to see, however, that the EC can retain political credibility in the eyes of the general public if it is seen that it has no policy in relation to unemployment and related social issues which form the stuff of debate throughout Western Europe at the present time. The issue of the functions of EC social policy in times of recession needs to be squarely faced.

Notes

1. Collins, D., *The European Communities. The Social Policy of the First Phase*. Vol. 2. *The European Economic Community 1958–1972*. Part Two, esp. Chapter 7 (London, Martin Robertson, 1975).
2. Comité Intergouvernemental créé par la Conférence de Messina, *Rapport des Chefs de Délégation aux Ministries des Affaires Étrangères* (Bruxelles, 1956), p. 58.
3. Roux, R., 'The position of labour under the Schuman Plan', *International Labour Review*, 65 (1952), 291, 311 *et seq.* See, too, Haas, E. B., *The Uniting of Europe* (Stanford, Stanford University Press, 1968), Chapter 6.
4. Roux, op. cit., p. 295.
5. Collins, op. cit., Vol. 1. *The European Coal and Steel Community 1951–1970*, esp. Chapter 3.
6. ILO, *Social Aspects of European Economic Cooperation* (Geneva, 1956).
7. For further discussion of this point, see Collins, op. cit., Vol. 2, Chapter 5 and Holloway, T.,

Social Policy Harmonization in the European Community (Farnborough, Gower, 1981), Chapter 3.

8. Shanks, M., *European Social Policy Today and Tomorrow* (Oxford, Pergamon, 1977), p. 30.
9. *Bull. EC*, Supplement 3/76, 'Action Programme in favour of migrant workers and their families'.
10. Dir 77/486/EEC, *OJ*, L199, 1977.
11. Dir 75/362/EEC, *OJ*, L167, 1975.
12. Dir 77/249/EEC, *OJ*, L78, 1977.
13. *Bull. EC*, Supplement 12/76, 'The preparation of young people for work and transition from education to working life'. Commission Recommendation, 6 July 1977, on vocational preparation for young people, *OJ*, L180, 1977. Resolution of Council of Ministers, 18 December 1979, on the need to develop linked work and training for young people, *OJ*, C1, 1980.
14. Commission of the European Communities, *9th Report on the Activities of the European Social Fund*, COM (81) 343 Final, p. 2.
15. Decision 71/66/EEC amended by Decision 77/801/EEC, *OJ*, L337, 27 December 1977.
16. Commission of the European Communities, *Supplement to the 8th Report on the Activities of the European Social Fund*, National Reports, Ireland, COM (80) 365 Final 3, p. 51.
17. *Bull. EC*, Supplement 3/78, 'Economic and sectoral aspects. Commission analyses supplementing its views on enlargement', esp. paras. 22, 31.
18. Commission of the European Communities, *Report on the Development of the Social Situation in 1977*, para. 23.
19. Recommendation 22 July 1975, *OJ*, L199, 1975.
20. *OJ*, C165, 1978.
21. Willis, F. R., *France, Germany and the New Europe 1945-1967* (Stanford, Stanford University Press, 1968), pp. 247-54.
22. Commission of the European Communities, *Report on the Development of the Social Situation in 1976*, paras. 33, 46.
23. Dir 75/117/EEC, *OJ*, L45, 1977.
24. Dir 76/207/EEC, *OJ*, L39, 1976.
25. 'Guidelines for the management of the European Social Fund during 1980 to 1982', *OJ*, C159, 1979.
26. Dir 79/7/EEC, *OJ*, L6, 1979.
27. See, for example, Commission of the European Communities, *Report of the Study Group on the role of Public Finance in European Integration*, 1977, p. 16.
28. Commission of the European Communities, *The European Social Budget 1980-1975-1970*, 1979, and Shanks, op. cit., Chapter 7.
29. *Bull. EC*, Supplement 2/74, 'Social Action Programme'.
30. *Bull. EC*, Supplement 8/75, 'Employee Participation and Company Structure in the European Community'; Supplement 6/79, 'Employee Participation in Asset Formation'; and Supplement 3/1980, 'Employee Information and Consultation Procedure'.

10   Free Movement of Workers[1]

SCOTT DAVIDSON

Introduction

The provisions relating to the free movement of persons are to be found in Part II Title III of the Rome Treaty and as such fall under the heading of 'Foundations of the Community'. Like free movement of goods,[2] free movement of persons is one of the means set out in Article 3 of the Treaty by which the EC's objectives, referred to in Article 2, are to be attained. A strictly literal interpretation of these articles would lead one to believe that the reason underlying the free movement of persons provisions was primarily economic; indeed the Spaak Report[3] described workers as one of the economic factors of production for which mobility was necessary in order to achieve an integrated economy. The economic rationale here is reasonably clear; if a shortage of workers in a particular field arises in one member state, then in the interests of the most efficient allocation of resources workers from another member state where there is a surplus of labour should be able to move in order to fill the shortage. It becomes apparent, however, that although the primary objectives of the Treaty are economic, the general approach of the ECJ in interpreting the relevant provisions has been to endow them with a human rather than a purely functional economic aspect. As Parry and Dinnage say,

> Although the economic considerations may originally have inspired the pro-visions on the free movement of workers, it is clear that these provisions now find a justification in the objective expressed in the preamble [of the Rome Treaty], of creating even closer relations between the people of the member states.[4]

The Treaty deals not only with free movement of workers but also with free-dom of establishment (that is, freedom to set oneself up in business) and freedom to provide services, but in view of the limitations of space it is proposed to discuss only the free movement of workers here.

The legal basis of free movement of workers

The Treaty basis of free movement of workers is to be found in Article 48 which secures the right of workers to move freely throughout the member states to accept offers of employment actually made, to reside in the member state where his employment is situated and to remain in that territory (subject to certain con-ditions) after his employment has terminated. These rights do not, however, apply to employment in the public service[5] and a member state may also, at its discretion, limit their exercise on grounds of public policy, public security or public health.[6] Article 48 also requires 'the abolition of discrimination based on grounds of nation-ality as regards employment, remuneration and other conditions of work and employment'. The precise extent of the application of Article 48 was discussed in the *French Merchant Seamen* case,[7] where the ECJ held that it was directly effective in the sense that it gave rise to rights which individuals could invoke not only before their own national courts, but also before the courts of other member states. The principle of direct effect is, discussed in detail elsewhere,[8] but it may be remarked here that it has proved to be a remarkably potent force in the area of the free movement of persons since it allows nationals of other member states to vindicate rights given to them by EC law before the courts of other member states.

The general framework of Article 48 has been fleshed out by a number of implementing regulations and directives passed by the Council. These implementing measures deal in detail with right of a worker and his family to enter, reside in, and to continue to reside in the place of the worker's employment after its termination. The provisions also deal in detail with equality of treatment in employment and the grounds on which a migrant worker may be refused entry or continued residence in a member state other than his own by an application of the public policy proviso contained in Article 48.3.

Of these provisions Directive 68/360[9] deals with the abolition of restrictions on the free movement and residence of workers and their families within the member states. Member states are to grant their nationals the right to leave their territory in order to take up activities as employed persons[10] and other member states are to allow entry to such persons upon production of a valid identity card or passport.[11] Several issues arise from an examination of Directive 68/360. First, who is a 'worker' for the purpose of the Treaty and the Directive since there is no definition to be found in either of those instruments? Second, the provisions deal only with the acceptance of offers of employment; they say nothing about an individual who wishes to look for work in another member state. Third, which members of the worker's family will be entitled to accompany him to his place of work?

Turning to the first question, the issue of whether an individual is a 'worker' within the meaning of the Treaty and implementing legislation is a matter of EC law.[12] In the recent case of *D.M. Levin* v *Staatssecretaris van Justitie,*[13] a request for a preliminary ruling[14] from the Dutch Raad van Staat (Council of State), the ECJ was faced with the question of whether a person whose income was below the minimum subsistence level as determined by Dutch law could be regarded as a 'worker'. The ECJ in an expansive interpretation of the relevant provisions held that the term 'worker' extended to include any person who was employed or who *intended* to take up employment. The Court held that the term 'worker' also meant a part-time worker but excluded persons whose activities were purely marginal and which could not be regarded as a real and genuine occupation. The decision of the ECJ in this case would seem to bear out the arguments of Hartley[15] to the effect that in determining who is to be classified as a worker the issue should be whether an individual is able to support himself or herself with the remuneration derived from their employment. It would also appear that the decision of an English magistrates' court in *R* v *Secchi*[16] is in conformity with the approach of the ECJ. In this case the defendant, an Italian citizen who was squatting in London and who occasionally undertook casual jobs such as washing up in restaurants, was charged with indecent exposure. He attempted to argue that he fell within the ambit of the free movement of workers provisions in order to prevent the magistrate from making a recommendation for his deportation. The magistrate, without making a reference to the ECJ on such a crucial issue, decided that someone who worked only a few hours on a casual basis could not be regarded as being a 'worker' within the meaning of the Treaty.

There is no explicit provision of EC law giving an individual the right to move throughout the EC to look for work, but when the Council was drafting Directive 68/360 it was agreed that individuals should be able to look for employment for a period of three months. But, as Hartley argues,[17] there are grave objections to reliance on this statement because 'the minutes of the Council are not published and this statement is only known through indirect means'. Nevertheless, measures implementing EC schemes for the provision of social security would seem to indicate that individuals are allowed three months to seek work in other member states.[18] Moreover, the member states themselves have introduced measures allowing entry for limited periods to persons seeking employment.[19]

As regards the members of a worker's family who may accompany him to his place of employment, Article 10.1 of Regulation 1612/68[20] gives the following categories of persons the right to install themselves with a worker:

(a) his spouse and their descendants who are under the age of 21 years or are dependants;

(b) dependent relatives in the ascending line of the worker and his spouse.

In addition, the member states are to facilitate the admission of any other member of a worker's family who does not fall within the categories described but who is nevertheless dependent upon the worker and who lives under his roof in the state whence he came.[21] Members of a worker's family will, however, only be allowed to install themselves with him if he is able to provide them with housing which is considered normal for national workers in the region where he is employed.[22]

Once a worker can produce an identity card or passport and a document of confirmation of engagement from an employer or a certificate of employment he is entitled to be issued with a residence permit as proof of his right of residence.[23] The worker's family is also to be issued with residence permits if they produce a valid identity card or passport together with a statement proving their relationship to or dependence upon the worker.[24] Unless the worker is to be employed for a period of less than twelve months (in which case a temporary residence permit will be issued), he and his family are entitled to be issued with a permit which must be valid for a period of five years.[25] Such a permit is automatically renewable for a further period of five years upon its expiration and it may not be withdrawn from a worker solely on the grounds that he has become voluntarily unemployed or incapable of work because of illness or accident.[26]

The principle of equality

As indicated above, Article 48.2 requires the abolition of any discrimination based on nationality as regards employment, remuneration and other conditions of work and employment. This particular aspect of the Treaty is implemented by Regulation 1612/68, Article 1 of which gives any national of a member state the right to take up and pursue employment in the territory of any other member state. The Regulation also prohibits particular discriminatory practices. These include, *inter alia*, special recruitment procedures for foreign nationals, the restriction of advertisement of vacancies in the press or subjecting it to conditions other than those normally applied to employers carrying on their activities in that member state, and the impeding of recruitment of individual workers where they do not reside in the territory of the state concerned.[27] When taken in conjunction with Article 7 of the Treaty these provisions amount to a sizeable weapon in the hands of an individual who considers that he has been discriminated against by virtue of his nationality.

Article 48.2 and Regulation 1612/68 not only deal with equality regarding eligibility for employment, but also with equality of treatment once employment has been secured. Article 7 of the Regulation provides that a national of one member state who is employed in the territory of another member state is not to be treated differently from national workers by virtue of his own nationality. This would seem to preclude both direct and indirect forms of discrimination.

In *Württembergische Milchverwertung-Südmilch* v *Ugliola*,[28] for example, an Italian national employed in the FRG was obliged to return to Italy to undergo a period of military service. On his return to work he found that his period of military service had not been taken into account when calculating his seniority. German legislation required national service in the Bundeswehr to be taken into account for such purposes. Ugliola argued that he had been discriminated against by virtue of his nationality. Despite the German Government's attempt to argue that both nationals and non-nationals were treated on a footing of equality on the entirely theoretical basis that a German citizen serving in the Italian army would not have his period of service taken into account, the German law was found to be inapplicable being in conflict with EC law.

However, where it is possible for a member state to demonstrate that differences in treatment apply to both national and non-national workers alike on an objective basis there will be no breach of EC law.

Regulation 1612/68 also provides that workers are to derive specific benefits as regards access to training in vocational schools and retraining centres;[29] the right to belong to and to vote in trade unions;[30] the enjoyment of social and tax advantages and the same rights and benefits as national workers in matters of housing.[31]

Workers' families are also to enjoy certain rights under Regulation 1612/68. These include the admission of the children of a worker to a member state's general educational apprenticeship and vocational training courses under the same conditions as nationals.[32] Thus it was held by the ECJ in *Casagrande*[33] that the son of a deceased Italian migrant worker was entitled to a grant to allow him to pursue his education. The ECJ by examining the overall scheme of the Treaty and Regulation 1612/68 has given it a very broad interpretation. For example, in *Fiorini* v *SNCF*,[34] French legislation allowed certain families to receive identity cards allowing railway travel at reduced fares. Fiorini was the widow of an Italian worker who had worked in France. The question arose as to whether the issue of such cards amounted to a social advantage for the purposes of Regulation 1612/68 and whether such advantages extended solely to workers or to their families. After examining the preamble of Regulation 1612/68 and the scheme of the legislation the ECJ decided that the freedom from discrimination extended to the worker and his family.

The public policy proviso

Article 48.3 provides that a member state may exclude persons benefiting from the Treaty provisions from their territory on the grounds of public policy, public security or public health. Such prohibition on entry must apply to the whole of the state in question and not only to parts of it, unless similar restrictions can be placed upon a member state's own nationals.[35] Article 48.3 is implemented by Directive 64/221[36] and both have been found by the ECJ to produce direct effects.[37]

Although member states are allowed discretion in applying the public policy proviso, the EC has made it clear that this discretion is circumscribed by EC law. The operation of the proviso may only be based exclusively on the personal conduct of the individual concerned and previous criminal convictions are not in themselves sufficient to allow its operation.[38] But if an individual's past conduct demonstrates that he has a propensity to behave in a particular way and that criminal convictions are evidence of personal conduct posing a present threat to public policy, he may be excluded or deported from the territory.[39] The individual's conduct must, however, constitute a genuine and serious threat to public policy and affect one of the fundamental interests of society.[40] Diseases which might endanger public health and diseases and disabilities which might threaten public policy or security are listed in an annex attached to the Directive and include, *inter alia*, tuberculosis, syphilis, drug addiction and profound mental disturbance.

The failure of an individual to comply with the requirements of obtaining a residence permit does not entitle a member state to deport a foreign national since the right of entry and residence is derived from the Treaty itself and is not dependent upon the issue of a permit.[41] This does not mean, however, that member states may not impose penalties on foreign nationals who fail to comply with immigration requirements, but penalties for violation of such requirements must not be excessive and must be proportionate to the offence.[42]

Conclusion

Plender has written[43] that the Vice-President of the Commission in 1968 discerned in the articles governing the free movement of labour not only an economic purpose but also '. . . an incipient form of European citizenship'. Certainly the liberal interpretation placed upon the Treaty provisions and EC legislation has reflected a wider concern than merely regarding labour as one of the factors of production. The decisions relating to the rights and benefits to be derived by the families of workers would seem to bear out this assertion. However, as Plender argues,[44] unless certain developments take place, '. . . The attempt to invest articles 48 to 51 with the significance of a citizen's charter will prove to be an exercise in legal mythology.'

One of the proposed developments which would surely act as a boost to the concept of European citizenship is that of the proposed passport union.[45] The Commission regards such a union as 'a natural extension of the principles of free movement'.[46] Despite the talk of the ideal of European citizenship, however, one must not lose sight of the fact that the Treaty provisions are essentially based on economic policy. The provisions exist to achieve both short-term economic and long-term political objectives and although it is difficult to disagree with Advocate-General Trabucchi's statement that 'the migrant worker is not regarded by Community law . . . as a mere source of labour but is viewed as a human being',[47] nevertheless it is hard to escape the conclusion that such a paternalistic view is generated by the assumption that the worker is an economic factor with a human face and that his rights and those of his family are derived solely from his status as a worker.

Notes

1. There are several general texts which deal with this area of EC law. See, e.g., Wyatt, D. and Dashwood, A., *The Substantive Law of the EEC* (London, Sweet & Maxwell, 1980), Chapter 13; Parry, A. and Dinnage, J., *Parry and Hardy: EEC Law* (London, Sweet & Maxwell, 2nd Edition, 1981), Chapter 16; Lasok, D., *The Law of the Economy in the European Communities* (London, Butterworths, 1980), Chapter 5; and Mathijsen, P. S. R. F., *A Guide to European Community Law* (London, Sweet & Maxwell, 1980),

Chapter 6. For an in-depth study of the law, see Hartley, T. C., *EEC Immigration Law* (Amsterdam, North Holland, 1978).
2. See Chapter 11.
3. Rapport des Chefs de Délégations aux Ministres des Affaires Etrangères (Brussels, Secretariat of the Intergovernmental Conference, 1956).
4. Parry and Dinnage, op. cit., p. 244.
5. Article 48.4 of the EEC Treaty (hereafter EEC).
6. Article 48.3 EEC.
7. Case 167/73, *Commission* v *France* [1974] E.C.R. 359; [1974] 2 C.M.L.R. 216.
8. See Chapter 5.
9. *OJ*, 1968, L257/15.
10. Article 2.1.
11. Article 3.1.
12. Case 75/63, *Hoekstra (nee Unger)* v *Bestuur der Bedrijfsverening voor Detailhandel en Ambachten* [1964] E.C.R. 177; [1964] C.M.L.R. 319.
13. Case 53/81 not yet reported.
14. For an explanation of this procedure under Article 177 EEC, see Chapter 5.
15. Hartley, T. C., 'The Internal Personal Scope of the EEC Immigration Provisions', *European Law Review*, 3 (1978), 191–207 and Hartley, op. cit.
16. [1975] 1 C.M.L.R. 383.
17. Hartley, *European Law Review*, op. cit.
18. Article 69 of Regulation 1408/71, *OJ*, 1971, L 149/2.
19. The period is six months in the UK; Statement of Immigration Rules for Control of Entry-EEC and Non-Commonwealth Nationals, House of Commons Papers, No. 81, 1972/1973. It should be noted also that the right to enter a member state was referred to in general terms by the ECJ in Case 48/75, *Procureur du Roi* v *Rover* [1976] E.C.R. 497; [1976] 2 C.M.L.R. 619.
20. *OJ*, 1968, L257/2.
21. Article 10.2.
22. Article 10.3.
23. Article 4.2 Directive 68/360.
24. Article 4.3.
25. Article 6.1.
26. Article 7.1.
27. Article 3.2 Regulation 1612/68.
28. Case 15/69, [1969] E.C.R. 363; [1970] C.M.L.R. 194.
29. Article 7.3.
30. Article 8.1.
31. Article 9.1.
32. Article 12.
33. Case 9/74, *Casagrande* v *Landeshauptstadt München* [1974] E.C.R. 773; [1974] 2 C.M.L.R. 423.
34. Case 32/75, [1975] E.C.R. 1085; [1976] 1 C.M.L.R. 573.
35. Case 36/75, *Rutili* v *Minister for the Interior* [1975] E.C.R. 1219; [1976] 1 C.M.L.R. 140.
36. *OJ*, 1964, 850. See Wooldridge, F., 'Free Movement of EEC Nationals: The Limitation Based on Public Policy and Public Security', *European Law Review*, 2 (1977), 190–207.
37. Case 41/74, *Van Duyn* v *Home Office* [1974] E.C.R. 1337; [1975] 1 C.M.L.R. 1.
38. Article 3.1 and 3.2. See also Case 67/74, *Bonsignore* v *Oberstadtdirektor* [1975] E.C.R. 297; [1975] 1 C.M.L.R. 472 and Case 41/74, *Van Duyn* v *Home Office* (note 37 above).
39. Case 30/77, *R* v *Bouchereau* [1977] E.C.R. 1999; [1977] 2 C.M.L.R. 800. On deportation see Barav, A., 'Court Recommendation to Deport and the Free Movement of Workers in EEC Law', *European Law Review*, 6 (1981), 139–61.
40. Case 36/75, *Rutili* v *Minister for the Interior* (note 35 above).
41. Case 48/75, *Procureur du Roi* v *Rover* (note 19 above) and Case 157/79, *R* v *Pieck* [1980] E.C.R. 2171; [1980] 3 C.M.L.R. 220.
42. Case 118/75, *Publico Ministero* v *Watson and Belman* [1976] E.C.R. 1185; [1976] 2 C.M.L.R. 552.
43. Plender, R., 'An Incipient form of European Citizenship' in Jacobs, F. (ed.), *European Community Law and the Individual* (Amsterdam, North Holland, 1976).
44. Ibid., p. 48.
45. On European citizenship and the proposed passport union, see Durand, A., 'European

Citizenship', *European Law Review*, 4 (1979), 3–14 and Evans, A. C., 'Entry Formalities in the European Community', *European Law Review*, 6 (1981), 3–13.

46. Implementation of Point 10 of the Final Communiqué issued at the European Summit held in Paris on 9 and 10 December 1974 concerning a Passport Union, COM (75) 322 Final, p. 7.23.

47. Case 7/75, *Mr and Mrs F.* v *Belgian State* [1975] E.C.R. 679 at 696; [1975] 2 C.M.L.R. 442 at 450.

11 Legal Aspects of the Common Market in Goods

SCOTT DAVIDSON

Article 2 of the Rome Treaty states that the EC is to promote a harmonious development of economic activities, a continuous and balanced expansion, an increase in stability, an accelerated raising of the standard of living and closer relations between the member states. At first sight it appears that the EC is concerned with economic issues, but the phrase 'closer relations between the member states' hints at a grander political design. In a sense the distinction between economic and political objectives is artificial, since the free market economy upon which the EC is based is in turn underpinned by the political assumption that a liberal capitalist economy best serves the interests of the people of Europe. The Treaty's scheme itself reflects the Spaak Report's[1] rationale that political integration naturally follows closer economic cooperation between the EC's member states.

The economic and political objectives in Article 2 are to be achieved by establishing a common market and approximating the member states' economic policies. It is clear from the non-exhaustive list contained in Article 3.f, which indicates the means by which the common market is to be attained, that 'common market' means a single internal market for the territory of all member states throughout which economic factors of production can move freely. Article 3 includes, *inter alia*, the elimination of customs duties and charges having an equivalent effect, the abolition of quantitative restrictions and measures having an equivalent effect, and the institution of a system ensuring that competition in the common market is not distorted. The ECJ has played an important part through its teleological interpretation of the Treaty[2] in ensuring that not only 'the law is observed',[3] but also that the Treaty's objectives are attained. Through this expansive interpretation of the Treaty the ECJ has acted as one of the most effective of the EC's institutions in advancing integration. An analysis of the ECJ's jurisprudence in the area of the common market in goods illustrates this. The ECJ has rigorously circumscribed unilateral state and individual action endangering the ideal of the single internal market.[4]

The notion of a single free market is based on certain underlying political and economic assumptions. These are that free competition between economic enterprises leads not only to efficient use of resources, but that it also satisfies consumer demand by ensuring that competing producers keep prices low and the quality of goods high in order to maintain the greatest market share and thus the highest profits.[5] Of course, this is a simplistic analysis of micro-economic theory, but upon these premises rests the justification for the common market in goods. Clearly there are two aspects to free competition within the common market: first, the creation of a single market throughout which goods can move freely, and second, the maintenance of an effective system of competition within that market. The first aim is to be attained by dismantling tariff barriers and eliminating quantitative restrictions; the second by ensuring that competition is not distorted.

The customs union: Articles 9–29[6]

The EC is based on a customs union covering all trade in goods[7] (which covers anything from pornographic literature[8] to art treasures)[9] and involves eliminating internal tariff barriers,[10] and member states adopting a common customs tariff in their economic relations with non-EC states.[11] The customs union takes economic integration one stage further than a free trade area. In the latter, although customs duties between members are abolished, no supranational body regulates duties or quotas on goods originating in non-member states. The customs union on the other hand, by creating a common customs barrier in respect of non-member states' goods, presents to the outside world the appearance of a single economic unit. In the EC this has been achieved by establishing a system of common external tariffs and eliminating internal tariffs.[12]

Customs duties are one of the primary obstacles to trade liberalization since they increase the price of foreign goods as they cross a state's border, thereby making them less competitive *vis-à-vis* domestic goods. Covert forms of protectionism are, however, more difficult to deal with, but the Treaty tries to do so by referring not only to the elimination of customs duties but also to 'charges having an effect equivalent to customs duties'.[13] As the latter is not defined in the Treaty, the ECJ has determined the nature of such charges. Claims by member states that pecuniary charges for veterinary and phytosanitary inspections[14] in conformity with domestic health regulations have been found by the ECJ to amount to charges having an equivalent effect, as was a tax on imported diamonds for the purposes of establishing a fund for retired diamond workers notwithstanding the Belgian Government's argument that the charge served no protectionist purpose.[15] The ECJ held that the Treaty did not require a protectionist intention to bring a charge within the ambit of charges having an equivalent effect.[16] Thus, the ECJ has rejected any charges interfering with intra-EC trade, irrespective of the name they were given or the purpose for which they were introduced.

The ECJ's broad interpretation of charges having an equivalent effect aims to prevent the imposition of charges which, although allegedly imposed for non-protective reasons, nevertheless have a protective effect or are used as revenue raising devices. In the *Statistical Levy* case[17] the ECJ, rejecting the Italian Government's argument that a tax imposed on both imports and exports for the purposes of gathering information about the flow of trade was not contrary to the Treaty, defined a 'charge having an effect equivalent to customs duties' as:

> . . . a pecuniary charge, even though minimal in nature, unilaterally imposed, regardless of its name or workings, imposed on domestic or foreign goods *by reason of their having crossed a frontier*, when it is not a customs duty properly so called. . . .[18]

This extremely wide interpretation which the ECJ repeated in substantially the same form in later cases, effectively precludes the imposition of any charges levied on imports or exports for any purpose within the EC and strictly curtails member states' ability to take unilateral action which might jeopardize the single market.[19]

Quantitative restrictions: Articles 30–37[20]

Quantitative restrictions are amongst a state's traditional weapons for protecting its domestic market.[21] They usually take the form of quotas whose effect is to predetermine the number or quantity of foreign goods placed in the domestic market. Any unilateral state action making it more difficult for foreign goods to penetrate the domestic market may be seen as a quantitative restriction. For example, increasing documentary requirements is a common device for deterring would-be exporters or importers.[22]

The Treaty not only provides for the abolition of quantitative restrictions[23] but also pre-empts the possibility of more subtle devices being used by member states to restrict the flow of trade by requiring the elimination of 'measures having equivalent effect to quantitative restrictions'.[24] Although the Treaty does not define this term the ECJ has interpreted it very widely. Finding that a Belgium law requiring imported spirits to be accompanied by documentation certifying their authenticity of origin was a measure having an effect equivalent to a quantitative restriction, the ECJ said,

> All trading rules enacted by member states which are capable of hindering directly or indirectly, actually or potentially intra-Community trade are to be considered as measures having an effect equivalent to quantitative restrictions.[25]

Using this formula the ECJ has found that national laws requiring certificates for the purposes of ensuring production quality in exported watch parts,[26] the maintenance of retail prices of alcohol[27] and the testing of imported produce[28] have all amounted to measures having an equivalent effect.[29] In these cases the existence of discrimination was a prerequisite to the finding that a measure had such an effect. In the *Cassis de Dijon* case[30] the ECJ radically departed from this view. Here, the German Federal Monopoly Administration refused to allow a firm, Rewe, to import the French liqueur Cassis de Dijon as it did not contain the minimum amount of alcohol required by German legislation. The FRG argued that its legislation, which was for the protection of health and safety, could not amount to a measure having an equivalent effect as it applied without discrimination to national and foreign products. The ECJ held that if the national measures favoured domestic goods at the expense of imported goods as the former could satisfy national requirements more easily, then the measures would be in breach of the Treaty. Neither the Commission, the Advocate-General, nor the ECJ mentioned the need for discrimination.[31]

Following *Cassis de Dijon*, the Commission issued a Communication[32] giving its view of the decision's implications, and noting how, in the light of it, it was likely to proceed with its programme of harmonization.[33] Although the Communication is not legally binding on member states, it indicates how the Commission views the law and consequently the way in which it anticipates member states should act.[34] The Commission's view is that a product lawfully produced and marketed in one member state must, in principle, be admitted to another member state. If this is so, the question arises as to what other national health and safety rules might legitimately exclude foreign goods not meeting national specifications. Total exclusion of foreign goods on the grounds of protection of public health, safety or morality may still be justified by Article 36 (below). But where national laws which constitute measures having an equivalent effect are non-discriminatory, the ECJ held that they must fulfil a 'mandatory requirement' (that is, the member state must show that the measures were designed to 'protect the consumer, to ensure fair trading, or to protect public health').[35] In essence these 'mandatory requirements' are similar to the provisions in Article 36, but since the ECJ created them, they have a wider ambit. In *Cassis de Dijon* the FRG argued that the rationale for a national law requiring alcoholic drinks to contain a minimum amount of alcohol was to protect consumers from the insidious effects of weak liquor which built up their resistance to alcohol! The ECJ pragmatically referred to the general practice of drinking spirits in diluted form, and deduced that the FRG's health and safety law was not a mandatory requirement.[36] This appears to have been borne out by subsequent case law: national health and safety laws must satisfy a very stringent test under EC law if they are to conform to the Treaty.[37] The test was, of course, devised by the ECJ and it shows again that it is prepared to interpret the Treaty very broadly to ensure that development of the common market is not frustrated.

What are the practical effects of *Cassis de Dijon* likely to be? It is reasonably clear, especially after the Commission's Communication, that specialized products of one member state should be freely available in other member states if they satisfy the requirements of their own national laws. This means that the Commission will not have to undertake large-scale harmonization since Article 30 becomes a much more effective weapon to deal with disparate national measures. Some now argue that 'the death-blow has been administered to notions such as "Eurobeer" and other "Europroducts" . . . [and] . . . that the common market should not become a melting pot in which national or regional specialities would disappear.'[38]

Derogation from the free movement of goods: Article 36[39]

In certain circumstances member states may derogate from the freedom of movement of goods provisions. They may do so on the grounds of:

> . . . public morality, public policy or public security; the protection of health and life of humans, animals or plants; the protection of national treasures possessing artistic, historic or archaeological value; or the protection of industrial and commercial property.

Derogation, however, must not constitute a 'means of arbitrary discrimination or a disguised restriction on trade between member states'. In practice the ECJ has interpreted Article 36 in a restrictive way. Attempted derogations by member states have often been revealed as illegitimate protectionism or revenue raising devices.[40] As noted above,[41] there have been several cases in which member states have attempted to levy charges for veterinary or phytosanitary tests on goods in conformity with national legislation. The ECJ held that Article 36 does not prohibit such tests, but it does not authorize charges for them.[42] However, EC members have discretion in certain matters such as import controls on obscene literature contravening national obscenity laws.

National laws protecting industrial and commercial property (intellectual property) give rise to conflict between individual property rights and functioning of the common market. Intellectual property consists of intangible property such as patents, trademarks and copyright. Article 36 permits states to derogate from the free movement of goods to protect such property, but as these rights are created by national law they may hinder trade liberalization. Notwithstanding Article 36 and Article 222 (which states that the Treaty shall in no way prejudice national laws governing property ownership), the ECJ has not allowed such national laws to hamper the creation of the single market, as the *Café Hag* case[43] illustrates. In this case, a German company had owned the 'Hag' trademark associated with decaffeinated coffee. After the Second World War, the Belgian and Luxembourg authorities sequestrated the trademark and it was transferred to Van Zuylen, a Belgian firm. In the early 1970s, the German company which had retained the trademark in Germany began selling coffee manufactured by them bearing the 'Hag' trademark in Belgium and Luxembourg. Van Zuylen sued in the Luxembourg courts to prevent infringement of its 'Hag' trademark. On a reference the ECJ held that the holder of a trademark could not rely on the exclusiveness of his mark to prevent the marketing of goods legally produced in another member state and legitimately bearing a trademark of common origin. The ECJ said:

> Such a prohibition which would legitimise the isolation of national markets would collide with one of the essential objects of the Treaty, which is to unite national markets into a single market.[44]

The main thrust of the ECJ's judgment was that the development of the common market could not be prejudiced by the application of national laws which jeopardized this objective. Here, the common market triumphed at the expense of national laws protecting trademark rights. Mann[45] criticized *Café Hag*, arguing that the ECJ had ignored the constraints of Article 222. He considered that the ECJ had stepped beyond the proper limits of its interpretative function saying: 'There is no such overriding principle as that of "the fusion of the national markets into one single market".'[46] Replying to Mann's criticisms, Jacobs[47] drew attention to the ECJ's teleological method of interpretation and pointed out that Mann had also missed the crucial distinction drawn by the ECJ between the existence of trademark rights and the exercise of those rights. Subsequent case law has refined this principle.[48] The *existence* of intellectual property rights remains unaffected by the Treaty provisions whilst the *exercise* of such rights are subject to EC control if they interfere with the free movement of goods or distort competition. Articles 36 and 222 only permit derogation from the principles of free movement if they protect the 'specific subject matter'[49] of property rights, by which is meant those rights which are given to it by national law and which endow it with its distinctive nature. For example, the specific subject matter of a patent right is the initial protection given to inventors to prevent their ideas from being pirated and to ensure that they receive recompense for development costs. But, once goods bearing a patent or trademark are legitimately put into circulation in the common market, the exercise of protective rights cannot be used to jeopardize the objectives of the Treaty.

The conflict between the protection of intellectual property rights and the ECJ's concern to develop the common market clearly called for a European resolution of the problem. Patent rights are now dealt with by an overlapping system or conventions. The Convention for the European Patent for the Common Market 1975 (The Luxembourg Convention)[50] creates for the EC a single patent within the wider framework of the Convention on the Grant of European Patents 1974 (The Munich Convention),[51] which deals with the creation of a European Patent for a greater number of European states. The Conventions have developed a unified system for granting, contesting, and protecting patents within Europe and these tasks are performed by the European Patent Office in Munich. The Common Market Patent is administered by a special section of the European Patent Office in The Hague and is subject to the jurisdiction of the courts of the member states who can make a reference to the ECJ for an interpretation of the Luxembourg Convention. National patent laws, however, still coexist with the European system so disputes concerning the protection afforded by patents granted under national law are still likely to arise.

Trademarks are not yet subject to European control, but in November 1980 the Commission published two proposals[52] for dealing with them at EC level. The

Commission viewed national trademark laws as an impediment to the free movement of goods and it therefore proposed harmonizing draft directive and draft regulation for the creation of a European Trademark to the Council. If these proposals come to fruition they will enhance the development of the common market. As Gormley noted:

> As a means of furthering economic integration and enabling the potential of mass production to be realised these proposals provide a further incentive to industry to think and act on a Community scale.[53]

Internal taxation of a discriminatory nature: Article 95[54]

Domestic markets may not only be protected by member states imposing customs duties and quantitative restrictions, but also by the application of discriminatory internal taxation. For example, a purchase tax applied at a higher level to foreign goods increases their price and makes them less competitive *vis-à-vis* domestic goods. Discriminatory internal taxation can therefore hinder the free flow of goods between member states. Frequently taxation of this kind reflects protection of traditional markets, as was well demonstrated in a number of actions brought by the Commission under Article 169[55] against certain member states because of the way they taxed alcoholic beverages.[56] In France and Italy fruit-based spirits were taxed at a lesser rate than grain-based spirits, whilst in Denmark akvavit was taxed at half the rate of other spirits. In the UK beer was charged at a lesser rate than wine. The mode of taxation in these states clearly favoured goods of national origin. The member states argued that this taxation of alcoholic beverages reflected social and economic peculiarities relevant only to themselves. The Commission and ECJ rejected this argument saying Article 95 did not allow exceptions based on such grounds.

Articles 95.1 and 95.2 envisage two situations where discriminatory taxation may occur: first where domestic and foreign goods are similar in kind and second where domestic and foreign goods compete with each other. The member states against whom the Commission had brought the actions argued that any notion of similarity depended upon the attitude of consumers. For example, the French Government argued that grain-based spirits were taxed differently because they were consumed as *aperitifs* whereas fruit-based liquors were drunk as *digestifs*. Not persuaded by this reasoning, the ECJ held that amongst spirits there existed an indeterminate number of drinks which must be regarded as similar for the purposes of Article 95. But even if the drinks could not be regarded as similar they were sufficiently similar in character to be in competition. The ECJ thus read Article 95 as a whole rather than as two paragraphs. Easson[57] has not only criticized this aspect of the ECJ's judgments but he also points out that the member states face great difficulties in altering their fiscal systems in order to comply with them. There can, however, be no doubt that the ECJ's decision was correct. Even if national traditions favour certain alcoholic beverages, it does not provide a justification for member states to prejudice the common market by applying discriminatory taxation. It is also arguable that if the markets in certain beverages are traditional, the reduction of taxation on foreign produce is unlikely to sway consumers.

The regulation of competition: Articles 85 and 86[58]

The authors of the Treaty recognized that to maintain a single market it was not enough to dismantle trade barriers and to prohibit quantitative restrictions as powerful private enterprises could also re-erect trade barriers. Hence the EEC Treaty requires 'a system ensuring that competition in the common market is not distorted'. Cartels of independent enterprises (undertakings) and monopolies are in a position to interfere with intra-EC trade. But the provisions relating to competition do not solely reflect the negative aspect of preventing private undertakings setting up their own barriers to trade, they also demonstrate a positive belief in the benefits to be derived from a free market economy. The Commission's First Report on Competition policy shows this to be the case:

> Competition is the best stimulant of economic activity since it guarantees the widest possible freedom of action to all. An active competition policy pursued in accordance with the provisions of the Treaties establishing the Communities makes it easier for the supply and demand structures continually to adjust to technological development. Through the interplay of decentralised decision-making machinery, competition enables enterprises continuously to improve their efficiency which is the *sine qua non* for a steady improvement in living standards and employment prospects within the Community. From this point of view, competition policy is an essential means for satisfying to a great extent the individual and collective needs of our society.[59]

As a statement of politico-economic ideology nothing could be clearer; competition is simply the best way to achieve the objectives of the EC.[60]

The Commission is charged with the task of carrying out the EC's competition policy. Its role in this area gives it an unusual status which Jacobs has described as: '. . . a federal agency operating directly within the territory of the Member States and having exclusive competence'.[61] Council Regulation 17/62 EEC[62] gives the Commission extensive powers in the area of competition policy which it uses not only to deal with individual cases, but also to shape an effective system of competition as required by Article 3.f. The Commission is empowered to investigate cases on its own initiative or following a complaint by a member state, an individual or an undertaking.[63] Investigations are inquisitorial with the Commission engaging in a fact-finding mission to determine whether a breach of the competition provisions has occurred. In its investigations it can visit an undertaking's premises and inspect documents. Should an undertaking be unwilling to disclose information, then, in addition to the natural inferences which may be drawn, the Commission may impose fines. If a prima facie breach of the competition rules is discovered by the Commission it must, according to the rules of natural justice, inform the undertaking in question and allow it to make representations before a decision is made.[64] If the Commission finds that the competition rules have been broken, it can require the termination of the infringement, and impose daily and punitive fines.[65]

The Commission also has certain implied powers under the Treaty and Regulation 17. For example, in several cases it has imposed fines on undertakings which, although not registered in the EC, nevertheless engaged in anti-competitive behaviour the *effects* of which were felt within the EC.[66] Such claims to jurisdiction are similar to those exercised by the US courts in anti-trust enforcement.[67] It is arguable whether the ECJ in considering these cases has fully accepted this 'effects' doctrine. Lasok considers that the principle has been established,[68] whilst Jacobs prefers to find that anti-competitive effects have been produced by the subsidiaries of foreign undertakings operating within the EC.[69]

The ECJ has also held that the Commission possesses an implied power to grant interim relief to undertakings likely to be irreparably damaged by prima facie anti-competitive behaviour of other undertakings.[70] Without prejudice to its final decision, the Commission can order an undertaking suspected of anti-competitive behaviour to take, or desist from taking, certain action. The complainant must agree to make good any loss suffered if the Commission makes an interim decision which subsequently proves not to be well founded.

It will be seen from this brief explanation of the Commission's powers and procedures that it undertakes a variety of functions: it is policy-maker, prosecutor, inquisitor and adjudicator. Whether it is able to fulfil all these roles effectively is arguable. Some commentators feel that the inquisitorial powers of the Commission need to be strengthened,[71] whilst others question whether it can simultaneously develop a coherent competition policy as well as make decisions in individual cases.[72]

Articles 85 and 86 of the Treaty prohibit certain types of anti-competitive behaviour. Article 85 deals with cartels whilst Article 86 deals with abusive monopolistic behaviour.

Article 85 catches a variety of anti-competitive practices. It prohibits formal agreements between undertakings and also informal modes of cooperation known as 'concerted practices'. The ECJ has defined such practices as:

> . . . a form of coordination between undertakings which, without having reached the stage where an agreement properly so called has been concluded, knowingly substitutes practical cooperation between them for the risks of competition.[73]

An example of a concerted practice can be found in the *Dyestuffs* case (1972),[74] where the ECJ found the major producers of aniline dyes in breach of Article 85 when they raised the prices of their dyes almost simultaneously.

But Article 85 also refers to 'decisions by associations of undertakings' and thus deals with trade associations which dictate measures to their members. For example, in *Frubo*[75] undertakings wishing to take part in fruit auctions in the Netherlands were obliged to conform to regulations made by an association of Dutch fruit importers. This was held by the Commission and ECJ to be contrary to Article 85.

The anti-competitive practices envisaged by Article 85 are not in themselves illegal; they will only be so if they have the capacity to affect trade between member states either actually or potentially. The Commission in establishing whether or not trade within the common market is actually or likely to be affected will examine the relevant market in goods and the patterns of inter-state trade, as the Treaty is equally concerned with potential and actual harm to intra-EC trade and its effects on the single market. Where the common market is not prejudiced the ECJ will exonerate undertakings who have entered into agreements which only affect the internal market of member states. Of course, such practices may breach national competition laws.[76]

The application of these rules may mean that undertakings may be unsure whether they infringe the competition rules. To dispel such uncertainty they may apply to the Commission for 'negative clearance',[77] a statement from the Commission that the undertakings' activities do not fall within Articles 85.1 or 86. Alternatively, undertakings may feel that although practices fall within the letter of Article 85.1, nevertheless economic benefits accrue to consumers. Where benefits can be shown to result, the Commission may grant the undertakings' exemption from the penalties attached to infringements.[78]

The Commission is able to develop the EC's competition policy in a pragmatic way by granting negative clearance on exemption. These procedures combine, as Temple Lang argues, a compromise between flexibility and certainty.[79]

Article 86 makes abuse of a dominant position illegal. It is not the existence of a dominant position but its abuse which is forbidden. Dominance is an indication that an undertaking has been a successful competitor and it is arguable that success should only be penalized when it becomes prejudicial to the maintenance of the single market. As Judge Hand said in the context of US anti-trust laws: 'The successful competitor having been urged to compete must not be turned upon when he wins.'[80] 'Undertakings are in a dominant position,' says the Commission, 'when they have the power to behave independently, which puts them in a position to act without taking into account their competitors, purchasers of suppliers.'[81] This definition has been affirmed by the ECJ in its subsequent case law. However, as in Article 85, the abuse of the dominant position must affect trade *between* member states in order to be in breach of the Treaty. Once again this reaffirms the ECJ's commitment to the development of the single market.

Abusive behaviour is varied and the list of types of abuse to be found in Article 86 is not exhaustive. Some examples of abusive practices taken from the ECJ's case law may be illustrative. In the *General Motors Continental* case,[82] for example, prices in excess of the economic value of services rendered were found to be contrary to Article 86. A breach was also found in the *United Brands* case,[83] where the undertaking was using different pricing policies in member states and making 30–40 per cent more profit than firms selling unbranded bananas. In the *Commercial Solvents* case,[84] a refusal to supply a chemical to another undertaking where Commercial Solvent's subsidiary company was the only source of supply was contrary to Article 86. One extremely bold use of Article 86 has been in its application to corporate mergers. In the *Continental Can* case,[85] Continental Can acquired shares in a smaller company which produced foodstuff containers. The Commission found that by acquiring these shares the company had abused its dominance and sought, by the acquisition of the smaller firm, to become even more dominant. Although the ECJ did not find that Continental Can possessed a dominant position, it held nevertheless that in theory Article 86 could be used to control mergers. As Swann says,[86] Article 86 is an imperfect instrument to control mergers since it requires the previous existence of a dominant position which is capable of being abused.

Korah has expressed concern about the way in which Article 86 has been used.[87] The Commission and the ECJ, she argues, have worked from the wrong premiss. They have examined the market share of a firm and if it has appeared that it has over 45 per cent of the market it has been treated as dominant irrespective of the amount of competition to which it is subject from other undertakings. Korah also fears[88] that the EC's competition rules are being used not to enable efficient firms to expand at the expense of the inefficient but to protect smaller and medium-sized firms from larger undertakings. An analysis of Commission and ECJ decisions bears out these criticisms.

Conclusion

The common market in goods, although only one aspect of the Treaty's strategy for European economic and political integration, is nevertheless crucial. 'The single market', M. Gaston Thorn told the European Parliament in February 1978,[89] 'is a priceless, irreplaceable asset. If it were destroyed the Community would not survive.'

Not only is the single market part of a wider strategy in the integration process, it is also a positive statement of belief in liberal-capitalism; a belief that a free market economy enjoying open competition is the best means of serving the peoples of Europe as well as attaining the EC's objectives. The ECJ has not been a passive instrument in this process, it has, through its case law, been highly effective in shaping and developing EC policy. The ECJ's teleological approach to interpretation of the Treaty has prevented national and individual measures from impeding the development of the common market. Such a policy-oriented approach has of course been criticized in some quarters,[90] but it cannot be doubted that the ECJ's activism has greatly enhanced the integration process.

To the traditional English lawyer judicial activism is anathema, but it is of course impossible for the judiciary to be apolitical.[91] Faced with an activist ECJ there is an uncomfortable feeling in many lawyers' minds that it has overstepped the limits of judicial propriety. A recognition of political and legal reality nevertheless dictates that the ECJ cannot ensure that the 'law is observed' by a purely literal approach to the Treaty. The EC is a developing structure and the ECJ has a role to play in its development. To date it has, by and large, fulfilled this role admirably—the cause of European integration will be best served if it continues to do so.

Notes

1. *Rapport des Chefs de Délégations aux Ministres des Affaires Etrangères* (Brussels, Secretariat of the Intergovernmental Conference, 1956).
2. See Chapter 5.
3. Article 164 of the EEC Treaty (hereafter EEC).
4. Usher, J., 'The Consequences of the Notion of a Single Market: Recent Decisions of the Court on the Free Movement of Goods', *Legal Issues of European Integration*, 2 (1977), 39–52.
5. See, e.g., Samuelson, P. A., *Economics* (Tokyo, McGraw-Hill Kogakusha, 1976), Chapter 3.
6. See generally Wyatt, D. and Dashwood, A., *The Substantive Law of the EEC* (London, Sweet & Maxwell, 1980), Chapter 9; Parry, A. and Dinnage, J., *Parry and Hardy: EEC Law* (London, Sweet & Maxwell, 2nd Edition, 1981), Chapter 13; Lasok, D., *The Law of the Economy in the European Communities* (London, Butterworths, 1980), Chapter 4; and Mathijsen, P. S. R. F., *A Guide to European Community Law* (London, Sweet & Maxwell, 1980), Chapter 6.
7. Article 9 EEC.
8. Case 34/79, *R. v Henn & Darby* [1979] European Court Reports (E.C.R.) 3795; [1980] 1 Common Market Law Reports (C.M.L.R.) 246.
9. Case 7/68, *Commission v Italy* (First Art Treasures Case) [1968] E.C.R. 423; [1969] C.M.L.R. 1.
10. Article 13 EEC.
11. Articles 18–29 EEC.
12. Swann, D., *The Economics of the Common Market* (Harmondsworth, Penguin, 1968), Chapter 3.
13. Article 12 EEC.
14. See, e.g., Case 46/76, *Bauhuis v The Netherlands* [1977] E.C.R. 5; (charges for veterinary inspections on the export of the bovine animals) and Case 39/73, *Rewe Zentralfinanz v Landwirtschaftskammer Westfalen-Lippe* [1973] E.C.R. 1039; [1977] 1 C.M.L.R. 630 (charges for phytosanitary inspections on import of apples from France).
15. Cases 2 & 3/69, *Sociaal Fonds voor de Diamentarbeiders v Brackfeld Chougol Diamond Co.* [1969] E.C.R. 221; [1969] C.M.L.R. 335.
16. Ibid., para. 11 of the Judgment.
17. Case 24/68, *Commission v Italy* [1969] E.C.R. 193; [1971] C.M.L.R. 611.
18. Ibid., para. 9 of the Judgment. My emphasis.
19. See further: Usher, op. cit.; Wooldridge, F. and Plender, R., 'Charges having an Effect Equivalent to Customs Duties', *European Law Review*, 3 (1978), 101–5.
20. See generally, Wyatt and Dashwood, op. cit., Chapter 10; Parry and Dinnage, op. cit.; Lasok, op. cit.; Mathijsen, op. cit.

21. See, e.g., Samuelson, op. cit., Chapter 35.
22. See, e.g., Regulations 19/82 and 20/82, *OJ*, L3/18, 1982 and L3/26, which lay down detailed rules governing the issue of licences for the export of sheepmeat to the EC by non-member countries.
23. Article 30 EEC.
24. Article 31 EEC.
25. Case 8/74, *Procureur du Roi v Benôit and Gustave Dassonville* [1974] E.C.R. 837; [1974] 2 C.M.L.R. 436, at para. 5 of the Judgment.
26. Case 53/76, *Procureur de la République v Boubelier* [1977] E.C.R. 197; [1977] 1 C.M.L.R. 436.
27. Case 83/77, *Openbar Ministerie of the Netherlands v Van Tiggele* [1978] E.C.R. 25; [1978] 2 C.M.L.R. 528.
28. Case 39/73, *Rewe Zentralfinanz v Landwirtschaftskammer Westfalen Lippe* [1973] E.C.R. 1039; [1977] 1 C.M.L.R. 630.
29. See further Page, A., 'The Concept of Measures having an Effect Equivalent to Quantitative Restrictions', *European Law Review*, 2 (1977), 105–17 and Meij, A. and Winter, J., 'Measures having an Effect Equivalent to Quantitative Restrictions', *Common Market Law Review*, 13 (1976), 79–104.
30. Case 120/78, *Rewe Zentral A.G. v Bundesmonopolverwaltung für Branntwein* [1979] E.C.R. 649; [1979] 3 C.M.L.R. 494.
31. See further Wyatt, D., 'Article 30 and non-discriminatory trade restrictions', *European Law Review*, 6 (1981), 185–93 and Barents, R., 'New Developments in Measures having Equivalent Effect', *Common Market Law Review*, 18 (1981), 271–303.
32. *OJ*, C256, 1980.
33. See further Gormley, L., 'Cassis de Dijon and the Communication from the Commission', *European Law Review*, 6 (1981), 454–9.
34. Ibid.
35. Case 120/78, note 30 (above) para. 13 of the Judgment.
36. Ibid.
37. Case 130/80, *Criminal Proceedings against Fabrick voor Hoogwaardige Voedings produkton Kelderman B.V.* Case 113/80 *Commission v Ireland*. Both cases are not yet reported, but see Dashwood, A., 'Cassis de Dijon: the line of cases grows', *European Law Review*, 6 (1981), 287–90.
38. Dr Mattera in *Revue du Marché Commun*, 1980, p. 510 (quoted by Gormley, op. cit., p. 459).
39. See note 20 above.
40. See Usher, op. cit., and Van Gerven, W., 'The Present Case Law of the Court of Justice Concerning Articles 30 and 36 of the EEC Treaty', *Common Market Law Review*, 14 (1977), 5–24.
41. See note 14 above.
42. Case 29/72, *Marimex v Italian Finance Administration* [1972] E.C.R. 1309; [1973] C.M.L.R. 486.
43. Case 192/73, *Van Zuylen Frères v Hag* [1974] E.C.R. 477; [1974] 2 C.M.L.R. 127.
44. Ibid., para. 13 of the Judgment.
45. Mann, F. A., 'Industrial Property Rights and the EEC Treaty', *International and Comparative Law Quarterly*, 24 (1975), 31–43.
46. Ibid., p. 37.
47. Jacobs, F., 'Industrial Property Rights and the EEC Treaty—A Reply', *International and Comparative Law Quarterly*, 24 (1975), 643–58.
48. See, e.g., Wyatt and Dashwood, op. cit., Chapter 21; Lasok, op. cit., Chapter 11; Parry and Dinnage, op. cit., Chapter 14 and Mathijsen, op. cit., Chapter 6.
49. The formulation was first used in Case 78/70, *Deutsche Grammophon v Metro-5B-Grossmärkte* [1971] E.C.R. 487; [1971] C.M.L.R. 631.
50. *OJ*, L17/1, 1976.
51. *International Legal Materials*, 13 (1974), 270. The Convention was negotiated under the auspices of the Council of Europe.
52. The proposal directive and regulation can be found in *OJ*, C351/1, 1980 and *OJ*, C351/5, 1980 respectively.
53. Gormley, L., 'The Commission's proposals on trademarks—Part II', *European Law Review*, 6 (1981), 464.
54. Wyatt and Dashwood, op. cit., Chapter 9; Lasok, op. cit., Chapter 4; Parry and Dinnage, op. cit., Chapter 22; and Mathijsen, op. cit., Chapter 6.

55. See Chapter 5.
56. Case 168/78, *Commission* v *France* [1980] E.C.R. 347; Case 169/78, *Commission* v *Italy* [1980] E.C.R. 385; Case 170/78, *Commission* v *UK* [1980] E.C.R. 417; [1980] 1 C.M.L.R. 716; Case 171/78, *Commission* v *Denmark* [1980] E.C.R. 447; Case 55/79, *Commission* v *Ireland* [1980] E.C.R. 481; [1980] 1 C.M.L.R. 734.
57. Easson, A., 'The spirits, wine and beer judgments: a legal Mickey Finn?', *European Law Review*, 5 (1980), 318–330; and also 'Fiscal Discrimination: New Perspectives on Article 95 of the EEC Treaty', *Common Market Law Review*, 18 (1981), 521–51.
58. See, e.g., Wyatt and Dashwood, op. cit., Part 6; Lasok, op. cit., Chapters 8, 9, 10; Parry and Dinnage, op. cit., Chapter 20; Mathijsen, op. cit., Chapter 6; Bellamy, C. and Child, G., *Common Market Law of Competition* (London, Sweet & Maxwell, 2nd Edition, 1980); and Korah, V., *Competition Law in Britain and the Common Market* (London, Elek, 1975).
59. Attached to the Commission of the European Communities Fifth General Report on the Activities of the EC.
60. See further Van Gerven, W., 'Twelve Years EEC Competition Law (1962–1973) Revisited', *Common Market Law Review*, 11 (1974), 38–61.
61. Jacobs, F., 'Jurisdiction and Enforcement in EEC Competition Cases' in Rowe, F. M., Jacobs, F. and Joelson, M. R. (eds), *Enterprise Law of the 80s'* (American Bar Association Press, 1980), p. 205.
62. *OJ*, L/87, 1962.
63. Article 3, Regulation 17/62.
64. Case 17/74, *Transocean Marine Paint Association* v *Commission* [1974] E.C.R. 1063; [1974] 2 C.M.L.R. 459. In this case the ECJ applied the English law rule of natural justice—*audi alteram partem*—which means that an individual should be allowed to make representations on his own behalf if he is involved in proceedings the outcome of which is likely to affect his rights. For further explanation of this principle see De Smith, S. A., *Constitutional and Administrative Law* (Harmondsworth, Penguin, 3rd Edition, 1977).
65. See generally Article 15, Regulation 17/62.
66. See, e.g., Cases 48, 49, 51–57/69, *ICI and others* v *Commission* [1972] E.C.R. 619; [1972] C.M.L.R. 557, in which the Commission imposed fines on ICI for anti-competitive behaviour, the effects of which were felt in the EC, at a time when the UK was not a member of the EC.
67. See Hawk, B. E., 'EEC and US Competition Policies—Contrast and Convergence' in Rowe, Jacobs and Joelson, op. cit., p. 39.
68. Lasok, op. cit., pp. 184–8.
69. Jacobs in Rowe *et al.*, op. cit., pp. 208–9.
70. Case 792/79, *Camera Care* v *Commission* [1980] E.C.R. 119; [1980] C.M.L.R. 334. Discussed by Korah, V., 'Commission has power to grant interim relief', *European Law Review*, 5 (1980), 135–9 and Temple Lang, J., 'The powers of the Commission to order interim measures in competition cases', *Common Market Law Review*, 18 (1981), 49–61.
71. For example, Lasok, op. cit., p. 183.
72. For example, Jacobs in Rowe *et al.*, op. cit., p. 209.
73. Case 48/69, *ICI* v *Commission* [1972] E.C.R. 619; [1972] C.M.L.R. 557 at para. 64 of the Judgment.
74. Ibid.
75. Case 71/74, *Frubo* v *Commission* [1974] E.C.R. 1031; [1975] C.M.L.R. 646.
76. Case 22/78, *Hugin Kassaregister* v *Commission* [1979] E.C.R. 1869; [1979] 3 C.M.L.R. 345.
77. Article 2, Regulation 17/62.
78. Article 85(3) EEC.
79. Temple Lang, J., 'EEC Competition policies: a status report', in Rowe *et al.*, op. cit., pp. 26–7.
80. *US* v *Aluminium Company of America* 148 Federal Reports 2d. 416 at p. 430.
81. *Continental Can Co. Inc.*, *OJ*, L7/25, 1972, para. 3.
82. Case 26/75, *General Motors Continental* v *Commission* [1975] E.C.R. 1367; [1976] 1 C.M.L.R. 95.
83. Case 27/76, *United Brands Company* v *Commission* [1978] E.C.R. 207; [1978] 1 C.M.L.R. 429.
84. Cases 6 & 7/73, *Instituto Chemioterapico Italiano and Commercial Solvents Corp.* v

Commission [1973] E.C.R. 357; [1973] C.M.L.R. 361; [1974] E.C.R. 223; [1974] 1 C.M.L.R. 309.

85. Case 6/72, *Europemballage Corporation and Continental Can Co. Inc.* [1973] E.C.R. 215; [1972] C.M.L.R. 690.
86. Swann, op. cit., p. 122.
87. Korah, V., *An Introductory Guide to EEC Competition Law and Practice* (Oxford, ESC, 2nd Edition, 1981), pp. 132–3.
88. Ibid.
89. *The Times*, 17 February 1982.
90. For example, see Hamson in *Judicial and Academic Conference*, Reports of the Conference held in September 1976, Luxembourg, Court of Justice, 1976 and Mann, op. cit.
91. See Griffith, J. A. G., *The Politics of the Judiciary* (Glasgow, Fontana/Collins, 1977).

12   Monetary Integration in the European Community

T. HITIRIS AND A. ZERVOYIANNI

Introduction

Twenty five years after the EC's establishment, and with a second enlargement under way, the task of uniting Europe is still unfinished. The progress the EC has made has been to a great extent in the sphere of the free movement of goods and services rather than in the sphere of economic policy integration, with the notable exception of the CAP. In fact, the Rome Treaty itself, although it expresses a desire for economic policy integration, goes into details only in its provisions concerning the common market objective. Its treatment of economic policy regulation is very general and there are but very few implementing provisions. However, it is true that the full realization of the aims of a common market, namely complete freedom of goods, services and factors of production, requires the fixity of exchange rates between EC member states and the replacement of national currencies by a common currency at a later stage. When exchange rates are not fixed, the possibility of changes in the values of national currencies *vis-à-vis* the other EC currencies always exists. Clearly, the consequent uncertainty has adverse effects on trade and impedes the free movement of goods, services and factors of production between member states. Even so, exchange rate fixity cannot be maintained unless the trend in nominal prices and productivity follows the same pattern in all participating countries. Thus, economic policy integration within a common market area is crucial because it can secure similar patterns in the trend of nominal prices while at the same time it tends to reduce the margin of differences in productivity trends.

As there was little pressure for economic policy integration in the EC when the Rome Treaty was signed, the greater emphasis on creating a common market is not surprising. At that time, economic fluctuations in Europe were relatively slight, the Six constituted a relatively 'harmonious economic and monetary grouping', and international monetary conditions were stable. Yet by the late 1960s the need for economic integration became pressing as inflation rates began to vary between member states, and as pressures on intra-EC rates began to threaten the achievement of a common market. Under these circumstances, the first concrete actions for greater economic and monetary policy coordination emerged with the Barre and Werner plans, and finally the 'Snake' agreement of April 1972. However, this first attempt to integrate policy through a scheme of lower permissible fluctuation margins between EC currencies failed to survive the destabilizing forces of 1973–5 which exacerbated divergence among EC member states over economic policies. Further efforts to promote integration culminated in the establishment of the EMS in December 1978. While, in its present form, its first objective is the creation of a zone of monetary stability, it can be developed as a step towards economic and monetary integration.

This chapter discusses progress towards economic and monetary policy integration in the EC and some aspects of the EMS. It also addresses such issues as the disadvantages of a monetary union from a national viewpoint and the possible paths to economic and monetary integration put forward at various times.

Historically, the view that 'monetary integration'—in the sense of securing exchange rate stability—should precede the integration of 'economic policy' has become dominant in the EC. Consequently, this chapter focuses on this preoccupation.

Monetary integration: scope and method

Article 2 of the Rome Treaty notes a desire for economic policy integration by setting the goal of 'progressively approximating the economic policies of member countries',[1] along with the target of establishing a common market which was the Six's primary concern. This is clear from the Rome Treaty as there are relatively few provisions for promoting policy coordination. Moreover, they are imprecise compared with those on the implementation of the common market. Thus, although Article 3(g) of the Treaty calls for '. . . the application of procedures by which the economic policies of member states can be coordinated',[2] the particular kind of procedures and the measures taken by the EC Commission to attain this are sketched only loosely in Chapter 2[3] which suggests '. . . the setting up of a Monetary Committee with advisory status to keep under review the monetary/financial conditions of the member states and to report to the Commission and the Council'. In fact, the perspective of a monetary union is not explicitly mentioned in the Treaty and one can hardly see any term imposing obligations and constraints on the member states' national monetary policies. This imbalance in the Rome Treaty is not at all surprising. On the contrary, it is quite justifiable given the prevailing stable international monetary conditions and the consequent weakness of internal pressure for greater monetary coordination inside the EC; and the satisfactory functioning of the Bretton Woods system of the adjustable peg. The USA was pursuing a consistent monetary policy and its slight balance of payments deficit provided Europe with the desired liquidity. As the member states' financial interchanges took place with and through a stable dollar, they did not face any pressure to create a European monetary bloc. In fact, there was an apparent monetary integration of the EC through the dollar which undoubtedly facilitated the development of both the common market and the CAP.

The first significant initiatives for European monetary integration came in the 1960s when international monetary conditions underwent intensive changes. Problems began in the early 1960s when a gradual weakening of the two reserve currencies (the dollar and sterling) began, leading to a gradual erosion of the foundations of the Bretton Woods system. Things became worse from the mid-1960s as the Vietnam war led to highly expansionary monetary policies in the USA resulting in an increasing American balance of payments deficit. This progressively undermined confidence in the dollar. When a two-tier gold market was established by the USA in March 1968 and the gold pool was abandoned, the disintegration of the Bretton Woods system became evident. At the same time, three European currencies were caught by speculative pressures. In November 1967, after substantial flows out of sterling, the UK authorities devalued the pound by 14.3 per cent. From May 1968 the French franc and the German mark came under pressure. This was resisted initially by the adoption of foreign exchange controls, but as the tide continued the French authorities were forced to devalue the franc by 11.1 per cent in August 1969, and the Germans to revalue the mark by 9.3 per cent in September 1969.

The revaluation of the German mark was a crucial factor in changing attitudes to the idea of monetary union. The changed intra-EC parities proved the fictitious nature of monetary integration in the EC based on fixed exchange rates to the dollar. There was considerable anxiety that a repetition of the 1968–9 crisis would undermine the CAP and the common market.

Against this background, the first concrete action on monetary integration in the shape of the Barre plan emerged. This called for more consultation and co-ordination of monetary and economic policies in general in the EC and proposed the creation of a short- and medium-term financial assistance programme to enhance the member states' existing credit facilities. More important was the EC leaders' statement at The Hague summit in December 1969. In it they formally expressed the EC's intention to proceed to a monetary union. Thus monetary integration was explicitly adopted as an EC aim. It was after this that various arguments for and against monetary union started to appear and alternative routes to monetary integration were debated, compared and evaluated.

Here three of the main arguments against monetary union, one political, the other two economic, are discussed. Concerning the political argument, it has been claimed that a full monetary union implies a wide transfer of economic powers from the national central banks to an EC Central Monetary Authority. Obviously, such a transfer of economic power requires a prior transfer of political powers at the expense of national sovereignty. Even if member states retain the right to have their own central banks, the commitment to keep exchange rates irrevocably fixed imposes constraints on economic policies which in turn inevitably imply some constraints in the political sphere. Thus, it has been argued that a monetary union either erodes national sovereignty or at best imposes political constraints on the member states. To a certain extent, this argument is correct and it can be said that a monetary union calls for significant compromises. For example, there must first be sufficient political convergence and political unification. Against this is the view that if economic advantages from monetary union are considerable, they may outweigh unfavourable political implications from a national viewpoint.

Of the two economic arguments, the first is based on the view that the exchange rate can be used as an instrument of policy. Then, the commitment to irrevocably fixed rates reduces the number of instruments available to the authorities for attaining domestic targets and especially curbing unemployment. However, a counter-argument to this is that nowadays the exchange rate as a policy instrument is, at best, effective only in the short run. This is because it is now recognized that expectations play a very important role in determining key economic variables. For instance, depreciation, which implies increases in the expected domestic value of imports, is most likely to lead to increased wage demands and hence to domestic price rises that in turn may reverse the initial favourable effect of depreciation. There will be only a short period in which the 'expenditure-switching policy' will be effective, and this period will be the shorter, the more rapidly expectations are embodied in current economic behaviour. From the long-run point of view, the only valid economic argument against an irrevocable fixing of exchange rates is related to the alleged necessity for exchange rate changes due to structural shifts. If the exchange rate is fixed, structural shifts will inevitably induce adjustments in a number of other key variables of the system, as for example in the level of output or other real magnitudes. In that case, certain member states would prosper, and others would suffer from the system of fixed exchange rates and only a proper regional policy on an EC-wide basis might be able to redress the balance.

Another subject of interest and dispute is the problem of currency unification (that is, the choice of strategy for monetary integration once agreement on setting up a monetary union exists). Several alternative routes have been proposed. The first, and more radical, favours the immediate establishment of the monetary union specifically by immediately setting up a Central Monetary Authority, pooling the members' reserves, and directly replacing national monies by a common currency. Although this method has the advantage of automaticity,[4] it is hard to see how such a radical change could be accepted by national governments in the absence of any significant external shock as it implies the immediate transfer of national powers to the Central Monetary Authority, and an immediate erosion of national sovereignty. Furthermore, this automatic route may also be very costly for the less prosperous member states. As they would have to adjust their inflation rates to the union's lower inflation rate at once, unemployment would result if the adjustment of price expectations is not instantaneous. The obvious solution is to announce this radical change well in advance in order for expectations to have time to adjust.

A different approach is the currency competition route, which has been presented in two versions. According to the first—survival of the fittest—version, all capital controls in the member states are abolished and all national currencies are accepted for use within the prospective union. With free competition among national currencies, only one currency—the relatively most stable—would survive in the long run and effectively become the union's common currency. Thus, monetary union would evolve through the market process. This method appears to have the advantages of gradualism avoiding costs consequent on the previous route. But it is also automatic as it is not based on successive negotiations and discussions between national authorities. It has a serious drawback as it gives rise to *seignorage* from the creation of international money which accrues exclusively to the monetary authority whose currency survives as the union's common currency. The second version of this approach attempts to overcome this drawback by suggesting the establishment of a parallel currency, probably a 'basket' currency consisting of all national currencies properly weighted. Accordingly, the parallel currency would be allowed to circulate alongside national monies, and if it proved more attractive than national monies, it would eventually become the union's currency. A parallel currency would preclude privileges attaching to a particular national currency. However, if the basket of parallel currency is to become the union's currency, it must out-compete both the weak and the strong national currencies. If the parallel currency is constructed in such a way as to have a more stable value than the weak currencies but a less stable value than the strong currencies, then eventually both the parallel currency and the strong currencies would survive and monetary integration would not ensue. A solution would be to guarantee the purchasing power of the parallel basket currency. In that case, if no special convenience attaches to national monies, it is likely that risk-averse economic agents would prefer to hold this stable currency in terms of purchasing power rather than the more unstable national currencies.

The last route put forward is the establishment of a monetary union by steps planned in a number of different ways and containing a number of different elements. For example, member states may decide to reduce initially exchange rate margins, at a second stage to eliminate exchange rate margins, at a third stage to pool all international reserves, and at a final stage to replace national currencies with an EC currency and to establish a Central Monetary Authority. On the other hand, the member states may decide that they will enter the scheme whenever they are ready (that is, whenever a harmonization of national monetary policies with the EC target has been achieved). Furthermore, it may be decided that member states would retain the right to withdraw from the scheme. In addition, the various steps of this scheme can be decided and well planned in advance or they can rest on successive negotiations. The attainment of monetary union by steps has an important desired feature, namely gradualism. In the case where all the steps are designed in advance and there is a firm commitment to stay in the scheme, automaticity is also present. However, if the members reserve the right to withdraw from the scheme, they may choose to follow their own monetary policies at a certain time when, for example, their national interests conflict with those of the union. Clearly, as a firm commitment to stay in the scheme imposes self-discipline on national monetary authorities, it is likely to lead to a monetary union. On the other hand, if the various steps are not decided in advance, this route has the drawback of relying on successive negotiation for the implementation of successive stages. It has been argued[5] that this increases the possibility of failure, as political will to support the scheme may vanish if member states' interests change over time.

European monetary integration

The gradual step-by-step approach was chosen by the EC at The Hague summit of 1969 as the way to attain European monetary integration. Subsequently, the Council was asked to draft a plan along these lines. Although all member states agreed to the principle of European Monetary Union, they disagreed over what these steps would involve.

One group of member states, namely the FRG and the Netherlands, argued that the first step should involve the setting up of EC targets, harmonizing national economic policies as an easy way of then fixing exchange rates to lead to the next step of establishing a Central European Monetary Authority, pooling reserves, etc. Other member states argued that the first step should be to narrow exchange rate fluctuation margins, pool reserves, and increase existing credit facilities to member states. They felt that the need to maintain a fixed exchange rate would impel policy coordination on member states.

These disagreements were clear among the members of the Werner Committee, set up to draft the plan for European monetary integration. Eventually, the Committee proposed establishing EMU by 1980 in stages involving rigid fixing of exchange rates, irreversible inter-convertibility of EC currencies and creating an EC Central Bank.[6] It was divided over the means and methods for achieving this. Thus, the final plan, adopted by the Council in March 1971, was a compromise: only the details of the first stage were outlined, but there was no binding commitment about how and when they should proceed to European Monetary Union. The first stage involved the gradual narrowing of exchange rate fluctuation margins, a two billion dollars increase in credit facilities available to member states, an attempt to coordinate national economic policies and a feasibility study on the creation of a European Monetary Fund.

The first stage of the Werner plan was not implemented immediately, primarily because of the highly unstable international monetary conditions prevailing at the time. In fact, during this time confidence in the dollar fell with continuous depletion of the US gold stock. After the US renouncement of its obligation to convert dollars into gold in inter-bank transactions, some EC member states left their currencies to fluctuate against the dollar. Finally, the Smithsonian arrangement was reached in December 1971, establishing a permissible ± 2.25 per cent fluctuation margin between the dollar and the other currencies.

It was after the Smithsonian arrangement that the first stage of the Werner plan was implemented. In April 1972 the EC member states entered the Basle Agreement, known as the 'snake', together with five other European countries. The permissible margin of exchange rate fluctuations between the participating countries was set at ± 2.25 per cent. The 'snake' agreement included an intervention mechanism and a monetary support scheme for participating countries. National governments reserved the right to withdraw from the 'snake' whenever they deemed it necessary. But the 'snake' soon came under pressure. The oil crisis of 1973–4 affected differently the various 'snake' countries and the self-discipline proposition did not work. The governments of the badly hit countries, facing unemployment, increased their money supply more than the preservation of exchange rate margins permitted. Soon a considerable divergence in inflation rates between the participating countries appeared forcing the member governments to leave the 'snake' at various times. It collapsed in March 1976 after France's withdrawal. Only countries with tight trade relations with the FRG stayed in. Thus, the EC's first steps towards monetary integration failed. The 'snake' proved unable to survive the destabilizing forces of the period, and the EC Committee set up in 1975 to evaluate the situation found no point in advancing to stage two. So the EC member states allow their exchange rates to fluctuate against each other—except for the Benelux countries and the FRG whose bilateral exchange rates remain stable.

It is worth assessing the functioning of the floating regime since it was dissatisfaction with it that led to the creation of the EMS. The floating exchange rates did help Western Europe considerably to cope with balance of payments and unemployment problems arising from or exacerbated by the oil crisis. However, the system's functioning was not as rapid and its outcome not as certain as its advocates had claimed. A number of countries complained that the balance of payments adjustment had been slower than expected and that the system was characterized by a certain degree of instability. In fact, many countries experienced sharp fluctuations of their exchange rates within short time periods, which could hardly be attributed to equivalent exchanges in any of the main determinants of the exchange rate as, for example, differences in inflation rates and in money supply growth rates. These fluctuations frequently led to real exchange rate changes that in some countries sustained the inflation rate and in others induced higher inflation and unemployment. Furthermore, at about this time, the 'vicious circle' argument was put forward, according to which a floating rates regime may prove more inflationary, the more open the economy. During this period and under the circumstances described, the proposition that exchange rate instability and rising inflation were the causes of low investment and growth rates in the EC won substantial support. Against this the EC took its second concrete step towards establishing a stable European monetary bloc.

In July 1978 the Bremen European Council agreed on the desirability of closer monetary cooperation and the establishment of a zone of monetary stability in Europe. However, in contrast to the Werner plan, full-scale monetary union was not mentioned. It seems that EC leaders of the day were reluctant to accept the significant institutional changes which a monetary union requires. Thus, the Commission drew up a plan for an EMS with far more limited objectives for the immediate future than a monetary union, although the plan did not preclude its future evolution into a monetary union. The final form of the system was agreed in December 1978 by eight EC member states. The UK was not satisfied by the plan and stayed outside the agreement.

The European Monetary System

The EMS in its present form should be considered mainly as an attempt to establish greater monetary stability within the EC. However, as there is nothing which precludes EMS[7] at least formally from gradually developing into European Monetary Union, it is worthwhile considering its performance thus far. The system has the following characteristics: central rates are established *vis-à-vis* the European Currency Unit (ECU) which is a weighted average basket of all EC currencies. The ECU, besides its function as a numeraire for fixing central rates, serves also as a denominator for operations under the intervention and credit mechanism and as a means of settlements between national central banks, with the potential to become the parallel currency for the EC.

From the central rates *vis-à-vis* the ECU, bilateral exchange rates are calculated and a permissible fluctuation margin of ± 2.25 per cent set (except for the Italian lira which is allowed a margin of ± 6 per cent *vis-à-vis* the other European currencies participating in the scheme). When two currencies hit the bilateral permissible margin, the two relevant central banks intervene to an unlimited extent to keep the rate within the margin. For that purpose the credit facilities available to participating countries have been extended substantially. In the short run, member states can borrow an unlimited amount. In addition, there are medium-term credit facilities available up to 14 billion ECU and long-term credit facilities up to 11 billion ECU.

Furthermore, a partial pooling of gold and dollar reserves of the EMS participating member states is established. Twenty per cent of the gold and dollar reserves of member states have been deposited in the European Fund for Monetary Cooperation and are to be transferred to a European Monetary Fund which initially was to be set up two years after the start of the EMS. Against these deposits, ECU can be issued and used as a means of payments in debt settlements between participating banks.

For each EMS country its exchange rate *vis-à-vis* the ECU serves also as a divergence indicator of the value of the national currency from the EC's average. A threshold of divergence is set at 75 per cent of the maximum permissible fluctuation margin *vis-à-vis* the ECU. This threshold is reached when that currency's market rate is at its intervention point against all other currencies in the EC. When the threshold is crossed, a 'presumption' that policy measures should be taken by the member's central bank is established. These measures can be either monetary policy or diversified intervention or even a change of its central rate. This latter element is crucial: each participating country retains the option of changing its central rate although the consent of all participating members is required for this. Finally, it is obvious that the EMS's philosophy is that the commitment to stable rates should impel coordination of national economic policies.

From the analysis of the intentions for establishing the system and the functions it is expected to perform, it can be said that the EMS represents a step forward in comparison to the 'snake' agreement. For instance, in the EMS there are provisions forcing central banks to intervene when bilateral permissible margins are crossed; a partial pooling of reserves; and much more extended credit facilities, etc., which make the system substantially more integrative than the 'snake'. However, three points must be remembered: first, that as in the 'snake', there is no commitment to irrevocably fixed central rates as the national central banks can always bargain for changes in the central rate. Then the problem is whether this characteristic strengthens the system by making it more elastic or weakens it by imposing on the members a smaller pressure for monetary discipline. If the system is very loose, continuous realignments of the central rates would be necessary, thus causing the EMS to fail as a step in the direction of European Monetary Union. Second, establishing a divergence indicator is a significant development. It has been argued[8] that divergence indicators provide an objective measure for deciding the need for inter-member state policy coordination. Hence, the introduction of divergence indicators may help realize the implicitly undertaken commitment for policy coordination which would lead the system towards European Monetary Union. However, it must be stressed that when the threshold of divergence is crossed, there is no firm obligation to adopt corrective measures. The agreement establishes only a 'presumption' that action should be taken. Third, although the ECU is to be initially used only as a means of payments between central banks, it may be the medium for establishing a parallel European currency to be used by the private sector. In its present form, the ECU can out-compete only the weak currencies and thus it can attract private investors only if they have to choose between it and the weak currencies. However, the establishment of a mechanism, whereby the ECU's purchasing power would be ensured, may allow the ECU to develop into the single European currency of the future.

The performance of the European Monetary System

A year after launching EMS, the EC claimed success:

A significant contribution towards a greater measure of monetary stability in Europe has come from the operation of the EMS. Exchange rate fluctuations have been greatly reduced among currencies participating in the exchange mechanism, largely as a result of active monetary cooperation between central banks.[9]

'The EMS . . . has operated in an exemplary fashion',[10] thus confounding sceptics who had predicted a probable collapse.[11] Not that the system has been entirely without strain. Contrary to expectations one of EMS's basic aims proved elusive from early on:

The economic divergencies between the States participating in the EMS have tended to widen, particularly in the areas of inflation and costs, and this meant that a readjustment within the EMS was necessary. The realignment is intended to ensure greater convergence between the economies of the Member States.[12]

In fact, a number of realignments in central rates have been made. In September 1979 the German mark was revalued by 2 per cent and the Danish krone devalued by 3 per cent against the other currencies in the system. A further 5 per cent devaluation of the krone was made in November 1979. In March 1981 the Italian lira was devalued by 6 per cent. In October 1981 the mark and the Dutch guilder were revalued by 5.5 per cent, while the franc and lira were devalued by 3 per cent. In February 1982 the Belgian franc was devalued by 8.5 per cent and the krone by 3 per cent. Nevertheless, the EC's verdict is that, despite these frequent but necessary realignments, the EMS 'has functioned satisfactorily'.[13]

Although it is rather early to judge the EMS's performance or to predict the future from current trends, it is worth examining how the system has worked so far.[14] Table 1 represents the market rates of EC currencies *vis-à-vis* the ECU and Table 2 represents the percentage changes of these rates over the preceding period. These changes reflect both market-induced variations and the effects of realignments.

Table 1   Values in national currencies of one ECU

Year	Belgium Luxembourg	Denmark	Germany	France	Ireland	Italy	Netherlands	United Kingdom*
	BFR	DKR	DM	FF	IRL	LIT	HFL	UKL
1978	40.06	7.02	2.56	5.74	0.66	1080.22	2.75	0.66
1979	40.17	7.21	2.51	5.83	0.67	1138.50	2.75	0.65
1980	40.60	7.83	2.52	5.87	0.68	1189.21	2.76	0.60
1981	41.29	7.92	2.51	6.04	0.69	1212.81	2.78	0.55
1982 Jan.	41.61	7.99	2.44	6.21	0.69	1308.88	2.68	0.57

*Not a member of EMS (not participating in the fluctuation margins).
Source: Eurostatistics, various issues, Eurostat Publications.

Table 2   Percentage changes of the values in national currencies of one ECU*

Period	BFR	DKR	DM	FF	IRL	LIT	HFL	UKL
1979–80	+1.07	+8.60	+0.40	+0.69	+1.50	+4.45	+0.36	−7.70
1980–1	+1.70	+1.15	−0.40	+2.92	+1.47	+1.99	+0.72	−8.33
1981–Jan.								
1982	+0.76	+0.88	−2.79	+2.81	−0.0	+7.92	−3.60	+3.64

*The sign + indicates depreciation, and the sign − appreciation, both *vis-à-vis* the ECU.
Source: Table 1.

Table 3   Average exchange rate changes *vis-à-vis* the ECU (per cent)

Group	1980	1981
EEC-9		
a. Absolute	3.10	2.35
b. Algebraic	1.17	0.15
EMS countries		
a. Absolute	2.44	1.48
b. Algebraic	2.44	1.36
EMS countries, excluding Italy		
a. Absolute	2.10	1.39
b. Algebraic	2.10	1.26

Source: Tables 1 and 2.

Table 3 represents the average percentage changes of the fluctuations of EC currencies, taken in groupings, *vis-à-vis* the ECU. For the three groupings examined (that is, the EC of the Nine, the countries participating in the EMS, and the EMS countries excluding Italy, whose currency fluctuates more than the currencies of the other members), the absolute variability and the algebraic sum of the variabilities recorded have been reduced between 1980 and 1981. But, despite this reduction in fluctuations, convergence in economic performance and economic policies, and in particular convergence in monetary policies, have not been achieved. Table 4 represents, as an example, the percentage changes in money supply of the EC member states over the periods 1979–80 and 1980–1. The data clearly show no tendency towards convergence over the period under consideration, at least as regards the money supply. However, it seems that an attempt at policy harmonization has already begun, which could be regarded as a first step toward achieving greater convergence in the future. Thus, from mid-1980, seven EC member states (Denmark, Belgium, Luxembourg, the Netherlands, Italy, Ireland and the UK), where inflationary pressures are relatively excessive, are applying restrictive budgetary and economic policies, while the rest are pursuing broadly neutral budgetary and monetary policies.[15] In addition, all member states give priority to policies to combat balance of payments problems.

Conclusion

Monetary union is necessary for progress towards economic and political integration in the EC. The process of monetary integration will lead in due course to a

Table 4   Money supply changes (over corresponding period of previous year) (per cent)

Year	1980	1981		
Quarter		I	II	III
Country				
Belgium	−0.1	2.4	5.8	3.7
Denmark	5.9	9.6	13.8	16.7
France	8.0	9.3	10.8	13.3
FRG	2.4	3.7	1.6	0.3
Ireland	4.6	17.9	15.9	14.0
Italy	15.9	14.2	12.2	. . .
Netherlands	4.2	5.7	3.8	0.9
UK	4.5	7.4	12.6	11.5
Greece	20.3	5.8	. . .	. . .

. . . not available.

Source: International Financial Statistics, April 1982, IMF.

single European currency, a European central bank, and a European monetary policy (that is, to 'some of the crucial elements of political union').[16] The EMS has resulted from political compromises and economic necessity, which dictated that some kind of balance between EC member states should be reached. As such, the EMS, in its present form, is not a substitute for EMU. The EMS has technically worked satisfactorily: the frequent and significant realignments have not caused undue stress to the system. Economically, the EMS has not as yet led to a degree of convergence in the EC member states' economic performance. With the UK and Greece outside the EMS, the political foundations for monetary integration are impaired. The EC's enlargement to include Spain and Portugal will obviously make convergence more difficult. However, nothing in the EMS can prevent it from developing into a system for European Monetary Union.[17] A central monetary authority can be established,[18] the ECU can in time become the European currency and the projected European Monetary Fund can develop into the central bank of the EC. But these institutional changes cannot be achieved without some degree of convergence of economic policy and performance which, in turn, require a genuine political commitment towards the unification of Europe. In conclusion, further progress towards monetary integration depends on the political will of the participating member states to unite.

Notes

1. Rudden, R. and Wyatt, D. (eds), *Basic Community Laws* (Oxford, 1980), Article 2.
2. Ibid., Article 3.
3. Ibid., Chapter 3.
4. See Vaubel, R., *Strategies for Currency Unification* (Tübingen, 1978) and Vaubel, R., *Choice in European Monetary Integration* (London, Institute of Economic Affairs, Occasional Paper 55, 1979).
5. Ibid.
6. 'Economic and Monetary Union in the Community' (The Werner Report), *Bull. EC*, Supplement 11–1970.
7. See Vaubel, op. cit., for different views.
8. See Thygesen, N., 'The Emerging European Monetary System: Precursors, First Steps and Policy Options' in Triffin, R. (ed.), *EMS: The Emerging European Monetary System* (Brussels, National Bank of Belgium, 1979).
9. *Bull. EC*, 4–1980, p. 34.

10. *Bull. EC*, 12–1980, p. 30.
11. See Brittan, S., *European Monetary System* (London, Hedderwick Stirling Grumbar, 1978) and Thornton, J., 'On Recent Trends, the EMS will probably collapse', *Euromoney* (August 1979), 117–19.
12. *Bull. EC*, 9–1981, p. 15.
13. *Bull. EC*, 12–1981, p. 16.
14. For similar exercises and on the EMS in general, see Zis, G. and Sumner, M. T. (eds), *European Monetary Union: Progress and Prospects* (London, Macmillan, 1982).
15. Emerson, M., 'Experience under the EMS and prospects for further progress towards EMU' in Zis and Sumner, op. cit.
16. Trezise, P. H., 'Political Commitment: The Central Question' in Trezise, P. H. (ed.), *The European Monetary System: Its Promise and Prospects* (Washington D.C., Brookings Institute, 1979).
17. For arguments for and against this proposition, see the papers and comments by van Ypersele de Strihou, J., Bryant, R. C., Emerson, M. and Cohen, B. J. in Trezise, op. cit.
18. At its 15–19 February 1982 part-session the European Parliament adopted a resolution calling for the creation of a European currency authority. See *Bull. EC*, 2–1982, p. 19.

13   The European Community and Africa, the Caribbean and the Pacific

CHRISTOPHER STEVENS

The foundations of EC Third World policy

Even though the EC is now in its third decade, it lacks many common policies. Yet several of them have a direct relevance to the Third World. As a result, Third World affairs have a higher profile in the EC institutions than they do in many of the member states. The most important common policies for the Third World are the EC's trade, agriculture and aid policies, although the last of these is only partly common. At the centre of the EC's formal relations with the Third World sits the Lomé Convention that covers a range of political, commercial and financial links between the EC and over sixty states in Africa, the Caribbean and the Pacific that are usually known collectively as the ACP.

The existence of a Common External Tariff (CET) means that the foundations of Europe's foreign trade regime are established at EC level. Thus the member states adopt a common position at meetings of the GATT and of UNCTAD and have negotiated at EC level a host of bilateral and multilateral trade agreements with Third World states. The CET's purity is reduced in practice as member states adopt to a greater or lesser extent national policies that influence trade flows. Most important are the growing number of non-tariff barriers (NTBs) to imports. Whereas the EC institutions have an unambiguous responsibility for setting tariff policy, their position on NTBs is much less secure. The member states have negotiated bilaterally numerous 'voluntary export restraints' (VERs) with developing countries. None the less, the most important NTB for the Third World, the Multi-fibre Agreement (MFA) which limits their exports of clothing and textiles, is still negotiated at EC level even though the EC's internal solidarity was heavily strained during the negotiations for the third MFA in 1981.

Many of the NTBs imposed by the Ten, either on a national or on an EC basis, are designed to limit Third World exports of manufactured goods. Relatively few are aimed at agricultural products. This is because the EC's agricultural sector already receives extensive protection against import competition through the Common Agricultural Policy (CAP)· which is the second major influence on the EC's Third World policy. The CAP tends to limit Third World agricultural exports to the EC to commodities (often unprocessed tropical products) that do not compete directly with EC produce, and to a small number of competitive products for which special agreements have been negotiated, e.g. sugar. These agreements are usually for limited quantities, and have been negotiated in the face of strong opposition from the EC farming lobby which keeps them under continuing pressure.

The third main element of the EC's Third World policy is the aid programme. Unlike trade and agriculture, this is only partially common. There are three main types of aid programme. There are multi-annual, EC-level programmes financed outside the EC budget. The European Development Fund (EDF), which finances the aid provisions of the Lomé Convention, is the largest of these, but the EC also has financial protocols to its commercial agreements with a number of other Third World states, most notably those in North Africa and the Middle East. Then there are annually-agreed aid programmes financed out of the EC budget. These include the food aid programme and the non-associates' aid programme that covers all countries lacking a specially negotiated, extra-budgetary aid agreement. Finally, there are the member states' bilateral aid programmes. Some of these tend to reinforce the geographical and political bias of the EC's programmes, but with some member states the reverse is true. Thus, the UK has used its aid to offset the EC's geographical emphasis on Africa and its neglect of South Asia. The proportion of aid channelled through EC and bilateral programmes varies widely between the member states. In 1979, 59 per cent of Italy's official development assistance (ODA), but only 6 per cent of Denmark's, went through the EC. For the four largest donors, the proportions in 1977 were: France, 8 per cent, Germany, 10 per cent, Britain, 12 per cent, and Holland, 9 per cent.[1]

The ACP and the 'Pyramid of Privilege'

The EC's commercial and financial links with the Third World are regulated by a set of over twenty bilateral and multilateral agreements (see Table 1). These

Table 1   The network of EEC relations with the Third World

	Countries	Agreement
(1)	African, Caribbean and Pacific countries	Lomé Convention (1980 for 5 years)
(2)	Applicants to the EEC:	
	Greece	Association Agreement (1962)
	Spain	Preferential Trade Agreement (1970)
	Portugal	Free Trade Agreement (1972)
(3)	Maghreb countries: Algeria, Morocco, Tunisia	Preferential Trade and Cooperation Agreements (1976 for unlimited period)
(4)	Mashreq countries: Egypt, Jordan, Lebanon, Syria	Preferential Trade and Cooperation Agreements (1977 for unlimited period)
(5)	Other Mediterranean countries:	
	Israel	Preferential Trade and Cooperation Agreement (1975 for unlimited period)
	Yugoslavia	Preferential Trade and Cooperation Agreement (1980 for unlimited period)
	Turkey, Malta, Cyprus	Association Agreements (1980, 1971 and 1973, respectively, for unlimited periods)
(6)	Other LDCs (except Taiwan)	Generalized System of Preferences
(7)	South Asia, Bangladesh, India, Pakistan, Sri Lanka	Non-preferential Commercial Cooperation Agreements (1976, 1974, 1976, 1975, respectively, for 5 years)
	ASEAN Indonesia, Malaysia, the Philippines, Singapore, Thailand	(One agreement, 1979 for 5 years)
	Latin America, Argentina, Brazil, Mexico, Uruguay	(1972, 1974, 1976, 1975, respectively, for 3 to 5 years)
(8)	China	Non-preferential Trade Agreements (1979 for 5 years)
	Romania	(1980 for 5 years)

Source: Stevens, C. (ed.), *EEC and the Third World: A Survey I* (London, Hodder & Stoughton, 1981), p. 61.

agreements form a pyramid: those at the top provide more favourable treatment than those at the base. The countries at the top have preferences not only over developed countries but also over other members of the pyramid. It is therefore a shifting pyramid, since improvements in the terms for some states can cut the value of concessions made to others. For example, improvements to the Generalised System of Preferences (GSP), which is at the base of the pyramid, with very broad geographical coverage and a relatively low level of trade concessions, may reduce the margin of preference accorded to other groups.

At the top of the pyramid sit the ACP. Their trade regime is more favourable than that offered by the EC to any other Third World group, and they receive more EC-level aid, both in absolute and in per capita terms (see Table 2). This

Table 2   Percentage share of the EEC in the Maghreb's total trade (by value)

		1969	1973	1978
Algeria	Imports	69.8	66.9	57.8
	Exports	81.1	64.7	38.1
Morocco	Imports	56.9	54.4	51.4
	Exports	66.1	64.6	56.4
Tunisia	Imports	58.2	62.9	65.2
	Exports	59.1	55.4	57.3

Source: UN Yearbook of International Trade Statistics, 1978 (Vol. 1).

concentration on one group of Third World states, primarily Black Africa, has drawn criticism from many quarters. Lomé has been attacked as a divisive instrument, weakening Third World solidarity. It is certainly true that under the terms of the Lomé Convention the ACP are allowed to comment upon the EC's annual proposals for the GSP and that in cases where the ACP have lodged an objection the EC has tended to limit the concession. Another related criticism is that the Lomé Convention is a neo-colonial device to maintain a relationship of dependence between Europe and Africa. Some European supporters of Lomé certainly believe that it creates a European 'sphere of influence'. This attitude, in turn, has provoked the criticism that the ACP are the wrong region. Concentration on Africa means the relative neglect of other regions of more 'interest' to the EC, however 'interest' may be defined: if in terms of poverty, the exclusion of India and Bangladesh is hard to justify; if in terms of commercial importance, the absence of South America and South-East Asia is odd; and if in terms of international politics and military strategy then, again, Africa plus some islands in the Caribbean and the Pacific is not an obvious focus.

The origins of the Lomé Convention

These criticisms need to be understood in the context of Lomé's origins, and evaluated in the light of its actual impact. The Lomé Convention grew out of the twin roots of the pre-existing relationship of the Six with France's African colonies in the Rome Treaty, subsequently modified after they became independent by the establishment of the Yaoundé Conventions, and out of the need to make provisions for Britain's former colonies when the Six expanded to Nine. Commonwealth LDCs were split into the 'associables' and the 'non-associables', and the former eventually joined the Yaoundé states to sign the first Lomé Convention in February 1975.

The Yaoundé Conventions were clearly neo-colonial arrangements by dint of their terms (notably the requirement that the African signatories provide reverse preferences for EC exports), the manner in which they were implemented (aid was distributed in very much a master-supplicant atmosphere), and the mercantilist ethos underpinning them (with an emphasis on static comparative advantage and little incentive to structural change). Partly as a result, the Six's negotiations with Nigeria and then with Kenya, Uganda and Tanzania to join Yaoundé proved largely abortive.

By the time of Britain's accession to the EC, the Yaoundé structure was under pressure. The EC's negotiations with the southern Mediterranean states (see Chapter 14) and its failure to agree terms with Nigeria and East Africa underlined the Yaoundé model's limited acceptability to other Third World states. Moreover, German and Dutch circles were critical of the French colonial-mercantilist approach. Finally, OPEC's success in raising oil prices in 1973 provoked a surge of interest in a New International Economic Order (NIEO). The opportunity was taken, there-fore, to negotiate an agreement to accommodate Britain's ex-colonies that claimed to be a qualitative departure not only from Yaoundé but also from other North–South agreements. Lomé I was described by the EC as a 'pioneering model of cooperation between equal partners' and by the Senegalese Finance Minister, Ousmane Seck, on behalf of the ACP as 'an exemplary type of cooperation'. During the negotiations the ACP exhibited an unexpected degree of coordination which contributed materially to the final outcome. This unity, which contrasted with the EC's somewhat disorganized and defensive posture, was due to a combina-tion of factors. Nigeria and Senegal established an early rapprochement that brought the Anglophones and Francophones together. Nigeria, in particular, flushed with oil wealth, was anxious to establish itself as a continental leader and could afford to take a hard line. Several other Anglophone states saw Lomé as a guarantee against discrimination by the EC in favour of their neighbours; they could afford, therefore, to see the negotiations falter, so long as the EC did not conclude with some of the states an agreement that excluded them. The Caribbean sugar-producing states had a strong interest in the negotiations because of their need to agree a successor to the Commonwealth Sugar Agreement under which Britain had imported cane sugar.

There was some justification for the claim that Lomé I marked a substantial improvement on the Yaoundés. But while Lomé I possessed valuable features and, putting aside the wider issue of those LDCs outside its charmed circle, represented a perfectly respectable deal for the ACP, it was in no sense a 'road to Damascus' conversion for either side. The continuity from Yaoundé II is as evident as the change. Writing of Lomé II, former EDF Director Jacques Ferrandi argued 'Elle ressemblera, comme une soeur jumelle à l'actuelle Convention de Lomé, laquelle ressemblait, comme une grande soeur, à la Convention de Yaoundé.'[2]

Institutions and individuals commonly tend to inflate their achievements, and usually no harm is done thereby. However, the Lomé II negotiations were made more difficult and more acrimonious than they need otherwise have been because both sides had been taken in by their own rhetoric. The ACP entered the negotia-tions with the stated aim of building upon Lomé I. A formal start was made to the negotiations at a ministerial conference in Brussels commencing 27 July 1978. The ACP negotiating posture, as spelled out by its spokesman, P. J. Patterson of Jamaica, was that 'the Lomé Convention always represented no more than a step, albeit a significant one, towards their goal. . . . Today our sole purpose here is to seek to make with you, our partners, another significant step towards that urgently needed goal.'[3] From the outset, it was clear that this view of the negotiations differed fundamentally from that held by the EC. The then chairman of the EC Council, H-D. Genscher, explained the EC's position in his welcoming address: 'The Convention has proved itself in practice. The negotiations will therefore not deal with sweeping changes or renovations, but with adjustments and improvements.'[4]

Four factors contributed to the sour atmosphere in which the negotiations were concluded. First and most fundamentally, the Nine were unwilling to make any major new concessions. In general, their perceptions of the continuing world recession urged retrenchment in dealings with the South rather than the kind of imaginative, large-scale transfers and concessions that were being widely recommended to facilitate trade expansion, break the protectionist spiral and unleash the dynamic forces of the market. Second, the EC has an in-built institutional bias towards impasse. The procedure is for the Commission to propose to the Council a set of negotiating positions, on the basis of which the Council issues the Commission with a 'mandate' for negotiation that provides only limited leeway for manoeuvre. Hence the Commission has to refer back to the Council whenever the negotiations reach a stalemate and a new initiative is required. Furthermore, Council members need on occasion to refer back to their national capitals before decisions can be taken. Because of the Nine's reluctance to make concessions, the Commission's negotiating mandate for Lomé II was much more tightly drawn than its Lomé I mandate. Moreover, it has been argued that the Commission omitted to take advantage of what little flexibility its mandate bestowed. Hence the third factor contributing to the bad feeling was the rigid and, according to some, high-handed attitude of EC negotiators. Whereas Commissioner Claude Cheysson, the political head of DG8 (the Directorate-General for Development), had played a leading role in formulating Lomé I, the negotiations for its successor were left largely in the hands of Commission officials. M. Cheysson only became closely involved after the talks had reached an impasse at Easter 1979. Finally, the ACP played their hand badly. At the early negotiating sessions they appeared to be in disarray, in sharp contrast to their position during the Lomé I negotiations. The result was that the EC's confidence in the strength of its position turned into over-confidence. The denouement came in May 1979 when, to the EC's demonstrable surprise, the ACP rejected its aid offer. Following this, M. Cheysson began to play a more active role, and partly because of his efforts the two sides returned to the negotiating table in June 1979. But after two days the talks broke up in confusion. The EC had been so confident of success that the then chairman of the Council of Ministers, French Foreign Minister, Jean François-Poncet, who left the meeting before it ended, gave a confident press conference at which he declared the negotiations to have been concluded successfully, only to be embarrassed a few hours later when the ACP spokesman, Senegalese Finance Minister, Ousmane Seck, firmly stated that the two sides had not reached agreement. From July to October, therefore, the talks were in a curious limbo. The EC officially maintained that they had been concluded; the ACP demurred. Throughout this time discussions continued at an official level, and even delayed the signing ceremony by two hours. Nevertheless, despite their revolt from May onwards, in the end the ACP signed on the dotted line on 31 October 1979 and agreed to terms that on essential points were very similar to those initially offered by the EC.

Two significant developments since the signing of Lomé II have been the accession of Zimbabwe and the failure of Angola and Mozambique to join. The possibility of Zimbabwe signing the Lomé Convention was discussed by Robert Mugabe and Claude Cheysson even before the transfer of power. The Zimbabwe Government's intentions were made public on Independence Day and its formal application to join was accepted by the summit of EC and ACP ministers held in Nairobi in May 1980. Until then all was plain sailing; but then the difficulties began. The principle of Zimbabwe membership was not in doubt. The problem concerned the terms of entry and focused on aid and trade. The aid package negotiated for Lomé II applies only to those states that signed on 31 October 1979. New entrants have to negotiate entirely new aid agreements. Zimbabwe's aid entitlement under normal EC criteria was fairly high. Some EC member states were reluctant to endorse a major new aid package for Zimbabwe so soon after agreeing to provide EUA 5607 million under the main Lomé II negotiations. France in particular was reticent about a large fund, to which it would perforce be a major contributor, for an English-speaking country outside its normal sphere of interest. Britain, which might have been expected to take a keen interest in Zimbabwe's case, was constrained both because of the Conservative Government's policy of cutting aid in general and because the Zimbabwe negotiations occurred at the same time as Britain began its attempt to reduce its contribution to the EC budget, which made it reluctant to press for any major increases in spending. On the trade front, problems centred on Zimbabwe's position as an exporter of commodities covered by the CAP. The prospect of Zimbabwe—a major producer of sugar, tobacco, and beef—benefitting from the Lomé trade concessions roused opposition in certain EC quarters.

On 16 September 1980, the Council agreed on its mandate, which was tougher than had been expected. The UK and Denmark pressed for generous aid and trade concessions during the Council deliberations, but other members were either hostile or ambivalent. France led the opposition, particularly on sugar, and was supported by Belgium. Zimbabwe's beef and tobacco exports worried Ireland and Italy respectively. Holland, which might have been expected to push Zimbabwe's case, was torn between its desire to increase aid to Southern Africa and its concern about the effects of Zimbabwean trade on the CAP, which it strongly supports. Germany was similarly ambivalent, having to balance its political interest in Southern Africa against the political imperatives of its forthcoming general election.

The first round of talks between the Commission and the Zimbabwe delegation took place on 22–4 September 1980 in Brussels. When the terms of the mandate were first announced there was speculation that Zimbabwe might call the EC's bluff by rejecting them outright. But it did not. Instead, the two sides came within spitting distance of each other on all major points except sugar. Even on sugar, remaining problems were more cosmetic than fundamental, and duly overcome by a largely cosmetic formulation. Zimbabwe formally signed the Lomé Convention on 4 November 1980, but its accession was not ratified finally by all EC member states until 1982.

In the run-up to Zimbabwean independence, there was hope in the Commission that Mozambique would join Lomé on Zimbabwe's coat-tails. Commissioner Cheysson encouraged both Mozambique and Angola to send observers to the Lomé II negotiations. However, Mozambique—like Tanzania and Zanzibar in the 1960s—has been caught up in the conflict between East and West Germany. The matter is exacerbated because Lomé signatories have to accept Annex 35—the 'Berlin' clause—which implies recognition of West Berlin as part of the FRG. The East Germans reportedly threatened to withdraw aid if Mozambique signed the

Convention. Whether for this or for other reasons, Mozambique decided not to apply for membership of the ACP. The FRG responded by opposing aid to Mozambique from the non-associates' budget and from the Southern Africa regional projects vote of the EDF.

The Lomé institutions

The Lomé Convention has had an impact on the EC's institutional arrangements in two ways. First, it has spawned a set of joint EC–ACP consultative institutions. In the euphoria following the signing of Lomé I, these were described as joint decision-making instruments of equal parties. In practice, they are nothing of the kind since the EC is usually the dominant partner and has tended not to perceive its interests as requiring it to give way to ACP positions. None the less, the institutions are useful as channels of communication and, sometimes, as a catalyst for EC concessions at the margin. Moreover, a number of Third World states outside the ACP have sought a similar set of institutions. The second type of impact has been on the EC's internal decision-making apparatus. The Lomé Convention has given the Directorate-General for Development a substantial policy to administer. This sets it apart from many other DGs, having little to administer, and it is one of the reasons why North–South relations tend to have a higher profile in EC institutions than in many of the member states.

The joint EC–ACP institutions include an annual ministerial council, an annual consultative assembly of parliamentarians supported by a semi-annual joint committee, and two special institutions, the Centre for Industrial Development and a Technical Centre for Agricultural and Rural Cooperation. In addition, there is a Brussels-based permanent joint committee of ambassadors, with the ACP ambassadors being serviced by an ACP Secretariat, that is potentially a valuable tool for the ACP in negotiations with the EC. However, this potential has only been realized partially, largely because of the Secretariat's relationship with the committee of ACP ambassadors. This is the reverse of the relationship between the EC's Council of Ministers and the Commission. Whereas the Commission can propose to the Council whatever it wishes, the ACP Secretariat can only investigate and make proposals on subjects referred specifically to it by the committee of ACP ambassadors. In practice, the committee has tended to be sparing in its instructions to the Secretariat and has consequently often been ill-informed in its negotiations with the Commission. A striking illustration occurred in 1981 when the April meeting of the joint Council of Ministers agreed cuts in the 1980 STABEX payments because claims on the fund exceeded the amount available. The ACP ministers agreed to the cuts believing them to be relatively small. In fact, cuts of about one-half were required. When the true picture emerged at a meeting of the joint committee of ambassadors in June, there were howls of protest from the ACP. Yet, because of the simple arithmetic on which STABEX payments are based, the scale of the fund's over-commitment (if not the precise amount) could easily have been estimated by the ACP in advance.

On the EC side, the two Commission DGs primarily responsible for Third World affairs are the Directorate-General for Development (DG8) and the Directorate-General for External Relations (DG1), although others, most notably agriculture (DG6) are also involved on specific issues within their portfolios. DG8's main task is to administer the provisions of the Lomé Convention which, since they cover trade as well as aid, draws it into the whole range of North–South economic issues. DG1's main task with respect to the Third World is in negotiating trade agreements outside the Lomé context such as the MFA and the GSP. On agricultural trade issues, such as the International Wheat Agreement, DG6 has a major involvement. The Lomé Convention gives DG8 a certain *esprit de corps* lacking in the Directorates-General that have no substantial policy to administer. Moreover, the Lomé aid programme, unlike many of the Commission's other major activities, is one that in principle, if not always in practice, is not subordinate to the dictates of the Council of Ministers. The financial aid for the ACP is not drawn from the EC budget. Instead, it is taken from the EDF which is voted by the member states every five years outside the framework of the annual budget. The Council of Ministers is fully involved in the process of fixing member states' contributions and the size of each EDF. However, in principle, once the EDF has been approved, disbursement is a Commission responsibility and the Council is entitled only to give an opinion on the desirability of particular projects. In practice, the Commission is jealous of its ultimate authority, but at the same time it recognizes the pragmatic need not to alienate the Council. When DG8 is satisfied with a proposed aid project, the EDF Committee examines it. The Commission insists that the EDF Committee, on which sit representatives of the Ten, can only express an opinion. But, if the opinion is unfavourable the Commission invariably takes it into account and re-formulates—or rejects—a project to accommodate the Ten.

DG8's *esprit de corps* has been bolstered by its Commissioner's prestige. Until he retired in May 1981 to become the new French Foreign Minister, Claude Cheysson was an influential Commissioner who tended to carry more weight on North–South issues than the Commissioner for External Relations, Wilhelm Haferkamp. Thus, the relationship between the development and external affairs departments is quite different in the Commission and in the member states. At both the official and the political level, the Commission's development department is at least the equal of its external relations department; in most of the member states this is not the case.

A particularly striking illustration of the power balance in the Commission is the fact that the EC's quasi-diplomatic representatives in a growing number of Third World countries are operationally responsible to DG8 and not to DG1. This break from the traditions of all the member states grew out of the original purpose of these overseas delegations, which was to act as on-the-spot auditors in the Yaoundé Convention countries and check on aid spending. With the 'new era' of the Lomé Convention, their number increased and their responsibilities were extended to make the Delegate a representative of the EC and not just a financial controller. The delegations have now spread beyond the ACP to other countries receiving EC aid, notably the Maghreb and Mashreq. DG1 and DG8 are now competing for control of future EC overseas offices in areas where aid spending is small; so far, DG8 has usually won.

Lomé in practice

It is probably too early to expect the Lomé trade regime to have had any major discernible impact on ACP–EC trade flows. Table 3 shows the share of EC trade accruing to the ACP, other developing countries, and the industrialized countries for the period 1972–80. Extreme caution is needed in drawing conclusions from such aggregate figures. EC–ACP trade is dominated by a small number of countries (eight account for nearly 70 per cent of ACP exports to the EC), and by relatively few commodities which have experienced sharp peaks and troughs in the 1970s affecting the value of ACP exports. None the less, the striking feature of Table 3

Table 3   EC–ACP Trade

EC Imports	1972	1975	1976	1977	1978	1979	1980
Total value	68.0	138.5	164.3	196.0	227.3	299.0	378.1
Per cent from:							
Western industrialized							
countries	55	48	47	48	52	51	49
Developing countries	36	44	45	44	40	40	42
ACP	7	7	7	7	7	7	7

EC Exports	1972	1975	1976	1977	1978	1979	1980
Total value	74.9	149.9	157.2	187.5	221.6	266.1	312.5
Per cent from:							
Western industrialized							
countries	61	51	53	52	52	54	53
Developing countries	28	37	37	38	38	36	37
ACP	6	7	7	8	7	6	7

Source: Eurostat.

is the consistency of the ACP's share of EC trade. ACP exports to the EC, in particular, have exhibited considerable stability.

This finding is consistent with what should have been expected as Lomé's trade provisions tend to reflect the nature of existing flows. It is not consistent, however, with EC claims that Lomé is a particularly liberal regime. In practice, it is liberal in four main areas. First, in cases where the commodities in question would enter the EC market duty free in any case, as the ACP are primarily exporters of raw materials (see Table 4), the proportion of goods falling into this category is very

Table 4   Commodity composition of ACP exports to EC (1977)

Product	% by value	Cumulative %
Oil	28.1	28.1
Coffee	16.1	44.2
Cocoa	10.2	54.3
Copper	7.6	62.0
Timber	5.0	67.0
Sugar	3.1	70.0
Iron Ore	3.0	73.1
Groundnuts	2.8	75.9
Aluminium	2.2	78.9
Cotton (excl. fabrics)	1.9	79.9

Source: Analysis of trade between the European Community and the ACP states. Series: Trade Flows (Eurostat, Luxembourg, 1979), p. 5.4.

high—in the region of 75 per cent. Over a quarter of ACP exports to the EC are accounted for by petroleum (mostly from the ACP's two OPEC members, Nigeria and Gabon), an import the EC would not normally want to restrict with or without a Lomé Convention!

The second area of Lomé trade liberalism concerns products lacking unrestricted access, but which would be imported in the normal course of events (because an EC demand exists which cannot be satisfied locally) but which need not be obtained from the ACP. Examples are cocoa and bananas, for which ACP exporters have a tariff preference over Latin American producers. In such cases the 'cost' of the Lomé privilege is borne not by the EC but by third party exporters.

The third area is where the ACP are ill placed to take advantage of the benefits on offer. This particularly concerns industrial products given free access under the Convention. The trouble is that the ACP's capacity to export industrial products is very limited. There are few obvious common factors linking the sixty or more countries scattered over three continents, and setting them apart from other LDCs. But one such link is the lower than average share of manufactures in their exports. This need not necessarily be considered a fault in the Convention, particularly if the trade concessions encouraged the development of processing and manu-facturing industries in the ACP. However, the signs are that where an ACP state is able to take advantage of its theoretical rights, it runs the risk of administrative action to discourage it. This has happened, for example, with clothing exports from Mauritius. Although it is a contractual agreement, the Convention is sub-stantially subject to the EC's interpretation.

The fourth area is the most significant. Some real access concessions are granted to the ACP which might not have been available without the Convention, and which are not necessarily obtained at the expense of other LDCs. These cover some of the products that fall within the purview of the CAP. This is a relatively small area—accounting for 9 per cent of ACP exports to the EC—but is of some impor-tance for particular countries, for example, Botswana (beef) and the Caribbean (sugar).[5] Not surprisingly, the trade concessions are complex and closely tailored to safeguard EC farming interests.

The main questions to ask of Lomé with respect to aid are: first, has Lomé increased the amount of aid spent either on the ACP or on LDCs as a whole; and second, is aid disbursed through the EC more or less effective than aid disbursed bilaterally or through alternative multilateral institutions such as the World Bank? The EDF's creation in 1958 and its subsequent replenishments have not perceptibly boosted the overall aid 'effort' of any EC member state; displacement has probably outweighed attraction. On the other hand, it is clear that, at the margin, the ACP countries, as opposed to the rest of the developing world, receive more aid thanks to the Lomé Convention than they would without it. An evaluation of comparative effectiveness is difficult both because the comparison is with a range of donors with different performance standards and because of the normative nature of the con-cept of 'aid effectiveness'. The EC spends its aid in two main ways: conventional project aid, and the trade/aid hybrid of STABEX. The money is technically held in an EDF, of which there have now been five. EDF I was created under the Rome Treaty, EDFs II and III under the Yaoundé Conventions, while EDF IV was co-terminous with Lomé I. The sectoral distribution of *commitments* under EDF IV until the end of 1980 is shown in Table 5. The EC likes to claim that the projects it funds are chosen by the recipient country. To an extent this is true, but so it is for other donors. It is hard to discern any justification in the EC's procedures and practice for the claim that the balance of power and choice between donor and recipient is significantly different from that obtaining with other donors. Whoever selects the projects, the result so far has been to emphasize schemes involving a heavy input of infrastructure. A detailed study of EC aid to Cameroon,[6] for example, shows that from 1958, when EDF aid first began, to 1975, some 53 per cent of EC aid was for transport infrastructure, followed by education (mostly school buildings) with 15 per cent, rural agricultural production (13 per cent) and health, again mainly buildings (6 per cent). Yet this period was one

Table 5   Sectoral distribution of commitments from EDF IV to ACP
up to 31 December 1980

Sector	Amount ECU m.	%
Development of Production	1,386.1	45
Industrial development	862.6	
Tourism	16.8	
Rural production	506.7	
Transport and Telecommunications		
Infrastructure	584.3	19
Social Development	380.8	12
Education and Training	227.8	
Health	47.4	
Water engineering, housing and urban administration	105.6	
Trade Promotion	32.6	1
Exceptional Aid	146.0	5
STABEX	374.0	12
Miscellaneous (including Delegations)	146.1	5

Source: EC Commission.

which saw a profound shift in many aid donors' thinking about the most effective
way of encouraging development. Table 5 suggests that the EC's current practice is
not as concentrated on infrastructure as the Cameroon example suggests, but it also
shows that infrastructure remains a high priority. The EC appears to have changed
its approach more slowly than some other major donors. The Cameroon study
concludes that:

> judged against the current criteria for aid effectiveness—sustained economic
> development, increases in local administrative competence, and improvement in
> the lot of the poor—the EDF's aid allocation mechanism seems to have missed
> the mark, predominantly because it failed to adapt to new circumstances and
> new development priorities.[7]

It is against this background of aid diversion and indifferent developmental
impact that the most publicized shortcoming of the EDF—its very slow rate of
spending—must be considered. By the end of 1980 (i.e. nine months after Lomé
I's expiry), 77 per cent of EDF IV had been committed but only 48 per cent
disbursed. By itself, slow spending is not necessarily a major fault, although at a
time of high inflation it underlines the limited importance of the global figures
included in the Lomé aid agreements. But, in the absence of any obvious attraction
of the EDF as compared with alternative aid channels, it casts doubt on the value
for the ACP of Lomé.

One of the major innovations of Lomé I that seemed to set it apart from other
aid programmes was the STABEX scheme, an aid/trade hybrid giving partial compensation to exporters of a limited range of commodities when their prices fall.
STABEX is financed from the EDF. Disbursement is governed by a complex set of
triggers and thresholds but, in theory, is automatic provided that requirements are
met. In practice, the Commission has some discretion in making an award and, of
more significance, claims on STABEX may be scaled down if the total claim exceeds
the funds available as it did in 1981 and will do again in 1982. The scheme's main

raison d'être was removed before it ever came into operation under Lomé I, because in 1975 the IMF extended the size and scope of its much larger compensatory financing facility which has similar aims, and because during the Lomé negotiations one of the unique features of STABEX, which would have channelled payments to the afflicted commodities, was dropped at the ACP's insistence. None the less, STABEX is extremely popular among the ACP. Even states gaining little or nothing from it have pressed not for its abolition but for its extension so that they, too, can benefit. The attractions of STABEX are obvious. Unlike the rest of the EDF it is a fast spender. Moreover, the transfers are effectively free foreign exchange for the recipients, allowing them the maximum flexibility in their use. And for the poorest countries the money is a grant. This cheapness is one reason why STABEX is much preferred by the ACP to the IMF's compensatory financing facility. The other is that the EC does not poke around the dusty corners of the recipient's economic policy and recommend painful adjustments.

The EC's relationship with the ACP has been seen by some as a model for others to follow and by others as a potent extension of neo-colonialism. It is neither. To a large extent the first Lomé Convention reflected the existing links between the EC and the ACP, even though it does contain innovations. Had the politico-economic climate in the EC in the second half of the 1970s been more sympathetic towards the South, the Convention might have provided a framework for significant improvements in its relations with one group of developing countries. But, in the event, it has not done so. None the less, the Lomé Convention may, in an indirect fashion, have produced a greater impact on the EC's Third World policy than this analysis suggests. By strengthening DG8 within the Commission, it may have had an impact on the Commission's overall stance on North–South relations.

Notes

1. House of Lords Select Committee on the European Communities, *Development Aid Policy* (London, HMSO, 1981), Table 3.
2. Ferrandi, J., 'De Lomé I a Lomé II', *Marchés Tropicaux*, 28 (September 1979), 2612.
3. 'Statement by the President of the Council of ACP Ministers on the occasion of the Opening of the Negotiations of the Successor Agreement to the Lomé Convention', ACP Group (Brussels, 24 July 1978), p. 5.
4. 'Speech delivered by the President of the Council of the European Communities, on the occasion of the opening ceremony of the negotiations for the new ACP–EEC Convention', ACP–CEE/95 e/78, p. 5.
5. The sugar concessions are not actually part of the Lomé Convention, but are detailed in a separate protocol; nor were they formally subject to renegotiation in 1978/9.
6. Outlined in Hewitt, A., 'The European Development Fund as a development agent: some results of EDF aid to Cameroon', *ODI Review*, 2 (1979), 41–56.
7. Ibid., p. 55.

14   The European Community and the Mediterranean

ROY HOWARD GINSBERG

Introduction

The chief aim of the EC's Mediterranean Policy—usage of balanced, equal and non-discriminatory trade-and-aid packages for the Mediterranean states to foster economic interdependence and regional stability—will be compromised by Spanish and Portuguese accession to the EC by 1985. The Mediterranean Policy's own limited success to date will foil its original goals. Southern enlargement is a natural outgrowth of the Mediterranean Policy (known hereafter as the Policy). The Policy encourages close contractual trade relations between the EC and the non-member Mediterranean states (known hereafter as the Basin states). These contracts take two forms: (1) *association* leading to customs union and possible membership (Greece joined in 1981, associated Malta, Cyprus and Turkey may seek membership in the future); and (2) *cooperation accords* including provisions for reduced tariffs and development aid (Portugal, Spain, Israel, Mashreq and Maghreb).[1] Enlargement will bring the entire northern Mediterranean littoral (minus Yugoslavia and Albania) into the EC. As a result, the EC will become self-sufficient or over-supplied with Mediterranean-type farm products and some manufactured items such as textiles. Table 4 depicts EC self-supply rates for fresh and processed fruits and vegetables. The EC will no longer need to import its historically high levels of these products from the non-European Basin region as Spain and Portugal join the other Mediterranean members—Greece, Italy and France—in the expanded Community, and enjoy the benefits of the customs union denied non-members. Moreover, the sixty-five members of the Lomé Convention already enjoy a wide variety of special EC-granted trade benefits which are broader in scope and level than those offered to Basin states.

Economic instability is likely to result within and among Basin states as they lose historically high market shares in the expanded EC to competitors in the new (and old southern) member states. Intra-regional competition for the EC's shrinking contractual horticultural import market will sharpen and aggravate the delicate regional balance of economic power the EC has fostered over the past decade. The Basin remains volatile as one of the world's most war-prone and thus militarized regions. It is Europe's soft under-belly. Trade losses will exacerbate all Basin states' burgeoning trade deficits with the EC. (See Table 3.) Vital foreign earnings will drop as exports to the EC and money that millions of Mediterranean migrant workers in the EC send home to their families fall. After accession, the numbers of Spanish and Portuguese workers in the EC are expected to rise above their already high levels. They will enjoy the free movement of labour provisions of the Rome Treaty. Non-member migrants will not. EC unemployment levels will remain high and Basin governments will face the return of perhaps tens of thousands of migrant nationals to already employment-scarce economies.

Does the EC have the economic means, in a time of global recession, and political audacity to accommodate the mutually inclusive export needs of its new Mediterranean members and historically close non-members with whom it is highly interdependent? If it does not, will the expanded EC become a protectionistic regional trade bloc? Neofunctional integration theory, particularly its concept of 'externalization', suggests that, given the EC's exclusive nature, it can be expected to safeguard the interests of its new and old southern Mediterranean members at the expense of non-member interests.[2] From a juridical standpoint, and due to the very nature of the customs union, member states' products are always to be preferred over outside competition. Enlargement is a trade-off between internal benefits for the new states and external costs for close non-member Basin states.

EC and the Mediterranean: historical record

The close relationship between the EC and Basin states is the result of centuries of intense interdependent human, political, commercial, cultural, security and geographic links, dating back to the Roman Empire when both regions were one functional and administrative unit. Roman civilization enveloped the entire Mediterranean region. The Basin itself is *the* cradle of Western civilization. Greek civilization brought Europe to Egypt and the Levant. Trade brought Italian city-states to the Mediterranean and Middle East.[3] Recent ties are rooted in the colonial era of the nineteenth and early twentieth centuries. Algeria, Tunisia and Syria were occupied by France; Egypt, Cyprus, Gibraltar, Malta and Palestine by Britain; and Libya and the Dodecanese Islands by Italy. The British Navy spanned the Mediterranean Sea largely unchallenged. Renewed European interest in the Basin during the colonial period was due to its revival as a 'highway of commerce'.[4] The Basin is at the crossroads of three continents where much world trade converges. Europe depends on the Basin as an outlet for its products.

In the post-war period the Basin became increasingly *vital* to the security of the EC states in commercial and geostrategic terms. Trade and human ties dominate the EC–Mediterranean relationship. Table 1 shows that Basin states take roughly 15 per cent of total extra-EC exports compared to America's share of roughly 12 per cent. The EC enjoys a trade surplus with all Basin states, to the latter's chagrin. Table 2 shows that the value of EC imports from Basin states is some 9 per cent of total extra-EC imports compared to America's share of roughly 16 per cent. In the mid-1970s, a peak of roughly four million Mediterranean migrants worked in the EC. The EC has a vested interest in a stable political environment in the Basin region.

The Basin is both a strategic asset and liability for the EC. As an asset, the region is *vital* to the physical and economic security of the EC. Most EC oil imports come from the Persian Gulf. Regional instability likely to impede this vital trade, investment and transport route is of constant concern to the EC. As a strategic liability, the region is excessively unstable. Nearly every southern littoral state has engaged in some form of military and/or political conflict with one or more of its neighbours since 1945. The US Fifth Fleet assumed naval primacy in the region after Britain relinquished that role to the US after 1945, but US naval supremacy is seriously challenged by the growing strength and presence of the Soviet Fifth Escrada Fleet.[5] Since the Tsar, Russians have coveted the Basin region in their search for warm water ports. Social and economic upheaval that is expected to arise from EC enlargement may invite Soviet expansionism to test Western resolve.

Basin states depend on the EC for economic survival, but are divided and cannot employ the weight of collective regional power to extract economic dividends from

Table 1   Trends in extra-EC-9 exports to ten largest Mediterranean contract trade partners and US[6]

Trade partner	value MIO ECU					value	Percentage						Rank					
	1958	1976	1977	1978	1979	1980	1958	1976	1977	1978	1979	1980	1958	1976	1977	1978	1979	1980
Extra-EC exports	22,102	141,300	164,288	173,893	194,182	224,446	100	100	100	100	100	100						
US	2,662	16,247	20,499	23,142	25,048	26,564	11.9	11.5	12.5	13.3	12.9	11.8	1	1	1	1	1	1
Spain	338	4,816	5,335	5,001	6,524	7,581	1.5	3.4	3.3	2.9	3.4	3.4	16	6	7	8	5	5
Algeria	1,025	2,759	3,677	3,638	3,812	4,710	4.6	2.0	2.2	2.1	2.0	2.1	4	14	11	13	12	11
Greece	290	2,465	2,897	3,139	4,077	4,214	1.3	1.7	1.8	2.1	2.1	1.9	21	17	15	16	11	13
Yugoslavia	219	2,686	3,566	3,708	4,410	4,131	1.0	1.9	2.2	2.3	2.3	1.8	25	16	12	12	9	15
Egypt	193	1,520	1,682	1,821	2,324	3,105	0.9	1.1	1.0	1.2	1.2	1.4	27	25	26	26	22	20
Portugal	259	1,649	1,952	1,922	2,230	2,895	1.2	1.2	1.2	1.1	1.2	1.3	24	24	24	22	24	22
Turkey	182	2,292	2,157	1,563	1,588	1,821	0.8	1.6	1.3	0.9	0.8	0.8	29	19	21	30	33	30
Israel	153	1,287	1,484	1,634	1,777	1,676	0.7	0.8	0.9	0.9	0.9	0.7	33	29	28	28	31	32
Tunisia	121	837	978	1,121	1,233	1,541	0.6	0.6	0.6	0.6	0.6	0.6	37	38	36	34	39	33
Morocco	282	1,317	1,537	1,343	1,676	1,479	1.3	0.9	0.9	0.8	0.6	0.5	20	26	25	30	32	34
Totals (exc. US)	3,062	21,628	25,265	24,890	29,651	33,153	13.9	15.2	15.4	15.3	15.3	14.5						

Table 2 Trends in extra-EC-9 imports from ten largest non-member Mediterranean contract trade partners and US[7]

Trade partners	value MIO ECU					value	Percentage						Rank					
	1958	1976	1977	1978	1979	1980	1958	1976	1977	1978	1979	1980	1958	1976	1977	1978	1979	1980
Extra-EC imports	23,654	159,590	171,743	178,386	218,011	271,552	100	100	100	100	100	100						
US	3,952	25,342	25,736	28,276	33,857	44,250	15.5	15.9	15.0	15.9	15.8	16.3	1	1	1	1	1	1
Spain	348	3,974	4,771	5,486	6,674	8,050	1.5	2.5	2.8	3.1	3.1	3.0	20	10	8	9	8	8
Algeria	507	2,153	2,099	2,006	2,761	4,027	2.1	1.4	1.2	1.1	1.3	1.5	11	21	22	22	21	19
Greece	135	1,417	1,517	1,725	2,202	2,301	0.6	0.9	0.9	1.0	1.0	0.9	37	26	27	25	24	24
Yugoslavia	172	1,459	1,569	1,588	1,967	2,059	0.7	0.9	0.9	0.9	0.9	0.8	32	24	26	27	26	26
Portugal	125	924	1,004	1,175	1,617	1,961	0.5	0.6	0.7	0.7	0.7	0.7	41	34	35	33	31	28
Egypt	77	678	703	945	1,183	1,746	0.3	0.4	0.4	0.5	0.5	0.6	54	45	46	39	38	34
Israel	69	816	1,000	1,186	1,350	1,599	0.3	0.5	0.6	0.7	0.6	0.6	56	44	39	32	35	36
Morocco	351	840	838	845	1,011	1,168	1.5	0.5	0.5	0.5	0.5	0.4	21	43	50	42	40	44
Tunisia	130	412	561	569	790	1,098	0.5	0.3	0.3	0.3	0.3	0.3	42	50	58	49	44	45
Turkey	117	873	820	836	942	996	0.4	0.5	0.5	0.5	0.4	0.3	43	42	51	43	42	48
Totals (exc. US)	2,031	13,546	14,882	16,361	20,497	25,005	8.4	8.5	8.8	9.3	9.3	9.2						

Table 3   EC-9 trade with Mediterranean contract trade partners 1978–80[8]

Trade partner	type	year	Imports					Exports				
			Total mio USD	of which: EC-9 mio USD	%	main non-EC supplier	%	Total mio USD	of which: EC-9 mio USD	%	main non-EC supplier	%
Greece	A	78	7,556	3,309	44	Japan	13	3,335	1,695	51	Saudi Arabia	6
		79	9,537	4,160	44	Japan	9	3,855	1,892	49	US	6
		80	9,729	3,861	40	Japan	11	4,751	2,262	48	US	6
Turkey	A	78	4,598	1,873	41	Iraq	11	2,288	1,090	48	US	7
		79	5,683	2,042	36	Iraq	11	2,472	1,215	49	USSR	6
		80	6,264	2,061	33	Iraq	14	2,748	1,136	41	USSR	5
Cyprus	A	78	758	385	51	Greece	6	341	103	30	Saudi Arabia	10
		79	1,009	477	47	Greece	7	453	146	32	Lebanon	9
		80	unavail.					unavail.				
Malta	A	78	516	353	68	US	9	289	196	68	Lebanon	11
		79	575	417	73	US	6	342	240	70	Lebanon	8
		80	780	568	73	US	5	434	311	72	Lebanon	7
Spain	P	78	18,713	6,496	35	US	13	13,118	6,072	46	US	9
		79	25,386	9,120	36	US	12	18,197	8,730	48	US	7
		80	34,177	10,493	31	US	13	20,824	10,260	48	US	6

Country		Year										
Portugal	P	78	4,981	2,169	44	US	10	2,029	1,049	52	US	7
		79	5,171	2,368	46	US	12	2,440	1,354	55	US	7
		80	6,543	2,718	42	US	12	3,486	1,955	57	US	6
Yugoslavia	C	78	9,988	3,833	38	USSR	14	5,668	1,306	23	USSR	25
		79	12,861	4,828	38	USSR	14	6,492	1,691	26	USSR	22
		80	14,028	4,711	34	USSR	18	8,364	2,659	32	USSR	26
Algeria	C	78	8,667	5,115	59	Japan	9	6,126	2,307	38	US	51
		79	8,407	5,236	62	US	6	9,863	3,620	37	US	52
		80	unavail.					unavail.				
Morocco	C	78	2,967	1,458	49	Spain	10	1,503	856	57	Spain	7
		79	3,807	1,911	50	Spain	9	1,873	1,108	59	Spain	6
		80	unavail.					unavail.				
Tunisia	C	78	2,120	1,381	65	US	4	1,090	625	57	Greece	9
		79	2,844	1,378	55	US	6	1,771	1,031	58	Greece	16
		80	unavail.					unavail.				
Egypt	C	78	6,727	2,587	38	US	16	1,737	576	31	USSR	17
		79	3,837	1,489	39	US	18	1,840	932	51	USSR	8
		80	unavail.					unavail.				
Israel	C	78	7,448	2,707	36	US	20	4,546	1,703	37	US	16
		79	8,024	2,682	33	US	19	5,540	2,121	38	US	16
		80	unavail.					unavail.				
Lebanon	C	78	2,245	847	38	Saudi Arabia	8	814	41	5	Saudi Arabia	35
		79	3,197	1,238	39	Saudi Arabia	9	884	60	7	Saudi Arabia	31
		80	unavail.					unavail.				
Syria	C	78	2,443	862	35	Rumania	7	1,053	470	45	USSR	9
		79	3,309	1,195	36	Iraq	15	1,634	850	52	US	10
		80	unavail.					unavail.				
Jordan	C	78	1,499	549	37	Saudi Arabia	9	295	4	1	Saudi Arabia	20
		79	2,135	769	36	US	16	259	25	10	Saudi Arabia	22
		80	unavail.					unavail.				

the EC. As much as the EC depends on the region for its own physical and economic security, Basin states without raw materials or close connections with Arab League oil producers are more dependent on the EC than the converse. Political scientists call the relationship 'interdependent' with an asymmetric slant favouring the EC. There is more Mediterranean dependence on, rather than interdependence with, the EC. Arab Mediterranean states, however, are beginning to realize their 'trump card' *vis-à-vis* the EC. Development of the Euro-Arab Dialogue may give Arab Basin states the clout they need to deal with the EC on a more even basis. Arab Basin states with close ties to big OPEC members may be able to strike a more symmetric interdependent relationship with the EC. Table 3 shows that most Basin states depend on the EC as their *primary* market outlet. Mediterranean horticultural and textile products have enjoyed an historically healthy market in the EC (see Table 5). Basin states depend on imports of European capital goods, technological know-how, and development aid in its various forms. EC aid is essential for Basin state economic development.

Between 1958 and 1972, the EC–Mediterranean relationship lacked a framework for cooperation. After 1957, close non-member Basin states began to court the Six to negotiate trade accords to protect their historical market shares and otherwise minimize anticipated losses in the new regional trade bloc. The EC did not initiate negotiations for these accords. Yet Articles 113 and 238 of the Rome Treaty provide for contract trade with third countries and a form of association with members' former colonies which extended many of the trade advantages of the common market itself. A patchwork of unrelated EC preferential trade agreements rather than a common policy developed. Bilateral trade accords between individual EC members and their Mediterranean clients were *belatedly* replaced by multilateral accords involving the entire EC and individual Basin states in the late 1960s. The Six then concluded trade accords with many, but not all, Basin states. These were strictly commercial and lacked the kind of generous tariff preferences and financial, development, technical and other protocols that typify current accords.

Table 4   EC–9 self-sufficiency rates for selected farm products[9]

	Rate of self-sufficiency for the	
Product	EC-9	EC-12
(1) fresh and processed fruit	78%	95%
oranges	47	86
mandarin and other small fruit	39	96
(2) fresh and processed vegetables	92	100
potatoes	98	99
tomatoes	93	99
wine	108	112
olive oil	88	109
(3) sugar	113	109

The EC's Mediterranean relationship prior to 1973 was less the result of a preconceived strategy than a random outcome of intra-Community trade-offs. The Mediterranean Policy that emerged in the mid-1970s was the first successful attempt by the EC at preconceived foreign policy. It was spurred by the first EC enlargement on 1 January 1973 to include the UK, Ireland and Denmark, and by the October 1973–March 1974 Arab oil embargo. After the first enlargement

Table 5   Non-member Mediterranean countries affected by enlargement[10]

States negatively affected by EC enlargement (in order of hardest-hit)	Percentage of total exports to the EC affected by enlargement	
(1) Cyprus	68	(potatoes, wine, citrus fruits)
(2) Malta	58	(textiles, clothing)
(3) Morocco	51	(citrus fruit, tomatoes, canned fruits and vegetables, canned fish and textiles)
(4) Tunisia	48	(divided almost evenly between farm and industrial products)
(5) Turkey	43	(break-down unavailable)
(6) Israel	33	(of which 21% farm products and 12% industrial products)

relations changed. All previous contracts due to expire were renegotiated; between 1973-7, the EC either renegotiated or negotiated for the first time trade-and-aid accords with all but two Basin states.[11] Prior accords were replaced by new agreements based on the principles of the post-1973 Policy. British influence led to a more generous tariff-cutting EC mood toward Basin states. When Britain, as the main customer for Mediterranean horticultural exports, acceded to the EC's much higher external tariff, Basin states dependent on the lower tariff British market feared loss of sales in it. The EC compensated them by offering tariff preferences and other trade concessions as part of the emergent Mediterranean Policy.[12] Enlargement stimulated a new relationship with Basin states. However, the Arab oil embargo and OPEC's rocketing petroleum prices just months later highlighted the EC's vulnerability. The Mediterranean Policy was expedited as the EC was reminded of the importance of the Basin and adjoining Middle East and Persian Gulf to its strategic security and economic welfare. As a continent poor in raw materials, Europe relies heavily on imports of many primary products. Concern for secure supplies of petroleum convinced those EC members still doubting the need for a Mediterranean Policy to agree to cooperation accords with Arab countries around the Mediterranean seaboard.[13] Positive EC treatment of Arab Mediterranean countries would be seen quite favourably by the wider Arab community. The EC's credibility in the Arab world hinged on how it handled ties with the Arab Mediterranean states as most of the twenty-one member Arab League live in the Maghreb and Mashreq states.[14]

Overall Mediterranean Policy: theoretical assumptions versus practical realities

The theory behind the Policy is very convincing. Through the overall Mediterranean Policy, the EC seeks to use its immense economic power—the lure of accessibility to the world's largest import market, development and financial aid, reduced farm import levies (within defined limits), and industrial free trade access (with exceptions)—to: promote regional stability, balance of economic power, and peaceful economic coexistence among the area's many political rivals; project itself as a force for moderation and as a fair player in relations with the Basin's many active and passive belligerents; avoid disruptions of normal trade patterns; secure and expand profitable market outlets and ensure fair market accessibility; ensure that it remains an influential *civilian* actor in the region; and check Soviet expansionism on NATO's exposed southern flank.

By offering roughly equal and balanced economic incentives through cooperation and association accords, the EC hopes to make Basin states feel that, in spite of their mutual diversity and hostility, they have equally important stakes in maintaining the delicate regional balance of economic power struck by the EC. By promoting a sense of mutual relevance and dependence, the EC hopes that Basin states will be too involved in the growing regional prosperity to jeopardize peace. For example, by balancing trade-and-aid benefits between Israel and the Mashreq states, the EC believes that a form of peaceful coexistence may develop between the belligerents as a step toward political conciliation. By not offending parties to any one of the many intraregional disputes, the EC maintains good relations with all states and thus may influence them to effect peaceful change. The EC aspires to become a source of moderation and objectivity in a region renowned for neither. It is careful not to play favourites among the Basin states: some could cooperate in future trade disruptions, such as embargos, either as a supplier or as a territory through which an embargoed item travels. By stressing mutual needs, the EC hopes to create a climate congenial to its vested physical and commercial interests. However, the Policy's assumptions are somewhat simplistic and, for reasons predating the second enlargement, the Policy has fallen short of its original economic goals. The EC over-extended itself with promises of tariff concessions and financial aid. It did so, with good intent, in the late 1960s and early 1970s during times of economic growth and prosperity. Now, long-term, low economic growth and severe austerity do not leave much room for generosity.

In spite of its shortcomings in the economic sphere, the Policy has shown its vast potential in enabling the EC, when and where it can, to play a stabilizing political role in the region. While it has failed to effect a peaceful resolution in the crisis on Cyprus, it has handled relations with parties to the Arab–Israeli dispute on the basis of equanimity and had high hopes for its own Middle East peace initiative. Just before President Tito's death, the EC tried to improve the terms of its cooperation accord with Yugoslavia to help stabilize it in the post-Tito period and to steer away the Soviets. The Policy has had some success in that Basin states are attracted to, not repelled by, the EC. The EC scored a major political success by helping to stabilize the nascent democracies of southern Europe through the lure of EC membership. One hesitates to think, for example, of Portugal's political fate in the mid-1970s had it not been for EC members' support. Ironically, success will have negative economic and political repercussions on Mediterranean states outside the EC.

The Policy's real strength and sense of purpose will be tested as it grapples with how the EC will deal with the negative implications of southern enlargement to Basin states who have been unsatisfied with the way in which their cooperation accords have been implemented. Their concern is less with the EC's overall Policy goals than the smooth-functioning of and benefits reaped from the cooperation accords. The following problem areas underscore the EC's difficulty in translating the Policy's theoretical assumptions into practical realities:

(1) *Industrial free trade*. Industrial free trade access only benefits developed industrialized Basin states, such as Spain and Israel, and not the agrarian-based export economies of Basin states. Industrial free trade access has not yet had the desired effects for most of the Basin states. It was designed to encourage Mediterranean industrialization to offset limitations imposed on farm exports to the EC. Industries which could have produced export growth were precisely those on which the EC took protectionist measures (due in large part to the recession). The EC has imposed so-called 'self-limitation agreements' on textile and clothing imports from

Basin (and other) states. Mediterranean industrial exports of these products could not develop as planned. Protectionist measures result in a crisis of confidence in the EC by its Basin trade partners.

(2) *Farm trade.* Agrarian export economies need wider free access to the EC which protects its farmers from outside competition through the CAP. The EC's Mediterranean tariff preferences generally cover items lacking a common market organization. Competing interests of Basin and southern EC farmers make it hard to devise EC import policies acceptable to both. Given the importance of Mediterranean-type farm produce to southern EC members, imports of like produce from non-member Basin states will remain limited. The EC is becoming self-sufficient in many non-grain food items. Prospects for increasing or maintaining the current level of non-member Basin food exports to the EC remain grim.

(3) *Balances of trade and payments.* During the Policy's existence, Basin states' balances of trade and payments with the EC have drastically worsened. In response, several Basin states have restricted imports of some EC capital goods.

(4) *The Basin's lack of homogeneity.* The Policy is based on the false assumption that the Basin states can be treated as one homogeneous region with the same interests in one another and in the EC. Basin states share dependence on EC markets but Arab Mediterranean states owe allegiance to the Arab League and see the emerging Euro-Arab Dialogue as a better forum for cooperation with Europe than their EC accords. Most non-Western Basin states are linked closely to the Third World. Because the region is heterogeneous, it is hard to apply a standard policy towards them and, for the EC, the Mediterranean takes on broader relevance as a regional unit than as individual states.

(5) *Migrant workers.* The EC has yet to formulate its own common migrant labour policy to regulate the movement and conditions of all Mediterranean migrant workers in the various member states. The Policy omits these matters. EC members regulate migrant workers and related issues through bilateral arrangements with the sender countries, but the Policy will fall short of its goals until it tackles these issues.

(6) *The regional and economic milieu.* The Policy devised in the boom of the late 1960s could not succeed in the leaner years of the post-1974 period. Goals have been frustrated by world recession, internal EC economic problems and regional problems with the EC's own Mediterranean farm producers. There is a close correlation between the success of the Policy and the economic conditions under which it must function.

(7) *The lack of EC–Mediterranean complementarity.* There is an inherent conflict in the Policy between simultaneous development and growth of the Mediterranean region in and outside the EC. The EC and non-EC Mediterranean areas are not economically complementary: they bitterly compete for the same northern European markets. The conflict between addressing the identical export needs of Mediterranean countries in and outside the EC will remain unresolved without one side undertaking structural changes away from horticultural production.

Repercussions of enlargement on the Basin states

The *existing* difficulties facing Basin states in exporting goods and workers to the EC will be compounded by enlargement. Since even the EC admits that the Policy is not operating as it should, problems in it should be worked out before, not in response to, enlargement. Even if enlargement were not to occur, the Policy needs a major face-lift to survive. Enlargement by 1985, like that of 1973, is again seen as a catalyst for change. In 1973 the change resulted in new benefits for Basin states. Since then, those benefits have been substantially eroded. Changes by 1985 will not benefit the Basin. The problem is how to devise a plan to prevent the costs of enlargement being borne disproportionately by Basin rather than EC and accession states. The US could give economic aid to Basin states as enlargement is in the interests of NATO and overall Western political and strategic security.

In reports and memoranda to the Council since 1979, the Commission has identified the major economic, social and political problems facing the Basin following enlargement. Commission Policy prescriptions have been few and inconclusive as in the final analysis they hinge on the political will of EC members, not the good will and sympathy of EC institutions.

Lorenzo Natali, Commissioner for enlargement and the Mediterranean Policy— no easy job—wrote eloquently in his mid-1982 communication to the Council on the need for a new global Mediterranean Policy to deal effectively with the consequences of enlargement.[15] A point-by-point presentation of workable solutions to the Basin's many problems was left to a future study. The report was sympathetic towards the Basin states' relative position to the accession states but offered few concrete solutions to their problems. It accepted the EC's historical responsibilities toward the Basin. It must prove itself a reliable partner whose trade and aid policies can be counted on when the going gets tough. There can be no vacuum left in the region. If Basin states lose their natural markets in West Europe, they will look elsewhere, perhaps to COMECON, with all this involves, for Western security. While development of trade agreements does involve costs to southern EC regions, the balance overall is clearly in favour of the Mediterranean Policy and the mutual utility for both regions. Solutions cannot be found solely in cooperation agreements. The EC, by constructive adjustments to internal policies and by closer commercial, financial and technical cooperation with the Basin states, must ensure that enlargement is not undertaken at the Basin states' expense. The Policy's success depends on EC efforts to face problems in its own Mediterranean region: Commission proposals to develop the EC's southern regions have already been passed to the Council. The Natali report calls for a new global Mediterranean Policy to strike a new balance between Europe and the Basin states; continued trade and cooperation via current accords, bolstered by regular trade consultations on sensitive products and more financial and development aid; consultations to regulate EC–Mediterranean trade on sensitive products such as textiles and farm produce so that both sides can avoid problems of structural oversupply; mobilization of large amounts of funds by drawing on EC financial instruments and borrowing on international markets to provide financial aid to the Basin states to restructure agriculture and industry to produce items not in over- or self-supply; reform of the CAP and stopping EC quantitative restrictions on textiles, processed foodstuffs and other items which are the only sectors where the emergent industries of the Basin states are competitive and enjoy the benefits of industrial free trade access.

What can Basin states do to check the ill-effects of enlargement? Their options are limited and depend on the outcome of enlargement. They include: meeting trade restrictions with trade restrictions; stressing the Basin's strategic importance to West Europe and the fact that the world balance of power depends on who controls the vital shipping routes in and out of the region; hinting, as Malta has, of further political and economic alignment with non-European groupings, such as the Soviet bloc, Third World, or Arab community; insisting that the EC stick to its commitment to hold regular consultations on the development of their cooperation accords in parallel with enlargement negotiations; negotiating aggressively to improve their cooperation accords prior to, not after, enlargement; aggressively marketing their products in the EC and improving product quality; securing new non-EC market outlets such as the Middle East or Persian Gulf states (some have already attempted to do this. They cannot succeed in the short term. Non-EC markets can only serve as small, supplementary outlets for some of their farm products, and world demand is limited); highlighting the very real likelihood that Basin demand for EC capital goods will fall as a direct function of decreasing sales of Mediterranean farm and industrial products in the EC; and appealing to northern, more sympathetic EC member states to protect their tariff preferences in the face of southern European pressure to reduce or eliminate them. One possible, though not very practicable, solution to retain the Basin states' historical market shares in the EC exists but, if undertaken, would simply pass the cost of enlargement on to another group of nations, i.e. non-associated LDCs. The EC *could* permit continued high levels of Mediterranean imports at preferential rates *if* it is willing to confront high oversupply rates for such products as a matter of internal resolution through the CAP.

The EC could import largely unneeded horticultural products from Basin states but expanded use of export subsidies would require major revisions of the CAP. The CAP favours northern European farm products. The EC tries to protect Greek raisins and dried figs by incorporating them into existing common market organizations for processed fruits and vegetables. The EC might accommodate Spanish and Portuguese Mediterranean farm products by either creating new common market organizations (e.g. fresh fruits and vegetables) or adding horticultural products to existing common market organizations. Ironically, the CAP could provide export subsidies which may help to alleviate surplus horticultural supplies. They may enable the Basin states to retain the integrity of their market shares in the EC. However, this only passes a regional trade surplus on to the world market. Export subsidies are an expensive way of dealing with oversupply and promised levels of imports from close third countries. The EC has been dumping surplus produce on to the world market while importing those same products from politically close third countries for years. Even though the EC has self- or over-supply rates for products such as sugar, textiles, and dairy by-products, it imports them—even at preferential or other concessional rates—from close third countries. For example, despite the EC's serious oversupply of dairy products, it permits the British to import regulated amounts of New Zealand butter because of the close relationship with that country and of the central importance of that product to the New Zealand economy.[16] *If there is a sufficiently high level of political will among influential member states to permit continued imports of products from close third states for which the EC as a whole is in a surplus situation, then the sacrifices will be made.*

Conclusions: the US and EC in the Mediterranean Basin

This discussion has shown that because of the conditions existing before and exacerbated by southern enlargement, the Mediterranean Policy's original goals will be foiled. Southern enlargement will involve the EC even more closely in Mediterranean affairs. It cannot expect to provide for its own economic and physical security if it allows Basin states to suffer unduly as a result of enlargement. These countries will need a massive influx of capital to redevelop and restructure their export economies if they are going to continue exporting products to Western Europe. Since enlargement will create economic, political and social upheavals in the Mediterranean region—the kind of atmosphere of which the Soviet Union is known to take advantage—the US will want to check any possible Soviet actions likely to destabilize the region. The US shares the EC assumption that enlargement will bind the applicant states—Spain and Portugal—to the West and NATO. While the EC should be encouraged by the US to exert itself as a civilian actor in the Basin region on behalf of Western interests, the EC's increased influence in the Basin after enlargement will closely involve it with the US in an area traditionally reserved for the US. EC–US conflict over the strategic role of the Basin in Western security is inevitable. Greater EC involvement in the region may add a divisive factor in the already strained US–European relationship. The US and EC members differ over the Middle East. Both would see the Basin's strategic role differently during future conflicts given the EC's greater dependence on oil imports from the Persian Gulf, markets in the Arab world, and closer ties with the Arab states through the Euro-Arab Dialogue. Nevertheless, the region's strategic security will remain a primary US responsibility.

The ill-effects of enlargement on the Basin states present both the US and its NATO allies with some important questions. Since the EC has taken the ambitious step of expanding membership to poorer southern European states, its ability to accommodate the needs of closely associated non-member Basin states will be compromised. At the same time, the EC's mere geographical expansion along the northern Mediterranean seaboard inextricably ties it to the Basin's political and security affairs. Since the EC will not be able fully to accommodate Basin non-members' needs, the US may be obliged to grant special development aid and improved market accessibility for certain Mediterranean products. US and EC grants, loans and technical expertise to help Basin states modernize and industrialize could help stabilize the delicate balance of interests in the region and repulse Soviet intervention to foment political unrest. Given possible disenchantment with the EC and the 'West' as a result of the ill-effects of enlarggement on their political economies, Basin states will be prime targets for Soviet interference. This must be checked by the continuous strong US naval presence in the region. The US has an important security stake in enlargement. For years the US officially opposed EC trade contracts and their provisions for tariff preferences and industrial free trade access with Basin states as they allegedly discriminated against US exports to these countries and to the EC. EC trade-and-aid packages—when their provisions are carried out—go a long way in helping to ease regional tensions and create a kind of regional economic balance of power. It is in US interests to support close trade-and-aid arrangements between the EC and Basin states and, where the EC simply cannot deliver, to step in and provide direct aid to bolster the Mediterranean states. Enlargement will only strengthen NATO and EC security if it does not create the expected social and economic unrest in the Mediterranean. The EC must seek US help in securing Basin stability. The US must respond if Western interests are to be preserved and if the EC is to remain an influential civilian power in the region.

Notes

1. Mashreq refers to Arab countries of the eastern Mediterranean: Egypt, Lebanon, Syria and Jordan. Maghreb refers to the former French colonies of northern Africa: Morocco, Tunisia and Algeria.

2. For further discussion on the question of the neofunctional explanation of enlargement, consult Ginsberg, R. H., 'Southern Enlargement of the European Common Market: Integration Theory Revisited', International Studies Association 22nd Annual Convention, Philadelphia, 18 March 1981.

3. For an excellent historical analysis of the European–Mediterranean connection, consult Pouns, N. G., *Europe and the Mediterranean* (New York, McGraw-Hill Book Co., Inc., 1953).

4. Ibid.

5. For further discussion consult Lewis, Jr, J. W., *The Strategic Balance in the Mediterranean* (Washington, DC, American Enterprise Institute, 1976); and Luttwak, E. and Weinland, R., *Sea Power in the Mediterranean: Political Utility and Military Constraints* (Washington, DC, Center for Strategic and International Studies, 1979).

6. Statistics extracted from *Monthly External Trade Bulletin, 1958–1980* (Luxembourg, Statistical Office of the European Communities, 1981), p. 10.

100 ECU = USD

Year	Value
1958	109,670
1976	111,805
1977	114,112
1978	127,434
1979	137,065
1980	139,233
1981	111,645

7. Ibid.

8. *Monthly External Trade Bulletin*, p. 10.

9. Figures extracted from *Agence Europe*, 27 June 1979, p. 10, and *The Agricultural Situation in the Community* (Brussels, Commission of the European Communities, 1980, p. 116.

10. *Agence Europe*, p. 11.

11. Libya and Albania have chosen not to engage in contract trade with the EC.

12. For a detailed study on tariff preferences and preferential trade accords, consult Tovias, A., *Tariff Preferences in Mediterranean Diplomacy* (New York, St Martin's Press, 1977).

13. Taylor, R., *Implications for the Southern Mediterranean Countries of the Second Enlargement of the European Community* (Brussels, Commission of the European Communities, 1980), p. 5.

14. Ibid., See also Seers, D., Vaisos, C. and Kiljunen, M-L., *The Second Enlargement of the EEC: The Integration of Unequal Partners* (London, Macmillan, 1982).

15. *Commission Communication to the Council on a Mediterranean Policy for the Enlarged Community* (Brussels, Commission of the European Communities, 1982).

16. See Lodge, Juliet, *The European Community and New Zealand* (London, Frances Pinter, 1982).

15 The European Community and the United States of America

ROY HOWARD GINSBERG

Introduction

A storm has broken again over the usually calm waters of the North Atlantic. The troubles now besetting US–EC relations are among the most intractable yet. The current global recession has exacerbated bitter US–EC disagreements over alleged restrictive trade/monetary practices and competition for scarce third country markets.

Equally divisive is the EC's increasing assertiveness and foreign policy independence from the USA. The patron–client years, when the US dominated and led an acquiescent Europe into economic reconstruction and transatlantic prosperity, are over. They ended in the 1960s with the EC's implementation of the Common Agricultural Policy (CAP), which cut historical market shares of selective US farm exports to the EC and led to the notorious Chicken War; with the French decision to withdraw from NATO's military wing; US entry into the Vietnam War; and the advent of East–West *détente* in Europe. Any lingering doubt about the irrevocability of the post-war US–European 'detachment' ended in 1971 and 1972.

In 1971, the US Government abruptly and unilaterally suspended the dollar's convertibility into gold and imposed a 10 per cent surcharge on all imports not already subject to quotas and duties. These served important US national interests but violated the spirit of US–European cooperation on mutual trade/monetary relations, formally ended the official functioning of the international monetary system known since 1944 as the Bretton Woods agreement, and signalled the end to unqualified US acceptance of costs to its foreign commerce in exchange for the benefits of a prosperous and unified European partner to defend the West against communism. In 1972, the UK altered its special relationship with the US in joining the EC.

The EC is now an international civilian power in its own right, an economic competitor of the USA in many third country markets, and a potential 'third force' challenging US primacy in the Western World. Three central themes underlie US–EC relations.

First, although individual trade *issues* between the two sides have always been as variable as the wind, most trade *problems* are as much in evidence in the 1980s as they were in the 1960s. Not much has changed! For every item on the current list of disagreements, there was an equivalent in earlier years. There have been periods, for example, during the early 1970s, when mutual complaints came as thick and fast as they do at present.[1]

What has changed in the 1962–82 period are three important structural developments:

(1) bitter trade competition has largely shifted from the EC to third country markets, many once US-dominated;

(2) the relative importance of the US market to the EC since the mid-1970s has declined. Although the USA remains the EC's largest *single* market, Mediterranean basin and OPEC countries have become larger *regional* markets for EC exports;[2]

(3) in many respects, the EC is now a larger trade/economic entity than the USA. The value of EC exports during 1976–80 was 8 per cent higher than those of the USA; the value of its imports was 26 per cent higher. The combined GNP of the EC is now higher than that of the USA.

What has not changed is:

(1) sharp disagreement over each other's farm support programmes/practices to protect domestic producers from the vicissitudes of world market conditions. Both interfere with 'market forces' to support farming but do so differently;[3]

(2) bitter competition for scarce foreign markets and petrodollars continues. The EC's historically high dependence on export/import trade, in comparison to that of the USA, puts it at a comparative disadvantage and renders mutual understanding on world trade difficult. The EC's export dependency is almost twice as high as it is for the USA; its import dependency is nearly one and a half times higher. The EC imports about 75 per cent of its energy and raw materials compared to America's 25 per cent.

(3) the effect on the European economy of swings in the value of the US dollar, interest rates set by the US Federal Reserve Board, and negative balances of trade with the USA make the EC dependent on US economic policy and performance.

Second, unlike the persistence of trade/monetary problems, political-diplomatic-security problems have arisen in the past ten years which were non-existent or dormant in the 1950s/60s. The latter arose as US–EC trade relations became more politicized, as the EC continued to assert itself in international diplomacy and translated its global economic power into political clout abroad, as European and American approaches to international economic/political problems diverged, and as world politics and commerce became increasingly inseparable. The extent of US–EC disagreement may be no greater than it was before. However, it causes greater disruption as a stronger Europe faces a relatively weaker America in the 1980s.[4] The current crisis is historically dangerous because mutual economic problems are compounded by serious political-diplomatic-security policy differences which could disrupt the normally stable NATO alliance; and the bases of the relationship in the 1950s/60s are beginning to weaken in the 1970s/80s.

Third, US–EC relations do not function in a vacuum. The international environment influences them enormously. US–EC problems must be seen in relation to American and European ties with the USSR, China, developing nations, other developed states and in connection with the international economic system. The international environment could promote good relations in times of economic prosperity and world peace; spur common action in the face of the Soviet threat to Western Europe; or sour relations in times of world recession and differing perceptions of how to handle relations with the non-Atlantic outside world.

Legal and discretionary underpinnings of EC foreign policy

The legal basis for the EC's common foreign economic policy is found in Articles 113 and 116 of the Rome Treaty. Article 113 calls for a common external tariff (CET) and empowers EC institutions to conduct trade relations with non-members on behalf of the member states. Article 116 calls for joint EC action at international economic organizations and empowers EC institutions to act at them on behalf of the members.

Foreign (political) policy is outside the Rome Treaty's purview. Yet, if interpreted broadly, and given the difficulty in clearly distinguishing between world trade and politics, these articles give the EC institutions a substantial degree of discretionary power in foreign affairs. The EC's foreign economic decision-making powers are underpinned by the members' vital political-diplomatic-security interests abroad. EC foreign policies can no longer be defined in strictly apolitical terms. The EC's founding fathers themselves probably did not expect the EC to become a non-political international entity. The EC cannot be the world's largest importer/exporter without exercising some concomitant political clout. The decision to grant or withhold foreign trade contracts, tariff preferences and other favourable trade terms, diplomatic recognition, and food-humanitarian-emergency aid to third countries entails political-diplomatic-security calculations on the Ten's part.[5] Finally, the Rome Treaty does not explicitly bind members to a common foreign (political) policy. Yet, the preamble, noting that members 'are determined to lay the foundation of an ever closer union among the peoples of Europe', implicitly suggests the prospect of a 'political union'. Thus, a common foreign policy could be a natural progression.[6] Neither implicitly nor explicitly does the Rome Treaty call for a common defence policy. The EC remains very much a civilian power.

Since the Commission's power to speak for the members with one voice outside Europe has been checked by some member states, and the Council is stymied both by constitutional constraints and often unyielding national governments, in 1970 EC members devised an intergovernmental forum for foreign policy cooperation. In European Political Cooperation (EPC), the members hold regular meetings of Heads of Government/State, Foreign Ministers, Ambassadors in foreign capitals and at international organizations, Political Directors from the national foreign ministries, and national civil servants to consult on common foreign policy issues and act jointly when practicable. Since EPC is not a treaty-bound body, its decisions are not legally binding on the members as are EC laws and regulations.[7]

Structure and function of US–EC relations

Transatlantic relations refer to all multilateral ties—military (NATO), economic (OECD, annual economic summits), trade (GATT, EC, international commodity agreements), energy (IEA), monetary (IMF, World Bank), non-governmental (Trilateral Commission), etc.—among the countries of, and institutions common to, North America and Western Europe. The term 'Western Alliance' in its broadest sense refers to the host of economic, political and social links among the developed, capitalist Western democracies which set them apart from the rest of the world. It may also refer to the spirit of shared beliefs and understanding among these nations. Somewhat different is the US–European relationship which refers to all multilateral and bilateral relations—economic, political and military—between the US and West European countries and their common institutions. Most specific (and technical) is the US–EC relationship which largely involves bilateral trade between the USA and EC member states who are legally represented by EC institutions. However, the US–EC trade relationship has been infiltrated and politicized by political-diplomatic-security issues in recent years. This is problematic from an institutional point of view. Outside NATO's regionally limited purview no bilateral institutional mechanism exists for coordinating foreign policies when practicable.

The dividing line between US–European and US–EC relations is becoming increasingly difficult to draw because of all the twenty West European nations, twelve are either members of, or applicants to join, the EC; the remainder are either affiliated with the EC through an industrial free trade area (EFTA) or by association agreements; trade relations interface with political-diplomatic-security issues. For example, of the EC members/applicants, all but neutral Ireland are NATO members (France is outside the NATO Supreme Command Structure). Of NATO members, all but the USA and Canada are either members of, applicants to join, or closely affiliated with the EC. An increasingly controversial overlap between the EC and NATO, much to the chagrin of the USA, is the discussion among EC Foreign Ministers within EPC of non-military aspects of western strategic security and disarmament/arms control talks with the Soviets.

As the EC asserts itself in international relations, it will become increasingly difficult to define US–EC relations in strictly apolitical terms divorced from broader US–European relations. This is exacerbated as US and EC governments often deal with each other on a bilateral basis on EC-related issues outside the EC institutional mode.

US–EC relations are conducted at the political-diplomatic level by the exchange of diplomatic missions and Heads of Delegations who have Ambassadorial rank and whose staffs enjoy diplomatic immunity. Senior officials of the EC Commission and US Administration meet semi-annually to consult on mostly economic (but on some political) issues. Members of the US Congress and European Parliament exchange official visits semi-annually to discuss mutual political and economic problems. An elementary 'crisis management' mechanism has been set up by the EC to handle EPC foreign policy deliberations which affect the interests of the USA and other non-members. When, in EPC, EC members discuss or act upon an issue vital to US interests, the EC Council President consults the US Government.

In terms of exchange programmes, the Eisenhower Exchange Fellowship Programme provides opportunities for mid-level Americans and EC officials to exchange visits and work with counterparts from one to six months. An annual US–EC media seminar takes place alternately in Europe and the US. It is sponsored by the EC's Washington delegation and the Foundation for American Communications. Two dozen prominent US and European journalists, high-ranking officials, and scholars participate in the meetings and discuss US–EC relations.

At the commercial level, mutual trade is regulated by the GATT in which the USA negotiates and conducts relations with the EC directly. There are five multilateral forums through which US and EC institutions/members interact but which are not directly linked to the US–EC relationship: (1) economic cooperation and development among the Western developed nations is promoted through OECD to which the USA and EC member states belong; (2) energy cooperation is attempted through their mutual membership of IEA (although France is not a member); (3) the EC Commission President joins the US President and other Western leaders to discuss mutual trade/payments problems and international politics at the annual economic summits and during the less regular senior-level consultations of the Trilateral Commission; (4) some international commodity trade is governed by multilateral agreements to which the USA and EC adhere; (5) consultation between the USA and EC members occurs at the follow-up meetings of the Conference on Security and Cooperation in Europe (CSCE).

Why study US–EC relations? What is its significance for both parties and for the outside world, and why is it timely to examine the relationship? From a policy-making point of view, it is worth studying US–EC relations because:

(a) both have huge stakes in world trade. Together they account for nearly one-half of all world imports/exports. Both favour a liberal free world trade order to varying degrees;

(b) both have huge stakes in the defence of the Western democratic political system against communism. NATO is weakened when trade disputes disrupt it. Both have equally vital stakes in balance between their trade and strategic security relationships;

(c) both face generally the same economic and social problems as the Western World's largest advanced industrial countries, so that their collaboration at all levels is vital to the future of their common security; and

(d) both share an intense economic and political interdependent relationship and are viewed as the two main pillars of the Western political/economic system. Both share comparable political and cultural experiences.

The security of developed non-NATO Western nations hinges on amicable trans-atlantic relations and prosperity. The US–EC trade relationship deeply affects the broader Western international economic system. To the Soviets, any cracks in the economic wing of the 'Western Alliance' could send the wrong signals and invite hostile tests of Western military resolve. To developing nations, US–EC cooperation in addressing North–South issues and on how best to coordinate foreign development aid is of paramount importance.

Examination of the relationship is timely because it is undergoing change: perhaps *the* final closing of the 'post-war period' in US–EC relations. The question of basic US–European compatibility is being raised. Was the US–European relationship which emerged after the Second World War more a temporary 'marriage of convenience' than a pliable long-term alliance capable of flexing with changing world realities forty years later? Did not the Soviet rejection of Marshall Plan aid and the US-sponsored international trade/monetary system deny Western Europe a natural market outlet to the East and force it into a costlier, perhaps less natural, trade dependence on the US? However, the very nature and process of European (not transatlantic) integration made US–EC trade and political conflicts inevitable.

Historical evolution

US–EC relations may be viewed in three periods: 1948–62; 1963–75; and 1976 to the present. Five observations apply to all:

(1) the USA has consistently supported EC integration. The relationship may be described in terms of 'allied rivalry';

(2) the USA assumed that a united Europe would share its burdens of defending the West and managing the international economic order.[8] Because the USA has viewed the EC as a component of its post-war policy, it has been unable to credit it with its own separate political and economic interests;[9]

(3) the relationship has a turbulent history. The most constant undercurrent in the trade relationship is its built-in propensity toward conflict. There has always been an incompatibility in US policy between the objective of a post-war multilateral, non-discriminatory and liberal economic order and support for EC integration which called for some trade discrimination against non-members;

(4) as a general rule, US and European leaders favour close/amicable trade ties. The biggest difficulty facing US and European leadership is to ensure that divisive trade disputes do not affect the more consensual military security relationship;

(5) what sustains the US–EC trade relationship is dependence on one another's vast internal markets; common democratic/economic beliefs; increasing isolation in a world of anti-Western hostility; common goal of a liberal world trade order given their large stakes in export trade; and the calming effect of the less divisive military security alliance.

During the 1948–62 period, the USA was a crucial driving force in the post-war reconstruction/integration of the European economy. The USA and EC countries were allies and partners (with the exception of the 1956 Suez crisis when the USA reacted strongly against British and French involvement). The roots of some current problems may be traced back to this period.

The USA envisaged a peaceful, unified European partner (not competitor) in its plan for a post-war, Atlantic-centred international trade/political order. The USA sought to rebuild Europe as a secure market outlet for its products and to incorporate it into a liberal and non-discriminatory world trade order. Sensitive to the economic nationalism and trade protectionism of the inter-war years, the USA was ready for a new approach to managing international economic relations. The US-initiated GATT in 1947 was designed to codify rules providing for fair and equal trade among its members. Support for a revitalized Europe as a bulwark against the spread of communism and as an indispensable participant in the emergent liberal world trade order became the cornerstone of post-war US foreign policy.

The EC was largely a by-product of US support for European reconstruction, based on the 1947 Marshall Plan—a massive injection of US economic aid.[10] Establishing the OEEC (now OECD) in 1948, the USA encouraged European governments to work together for economic reconstruction. The USA lent moral/diplomatic support to the European Payments Union (1950), ECSC (1951), EDC (vetoed by France in 1954), and EURATOM and EEC (1957). Barred from traditional Eastern markets, EC members were, therefore, thrust into a trade relationship with the USA. It was perhaps more costly and artificial than the more natural markets to the East. This later became a source of friction.

In return for a rebuilt and prosperous European partner, the USA tolerated (perhaps then underestimated) the expected costs to its foreign commerce of the EC's high tariff barrier, export subsidies, tariff reductions for close non-EC members, and competition with EC members in third markets. The seeds for future misunderstanding were sown with the EC's founding, as it is the nature of a common market with its customs union and CET to discriminate against non-members to some extent. Thus, it was no surprise that the EC would to some extent work against the US picture of a non-discriminatory Atlantic-based economic order. What brought the two sides together in the 1950s—a mutual fear of Stalinist Russia, Soviet rejection of US reconstruction aid and the GATT, and the need for one another's markets—began to unravel in the 1960s as both sides began to find other lucrative markets as the Soviet threat lessened and *détente* burgeoned.

By 1962, the USA had begun to lose its influence over European integration. Realizing that the EC could become a strong economic power (roughly equivalent to the USA) and a non-Atlantic foreign policy actor independent of the USA, President Kennedy announced his 'Grand Design' in July: an overambitious attempt to re-define US–European relations, calling on the EC to be an equal partner of the USA in managing transatlantic relations.[11] The Grand Design endorsed EC integration and called for British accession to the EC. However, the EC was not ready to shoulder the kind of burdens the USA would place on it. Moreover,

President de Gaulle opposed the Grand Design as he favoured the EC developing into a French-led 'third force' in international relations. America's high hopes for the Grand Design quickly faded as the two sides entered the tumultuous 1963–75 period.

In the 1963–75 period, the USA and EC gyrated between insensitivity and hostility as they tried to adjust to their changing relative positions in the world. By the 1970s, other centres of economic power had emerged (Japan, OPEC, and the EC); the USA was no longer in a position to dominate world trade. The strictly bi-polar 'we–they' world configuration of the 1950s simplified and required US–EC cooperation. The multipolar 'interdependent' world of the 1970s complicated and added new pressures to US–EC relations. The USA found that outside NATO its European allies had increasingly become competitors, in some cases even adversaries. Memories of wartime camaraderie and early post-war collaboration faded with the new generation of European youth; relations began to crack.

In the early 1960s, the relationship began to show its wear as the EC grew in strength and the USA began to feel threatened by it. The EC had secured the structural base upon which to assert itself *vis-à-vis* the outside world and became the vehicle through which member states projected their policies for attaining competitive equality with US industry, and remnants of their former world roles.[12] From the time the US balance of payments went into deficit in the late 1950s, the USA began to focus on its economic problems and considered a post-war unmentionable: unilateral solutions to international economic problems. All along, the USA had calculated that any damage from EC integration to its producers would be more than outweighed by its political advantages. US support faltered in the 1960s as the EC began to endanger its economic interests without corresponding political advantage and as EC members seemed to get richer at the expense of the USA while under its protection.[13] Six sore points emerge in hindsight:

(1) in the early 1960s, the EC began to extend tariff-cutting association and preferential trade agreements to former colonies and other historically close trade partners in Africa and the Mediterranean basin. The USA saw this as discrimination against its exports and opposed to its vision of liberal world trade;

(2) in 1963–4 the notorious Chicken War broke out. This remains the only actual trade war between the two sides. As a result of the newly created poultry CAP in 1963, import levies were set high to protect the EC poultry industry from outside competition. This had a devastating effect on traditional US shares of the EC poultry market. Pushed by its producer groups, the USA retaliated by imposing high tariffs on EC exports of high-priced brandy, Volkswagen pick-up trucks, dextrine, and potato starch to the USA.[14] Yet, poultry was less of an issue in the Chicken War than the CAP itself. By 1967 the CAP covered most major farm commodities. US exports of items covered by the CAP fell by 47 per cent in the last half of the 1960s just as intra-EC trade quadrupled and EC farm production grew;

(3) France's veto of US-supported British bids to join the EC (1963 and 1967), break with the military wing of NATO (1966), challenge to the authority of EC institutions (1965–6) and snub of IEA membership (1974) quickened US disenchantment with EC integration and severely lessened America's role in its future;

(4) the Kennedy Round of multilateral trade negotiations (MTNs) showed the EC's ability to be tough and united *vis-à-vis* the USA. EC resolve caught the US off guard;

(5) Europe's silence over, or condemnation of, US participation in the Vietnam War heightened US resentment toward its European allies, awakened America's realization that the EC members had their own foreign policy interests, and hastened the rift between US and European foreign policies;

(6) in the late 1960s, *détente* caused further conflict. EC members saw the benefits of *détente* partly in terms of new market opportunities in East Europe, whereas the USA viewed it in terms of SALT talks and other areas of 'high (international) politics'. Europeans were anxious (and felt helpless) over the new dialogue between the USA and the USSR and resented 'superpower bilateralism' on arms limitation talks in which their fate hung in the balance. EC members felt inadequately informed by the USA on these bilateral arms talks.

The Nixon Administration broke traditional US support for EC institutions, preferring bilateral relations with EC member governments. It avoided dealing directly with the EC which it saw 'as mystifying as the Tibetan theocracy'.[15] The USA can either facilitate EC institutional integration by dealing directly with EC bodies when appropriate, or detract from it by ignoring them in favour of the member governments on issues that come under EC purview. What the USA assumes about the EC will affect what it does.[16] A consistent US error has been to force relations with the EC into two familiar patterns: to treat it as if it were a nation state or regard it as just another international organization.[17] Coolness and indifference marked the relationship after the Kennedy Round in 1967 until the early 1970s.

In the 1960s, the USA ran increasingly large payments deficits due in part to massive economic and military aid to allies, European accumulation of dollar holdings and a gold drain caused by their conversion into gold. US deficits helped generate an economic boom in the Atlantic world by constantly increasing liquidity in the international monetary system.[18] In 1962, the US balance of payments problem prompted President Kennedy to attempt multilateral cooperation with the Europeans through his Grand Design. In 1971, the payments crisis moved the Nixon Administration in the opposite direction: unilateralism. Many Americans then began to question the high cost of stationing US troops in Europe. To relieve the acute balance of payments crisis, strengthen the weakened dollar and counteract domestic recession, the Nixon Administration took several 'revolutionary' unilateral steps between 1971 and 1973 without much prior consultation of its trade partners. It formally suspended gold payments for dollars; abandoned fixed exchange rates between the major currencies leaving them to float freely in response to market forces; imposed temporary import levies on products not already subject to quotas; and temporarily embargoed soyabean exports.

Legitimate American interests notwithstanding, these unilateral actions abruptly ended the agreements reached at Bretton Woods in 1944 and the post-war policy of a multilateral/cooperative approach to international monetary/trade relations.[19] Under the Bretton Woods agreement, an international monetary system was constructed in the form of a gold exchange standard based on the dollar. The USA functioned as central banker. Suspension of dollar convertibility caused European currencies to be revalued upwards against the dollar. For the first time since 1945, a US Administration treated the EC as it would a hostile state.[20] Offended Europeans were spurred toward greater trade, monetary and political independence from the USA. They saw the US 1974 Trade Reform Act as particularly protectionist and as an attempt by the USA to discharge a domestic problem on the outside world. The Act empowered the US President to raise, lower or eliminate US tariffs and simplified his authority to raise import barriers against states that restrict US exports. It also provided for adjusting import restrictions to help stabilize the balance of payments situation and to combat inflation.

The EC the UK joined in 1972 was a far different animal from that towards which the US had pushed the UK in the 1960s. British membership signalled America's increasing isolation and impotence *vis-à-vis* the course of EC integration. In 1973 there was a surprising, almost impetuous, brief turnabout in US attitudes towards EC (and NATO) members. With the end of involvement in Vietnam and new relations with the Soviets and Chinese, the Nixon Administration suddenly tried to reverse years of neglect of the European allies by announcing a Kennedy-like Grand Design, this time dubbed 'Year of Europe'. Articulated by Secretary of State Kissinger, the USA called for a new 'Atlantic Charter' to resuscitate US–European security and trade relations. The USA sought to guide European foreign policy in an Atlantic direction. Trying to keep Western policy formation centred in Washington, Kissinger insisted that the USA should be consulted on EC foreign policy decisions before they were taken. The compromise came in June 1974 with an informal agreement whereby EC member states agreed through the Council Presidency to inform allied or friendly governments of EC deliberations affecting them.

The 'Year of Europe' came at a time when EC members were stressing their own foreign political identity distinct from American patronage. Kissinger's inference that European interests were largely regional whereas the USA as a world power had global tasks offended the EC. The net effect of unilateral (and unfavourable) US action *vis-à-vis* the EC during 1971–3 was to reduce European trust in the USA. Europeans generally received the 'Year of Europe' with coolness if not suspicion, seeing the US approach and tone as patronizing and clumsy. Instead of a new Atlantic Charter, EC members responded months later with a Statement of Atlantic Principles (and a separate declaration for NATO) which fell drastically short of US hopes. Whereas Kissinger wanted to restore to the West a sense of common purpose, he only succeeded in highlighting its absence.[21] Controversy over the 'Year of Europe' was quickly overtaken by events in the Middle East in 1973/4.

One of the most serious splits in US and EC foreign policies came as a result of divergent responses to the October 1973 Yom Kippur War and the selective Arab oil embargo of October 1973–March 1974. The US military and political commitment to Israel sharply conflicted with the EC's attempt at a more even-handed, some would say pro-Arab, policy. The EC's immense dependence on Middle East oil imports makes it much more vulnerable than the USA to cuts in supply, so EC members took care not to offend Arab League members. US and European foreign policies towards the Middle East are complicated by the lack of an institutional forum in which to coordinate strategies: the Arab–Israeli conflict is outside NATO's regionally-limited purview. In 1973/4 the USA was angered by the EC's independent actions or inactions as the case may be, which in some cases openly conflicted with its own moves. Important examples include when: EC member states refused to put their air bases at US disposal in its effort to resupply the Israeli war effort in October; EC unity and resolve dissolved in its response to the selective Arab oil embargo; the EC communiqué of 15 December 1973 called on all sides to take into account 'the legitimate rights of the Palestinians';[22] France refused to join the other eight members and the Commission in IEA in 1974; EC and Arab League members created the Euro–Arab Dialogue in 1974.

Never before had EC members failed so miserably to act with resolve and unity on a trade issue (oil) under the EC's legal purview.[23] Treaty trade rules were suspended by some member states as they rushed to conclude bilateral trade agreements with Arab oil producers. But EC law bound them to work within EC rules and regulations. Commission proposals for joint responses to the embargo were rejected by two member states. Any last minute hopes for a common front fell apart at the Washington Energy Conference in 1974. France failed to join the other eight member states and the Commission in establishing the IEA and its petro-sharing plan for the oil-consuming developed nations. France viewed its formation as an attempt by Kissinger to confront the OPEC cartel. The USA roundly criticized the establishment of the Euro–Arab Dialogue to forge economic, financial, technical and cultural cooperation/links between the EC and Arab League members as against its more hardline approach to the OPEC cartel. The Dialogue was launched but the EC bowed to US pressure to keep discussions on a non-political level.

During the mid-1970s, US–EC relations were generally cordial if indifferent.[24] In 1975 two developments augured well for the future. Cooperation between the two sides which led to the conclusion of the CSCE accords in Helsinki showed how well they could work together in an area of mutual concern and on a basis of equality. In the Lomé Convention, the EC eliminated reverse preferences. In previous trade accords with the African associates, the EC not only offered tariff reductions for the signatories but itself received reciprocal preferences. These had been bitterly attacked by the US as discriminating against its trade with EC associates.

The current phase in US–EC relations began in 1976 when the Carter Administration took special steps to improve political ties with the EC. Goodwill generated then was replaced by the revival of old economic antagonisms and foreign policy differences with the arrival of the Reagan Administration in 1981, when divergent foreign policy interests and the worst transatlantic recession since the 1930s were bound to aggravate US–EC relations. However, the brusque approach of the Reagan Administration exacerbated matters.

Although many Europeans saw Carter's foreign policy as irresolute and direction-less, he concluded the tough-going Tokyo Round of MTNs, signed SALT II (both welcomed by Europeans) and supported the EC by paying an unprecedented official visit to the EC in 1978 which, although largely symbolic, went a long way in reconfirming US support for institutional aspects of European integration; directing the official foreign agricultural bureaucracy in Washington to accept the CAP as a *fait accompli* and to work with rather than against it;[25] approving partici-pation by the EC Commission President at the annual Western economic summits beginning in 1977; assigning importance to the new biannual high level US–EC consultations; and being the first US Administration to bless EPC, previously considered anathema to America's control over Western policy.

Even so, differences persisted over US and European policies toward the Middle East. Sceptical of the Camp David peace process, the EC called in 1980 for a Palestinian homeland and participation in peace negotiations and international guarantees of mutually recognized borders. The EC's unified position on the Middle East continued to exacerbate US–EC relations well into the 1980s. One bright spot in the relationship occurred in 1981 when EC members endorsed a plan to provide troops for a US-supported multilateral peacekeeping force for the Sinai, considered an integral part of the Camp David agreement. The EC backed the participation of token units of troops from four member states, without which the Force would have lacked a genuine international (and certainly European) character and credibility. However, the EC's reluctant response to the hostage crisis in Iran (1979–80) angered the USA which expected more forceful sanctions. Divergent American and European approaches to East–West relations were aggravated by their reactions to the Soviet invasion of Afghanistan in late 1979. Again the USA was deeply disturbed by the EC's reluctance to impose more forceful and comprehensive sanctions against the USSR. Nevertheless, the Carter Administration succeeded in creating goodwill toward the EC. It was a brief interlude which bridged the gap between developing problems of 1963–75 and their belated effects in the early 1980s.

Current problems are similar to those of the 1963–75 period: a close trade/security alliance whose post-war consensus and margin of commonality are dwindling as a result of several factors. They include: a changing international environment in which the EC's clout rose and America's declined; differing international outlooks predating the relationship;[26] and changing world trade patterns.[27] What has changed is the nature of US–EC problems whose solutions seem more unattainable and whose stakes are higher than ever before. These problems may have much to do with their adjustments to the final closing of the immediate post-war period. While the USA is withdrawing from its pre-eminent role in the world, and adjusting to a new position as one of several major powers, the EC is grappling with its new-found world economic power and diplomatic influence. Both do not yet have a clear concept of how to handle their new or adjusted roles, so confusion spills over into their mutual relations.[28]

The USA has begun to emerge out of the introspection and neo-isolation of the post-Vietnam War era committed to rebuilding its own and NATO's military strength *vis-à-vis* the USSR. It takes a hard line on relations with the USSR, is sceptical of *détente*, links Soviet actions in the world to progress in East–West trade liberalization and arms control, and uses trade, if necessary, as a tool against its adversaries. The EC does not share the US view of *détente* as a matter involving all relations between East and West. More sensitive to export trade, it is wary of using trade as a lever in East–West relations. There are US–EC disputes over El Salvador, Poland and the Middle East, and trade relations have sunk to an all-time low. The most intractable recession since the Great Depression and calls from producers and workers on both sides of the Atlantic for beggar-thy-neighbour-type trade practices—reminiscent of the inter-war years—greeted the Reagan Administration's arrival in 1981. It too supports a united Europe and a strong Atlantic Alliance, but is a no-nonsense protagonist of US producer interests. Like its predecessors, it is hesitant to take the EC to task over every complaint of US producer groups as it wants to avoid confrontation while vociferously attacking discriminatory effects of EC internal and external policies.[29]

Averting trade war: the challenge of steel and agriculture

Trade disputes in agriculture and steel are as old as the EC. Since 1981, US officials have argued with the EC over the CAP's protective and export support mechanisms. EC officials defend the CAP as crucial to the EC's survival and point out that aspects of US farm and related policies are discriminatory.

Both sides have different reasons for and methods[30] of protecting farm incomes from cheap food imports, subsidizing exports (either directly or indirectly) and spending huge sums of public money on their farmers. They differ widely over whether societal and structural problems should be addressed by price support programmes.[31] Agriculture's historical and political role in the USA and EC explains the divergences. The CAP guarantees a return to profit for all EC farmers. It is a social policy supporting low rural incomes and standards of living. There are 7.8 million EC and 3.3 million US farmers. The EC has more small and inefficient farms than the USA. Consequently, Europeans see the CAP as promoting structural transformation. The voluntary US farm price support policy, much less encompassing than the CAP, guarantees a return to the cost of production only (not a profit) for those participating farmers in any of the ten price support programmes who agree to their various provisions (such as acreage set aside during times of anticipated oversupply). The USA has long since separated its rural, social and economic problems from farm support policy.[32] Both sides are sensitive to their powerful farm producer lobbies who influence foreign economic policy.[33]

There are two important facts of foreign agricultural trade with which the USA must come to terms in the years ahead when agricultural technology will increase output,[34] world trade will grind to a halt, and competition for foreign markets will grow with major implications for US–EC relations:[35]

(1) *The EC is becoming an increasingly serious agricultural trade competitor of the USA.* Between 1973 and 1980, EC and US farm exports rose by 21 per cent and 13 per cent, respectively. EC sales account for 11.4 per cent of the current world food market against 9.5 per cent in 1975. The US world market share stayed at 17 per cent. It still holds one-half of the world grain market; the EC has 20 per cent but is gaining ground. The EC has overtaken Australia as the world's largest beef exporter and is challenging it as the world's third largest wheat exporter. During the 1962–82 period, the EC went from being the world's largest poultry importer to being its largest exporter. EC sugar exports doubled during 1976–81, taking about one-fifth of the world sugar market. EC enlargement to include Spain and Portugal will increase its farm export strength and could cut imports of Mediterranean-type products from the USA.

(2) *The EC is declining as America's main food customer.* Even though the USA has a huge farm surplus with the EC (last year it rose to about $8 billion), the EC has been declining as a share of US farm export market from over one-quarter to about one-fifth since 1975. In 1980–1, Asia was America's main farm export market. Agriculture has declined as a proportion of US–EC trade from over 17 per cent in 1976 to about 12.5 per cent in 1980. The largest item in US farm trade with the EC—grain (and products)—fell from 15 to 10.6 m. tons during 1976–81; US exports of feedgrains, mostly corn, from 13 m. tons in 1976 to 9.4 m. tons in 1980; wheat exports from 2.5 to 1.5 m. tons. US soyabean and corn gluten feed (a cheap feedgrain substitute) exports, which are not subject to the CAP's variable levy, have risen in value to about $4 billion from 1976 to 1981. US soyabean exports rose from 5.7 m. tons in 1976 to 9.6 m. tons in 1981; soyabean meal from 2.6 m. tons to 3.8 m. tons.[36] The increase in US farm exports to the EC since the founding of the CAP has occurred because gains in farm export items not subject to the CAP's variable levy system have more than offset the decline in items that are.

The Reagan Administration has revived a catalogue of US complaints against the CAP.[37] It hopes to change EC farm policy through direct pressure and/or official complaints at the GATT,[38] and objects to the EC's:

— export subsidies (the main bone of contention in US relations with the EC). The USA claims that the EC dumps surplus produce on to the world market using 'export restitutions'. Subsidized exports allegedly cause gluts, depress world prices and put US exports at comparative disadvantage, particularly in traditional US markets in Latin America, Africa and the Middle East. The EC is accused of violating a GATT agreement with the USA not to use export subsidies to capture unfairly third markets beyond traditional shares. The USA wants GATT to fix levels of farm trade for EC-subsidized exports but the EC expectedly refuses;[39]

— high import levies that shield the EC from world market forces and make US exports to it more costly;

— high price support levels on open-ended production (often set above world prices) leading to surpluses of wine, dairy products and sugar that are then subsidized for possible export;[40]

— tariff preferences on most Mediterranean horticultural exports to the EC discriminate against US exports of Mediterranean-type products, particularly citrus fruits;[41]

— subsidized export credits to keep interest rates on export financing (to promote foreign sales) on average 2 per cent below US rates. USA and EC disagree on new ground rules for official export financing.[42]

Steel is the other main source of friction in US–EC trade relations. The stakes are again high. Steel is among the largest employers in both economies, and vital to the construction and automobile industries. Unlike farm matters, steel trade disputes principally involve producers. The Carter Administration averted confrontation with EC steel producers. It appeased its own manufacturers, bent on protectionism, with a package of benefits and compromises all short of imposing new tariffs and/or quotas. It offered to protect its steel industry in 1977 with a so-called 'trigger price mechanism', a floor price set to keep cheap foreign supplies from undercutting US prices. If foreign prices fall below the trigger price mechanism, a quick anti-dumping investigation is undertaken automatically. If the US International Trade Commission and Department of Commerce determine that dumping and/or price undercutting occurred and resulted in material trade injury, the US Government may impose import restrictions to protect domestic industry. The trigger price is calculated on the basis of production and export costs of the most efficient foreign competitor—Japan. Europeans view the trigger price mechanism as a disguised subsidy for the US steel industry since it checks cheap imports.

In spring 1981, the US steel industry—America's fourth largest industry operating at about 50 per cent of capacity with one-third of its workforce either laid off or under-employed[43]—began sustaining huge sales, production, profits and job losses. The EC steel industry, highly dependent on US orders, is operating at about 30 million tons of over-capacity, with depressed prices, lost jobs and shrinking consumer demand both at home and abroad. Steel industries on both sides have outdated plants, high labour costs, and other structural problems. The EC has restructured its steel industry to alleviate some of these problems. Falling European currency values against the dollar in the past two years increased the competitiveness of EC steel exports and the chance for some to export profitably below the trigger price mechanism. Imports rocketed after the USA suspended the trigger price mechanism for an indefinite period from January 1982.

In the first half of 1982, major US steel producers tabled a flood of anti-dumping and countervailing duty suits with the International Trade Commission and the Department of Commerce against steel manufacturers in seven EC member states. They allege that EC producers have an unfair share of the US market. Nearly 90 per cent of all EC steel exports to the US are covered by these suits. The US steel industry wants the Department of Commerce either to impose import restrictions or preferably new additional levies. The USA wants to avert a trade war with the EC by negotiating voluntary export restraints: a more punitive response could trigger EC retaliation by unbinding the zero-rate duty on US profitable soyabean and corn gluten feed exports.

In preliminary rulings, the International Trade Commission agreed that EC steel imports caused material injury to domestic industry; and the Department of Commerce ruled that EC producers with government subsidies of 15–40 per cent of production costs dumped subsidized steel on the US market. The Department of Commerce imposed countervailing and anti-dumping duties on these EC producers in June and August 1982, respectively. They must pay tariffs of up to 40 per cent to make up the difference between their production costs, plus a profit margin, and their sales prices in the US. EC producers misjudged US resolve to limit imports. The Department of Commerce could price EC steel out of the US market. EC producers feel that the US exploits its advantage as an importer by 'artificial import limitations'.[44] US producers claim that the EC exports its steel unemployment. Final International Trade Commission and Department of Commerce rulings are due in late 1982. If EC producers are found to be either dumping and/or undercutting the fair market value of steel, the USA may impose punitive duties or quantitative restrictions. Importers would have to pay accumulated duties retroactively to the Department of Commerce's preliminary rulings.

By singling out producers in some (but not other) EC member states rather than uniformly imposing retaliatory duties on the EC as a whole, the USA split and weakened the EC, set its members against one another and ridiculed the EC's legal competence in steel trade. Some Europeans accuse the USA of using 'divide and rule' tactics to break the EC's back. US officials retort that EC members were unable to agree on export restraint levels acceptable to EC producers. Negotiations between all involved parties have so far failed to agree on voluntary export restraints to the USA.

Trade disputes will continue as long as both parties produce the same kind of products, compete for the same markets, support industry differently, and pursue contradictory economic/monetary policies. Trade problems will always exist. They become disputes when governments are pressurized into unilateral protectionism.

Political/security relations will always be captive in part to the mercantile interests of powerful domestic producer groups so long as the USA and EC remain open capitalist democracies. Narrow commercial interests often conflict with broader national interests.[45] The USA and EC must strike a balance between satisfying legitimate internal commercial interests and pursuing amicable political and security ties. Trade must be handled skilfully so it does not contaminate the entire Atlantic world.[46] The political and security relationship has, with some exceptions, kept the trade peace for thirty years. As political malaise deepens in the Atlantic Alliance, the trade relationship—always controversial—may be subject to further disruptions.

Politicization of trade relations

Many aspects of the US–EC trade relationship have become politicized in recent years. In many cases, international trade and politics have become so interlocked that conduct of one may affect the outcome of the other. The USA and EC disagree over trade and other ties with the Soviet bloc, over how serious the Soviet danger to Western Europe is, and how it should be met and by whom. That they bicker over NATO's enemy underscores the irony of the current intra-alliance dispute over East–West relations.

America and Russia were rivals long before the founding of the Atlantic Alliance. In 1949, Western Europe joined the US in its historical animosity towards Soviet Russia. However, with *détente*, Western Europe sought to renew commercial and human links with the East. For a while, many Americans welcomed the concept of *détente* but by the mid-to-late 1970s it was discredited, given international Soviet aggression either through Cuban surrogates in Africa or by direct military invasion of Afghanistan. Yet, for most West Europeans, it was still business as usual with the USSR, with some exceptions, based on the belief that 'European *détente*' was unlinked to 'superpower *détente*' outside Europe.

US trade with the Soviet bloc, barring grain and high technology sales, is limited. The US Government believes the Soviet economy is vulnerable to immediate outside economic pressure. So, unlike the EC, it uses trade as a lever over Soviet actions, such as denying 'most-favoured-nation' treatment until more Soviet Jews and others suffering religious persecution are allowed to emigrate. Although the Soviet bloc takes only 3 per cent of EC total exports (about 6 per cent for the FRG), the EC wants to expand this. The fact that COMECON and the EC do not officially recognize one another inhibits EC penetration of East European markets. While trade with the Soviet bloc is proportionately small, some key industries and sectors depend on it.

EC dependence on imported energy (Siberian natural gas could help), export markets (East Europe looks attractive) and geographical proximity to the Warsaw Pact (heightens its vulnerability to enemy pressure) explains why the EC seeks low-key cordial relations with the Soviet bloc. West Europeans tend to take a longer-term view of East–West relations than do Americans, many of whom see West Europeans as too captive of their commercial pursuits without sufficient concern for their own physical security.

The following disagreements illustrate the stunning differences between the close allies:

(1) *1979 Soviet invasion of Afghanistan*—The US imposed sanctions against the USSR, including a partial grains embargo and a boycott of the Moscow Olympics. EC responded less speedily with milder sanctions by preventing its exports to the USSR from replacing the suspended US supplies. It disregarded resolutions of the European Parliament for broad economic sanctions and an EC-wide boycott of the Olympics. The EC's response appeared indifferent and infuriated the US.

(2) *1981/2 Soviet-instigated imposition of martial law in Poland*—The US quickly imposed mild sanctions against the Polish Government; suspended government food aid shipments, commercial credits for non-food sales and Polish fishing rights in US waters, and postponed talks on rescheduling Poland's official debt. Slow-to-respond EC members bowed to US pressure and adopted NATO sanctions previously imposed. The US banned sales of General Electric turbine parts and caterpillar pipelayers earmarked for the Siberian natural gas pipeline. USA took other punitive actions, suspended export licences for high technology equipment and landing rights in the US for the Russian state airline. USA was angered and disappointed by the EC's belated mild symbolic sanctions: import quotas on about half of all luxury/manufactured products, amounting to 2 per cent of all Soviet exports to the EC.

(3) *Construction of Soviet pipeline linking Siberian natural gas to Western Europe—*

Participation by some EC member states in manufacturing parts for the construction of the pipeline and in arranging long-term contracts for the sale of natural gas met strong US resistance because it would make part of Europe dependent on the USSR for natural gas; and would earn the USSR the hard currency revenues it needs to expand its military strength *vis-à-vis* NATO. The USA claims that by denying the Soviets the needed bank credits, equipment and technology for the pipeline, they would be forced to divert their own huge resources away from defence. This would reduce military pressure on NATO in the years ahead. The EC's members claim American overreaction and interference in their internal affairs. Days after the Versailles economic summit of 4–6 June, on 18 June 1982 the USA extended its pipeline-parts embargo of the USSR to foreign subsidiaries of US companies and to foreign companies granted licences to produce pipeline equipment with US technology. This angered Europeans involved in the project who claimed that the prohibition on licences was illegal under international law.

(4) *Subsidized export credits/loans to the Soviet bloc*—The USA strongly opposes EC member governments' subsidized export credits/loans to the Soviet bloc as they enhance Soviet military and industrial power. At the Versailles economic summit, the two sides agreed only to surveil all Western commercial and financial relations with the Soviet bloc through OECD and to limit EC credits on the basis of 'commercial prudence'. The gap between US and European positions remains very wide.

(5) *Planned deployment of US cruise and pershing II missiles in Western Europe by late 1983*—A 1979 NATO agreement to deploy these missiles may be delayed by an upsurge in popular anti-nuclear, pro-neutral sentiment in parts of Western Europe. The problem is complicated by a growing fear among many Europeans that the USA would not come to their aid in the event of a Soviet invasion or threat of one.

(6) *Civil war in El Salvador*—Material and political support by the Reagan Administration for the anti-communist El Salvadorean Government against leftist guerrillas is strongly opposed by some EC member states, notably France and Denmark, who point to the oppressive nature of the regime. The US sees the war as an East–West confrontation and is upset by hostility or ambivalence among the European allies for its efforts to bolster the pro-Western Government.

The USA and EC also disagree over a joint Western approach to the North–South dialogue. Both realize the utility of a common negotiating stance *vis-à-vis* the Group of 77 (UN group representing about 115 developing countries). It would help them to moderate the more impractical demands of the less-developed countries (LDCs), strike a deal with which they can both live comfortably, improve the West's standing in the developing world, and avoid further cleavage in their foreign policies. But they cannot agree on how to accommodate Group 77 demands for the so-called 'new international economic order' (NIEO). US–EC agreement on Third World policy could be the key to improving the overall North–South relationship.

Disagreements over Third World policy are predictable since they are based on different historical and current trade relationships with the LDCs. The EC's well-formed foreign development policy is heavily influenced by the member states' close extensive ties with former colonies and their dependence on import/export trade with the LDCs. Its innovative development policy combines substantial tariff reductions with economic aid to seventy-five Lomé Convention and Mediterranean

Chart 1 US–EC relations: the balance sheet

Aspects of the Relationship	Centripetal Forces	Centrifugal Forces
Civilization	Common heritage —political culture moral/social values —ideology	Immediate post-war era of unquestionable US–European cohesion has ended; different historical ties with third countries cause current foreign policy disputes over ties with LDCs, Soviet bloc.
Historical experiences	Wartime and post-war camaraderie —cohesion Long-standing ethnic links —trade ties	
Political–economic systems	Pluralist democratic —mixed capitalist common socio-economic problems	Pluralist political–economic systems allow unreasonable producer group demands for government imposed protectionist trade measures to disrupt overall relationship.
Strategic security	Collective self defence arrangement (NATO) Equal stakes in defence of the Western Democracies against the common enemy	West Europe ultimately *dependent* on US for military security; rising pacifist–neutralist sentiment in West Europe; declining spectre of Soviet invasion; scepticism about US commitment to defend West Europe; questioning of original urgency behind and basis for alliance; EC's geographic proximity to USSR makes it more vulnerable and sensitive to pressures not immediate to US.
Interdependence[47]	Symmetric trade interdependence Symmetric political interdependence	Asymmetric monetary interdependence Asymmetric strategic security interdependence.

International trade	Common stakes in liberal world trade order—huge world trade shares	Politicization of world trade heightens number and area of US-EC conflicts; EC's heavy dependence on import/export trade makes it more vulnerable than US to international pressures.
Bilateral trade	Heavy dependence on each other's huge internal markets	Declining relative importance of each other's import markets; bitter commercial rivalry; huge EC trade deficit with US; differences over scope-level of government supports for private industry.
Leadership	Strong leaders capable of balancing US-EC trade-security interests; committed to smooth-running relationship	Weak leaders more susceptible to producer groups' protectionist calls; less capable of providing balance to relationship.
Foreign policy	Broad agreement on long-term Western goals; increasing isolation of US and EC in anti-Western international system spurs mutual foreign policy sensitivities	EC foreign policy independent of and conflicting with US; disagreement over foreign policy methods; lack of mechanism to coordinate non-NATO US-EC foreign policies; lack of coherent policies toward one another; lack of division of labour in the conduct of Western foreign policy interests.

basin countries. These trade/aid packages are highly regarded in the Third World. Through them the EC has been able to foster its own diplomatic and security goals independent of the USA, and given the developing countries their own forums to discuss bilateral trade problems and economic development matters with the EC. Its close contractual links and diplomatic relationships with a majority of the world's LDCs heightens its sensitivity to their problems. The EC takes a forward-looking position on many of the issues involved in the North–South negotiations. Other Western countries, including a reluctant America, often adapt their negotiating positions to those of the EC. Many LDCs see the EC as a conduit for pressuring the US into taking a more liberal view. The Lomé Convention has already incorporated some Group 77 demands for a NIEO. EC foreign development aid is granted largely independent of the East–West conflict. Since the EC is not a military superpower, many LDCs are more comfortable with EC aid than with US, Soviet, or even individual EC member state aid.

The US relationship with the Third World reflects its historical experience. The USA is less dependent on Third World trade than the EC and favours non-discriminatory world trade. The quality and quantity of its Third World links are limited. As a superpower, the US views Third World development more in terms of the East–West conflict than the North–South dialogue. Economic development alone was not the sole purpose of extensive US aid to its largest recipients: Egypt, Israel and Turkey. While it has its own extensive network of bilateral and multilateral foreign aid commitments, the USA lacks the EC's commitment to and experience of Third World economic development problems. Since its image in the Third World is very poor, its ability to influence events there is quite limited. The USA provides a smaller amount of official foreign aid as a percentage of GNP than do most of the other OECD countries. It is less accommodating in North–South negotiations than the EC, believing that many LDC problems should be addressed through existing bilateral and multilateral arrangements rather than new international development institutions.

The USA may gain by following the EC's lead. A ray of hope was injected into the US–EC impasse over North–South relations at the Versailles economic summit. The USA agreed to join an anxious EC in working toward the launching of a new round of North–South negotiations on proposals tabled by Group 77 at the UN. The USA and EC disagree not so much on the ultimate outcome of East–West and North–South relations—commercial and military security for the Western countries—as over the methods to achieve the same general ends.

US–EC relations: the balance sheet

Do the disruptive outweigh the unifying forces in the US–EC relationship? Are current disputes more destabilizing than their predecessors and, if so, is the relationship undergoing fundamental change?

The balance sheet (see Chart 1) shows that the US–EC relationship traverses a very fine dividing line between forces which hold it together (centripetal) and those which pull it apart (centrifugal). The existence of the relationship depends on the balance struck between those forces by committed Atlantic leaders. The centrifugal forces have grown in number and substance over the past decade. Yet, the Atlantic leaders have thus far been able to balance them by underscoring the importance of the centripetal forces. Whether they will be able to continue to maintain the balance is the most critical question facing US–EC relations today. However, many centrifugal forces cannot be controlled. The current round of disputes is unprecedented in the history of the relationship as the trade quarrels are compounded by foreign policy differences.

Are these divisions penetrative or largely cosmetic? Divisions over different historical experiences as they affect current behaviour and pressures borne by the relationship from the changing international environment result in more penetrative than cosmetic differences. However, the USA and EC disagree more often over methods than goals of each other's foreign policies. Such differences are more cosmetic than deep-seated. That the two complain about one another's unilateral actions so ferociously and often underscores the extent to which they are mutually relevant and dependent as key trading and security partners. The more inter-dependent the relationship, the more likely the two sides are affected by what the other does and says. Seen from this perspective, their differences are more cosmetic than substantive.

The relationship is undergoing fundamental change. Its future hinges on many unforeseen exogenous and endogenous developments. However, the two sides will be hard pressed in the 1980s to find the same kind of unifying missions to keep them as closely bound as they were in the 1950s.

Notes

1. *The Economist*, 27 February 1982, p. 11.
2. See *Monthly External Trade Bulletin 1958–1980* (Luxembourg, Statistical Office of the EC), 1981.
3. For a comparison of US and EC farm support policies, see Gardner, B., 'Agricollision', *Europe* (January/February 1982), p. 13.
4. *The Economist*, op. cit., p. 12.
5. On the development of a European foreign (political) policy, see Ginsberg, R. H., 'Political Economy of Cooperation: European Foreign Policy in the Making', paper presented to the Third International Conference of Europeanists, Council for European Studies, Washington DC, 1 May 1982.
6. *Treaties Establishing the European Communities* (Brussels, Office for Official Publications of the EC, 1978), p. 213.
7. On EPC, see da Fonseca-Wollheim, H., *Ten Years of European Political Cooperation* (Brussels, Commission of the European Communities, 1981).
8. For an exposé of US–European relations, see Morgan, R., 'The Transatlantic Relationship' in Twitchett, K. J. (ed.), *Europe and the World: The External Relations of the Common Market* (London, Europa, 1976).
9. Warnecke, S., 'The Political Implications of Trade for European–American Relations' in Czempiel, E-O. and Rustow, D. A. (eds), *The Euro-American System: Economic and Political Relations between North America and Western Europe* (Boulder, Westview, 1976).
10. Johnson, H. S., 'EC–US Relations in the Post-Kissinger Era' in Hurwitz, L. (ed.), *Contemporary Perspectives in European Integration* (Westport, Greenwood Press, 1980).
11. See Kraft, J., *The Grand Design: From Common Market to Atlantic Partnership* (New York, Harper, 1962).
12. Warnecke, op. cit., p. 79.
13. Morgan, op. cit.
14. Talbot, R., *The Chicken War: An International Trade Conflict between the United States and the EEC* (Ames, Iowa State University Press, 1978).
15. On Nixon–Kissinger foreign policy towards the EC, see Schaetzel, R. J., *The Unhinged Alliance: America and the European Community* (New York, Harper & Rowe, 1975), p. 143.
16. Diebold, Jr, W., 'Economics and Politics: The Western Alliance in the 1970s' in Hanrieder, W. (ed.), *The United States and Western Europe* (Cambridge, Winthrop, 1974), p. 145.
17. Schaetzel, op. cit., p. 95.
18. Calleo, D. P., 'American Foreign Policy and American European Studies: An Imperial Bias?' in Hanrieder, op. cit. Calleo offers a 'revisionist' approach to analysing events surrounding US actions in August 1971.

19. Ibid.
20. Schaetzel, op. cit., p. 78.
21. Aron, R., 'Europe and the United States: The Relations between Europeans and Americans' in Landes, D. S. (ed.), *Western Europe: The Trials of Partnership* (Lexington, D. C. Heath, 1977).
22. *European Political Cooperation* (Bonn, Press and Information Office, 1978), p. 79.
23. Etienne, H., 'Community Integration: The External Environment', *Journal of Common Market Studies*, 18 (1980), 289–312.
24. Cooper, R. N., 'Trade and Monetary Relations between the United States and West Europe' in Landes, op. cit., p. 327.
25. Observation based on the author's work experience in the international trade policy division of the Foreign Agricultural Services, United States Department of Agriculture (1977–9). While Carter directed farm trade bureaucrats to accept and work with the CAP as it is, built-in institutional bias against it persisted.
26. For further discussion, see *The Economist*, 27 February 1982, p. 12.
27. On changing US–EC trade patterns (1962–78), see Jacobsen, H. D., 'Trade between the European Community and the United States' in Feld, W. (ed.), *Western Europe's Global Reach* (New York, Pergamon, 1979).
28. Malmgren, H., 'Europe, the United States and the World Economy' in Warnecke, S. (ed.), *The European Community in the 1970s* (New York, Praeger, 1972).
29. This is not to say that the USA keeps its import trade market fully open. It does indeed limit imports such as cheese, sugar and steel which hurts EC trade.
30. Gardner, op. cit., p. 13.
31. Ibid.
32. Ibid.
33. Diebold, Jr, op. cit., p. 155.
34. Gardner, op. cit., p. 13.
35. The trade statistics quoted in items (1) and (2) are extracted from *Foreign Agriculture*, March 1982.
36. According to EC Agriculture Commissioner, Poul Dalsager, continuing growth in EC imports of cereal substitutes results in lower imports of corn and higher EC exports of cereals and poultry, with negative consequences for both the EC budget and US agricultural exports. See *Europe* (July–August 1982).
37. Diebold, Jr, op. cit., warns that, given the sensitivity of EC agriculture policy, any frontal attacks on the CAP calling for drastic change will not succeed. Reform is more likely to come from within rather from outside pressure.
38. For a detailed account of how the EC responds to US charges of agricultural trade discrimination, see *Europe* (July–August 1982), 16–21.
39. The EC refutes US contentions about export subsidies, maintaining that they are designed to bring domestic EC prices down to world level. The EC claims also that the USA subsidizes grain exports by offering long-term concessionary rate loan facilities to purchasers. But the USA considers its subsidized grain sales as part of its foreign aid assistance effort.
40. The EC in turn complains about the high level at which the USA sets dairy price supports which have resulted in the accumulation of huge surpluses of dairy products.
41. Tariff preferences, granted to nearly all Mediterranean countries on a roughly equal basis, contribute to regional economic and political stability in an otherwise volatile area. See Chapter 14.
42. The EC has been pressuring the USA to lower its interest rates which are making it difficult for European governments to reduce their own interest rates and achieve economic growth. As the dollar appreciates against the European currencies, oil purchases become more costly since they are paid for in dollars. At the same time, EC exports to the USA, such as steel products, become more attractive to its customers.
43. *The Economist*, 15 May 1982, p. 79. Figures are for March 1982.
44. For Europe's view of the US steel actions, see van der Ven, H., 'Steel Deadlock: A Primer', *Europe* (July–August 1982), 24–8.
45. It is possible that the steel and agricultural trade grievances will be sorted out through a package deal at the GATT meeting scheduled for November 1982. Potentially disruptive, from the European point of view, is the consideration being given to trade reciprocity legislation in the US Congress. Viewed as protectionist by the EC, such legislation would make a close connection between the way in which US products are treated by country 'x' and the way in which its products are in turn treated by the USA.
46. Schaetzel, op. cit., p. 118.

47. The USA and EC have a roughly equal (symmetric) interdependent trade and political relationship. That is, one side does not dominate the other with regard to trade and political relations. However, the EC's well-being and physical security are dependent on US monetary policy, economic growth, and its commitment to defend Europe from attack and provide a credible deterrent against such a possibility. The EC then has an asymmetric (unequal) interdependent relationship with the US over monetary affairs and strategic security.

16 The European Community and the East bloc

DAN HIESTER

EC relations with the state-trading countries of Eastern Europe and the Soviet Union provide a fascinating and important area of study for students of EC affairs not only because of their special nature within the more general range of external relations policy, but also because they highlight the contradictions in some of the more abstract goals of European integration. There are, in fact, no official relations between East and West at the level of bloc institutions, although contacts do exist. As part of its trade and commercial policy, the EC does have agreements with individual states of the East bloc, but state-to-state agreements between East and West constitute continuing and important exceptions to this policy. At a more fundamental level, the success of EC integration and the delicate nature of East–West relations in Europe highlight the lack of a more general pan-European integration, or, alternatively, the division of Europe into political and economic halves.

In a European context, the East bloc is generally taken to refer to the European members[1] of the Council for Mutual Economic Assistance (CMEA).[2] Yugoslavia and Albania are sometimes considered part of the bloc, but they remain outside the CMEA. The remainder of this chapter will concentrate on the CMEA members, but it should be noted that Yugoslavia has important agreements with the EC and remains a poignant exception to many of the generalizations made here on inter-bloc relations in Europe. Since the term 'bloc' appears to be firmly rooted in the literature, it will be employed here as a matter of convenience, although it is not entirely appropriate. While the EC may be seen as an integrating, cohesive economic grouping based on multilateral relationships with authoritative central decision-making institutions, the CMEA is based primarily on a series of bilateral relationships served by an intergovernmental secretariat based in Moscow. This essential difference in the nature of the two organizations has been a basic impediment to the establishment of formal institutional relations between the two blocs. More generally, of course, the term 'bloc' is used to denote the fundamental economic, social, and political differences between the Western and Eastern parts of Europe.

The formal competence of the EC to act in external relations arises principally, although not exclusively, from three main areas of the treaties: the Common External Tariff (CET), the Common Commercial Policy (CCP), and the Association Policy. In these areas the EC's authority to act is firmly established and remains generally unchallenged by the member states and is accepted as a political and legal fact of life by most of the international community.[3] Thus, for example, the EC represents the interests of the member states in international trade negotiations, most notably the GATT (General Agreement on Tariffs and Trade). In this area, EC competence and control over external relations appears firmly entrenched, based on the consensus that existed among the members at the time of the formation of the EC and subsequently accepted by applicant states.

The EC, or rather the member states of the EC, also attempt to form common positions on external relations/foreign policy through the system of Political Cooperation. Since this is discussed elsewhere in this volume, it will not be dealt with here. However, Political Cooperation is an increasingly important forum for discussion of the EC member states' relations with the East bloc. Their approach to the Conference on Security and Cooperation in Europe (CSCE) is a prime example of the use of this intergovernmental mode of cooperation in an attempt to forge common external positions. However, the main form of concrete inter-action between the members of the EC and the members of the CMEA has been trade and commerce and it is this aspect of inter-bloc relations that will be emphasized in this chapter.

At the present time, neither the CMEA nor most of the individual member countries officially recognize the EC, although they do engage in talks with its representatives and in certain cases conclude agreements with the Commission.[4] Initially, the countries of the East bloc were hostile to the existence of the EC, seeing it as yet another capitalist club allied closely to the USA. In 1972, however, Mr Brezhnev recognized the 'realities' developing in Western Europe (that is, the existence and development of the EC). Around the same time new goals for integration in the CMEA were announced[5] and preliminary negotiations were beginning which were to lead to the conclusion of the Helsinki accords in 1975. These negotiations had been facilitated in no small measure by the FRG's successful prosecution of its Ostpolitik. This new era in East–West political relations in Europe had been preceded by more than a decade of dramatic increases in trade and other forms of economic interaction between the two blocs, as can be seen in the accompanying table.

Table 1   EC exports to Eastern Europe (in millions of dollars)

	1958	1971
Bulgaria	25.0	192.0
Hungary	58.0	438.0
Poland	141.0	464.0
Romania	47.0	445.0
East Germany	34.0	178.0
Czechoslovakia	110.0	575.0
USSR	208.0	1,118.0
Total	623.0	3,410.0

EC imports from Eastern Europe (in millions of dollars)

	1958	1971
Bulgaria	26.0	153.0
Hungary	56.0	363.0
Poland	124.0	553.0
Romania	60.0	428.0
East Germany	33.0	171.0
Czechoslovakia	104.0	429.0
USSR	274.0	1,084.0
Total	677.0	3,181.0

Sources: Supplement to the Monthly Statistics of Foreign Trade, No. 5, 1972, and Foreign Trade Analytical Tables (CST), 1958.[6]

It might be expected, therefore, that trade and commerce with the East bloc would provide a prime example of a common EC external relations position based both on the Treaties, as noted above, and on the member states' interest in forming common political positions. The operation of the CCP in relation to the state-trading countries of the CMEA provides instead a glaring exception to the ability of the EC members to achieve common external policy positions. EC competence in this area derives mainly from Article 113 of the Treaty of Rome which gives the EC sole negotiating rights over commercial policy for the members after the transitional period. Since 1973, the EC has formally had exclusive competence over commercial agreements with the state-trading countries. From this time, the member states were to cease negotiating bilateral agreements with individual countries of the East bloc.

However, the success of the central institutions of the EC, primarily the Commission, in wresting this important area of competence in external relations from the control of the member states is more apparent than real. The commercial clauses of the Treaty have been interpreted narrowly by the member governments and significant areas of economic relations between individual member states of the EC and the CMEA are regulated by bilateral, long-term (up to ten years) co-operation agreements. These commercial and industrial cooperation agreements cover credit policy, technology exchange, co-production, and joint ventures. As a result, major areas of external economic relations remain outside the effective control of the EC's institutions and weaken its claim to exclusive competence in this policy area in relation to a region of vital interest to the member states.[7] To deal with this problem, the EC established in 1974 a consultative procedure for member states negotiating bilateral cooperation agreements with the state-trading countries of the CMEA. It did not really alter the basic position, however, which remains unsatisfactory from the point of view of the Commission and the European Parliament (EP).

The reasons for this situation are not difficult to discern. Commercial relations with the countries of the East bloc remain an important aspect of the foreign economic policies of the member states over which the individual governments are not willing to relinquish control to the central decision-making institutions of the EC. That this would be the outcome was not anticipated either by the architects of the Treaties or by integration theorists. In fact, Philippe Schmitter had put forward a quite contrary hypothesis to explain what was likely to happen in external relations. Externalization, the need to come to terms with external issues, would lead to increasing levels of policy integration in a group of already integrating states. To do this, they would rely increasingly on central institutions.[8] This has not happened for the EC in the issue area of East–West economic relations.

One possible explanation for this may be found in the burgeoning interdependence literature which focuses on international or global issues, emphasizing the increasing complexity of international life, especially in the area of economic interactions, and the mutual vulnerability of all states to these forces.[9] Whether global interdependence and regional integration are in some areas incompatible is a question raised most clearly by Ernst Haas in his monograph, 'The Obsolescence of Regional Integration Theory'.[10] Haas argued that the EC states had made no clear choice between national, European, or global action in dealing with industrial and post-industrial issues in a period he described as one of 'turbulence'. Institutions and forums for dealing with these problems proliferated; a situation which he described as 'asymmetrical overlap'. The point is that the members of the EC may choose to respond to this situation, which might be described as interdependence, in a number of ways and that EC methods and institutions may not always be the obvious choice. Analytically, the answer may be that integration theory is simply not relevant to an understanding of these problems and that looking to other areas of international relations theory may be more helpful.

The external issue of economic relations with the East bloc is an example of the tension that exists between the goal of regional integration and the pressure of international interdependence for the EC states. The Treaties and integration theory would seem to anticipate that all issues of economic relations between member states of the EC and the state-trading countries of the CMEA should come under the control of the EC within the scope of the CCP. In practice, only in those areas where a prior issue consensus existed, primarily the CET, has central EC control been successful. On most other matters, specifically cooperation agreements and industrial policy, bilateral East–West arrangements have been the rule. Because of the nature of East–West economic relations in Europe, this situation is unlikely to change and the EC will probably fail to bring commercial policy under central control. Put another way, bilateral cooperation agreements and industrial cooperation between East and West European governments, firms and enterprises represents an absence of policy integration on both sides.[11] The reasons for this absence are political as well as economic and related in part to the foreign policy objectives of the individual states.

The area of direct bloc-to-bloc links and official recognition remains clouded by disagreement. The main obstacles are the differences in character and purpose of the EC and the CMEA and the political implications that would accompany official mutual recognition. The EC sees itself as a comprehensive, integrating economic and political grouping with supranational powers. The CMEA is seen as a loose affiliation of disparate economies dependent upon, and dominated by, the Soviet Union. The two institutions are not, therefore, comparable and the EC negotiating position is to propose limiting prospective official links to exchanges of technical and statistical information. The CMEA wants the links to be comprehensive, covering all inter-bloc trade. The EC resists this since the CMEA does not have comparable legal powers and the separate economies of the bloc are too diverse in both size and level of economic development to be encompassed within an overall set of agreements. The EC, therefore, prefers bilateral agreements with each state of the bloc, tailored to the individual conditions. Moreover, the EC is not anxious to strengthen further the Soviet Union's control over Eastern Europe which the enhancing of the CMEA by mutual recognition would imply.[12] The incentive for the EC in the negotiations, however, is that signing of an agreement would signal official recognition of the EC by the CMEA and its members. This would end the contesting by East bloc countries of the EC's presence and status at international meetings and its standing in signing international conventions and agreements. During 1981, these negotiations reached an impasse.[13]

Relations between the two blocs can be summarized by breaking them down into three broad categories: (1) state-to-state bilateral relations, (2) EC-to-state relations, and (3) EC–CMEA relations. Analytically, this has important implications for intra-bloc cohesion and inter-bloc interactions.[14] The categories containing the most significant links will be important indicators to the likely success or failure of continuing EC attempts to form a comprehensive external position *vis-à-vis* the East bloc.

Relations in the first category, between governments in each bloc, are the most numerous and reflect the use of economic policy to further the separate foreign policy interests of the member states. These are the most difficult to bring under a common policy decided at the level of central institutions. This problem is clearly reflected in Commission and EP concern at the lack of effective EC control over cooperation agreements within the scope of the CCP.

Activity in the second category, in which the Commission represents the EC in links with individual East bloc countries, is gradually expanding. There are two problems here, the first being how much control over these links the member states are willing to yield to the central institutions. Put simply, it is a matter of which links will be moved from category one to category two. The second problem concerns the willingness of the East bloc countries to deal with the EC institutions directly rather than with the governments of the individual member states, implying thereby a *de facto* if not *de jure* recognition. The likelihood is that if the EC members can agree on a particular common position, then the CMEA states have no choice but to deal with the EC in cases of significant interest to the East bloc states. This was no more clearly demonstrated than in the fisheries negotiations when the Soviet Union, Poland, and the German Democratic Republic entered into negotiations with the EC.[15]

As has been explained, contacts in the third category are being explored only very tentatively. They contain the most far-reaching implications for the blocs, each having something to gain and something to lose by mutual recognition. Success in the negotiations has been blocked by the incompatible terms of agreement sought by each side. It is in this area of potential relations that the most fundamental problems are raised for the EC in terms of overall goals in Europe.[16]

The future of bloc relations is likely to be troubled by a number of contemporary issues. The 'crisis' over the imposition of martial law in Poland in 1981 caused considerable difficulty in East–West relations, at least at the level of political rhetoric. The lasting impact of the event is more difficult to judge and may be more significant for relations within the Western Alliance than for relations between East and West. Within the EC, the demonstrable difficulty the member states experienced in trying to agree a common approach to Poland may prove to be more of an impediment to future negotiations at the inter-bloc level than the 'crisis' itself.

A more basic and what may prove to be a much more difficult problem to deal with is the huge cumulative debt being built up by the East bloc with Western countries. The burden is most acute in the case of Poland but is faced by all the East bloc countries, including the Soviet Union. Since non-European countries, most notably the USA, are involved, the debt problem cannot be dealt with on a purely European basis, and this presents further challenges to the role of the EC in inter-bloc relations. The difficulties are compounded and made extremely complex by problems in the areas of currency convertibility, compensation arrangements, agricultural trade, dumping, and other market disturbances.[17] The ability to process and deal with all these issues is straining the capacity of national governments and EC institutions alike.

The future of EC relations with the East bloc will depend in large part on the future of the EC itself. Should a 'two-tier' Europe or 'Europe à la carte' emerge, then the three categories discussed above would need significant revision. A mixed and untidy set of relations may be the most likely outcome, not least because of the conflicting pressures of integration and interdependence. The fundamental problem is that the EC seems to be pursuing incompatible goals in its policies and relations with the CMEA and its members. It wants recognition, on its own terms to serve its own interests, from the individual member states of the East bloc, while refusing to offer the same status to the CMEA for fear of adding greater legitimacy and strength to the Soviet Union's influence over the economies of Eastern Europe. Moreover, if relations between the two blocs at a formal level were realized, it would tend to strengthen the symbolic impression that the EC was recognizing formally the economic division of Europe, which in the most general sense it should be dedicated to eliminating. EC external relations policies, which may seem on the surface to be of a technical economic nature, have the most profound political implications for all of Europe.

Notes

1. Bulgaria, Czechoslovakia, the German Democratic Republic, Hungary, Poland, Romania and the Soviet Union.
2. In the West, the CMEA is also sometimes known as COMECON.
3. See, e.g., Twitchett, K. J. (ed.), *Europe and the World: The External Relations of the Common Market* (London, Europa Publications, 1976), p. xiv.
4. See, e.g., Marsh, P., 'EEC Foreign Economic Policy and the Political Management of East–West Economic Relations', *Millennium*, 9 (1980), 41–54, and *EP Working Documents*, 'Report on the state of relations between the EEC and East European state-trading countries and COMECON', 89/78 (11 May 1978), 8–10.
5. Pinder, J., 'Integration in Western and Eastern Europe: Relations between the EC and CMEA', *Journal of Common Market Studies*, 18 (1979), 127.
6. *European Community*, No. 160 (Washington, DC, November 1972), p. 17. Figures for East Germany are low because all trade between East and West Germany is considered 'intra-German trade'. This creates major problems for the operation of the EC's external economic policies *vis-à-vis* the East bloc.
7. See the concern expressed in *EP Working Documents*, 89/78, op. cit. and in *EP Working Documents*, 'Report on relations between the European Community and the East European state-trading countries and the CMEA (COMECON)', 1–424/81, 28 August 1981.
8. Schmitter, P. C., 'Three Neo-Functional Hypotheses about Regional Integration', *International Organization*, 23 (1969), 165. See also Schmitter, P. C., 'A Revised Theory of Regional Integration', *International Organization*, 24 (1970), 848, and Nye, J. S., *Peace in Parts: Integration and Conflict in Regional Organization* (Boston, Little, Brown & Co., 1971), pp. 92–3.
9. See, e.g., Nau, H. R., 'From Integration to Interdependence: Gains, Losses and Continuing Gaps', *International Organization*, 33 (1979), 119–47.
10. Haas, E. B., *The Obsolescence of Regional Integration Theory* (Berkeley, University of California), 1975.
11. For an important discussion of the whole question, see Pinder, op. cit., pp. 114–34.
12. *EP Working Documents*, 89/78, op. cit., p. 29.
13. *Agence Europe*, No. 3173, 6/7 July 1981, p. 11.
14. For an interesting discussion of the interaction of blocs, see Kaiser, K., 'The Interactions of Regional Subsystems', *World Politics*, 21 (1968), 84–107.
15. *EP Working Documents*, 89/78, op. cit., p. 8.
16. Ibid., p. 29.
17. For extensive discussion of these problems, see *EP Working Documents*, 89/78, op. cit., and *EP Working Documents*, 1–424/81, op. cit.

17 The European Community and Canada

ROBERT BOARDMAN

The EC's economic and commercial cooperation agreement with Canada, signed in 1976, filled a residual and somewhat obscure gap in the external relations network.[1] Canada tended to lack the definition and visibility which British membership negotiations had earlier given to Australia and New Zealand. Frequently concealed in the glare from Washington, moreover, Ottawa did not in the early 1970s appear to present problems calling for a new lens with a higher magnitude of resolution. That Canada and the EC were able within a relatively short span of time to create this novel instrument can be attributed to three main sets of factors: first, a push by Canada for some kind of working relationship with the EC that would set the seal on a search for greater diversification in its foreign economic relations; second, the growing importance in international relations generally during the 1970s of resource issues, which served to focus European attention on Canada as a politically stable and like-minded supplier state; and third, a set of political circumstances in the EC conducive to member state acceptance of the kind of link with Canada being pressed, in its turn, by the Commission.

Relations between Canada and Europe are long standing. There are historic ties with Britain and France, and connections of varying degrees of political significance with Italy, the FRG and other member states created by immigrants to the country. Until 1982, Canada's Commonwealth membership was underscored by its constitution's status as an Act passed by the Parliament of the United Kingdom. Economic relations, in the form of the Grand Banks fisheries off Newfoundland from the late fifteenth century, pre-date the existence both of the EC and of Canada. Canada in 1976 was part of the common military alliance framework linking it with the majority of the EC's member states. There are even common ocean boundaries: with Denmark by way of Greenland, and with France by way of the islands of Saint-Pierre and Miquelon. However, with one important exception —the 1959 agreement on uranium supply between Canada and EURATOM—no formal relations between the EC and Canada existed until the developments of the mid-1970s which form the subject of this chapter.

Origins of the Canada–EC Framework Agreement

The events which led to this relationship can be summarized very briefly. An initial series of Canadian overtures for what came to be known as a 'contractual link' having met with a mixed reception in Europe in the early 1970s, the EC Commission was then instrumental in giving shape and meaning to the impulse, within limits set by what was acceptable to member states and what was permissible according to the provisions of the Rome Treaty and the GATT. Slips 'twixt cup and lip' being as common as they are in international politics, however, the outcome of the Canadian Government's initiative remained uncertain until well into 1975.

Assessments of the impact on Canadian interests of the EC, and particularly of the CAP, had appeared occasionally in Canada since the late 1950s. However, before British accession to the EC, the various issues involved were not central to Canada's foreign policy makers. British membership of the EC from 1 January 1973 coincided with the final phases of a period of reappraisal by Ottawa of Canada's future position in world affairs, and more especially within the grouping of Western industrialized nations. The navel-gazing was prompted by events not in Europe so much as in North America. A quest for new directions marked the general approach to foreign policy matters taken by Prime Minister Trudeau's Liberal Government in the first few years following the 1968 election. While the broad question of relations with the giant neighbour to the south is a perennial one for Canadians, it was President Nixon's foreign economic policies of 1971 which made this question again an immediate and compelling one.[2] The so-called 'third option' for Canadian foreign policy meant a search for a more diversified set of economic relations with other countries, a mix of partnerships that might serve to deflect some of the costly effects of over-reliance on one. Somewhat discredited in the changed atmosphere of the later 1970s, the phrase at this time was used to lend coherence, visibility and perhaps even a sense of mission to Ottawa's approaches to Brussels. At no point, though, did it imply a wish to set Canada adrift from its American marker buoy. Such an intent would in any case have been counter-productive, as the soundings of Washington's reactions taken later by Bonn and London indicated.

Leaving aside the provisions of Article 238 of the Rome Treaty, on association agreements, the bulk of the EC's external relations role has been constructed on the limited foundations of Articles 111 and 113, which deal with commercial policy. This was not an adequate basis for the kinds of relations with the EC envisaged by Canada. Moreover, the GATT stood in the way of some possibilities. It appeared to rule out any form of preferential trading agreement; and the alternative of a non-preferential agreement ran up against the objection that this would be meaningless. A general statement of principles, aired as one option in Europe, would not have satisfied Ottawa (and the Paris summit of 1972 had already spoken of the need for a 'constructive dialogue' with Canada). Economic cooperation, though more conventional, proved a more satisfactory lever.

Establishing formal mechanisms for the promotion of economic cooperation between the EC and Canada, however, clearly raised issues of competence. In the event, the more open-ended provisions of Article 235 of the Rome Treaty were exploited as a legal underpinning of the 1976 Framework Agreement. Of the member states, objections on the grounds of EC competence came most forcefully in 1974–5 from Britain and France. Hence a crucial feature of the agreement, Article III(4) stated that the agreement and action resulting from it 'shall in no way affect the powers of the member states of the Communities to undertake bilateral activities with Canada in the field of economic cooperation and to conclude, where appropriate, new economic cooperation agreements with Canada.'[3] Insertion of this compromise formula was a key factor leading to accommodation of French and British concerns, and to the start of formal negotiations between Canadian and Commission officials in 1976. Without it, the Commission's active pursuit from the late summer of 1974 of a Canadian connection might well have come to nothing. Though Canada's own proposals were in themselves inadequate, it argued, a wider concept was both desirable and feasible.[4] Apart from the EC-building character of the proposed arrangement—foreign policy competence would be extended, and an EC role in certain areas of economic cooperation arguably had implications for industrial policy within the EC—the Commission pointed to the importance of Canada as a supplier of raw materials in a world of mounting uncertainties. It was this point that the European Parliament (EP) found particularly attractive.

The eventual success of these various moves depended on a combination of factors in the EC. While facilitating agreement, these nevertheless ensured that the resulting document did not depart too radically from existing norms. Canadian diplomacy at the highest governmental levels, including visits to Brussels and member state capitals by Trudeau, the personal support of leading Commissioners, mediatory activity by the Dutch and others—all played a part in securing a green light for the start of negotiations from the Council of Foreign Ministers. While not unduly perturbed by the competence question, however, states other than France and Britain had qualms. Even the Dutch had been somewhat sceptical observers of Canadian approaches in 1974. Denmark in 1975 linked the issue with continuing oil-pricing negotiations in Paris, and held up the start of negotiations by demanding that Canadian concessions in this more important forum should come first. Lingering fears that Canadian defence cutbacks in the late 1960s might augur a more pervasive spirit of withdrawal from European security affairs coloured the German response. The linkage with defence issues was explicit in Bonn's approach, and occasions such as Trudeau's visit in late 1974 to NATO headquarters were thus direct contributing factors to the conclusion of the agreement.

Its text was short. Exploratory rather than entangling, it stimulated the palates of supporters while reassuring critics, worried about the indigestible meal to follow, that the enterprising chefs had probably ransacked the larder even to get this far. The preamble recognized, *inter alia*, 'that the European Communities and Canada desire to establish a direct link with each other which will support, complement and extend cooperation between the member states of the European Communities and Canada,' and made the point 'that such cooperation should be realised in evolutionary and pragmatic fashion, as their policies develop'. The main body of the agreement (Articles II and III) then consisted of a brief statement of objectives and of possibilities with respect to commercial and economic cooperation. On the first, the parties undertook 'to promote the development and diversification of their reciprocal commercial exchanges to the highest possible level.' As part of this, they would 'take fully into account their respective interests and needs regarding access to and further processing of resources.' In relation to the second, various objectives were defined, including the encouragement of technological and scientific progress, the opening up of new sources of supply and new markets, and the reduction of regional disparities; and the parties agreed to encourage and facilitate such means as broader inter-corporate links, 'especially in the form of joint ventures', increased and 'mutually beneficial' investment, technological and scientific exchanges, and joint operations by their respective firms and organizations in third countries. Finally, a Joint Cooperation Committee (JCC) was created in Article IV 'to promote and keep under review the various commercial and economic cooperation activities envisaged between the Communities and Canada.'[5]

The workings and significance of the Agreement

The Framework Agreement of 1976 did not represent an abrupt transition in relations between Canada and the EC. A Canadian mission to the EC had begun operating in Brussels as early as April 1973; a series of semi-annual high-level consultations between the two sides was already underway (and continued to run parallel with meetings organized under the JCC machinery); some mechanisms existed for negotiation on contentious issues, for example, those arising from Canadian demands for compensation under GATT provisions for loss of markets caused by British membership of the EC; regular exchanges had been initiated between the European and Canadian parliaments; and some of the kind of exploratory work referred to in the agreement had been begun—a forest products mission of 1974 was followed by two during 1975 dealing respectively with the uranium industry and non-ferrous metals. What was new was the commitment to create an institution specifically charged to investigate the potential for collaboration between Canadian and EC industries.

The JCC's Sub-Committee for Industrial Cooperation began meeting in March 1977.[6] A set of Working Groups, changing over time, constituted the nervous system of the skeletal framework described in Article IV of the agreement. The choice of sectors to be singled out for special attention reflected discussions and tacit understandings of the mid-1970s. These acknowledged in part Ottawa's requirement that certain high technology areas in which Canada had both expertise and export potential should find a place in JCC probings, along with the primary and extractive industries that had originally helped to fire the Commission with enthusiasm for the venture. Initial emphasis centred upon forest products, peri-informatics and telecommunications, aerospace, nuclear industries, and metals and minerals.

The machinery has thus constituted a forum for joint enquiry by Canadian and EC officials and industry representatives of problem areas and obstacles as well as of sectoral possibilities ripe for further development. Urban transportation, for example, was identified in meetings of the Industrial Cooperation Sub-Committee in 1980–1 as a new and promising area. The Canadian side has made use of such meetings to highlight specific EC policies which have repercussions on Canada. The question of building code harmonization in the EC, for example, has been raised in the timber frame construction group, in part as a result of provincial overtures, and the point made that the future growth of processed and semi-processed exports from Canada to the EC in the forest products sector was contingent upon the pace of change in EC policy.[7] However, on balance, the number of specific outcomes that can be attributed to this process has tended to be small. By the end of the 1970s, Canadian and EC officials had concluded that no further purpose would be served by continuing to hold working group meetings in the aerospace and peri-informatics sectors, even though it was argued that opportunities still exist for cooperation in these fields. On the other hand, European interest in Canada's 'energy bus' system of on-site analysis of energy efficiency and conservation in industry led to the signing of the Canada–EC memorandum of understanding on related energy-saving matters.[8]

Of the difficulties encountered in this stage of implementation of the 1976 agreement, one recognized early in the game has proved especially stubborn. It concerns the nature of the exercise. Neither Canada nor the EC run centrally-planned economies. Government is limited in its persuasive power in relation to industry. Some Canada–EC missions since 1974 have generated productive contacts between businessmen on either side. But the constraints, in this art of the potential, are much in evidence. Larger companies, for example, in the Atlantic provinces fisheries sector in Canada or in the British Columbia forest industries, have tended to rely on their own infrastructure of relations with concerns and associations in the EC. Smaller enterprises in Anglophone Canada have been reluctant to stray from traditional North American grounds because of the common language, familiar business practices, ingrained doubts about the wisdom of allowing governments into the market-place, and criticism of the impact on their competitive position of certain EC policies. Encouragement in the 1976 agreement of joint ventures and other investment opportunities has been checked, according to some European critics, by Canadian policy, notably that implemented by the Foreign Investment Review Act (FIRA) machinery. The complaint here related not so much to the risk of rejection—Ottawa's approval rate has tended to be high—but rather to the red tape of the application process and unacceptably slow decision times. In the face of these kinds of problems, the Canada–EC joint committee has not been able in practice to move ahead as quickly as some hoped in 1976. Hopes, for example, that the Business Cooperation Centre (BCC) of the EC and Canadian officials might together be able to foster cooperation between smaller and middle-sized companies on either side seem to have proved unfounded.

An early example of the way in which the 1976 agreement was vulnerable to developments outside its ambit was provided by uranium supply issues. Progressive tightening by Ottawa of its nuclear safeguards compelled consumers, including the EC, to engage in 1976 in fresh negotiations on the conditions of supply. Canada instituted an embargo on deliveries to the EC in 1977 following the breakdown of a provisional agreement.[9] Subsequent exchanges on the uranium question became a high priority in Canada–EC relations. Two points in particular are worth noting. First, negotiations on the resumption of supplies fell outside the formal structure of the 1976 agreement, the uranium industries work of the JCC machinery having a much more specific and largely unrelated mandate. The matter did arise, though, in the semi-annual high-level consultations, and an attempt was made during 1977 meetings of delegations of the Canadian and European Parliaments to resolve the deadlock.[10] Second, the Canadian move does not appear to have been made in the light of the impact it might have on the 'contractual link' process; coming as it did in the wake of an economic cooperation agreement, one pillar of which was arguably stability in the supply of raw materials, the embargo provoked sharp criticism from the Commission.

As noted earlier, the CAP has been a focal point of Canadian evaluations of the EC for a long time. In the late 1970s, the EC was the largest customer for Canada's agricultural products, with 1977 sales valued at $907 million.[11] Canadian concern, expressed by farmers and by agriculture and trade officials, has centred on the protection afforded to EC producers and on distortions in EC markets. It has been argued also that the system has generated surpluses thrown on to the international market, sometimes in effect at dumping prices, and that this therefore creates a further kind of distortion of competition for Canadian agricultural exports. This, too, represents a crucial area in Canada–EC relations that falls in practice largely outside the confines of the Framework Agreement, which leads in turn to criticism in Canada that that accord has done little to further Canadian interests in a vital area. Canadian attempts to press for substantial tariff reductions in the Geneva multilateral trade negotiations came to little. Concessions given by the EC to the United States in some areas—certain beef products, almonds, rice and certain tinned fruits, for example—did not spill over into products of concern to Canadian farmers; despite the Framework Agreement, it was alleged, Canada was being given second-class treatment by the EC.[12]

Conclusions

The capability of the EC to create productive commercial and economic links with countries outside the perimeter of its immediate concerns depends in part on the perceptions such countries have of the EC. China, for example, made little secret during the 1970s of its admiration for what it saw as the EC's staunchly anti-Soviet character.[13] For Ottawa, the EC represented not so much an alternative to the United States as a significant economic grouping closer ties with which could ease some of the strains being encountered in Canadian–American relations. The Framework Agreement of 1976 between Canada and the EC generated some expectations which could not be fulfilled. Though both Canadian and Commission officials placed emphasis at that time on the evolutionary, pragmatic and longer-term nature of the accord, the relationship in practice for the next few years was dominated more by protracted negotiations on contentious issues—uranium supply, fisheries—than by the patient, step-by-step fostering of links. In the 1980s, then, the joint Canada–EC machinery set in motion in 1976 can more realistically be regarded as one facet among several in the relationship between the two.

This is partly because circumstances have changed. The politics of link-making in 1975–6 edged Canada into a more prominent position for EC institutions. Implementing its somewhat vague terms has been a process which has inevitably lacked the gloss, especially given the EC's major preoccupations during the second half of the 1970s. And attention to Canada has brought criticism, for example, of its energy pricing system and of plans for greater 'Canadianization' of the energy sector.[14] For its part, too, Canadian opinion has undergone change. The concerns of this period were largely internal, more focused on problems of nation-building within Canada than on foreign policy. The consolidation of relations with the United States was a more broadly acceptable option, and there was renewed interest in continental free trade arrangements. Canada's role as a Pacific rim, rather than an Atlantic country also received considerably more attention. Moreover, since constitutionally in Canada policy on resource exploitation falls under provincial jurisdiction, a more thoroughgoing development of the Framework Agreement's potential has been to some extent dependent upon the state of relations between Ottawa and the provinces, which have not been at their most harmonious since 1976.

Notes

1. For a recent evaluation of the subject in general, see Soldatos, P., 'La politique extérieure', in Lasok, D. and Soldatos, P. (eds), *Les Communautés Européennes en Fonctionnement* (Bruxelles, Bruylant, 1981), pp. 477–97.
2. On the sources of Canada's EC policy, see Mahant, E. E., 'Canada and the European Community', *International Affairs*, 52 (1976), 551–64.
3. *OJ*, 24 September 1976, No. L 260/23–5. On the course of the negotiations, see Pentland, C., 'Linkage Politics: Canada's Contract and the Development of the EC's External Relations', *International Journal*, 32 (1977), 207–31.
4. Ibid., pp. 218–19.
5. *OJ*, op. cit. See further Boardman, R., 'Canada and the Community: One Year After', *The World Today*, 33 (1977), 395–404; and 'Initiatives and Outcomes: The EC and Canada's "Third Option" ', *Journal of European Integration*, 3 (1979), 5–28.
6. *Canada–Communauté Européenne, Comité Mixte de Coopération. Deuxième Réunion: Rapport. Ottawa, le 8 mars 1978*, p. 2.
7. *Canada–Communauté Européenne, Comité Mixte de Coopération. Quatrième Réunion: Rapport. Ottawa, le 6 juillet 1981*, pp. 2–3.
8. On this and other developments see *EC–Canada, JCC. Third Meeting: Report. Brussels, December 17, 1979*, pp. 3–9.
9. Boardman, R., 'Canadian Resources and the Contractual Link: The Case of Uranium', *Journal of European Integration*, 4 (1981), 299–326.
10. *Fifth Inter-parliamentary Meeting of Delegations of the European and Canadian Parliaments, Ottawa and Toronto, June 19–25, 1977*, pp. 11–12.

11. Fischer, L. A., 'The Common Agricultural Policy of the EC: Its Impact on Canadian Agriculture', *Journal of European Integration*, 3 (1979), 37.
12. Ibid., p. 47.
13. Boardman, R., 'Guns or Mushrooms: Relations between the EC and China, 1974–80', *Politica: Tidsskrift for Politisk Videnskab*, 13 (1981), 50–79.
14. *Bull. EC* 4–1981, point 2.2.48, p. 44.

18 The European Community and Australia

J. D. B. MILLER

In relation to the EC, Australia is one of a heterogeneous group of countries which might be called 'unassociables' (that is, those which are so similar to the EC member states in terms of agricultural production as to be incapable of inclusion in the CAP, and therefore incompatible with the EC's economic policies).[1] Other states within this category include Canada, the USA, New Zealand and (on other than agricultural grounds) Japan.

Australia's situation in the world economy can be described as follows. Australia exports food, fibres (especially wool) and raw materials (especially minerals) in order to pay for imports, and repay the interest and profits on foreign investment. It constantly needs new investment capital to make up for the deficiency on current account caused by its appetite for imports, as well as to finance new development. Until well after World War II it was heavily dependent on Britain for markets and investment funds, and especially dependent on preferential entry into the British market for foodstuffs such as butter, cheese, fruits and meat. Much of its rural structure depended on the sheltered British market, although the major rural product, wool, did not require preference. It has shown intermittently a strong demand for immigrants, the great majority of whom have come from Britain; the British still provide the biggest single contingent, but there is also substantial immigration from other EC member states, notably Greece and Italy. In looking to the future, Australian planners set great store on the country's capacity to sell raw materials to expanding industrial economies, whether these be in Europe, East Asia or North America.

In political terms, Australia is part of the Western Alliance, but its role is largely that of a junior partner to the USA. In the 1950s and 1960s there was considerable military cooperation with the British effort East of Suez, but now there is little such contact, since neither Britain nor any other European power wishes to operate militarily in Asia and the Pacific. The one possible exception is France, which retains its colonial empire in the Pacific Islands; but cooperation with France is inhibited by Australia's close connection with island states such as Papua New Guinea and Vanuatu (the former New Hebrides) which are against the continuance of French colonialism.

Certain problems have arisen for Australia following Britain's entry into the EC. For example, there was a decline in the British market for Australian exports. Thirteen per cent of Australian exports for farm products went to Britain in the three years ended 1971–2; the figure had fallen to 3 per cent in the three years ended 1976–7. Wheat, meat and dairy products were the main sufferers. Fortunately, markets improved in East Asia for some products and in the USA for others. Furthermore, while the other EC member states provided no access for foodstuffs, they were a market for some of the products of the mining industry. In an overall sense, then, British entry to the EC did not cause a disaster, though it disturbed a number of rural industries and called for some adjustment of mind.

More serious has been the effect on Australia of the EC's export policies, following upon the achievement of self-sufficiency under the CAP, and the appearance of gluts in certain products. It is a long-standing Australian complaint (echoed by some of the other 'unassociables') that the EC solves its farm problem at home by creating problems for them abroad—that is, that it subsidizes surplus foodstuffs and then sells them in markets which were previously the preserve of others. In recent years Australia has experienced aggressive competition from EC exports of wheat (especially in the Middle East and South America), flour (Sri Lanka, Saudi Arabia, Mauritius and Malawi), beef (the USSR, Sweden, Greece and the Middle East), and dairy products (the Middle East, Latin America, South East Asia and Japan). In Sri Lanka, the Australian Prime Minister pointed out in 1977, Australia used to have a virtual monopoly of the market for flour; but EC subsidies (running at about $100 per tonne) had enabled EC exporters to undercut Australia by $36 per tonne, and thereby reduce the Australian market to a quarter of what it had been previously.[2] A particularly annoying experience for Australia was being undercut by the EC in the export of sugar to Papua New Guinea, a former Australian dependency.

The effects of the CAP are the main source of Australian complaint. However, there have also been complaints about the EC's disinclination to admit imports of Australian coal and steel, at times when the European and Australian industries, like those of other countries, were in a depressed condition. In reply, EC spokesmen have pointed to Australia's traditionally high industrial tariffs.

It is easy for Australia and the EC to accuse one another of protectionism, since both are highly protectionist in practice. The EC, on the one hand, which is supposed to be an outstanding example of the free movement of resources, goods, services and funds across frontiers, is a rampant case of agricultural protectionism. Australia, on the other hand, has traditionally operated systems of protection for both farm and factory products, and shows little inclination to reduce tariffs for such goods as clothing, textiles and motor cars. The basic situation seems to be that states (or groups of states like the EC) that do not need to protect manufactures can be scornful about those that do, while those that do not need to protect particular foodstuffs can take the same attitude towards their opposites. In a world in which all the major manufacturing centres except perhaps the British have been built upon protectionism, and in which every state protects and subsidizes its farmers, there is ample room for complaint, but not much result from it, except in placating domestic opinion.

The problems which Australia has with the EC are not, however, the whole of the story. It is notable that no major difficulties have occurred with any member of the EC about immigration, in spite of the large numbers involved, and the diversity of problems arising from such issues as citizenship, deportation, availability of social benefits, liability to military service, differential taxation, and divided families. Many of these problems are not fitted to treatment at the diplomatic level; none the less, it is remarkable how well the Australian and European governments have understood each other's problems.

Again, it is something of an achievement that Australia has not found itself in confrontation with France over issues in the Pacific, including the future of New Caledonia. As indicated above, the possibility of divergence between Australian and French policy comes not so much from Australian interests in themselves (Australia trades heavily with New Caledonia, being the nearest industrialized country, but also trades heavily with other Pacific island states), as from the pressure of relatively new states in the Pacific, especially Papua New Guinea, the Solomon Islands, and Vanuatu, which have ethnic connections with the Melanesians of New Caledonia. Australia is prominent in the South Pacific Forum, an assembly of Australia, New Zealand and their former dependencies, together with Britain's former Pacific colonies; France and the USA, the remaining colonial powers in the South Pacific, are not members. The emphasis in the Forum is very much upon self-determination. In relation to France, Australian influence has been towards moderation.

Again, it is notable that, on major foreign policy issues, Australia normally finds itself agreeing with what emerges as consensus amongst the EC member states. This is especially true of Middle East issues. It is also broadly true in respect of the world economy. Australia, as a member of OECD, has been involved in the attempt to reduce American interest rates and to persuade the USA to follow a more generous policy towards the Third World. In this regard, the disputes between Australia and the EC over trade and the dumping of agricultural products seem less important than the two sides' common desire to influence American economic policy in the direction of expansion. While the Australian Government under Mr Malcolm Fraser (Prime Minister since November 1975) has shown more enthusiasm for the Common Fund and other elements of the proposals for a New International Economic Order than its counterparts in the EC, it is still the case that Australia has little difficulty in adjusting its views on the world economy to those of the EC member states. In the same way, overall political analyses tend to be similar: the USSR is seen as a possible threat, China as a source of opportunity, and Third World countries as awkward but essential associates.

A notable example of cooperation in matters of mutual advantage has been in respect of nuclear safeguards. Australia is a major producer of uranium, which, it is widely hoped, will be a source of external income for many years, in spite of some hesitancy in the Australian labour movement about whether the substance should be mined at all. From 1977 to 1981, a series of negotiations between Australia and other countries—including the EC member states and EURATOM—produced a series of treaties which should effectively prevent the fear of nuclear proliferation from spreading.[3]

One can thus see relations between Australia and the EC as essentially mixed, and likely to remain so. In those matters in which there is a basic clash of interest —especially but not exclusively the trade in farm products—we can expect to see continued friction. In those larger matters which involve the super powers and the Third World, one can expect broad agreement, since Western Europe and Australia are likely to have the same allies and antagonists, and to disagree about methods rather than aims.

Such an outcome might have been predicted at the time of the British EC entry negotiations in 1962, but few mentioned it. As already indicated, Australia's ties with Britain were then tighter and more numerous than they are now. A dominant state of mind, backward-looking in many ways but understandable in terms of fairly recent experience, was characteristic of many political and community leaders. As exemplified by the Prime Minister of the day, Sir Robert Menzies, it did include an awareness of the economic importance to Australia of Japan and the USA, and of the strategic significance of the USA as the only great power capable of coming to Australia's assistance in time of trouble. Primarily, however, it involved loyalty to British values and institutions, and often to Britain itself as symbolized by the monarchy and by the multitude of connections which had arisen from the settlement of Australia, the joint efforts in two world wars, and the cultural links in sport, religion, and education. It was a state of mind which could be expressed in maudlin and obsequious terms, but also in terms of sober pride at what a British people had achieved across the seas, and of gratitude for the British legacy.

The British proposal to enter the EC seemed to many Australians to be a contradiction of their previous understanding of Britain, a denial of British effort overseas, and an affirmation of a narrow, inward-looking, Euro-centric point of view. To some extent, of course, this was true; to some extent, however, it neglected the situation in which Britain found itself. It was also, by implication, a denial of Australia's own situation, which, in both strategic and economic terms, could no longer be one of dependence on Britain. Even in ethnic terms, Australians were becoming significantly less British, and were to continue in this direction, just as they were to become less concerned with the British market and British defence policy.[4]

To understand how this dominant state of mind changed in twenty years to one in which Britain no longer seemed of major importance, and the EC became a normal though rarely appreciated feature of the international scene, we have to recognize the interaction between political opinion and economic change. For a very long time—certainly from the beginning of the century, and further back in less organized terms—Australians had been told that their prosperity depended on the British market and British investment. What happened in the 1960s and 1970s was that this proved to be no longer the case. Japan became Australia's biggest trading partner; new markets appeared in East Asia and the USA; Australian enterprises found that not only British, but also American, German and Japanese investors were interested in deals. The Australian economy itself, while still heavily dependent on the rest of the world, achieved a certain maturity in its own right, a certain capacity (still untested in any critical situation) for self-sustained growth. At the same time, Britain's need for Australian products and for Australian political support became steadily less apparent as Britain immersed itself more in Europe, both economically and politically. The seeds of change for both Australia and Britain had been sown well before Britain entered the EC; but they had taken time to sprout, and awareness of them lagged behind.

One can ask what possibilities there are for future relations between Australia and the EC, given that the direct connection between Australia and Britain is no longer of primary importance. On the whole, the answer is that relations will probably be very much as they are now, only more so. There may yet be trouble arising from France's colonial possessions (and nuclear tests) in the Pacific; these, however, are likely to cause more excitement in newspaper headlines than in official links between the two countries, and will hardly cause a commotion at the headquarters of the EC. Otherwise, political relationships show no sign of deterioration.

However, there could be further heated argument about trade questions. It is not impossible, for example, that Australia and New Zealand might join forces in complaints about certain EC policies, such as moves restricting the import of sheepmeats. It is inevitable that there should be disputes of this kind, just as it is inevitable—unless the CAP is changed in ways which at present seem far-fetched —that there will be disputes about dumping in 'third country' markets.

Most questions about future relationships rest upon whether the current recession will be halted, and when. If conditions improve, Western Europe will need more of Australia's minerals, and Australia will need more of Western Europe's money. In such a context, the EC member states are the operative bodies, rather than the EC Commission or Council of Ministers: it will be in Bonn, Paris, Rome and London that the discussions will take place, rather than in Brussels.

This raises the question of how Australia stands in relation to the institutions of the EC. Like other foreign countries, it has little to do with the EP or the Court of Justice. It does, however, have constant contact with the Commission, in Brussels itself (where an Australian ambassador has been accredited to the EC for many years) and in Canberra (where a Commission office was established in 1981). It has contact with the Council of Ministers through its embassies in each of the member states, and also through EC member governments' missions in Canberra. This aspect of contact can be of greater importance than contacts with the Commission, depending on the matter in hand. Much Australian diplomacy with EC member states is a mixture of bilateral and multilateral diplomacy, in the sense that there are questions of bilateral trade and investment to be settled, along with multilateral issues of EC policy, especially in respect of the CAP. If Australia (like Canada or Japan or New Zealand) can prevail upon a sufficient number of member states to recognize certain common interests, then it may be able to enlist the aid of those member states on the multilateral issues to be decided by either the Commission or Council.

The earlier notion that Australia and other Commonwealth countries would conduct their diplomacy with the EC largely through Whitehall has become outdated by the combination of lessening British interest in the Commonwealth—and specifically in Australia—with the greater interest being displayed by other EC member states. Britain may still be useful as an advocate in matters arising from the original conditions for its entry into the EC, and in other matters about which it has been agreed bilaterally that interests coincide. There is no longer substance, however, in the idea of a 'Commonwealth front' in negotiation with other EC member states.

Thus, in relations with the EC and the member states, Australia is set a complex and potentially exhausting task of both bilateral and multilateral diplomacy, but one which must be performed. Diplomacy can, of course, go only so far where international economic conditions are concerned. It cannot provide demand where it does not exist, or guarantee investment that may fail because of faulty economic analysis. The international economic climate is the arbiter of how effective economic diplomacy can be.

Australia is not confined to the European sector of the world economy in its search for profitable markets and sources of investment. There is considerable academic and business support for the idea of a 'Pacific Economic Community' which, in one form or another, would enable Australia to work more closely with the rapidly growing economies of East Asia, and in due course with China.[5] The proponents of such schemes do not envisage a break with Western Europe, but they see the European market as expanding more slowly than the markets of South Korea, Taiwan and Malaysia. If Australia can combine successful economic diplomacy in Europe with equally successful diplomacy in the Pacific, its future will be bright. However, it is important to emphasize that in such procedures Australia and Western Europe (which is also deeply interested in economic growth in East Asia) will probably sink or swim together. World-wide recession is no recipe for any state's growth. If the recession lifts, there will be room for all.

Notes

1. See Miller, J. D. B., 'The Unassociables', *The World Today*, 30 (1974), 327–34.
2. *Australian Foreign Affairs Record (AFAR)*, 48, 6 (1977), p. 314.
3. *AFAR*, 52, 9 (1981), where there are particulars about the agreements with France and EURATOM.
4. Sources for the state of opinion in Australia in the early 1960s include Fletcher, B. H., 'Australian Opinion on the Common Market' in Bell, C. (ed.), *Europe Without Britain* (Melbourne, Cheshire, 1963); Gelber, H. G., *Australia, Britain and the EEC 1961–1963* (Melbourne, OUP, 1966); and Miller, J. D. B., *The EEC and Australia* (Melbourne, Nelson, 1976).
5. A source of information on Australian interest in these schemes is Crawford, Sir J. (ed.), assisted with Seow, G., *Pacific Economic Cooperation: Suggestions for Action* (Selangor, Heinemann Asia, 1981), especially Readings 1, 8, 9, 10, 11.

19 The European Community and New Zealand

JULIET LODGE*

When Britain joined the EC in 1973, New Zealand was granted special privileged access to the British market for its dairy exports. This access represented a derogation from EC rules and the terms governing it were set out in Protocol 18 to Britain's Treaty of Accession. In essence, they provided for special access for butter and cheese for a transitional period, which ended in December 1977, and stipulated the maximum quantities of butter and cheese that New Zealand could export to Britain at a fixed price during the 1973-7 period.

Whereas a number of EC member states have argued that Protocol 18 was strictly a transitional arrangement, it has always been the opinion of the New Zealand Government that, given the level of New Zealand's dependence on dairy outlets in Britain, the special arrangement with the EC should be one subject to 'continuing review'. In other words, the New Zealand Government's position since Britain's first bid to join the EC, when Sir John Marshall began seeking special assurances in respect of New Zealand's exports to Britain, has been that special arrangements must continue until such time as New Zealand is able to find alternative market outlets. This in itself is difficult, not least because demand for dairy products is limited. Diversification has met with some success. Whereas in 1960 Britain took 53 per cent of New Zealand's exports, in 1976 this figure had fallen to 19 per cent. However, dairy products pose a particularly difficult problem because, on the one hand, 15 per cent of New Zealand's total agricultural exports (which account for 70 per cent of its total exports) comprise dairy products and Britain remains the major market, and because, on the other hand, the EC has substantial dairy surpluses. In July 1977, the Prime Minister of New Zealand, Mr Robert Muldoon, pointed out that in his view there were no alternative outlets for New Zealand's butter, for a significant proportion of its cheddar cheese exports, and for the larger proportion of its lamb exports.[1] Not surprisingly, therefore, New Zealand has concentrated on securing further derogations in respect of butter and cheese and arguing against implementation of the common sheepmeat regulation by the EC. Agricultural issues have dominated New Zealand's thinking on the EC for a long time.

The Luxembourg Agreement

Apart from seeking to extend special arrangements, New Zealand officials have been concerned with securing price increases for the annually decreasing quantities

*I wish to thank Mrs Liliana Brisby, the Editor of The World Today, for her kind cooperation in granting permission for the publication of a revised version of my article on 'New Zealand and the Community' published in The World Today in August 1978. The World Today is issued under the auspices of the Royal Institute of International Affairs and published monthly by the Oxford University Press.

of butter exported to Britain. Indeed, dissatisfaction with the pricing arrangement for butter was expressed in 1971, when British Ministers and officials, in consultation with their New Zealand counterparts, negotiated with the EC the so-called Luxembourg Agreement—which became Protocol 18. Then it had been decided that a fair price for butter would be one that represented the average price for butter over the 1969–72 period. Subsequent inflation and the oil crisis resulted in this price appearing less generous. Indeed, even before Britain joined the EC, steps were taken to try to amend the pricing formula which was supposed to last for the duration of Protocol 18.

Both in terms of the formal negotiation of Protocol 18 and in terms of the formal discussions for amending the pricing formula, New Zealand's role *vis-à-vis* the EC has been indirect. This has meant that its case has had to be argued on its behalf by British representatives, as had been the case in respect of the Luxembourg Agreement. This has had two implications. First, it has resulted in a tendency at the political level to underestimate the importance of the EC Commission's role and position in EC decision-making and to misinterpret the nature of a supranational Community on the part of New Zealand. Thus, for example, stereotyped images of the EC and of France's role in it have persisted in New Zealand. Even before the important Dublin EC summit of 1975, special representations had to be made to the New Zealand Government in order that the Labour Prime Minister, Mr Wallace Rowling, might not omit the Brussels Commission and Irish Government during his tour of European capitals as he had originally intended. Secondly, the fact that Britain has been responsible for putting New Zealand's case to the Commission and Council of Ministers has meant that New Zealand has been comparatively slow in developing and intensifying its own relations with the Commission and other EC bodies, even though New Zealand Ministers and officials regularly visit EC member states. Not until 1976 did a group of New Zealand MPs visit the EP, and not until 1975, after Lord Soames's visit to New Zealand in 1974, was a consultative procedure established to facilitate informal talks between Commission and New Zealand officials from government departments and European embassies.[2]

Since 1973, New Zealand's relations with the EC have been dominated by the question of access to the British market for butter and cheese, and more recently sheepmeat. Essentially, discussions have hinged upon four things: the revision of the pricing formula, the determination of quota levels, special access for butter and cheese after 1977, and avoidance of a common sheepmeat regulation. As will become apparent, the first two of these items have been closely related and have affected the third.

The pricing formula revision

Technical discussions over the revision of and application of the contentious pricing formula began soon after its having been agreed upon by the EC's six founder members. It is difficult to discover with whom the formula originated, but it has proved to be the key to a number of subsequent negotiations and 'understandings' on the levels of New Zealand's butter exports—irrespective of the formal levels set out in Protocol 18. There are good reasons for believing that the Six particularly favoured the pricing formula. These reasons were not unrelated to their views of the relationship between prices and quantitative guarantees—a relationship that had been made clear in 1971, and which itself was linked to the level of Britain's budgetary contributions to the EC. Paragraph 9 of the agreement on New Zealand, accepted in Luxembourg in June 1971, noted that 'because of the financial impact of this exceptional system' the proposal on New Zealand was to be 'subject to a satisfactory agreement on the amount of the British contribution to Community finances'.[3] The significance of this was to be highlighted during Britain's 'renegotiation' of its terms of accession, and specifically of its budgetary contributions.[4] It may be suggested that the pricing formula agreed upon in 1971 —a formula that provided for New Zealand to receive a price *representing* the average of prices over the four years 1969–72—strengthened the EC's bargaining position *vis-à-vis* New Zealand to the extent that modifications to that formula could be traded off against a reduction in imports of New Zealand butter by Britain. That the formula was not as inflexible as commonly assumed was evinced by both New Zealand's insistence that the possibility of amendment was implied by the term 'representing'; and by the EC's willingness to consider trade-offs against actual butter deliveries.

From the outset New Zealand insisted that the intention behind the pricing formula of the Luxembourg Agreement was to assure New Zealand of a 'real' return for its exports; that world inflation had prevented this; and that, therefore, New Zealand had a legitimate claim to an increase in the price paid for its dairy exports to take account of increased production and freight costs. To get higher prices the agreement of both the EC and Britain was needed. In 1973, political pressure was exerted on the British Government to agree to the Commission proposal to apply Monetary Compensatory Amounts to New Zealand's exports[5] in order to compensate it for sterling's devaluation; the British agreed and New Zealand's returns increased. However, it was stated in the Commission report on New Zealand that no allowance could be made for price differences occasioned by revaluations of the New Zealand dollar.

Further amelioration in the pricing arrangement was achieved when the Council of Ministers agreed to increase the prices New Zealand exporters received by 18 per cent as from 1 January 1975. The Prime Minister, Mr Rowling, expressed his satisfaction but noted that 'while the increase is less than we think justified by the facts, nevertheless it is a substantial and welcome improvement in our trade with the EC.'[6] However, the price increase was contingent upon the level of butter exports to Britain. New Zealand's failure to meet its guaranteed quota levels, due to domestic production figures associated with the drought and to its ability to find alternative and more lucrative markets elsewhere, meant that the EC could trade off an increase in the price with an agreement from New Zealand to limit its actual deliveries to a level below that set out in Protocol 18 for the year 1975.

Again in 1975, New Zealand sought price increases as part of a similar quid pro quo. The issue featured in talks between Mr Rowling and Mr Harold Wilson in March 1975 prior to the British referendum and the formal review of the application of Protocol 18 scheduled for 1975. The matter was raised further by New Zealand's Minister of Foreign Affairs, Mr J. Walding, during his September visit to the EC. It was reported that New Zealand was seeking a 25 per cent price increase, but British and EC observers anticipated a smaller increase. In the event, agreement was reached eventually under Mr Brian Talboys, Minister of Foreign Affairs in the New Zealand National Government, whereby New Zealand received an 18 per cent price increase in exchange for a 'secret' agreement to limit deliveries.[7] In September 1977, New Zealand secured a further 10 per cent price increase; this was much less than it wanted but was not subject to any understandings on quantitites. The Commission's position is that New Zealand should not be accorded higher price increases than EC farmers.

The butter quotas

It was also under Mr Talboys, in 1977, that a series of butter quotas for the period 1978–80, that is, beyond the five-year period established in Protocol 18, were negotiated. These negotiations illuminated a number of misunderstandings that had arisen in New Zealand over the provisions of Protocol 18. Three points in particular gave rise for concern. First was the question of 'degressivity': the notion that over a number of years New Zealand's actual butter deliveries should decline; second, the question of whether or not further butter quantitative agreements could be negotiated; and third, the question of whether or not some arrangement could be found that would permit the continued export of cheese to Britain on a special access basis after the quota provisions lapsed at the end of 1977. The latter question was dealt with under GATT, and special access was not, therefore, extended. However, the first two issues were cleared up in the course of the discussions arising out of the 1975 Review, discussions which actually culminated in 1976.

Throughout 1975 and 1976, New Zealand politicians created the impression— possibly deliberately for domestic political reasons—that Protocol 18 was inflexible and that tough bargaining was ahead if Protocol 18 was to prove more than a transitional arrangement. The New Zealand Government set out to obtain a new series of quotas permitting, according to the Dublin Declaration,[8] the effective marketing of New Zealand butter. In so doing, it contested the principle of degressivity—unsuccessfully as it happened, since this was implicit in the Protocol and had been applied in respect of the 1973–7 quota levels.

The quotas obtained for 1978–80 were generally deemed satisfactory by the New Zealand Government. They had been negotiated after the Review and lengthy wrangling between the Commission and the Nine—New Zealand having rejected the Commission's original proposals as unsatisfactory and having gained a readjustment of the proposed quotas, so that the quota for 1980 was somewhat higher and the earlier ones lower. In effect, New Zealand obtained a redistribution of the total allocation among the three-year quota period. The quantities finally adopted by the Council of Ministers in June 1976 were 125,000, 120,000 and 115,000 tonnes respectively for the three years in question—the Commission having made proposals to the Council of Ministers in June 1975 for the expansion of butter arrangements under Protocol 18 until 1980.[9] The implicit degressivity again gave rise to concern, not least because Mr Walding had remarked in 1975 that continued progressive reduction would result in New Zealand butter being phased out of the British market by the 1990s. There can be no doubt that this is what some member states within the EC desire.

In addition, it is important to note that, under Article 5 of the 1976 Regulation, New Zealand's share of the British butter market for direct consumption is limited to 25 per cent. This, too, gave rise to concern given declining butter consumption in Britain. Butter in excess of the 25 per cent limit is subject to a special levy and must be used for other purposes.[10] The quid pro quo bargaining tactic on higher returns in exchange for lower deliveries has marked subsequent negotiations between New Zealand and the EC. New Zealand's aim has been to secure progressively higher prices while making but token cuts in actual butter deliveries to Britain. It has also unsuccessfully called for a 'communitization' of its butter exports in the hope that its access would cease to be limited to the British market and extend, instead, to the whole of the EC. Annual bargains have been struck but renewed EC surpluses have realerted EC farmers to the level of New Zealand's shipments to Britain. Latterly, British butter consumption has so declined that

New Zealand's share of the UK butter market far exceeded the 25 per cent limit and provoked renewed calls for ending the derogation in New Zealand's favour. However, acute problems remain both for New Zealand and the EC as world demand for butter is rather inelastic and alternative reliable, remunerative outlets to those in Britain are non-existent. Furthermore, New Zealand wishes to keep the British market as a fall-back position, and is keen to supply it even when an alternative (but possibly temporary) market is found. A few years ago, New Zealand found itself shipping large quantities of butter to the USSR and importing similar quantities from the USA. More recently, New Zealand has resumed the battle to retain its British outlets. Complicated and prolonged discussions have ensued. Clearly, from the EC's point of view, continuing butter access to the British market for New Zealand makes little if any economic sense. Yet, political desiderata impel it. Not only is New Zealand an important, if small, actor in the increasingly significant South Pacific arena, but the New Zealand Government has not faltered in supporting the British Government, notably over the Falklands crisis. Loyal allies, New Zealand argues, should help each other: Britain has a moral duty to safeguard New Zealand's trading interests despite growing opposition from British farmers to continuing New Zealand access.

New Zealand has argued consistently that it has a moral right to continue exporting to the British market and some Ministers have suggested, albeit unrealistically, that minor shifts in EC production patterns would afford outlets for New Zealand. Given that the number of dairy cows in the EC has been falling while production has risen and that the EC has made efforts to deal more effectively with over-production,[11] it may prove extremely difficult to accommodate New Zealand over the longer term for two reasons: first, because of changing UK patterns of butter imports; second, because there is mounting and acrimonious farmer hostility in many EC member states to the imposition of co-responsibility schemes penalizing them for excessive production at a time when farmers from a non-member state have a special and guaranteed right to export to the EC a commodity in which the EC itself is self-sufficient. Remarks made during a debate on butter surpluses and their disposal in the EP on 9 March 1977 by Mr Gibbons on behalf of the Group of European Progressive Democrats summarized some members' feeling that the maintenance of dairy imports from third countries, in particular New Zealand, was creating an 'untenable position'.[12] By contrast, New Zealand has argued that the remedy lies in a reorganization of, and modifications to, the CAP. The logic behind this argument rests with the view of the CAP as protectionist, inefficient and discriminating against efficient third-country exporters. Mr Douglas Carter, New Zealand High Commissioner in London, noted in March 1977 that he deemed it grossly unfair that the levies imposed by the EC on New Zealand butter (29 cents per pound) meant that the higher price of butter to the consumer resulted in a drop in consumption.[13]

That New Zealand managed to obtain relatively favourable quantity arrangements for 1978–80 was partly due to Britain's 'renegotiation' and to the agreement in principle to divert New Zealand butter in excess of 25 per cent of Britain's needs to manufacturing. The extension of the commitment in Protocol 18 in respect of butter that this represented was achieved not simply because of the persuasiveness of New Zealand's arguments for a further extension, or because of the implicit provision for such an extension in Protocol 18, but because of the political undertaking to safeguard New Zealand's interests implied by the Dublin Declaration.

At the end of 1978, New Zealand began pressing for continued butter access beyond 1980. Not until April 1981 was agreement reached: Britain was authorized to import 70,250 tonnes of New Zealand butter from April–December 1981 and 92,000 tonnes in 1982. Before 1 October 1982, the Council of Ministers was to fix the 1983 quota in the light of EC butter production and world market trends. Indications were that as in 1981 (when a clause was inserted into the agreement allowing for a temporary cut in New Zealand butter deliveries to prevent serious disruption on the British butter market) fierce resistance to New Zealand among the EC's national and supranational farming lobbies would increase and result in New Zealand's 1983 entitlement being cut by at least 5,000 tonnes. These short-term arrangements are highly unsatisfactory from New Zealand's point of view. New Zealand has pressed for long-term accord. Before 1 August 1983, the Council acting on a Commission report and related proposal, is to review the 1981–3 arrangement with a view to determining the post-1984 arrangements. Commitments to New Zealand are politically rather than economically inspired. Economically, as we have seen, from EC member states' points of view there is little to warrant a continuation of the derogation in New Zealand's favour. Prospects for dairy access after 1983 are not hopeful.

Cheese and sheepmeat exports

Where cheese exports to Britain are concerned, New Zealand has not managed to secure additional arrangements. New Zealand cheddar exports to Britain ceased at the end of 1977 as per Protocol 18. However, cheese stored and debonded[14] in Britain in 1977 was sold. This was an important tactic by New Zealand since it failed to secure an interim bridging solution for its cheese exports to Britain between the ending of Protocol 18 and any measures arranged within the GATT multilateral trade negotiations. New Zealand did secure a small cheese quota of 9,500 tonnes per annum (within the GATT framework) which it could export to Britain in spite of the fact that such an arrangement was seen to endanger the expansion of British cheese production.

Although access for butter and cheese has been New Zealand's major pre-occupation, prospects for sheepmeat exports have also given rise to concern.[15] On the one hand, New Zealand had to adapt, while unsuccessfully resisting its stage-by-stage application to New Zealand sheepmeat exports, to the EC's 20 per cent Common External Tariff. On the other hand, New Zealand had hoped that the EC would not introduce a regulation governing sheepmeat lest this be to New Zealand's disadvantage at a time when its sheep industry accounts for 39 per cent of export income. However, there was considerable pressure for such a regulation from some EC member states—notably Ireland. The EC consulted New Zealand about a common sheepmeat regulation, but New Zealand argued against such a measure. After much wrangling, an EC sheepmeat regime became effective on 20 October 1980. As a result the tariff on New Zealand imports was reduced to 10 per cent, and New Zealand agreed to limit exports of lamb, mutton and goat meat to the EC (including Greece from 1 January 1981) to 245,500 tonnes per calendar year. The regulation, which basically allows free intra-EC trade in sheepmeats, guarantees producers incomes through production subsidies and/or intervention and ensures that imports are restricted through voluntary restraint agreements with third-country suppliers including New Zealand, lasts indefinitely but is to be reviewed by October 1983 in order that any changes may be agreed by April 1984.

The EC sheepmeat regulation affords New Zealand dependable guaranteed access for sheepmeat to the EC and facilitates diversification and planning. The cut in the sheepmeat tariff increases New Zealand's foreign exchange earnings and farmers' returns. Even so, New Zealand cannot afford to be complacent as EC sheepmeat production trends—the EC's self-sufficiency rate in sheepmeat is 75 per cent—may lead to pressure from within the EC to reduce third-country imports. Although New Zealand faces limited opportunities for its sheepmeat exports, the prospects for wool, which is not subject to regulations, are bright.

Although New Zealand's relations with the EC have been, and even now tend to be, characterized by obsessions with dairy quantitative guarantees and access for New Zealand's produce to the EC, there are a number of areas in which steps can be taken to improve and extend the relationship. This is beginning to happen already under the consultation procedure where discussions have also broached questions relating to commitments in the South Pacific, for example. However, if the relationship is to become more useful to both sides, then it is imperative for New Zealand to recognize that the EC is neither the only trader operating trade restrictions on agricultural produce, nor the major offender in this regard. EC agricultural exporters face formidable barriers on the North American and European markets; and EC manufacturing exports face barriers in New Zealand. While the need for reciprocity in trade is recognized, New Zealand still argues that access to the British market for butter and lamb is a matter of 'economic life and death'.[16] Indeed, in New Zealand, the notion of the country as a European farm in the South Pacific persists. Even so, the New Zealand–EC relationship cannot indefinitely be narrowly confined to butter and lamb. It is likely that political will and understanding will increase and that the relationship will develop satisfactorily. However, this does not mean that New Zealand's old demands concerning dairy and sheepmeat access will be accommodated indefinitely, but it does mean that the basis for a mutually rewarding relationship has been laid.

Notes

1. *New Zealand Foreign Affairs Review* (hereafter cited as *NZFAR*), 27 (July–September 1977), 33.
2. For details, see *NZFAR*, 24 (September 1974), 4.
3. Young, S. Z., *Terms of Entry: Britain's Negotiations with the European Community, 1970–1972* (London, Heinemann, 1973), p. 173.
4. See Lodge, J., 'New Zealand, Britain and the EEC in the 1970s', *Australian Outlook*, 29 (1975), 292–4.
5. Address by the Secretary to the Treasury, Mr H. G. Lang, to the New Zealand Institute of International Affairs, 25 August 1973, cited in *NZFAR*, 23 (August 1973), 22.
6. Ibid., 24 (November 1974), 37–8.
7. Ibid., 25 (December 1975), 41.
8. In the communiqué issued by EC Heads of Government at the Dublin summit on 11 March 1975, it was stated: 'As regards the annual quantities to be established by the Community institutions in the framework of the special arrangements after 1977, these should not deprive New Zealand of outlets which are essential for it.' See *NZFAR*, 25 (March 1975), 13 ff., for text of the Dublin Declaration; see also Lodge, J., 'New Zealand and the EEC', *New Zealand Economist*, 37, 1 (1975), 3–4; Lodge, J., 'Where we stand with the EEC', *New Zealand Economist*, 37, 11 (1976), 7–9; and Lodge, J., *The European Community and New Zealand* (London, Frances Pinter, 1982), pp. 102–7 and 114–15.
9. See Lodge, J., 'New Zealand and the EEC 1978–80: the butter quotas', *New Zealand Economist*, 38, 6 (1976), 10–11, and Lodge J., *The European Community and New Zealand*, op. cit., pp. 142–66.
10. See the Modified Proposal of 14 June 1976 under Article 149, Paragraph 2 (EEC) of Council *Regulation extending the transitional arrangements for the import of New Zealand butter into the United Kingdom*.
11. See *Bulletin of the European Communities*, Supplement 10/76, 'Action Programme (1977–80) for the progressive achievement of balance in the milk market', Brussels, Commission of the European Communities, 1976; also see *The Times*, 21 April 1977.

12.. *Debates of the European Parliament*, 1977–8 Session, Annex to the Official Journal of the European Communities, No. 214, March 1977, p. 39. In the same debate, another British MEP, Mr Howell, pointed out that in 1975 the EC was 98 per cent self-sufficient in butter production.

13. *New Zealand Herald*, 7 March 1977.

14. Debonded stocks are those on which the appropriate levies (charges applied to imports in addition to any tariffs or import duties) have been paid.

15. See Lodge, J., *The European Community and New Zealand*, op. cit., pp. 197–215.

16. New Zealand's Prime Minister, Mr Robert Muldoon, quoted in *The Times*, 28 April 1978.

20　The European Community and Japan

REINHARD DRIFTE

Historical background

At the end of the Second World War Europe became separated from the Far East in political as well as in economic terms. China turned to the Soviet Union, and Japan was occupied for seven years by the USA, which had a decisive influence on Japan's post-war orientation towards North America. Japan's former European allies, Britain and later the axis powers, the FRG and Italy, were seriously weakened and could not offer an alternative in Asia. Instead Europe concentrated on her economic rehabilitation and tried to solve her colonial problems. For these reasons Japan turned to the USA which was then the strongest power in the Far East and also closest to the political ideology of Japan's leaders. Whereas Japan concentrated on a comprehensive relationship with the USA and gradually turned to South East Asia for new markets since she had been forbidden the Chinese market, Europe developed the Atlantic partnership with North America and moved towards some form of integration of Western Europe. Although Europe and Japan were thus both allied to the same superpower this did not imply any link between them at that time.

This mutual disinterest was first terminated by a Japanese move. Japan became greatly worried when the EEC was founded in 1958, and followed by the establishment of the rival European Free Trade Area (EFTA) in 1960. Japan feared that European integration would bolster Europe's competitive power and exclude her from third country markets. In addition, closer Atlantic ties seemed to leave Japan out in the cold. In 1959, Japanese exports to Western Europe already amounted to 10.6 per cent of Japan's total exports. For these reasons Japanese Prime Ministers visited Europe in 1959 and 1962, followed by many other political leaders and business delegations.

However, Europe was not yet prepared to accept Japan as an equal political or economic partner. Resentment against Japan as a result of the war was still very deep-rooted in many Western European countries. Europe had not forgotten aggressive Japanese trade practices in the pre-war era and was still afraid of Japanese low-wage products, trademark and patent piracy and dumping practices.[1] It is still vividly remembered in Japan that President Charles de Gaulle referred in 1962 to visiting Japanese Prime Minister Ikeda as the 'transistor merchant'.

As a result it proved very difficult for Japan to obtain the non-discriminatory commercial treatment of the General Agreement on Tariffs and Trade (GATT). She was accepted to this body in 1955, only after having submitted her candidacy in 1952. Even then fourteen countries still invoked Article 35 of the Agreement which provides for the non-application of the Agreement between particular contracting parties if either of them does not consent to its application to the other at the time of either becoming a contracting party. Britain withdrew as the first European country the application of Article 35 against Japan in 1963 when she concluded a Treaty of Commerce which replaced the offending Article by safeguards of a selective nature. Other EC member states followed in 1964.[2] In 1964 Japan was also admitted to the Organization for Economic Cooperation and Development (OECD).

Replacing the application of Article 35 by safeguard measures was considered by Japan as an improvement but could not entirely satisfy her wish to get equal treatment. The dialogue between Japan and the EC Commission started in 1961 with the visit of Commissioner Jean Rey to Japan, but it was only in July 1970 that the Council of Foreign Ministers mandated the Commission to negotiate a trade agreement with Japan in accordance with Article 113 of the Rome Treaty. The negotiations between Brussels and Tokyo broke down over the European insistence on the inclusion of some safeguard agreement. The Japanese side considered instead Article 19 of the GATT as sufficient safeguard. It is here where the problem of the not yet concluded trade agreement between Japan and the EC still rests today despite the Commission's efforts to secure a mandate to reopen negotiations in July 1980.[3]

At the end of the 1960s, the impact of Japan's economy began to be felt in Europe and could no longer be ignored by the EC. In 1966, Japan's Gross National Product (GNP) overtook the Italian one, in 1967 it overtook the British, in 1968 the French and in 1969 finally the German GNP. Moreover, since 1968, the EC no longer enjoyed a trade surplus with Japan as had been the case before. During the 1968–77 period, Japanese exports to the Nine increased at an average compound rate of 25.9 per cent (Japanese imports from the EC increased at 18.1 per cent in the same period), while the share of imports from Japan in the EC's total imports remained very low at 2 per cent. In addition, the Japanese concentrated on a limited range of products where they could achieve outstanding results.[4]

In order to augment understanding of the EC–Japan relationship I propose to analyse it first on an economic and then on a political level. On the economic level we are concerned with four problem areas: (i) Japan's trade surplus with the EC; (ii) Japan's export pattern; (iii) Japan's import pattern; and (iv) the accessibility of the Japanese market.

(i) *Japan's trade surplus with the EC*

Japanese exports to the EC increased at an average compound rate of 25.4 per cent during the period 1970–6, while the comparable rate for Japanese exports to the USA was 17.6 per cent.[5] Although Japanese exports to the EC started from a lower level, from the beginning of the 1970s they expanded at a much faster rate than Japanese exports to the USA. As a result, the EC's trade deficit with Japan has been steadily growing worse since 1973 to reach almost $13 billion in 1980 and $14.4 billion in 1981, since Japanese exports to Europe were not matched by corresponding European exports to Japan as the following table shows.

In terms of shares Japan is not an important trading partner for Europe. Only 4.4 per cent of the EC's imports in 1979 came from Japan, making Japan her fifth main supplier after the USA, Saudi Arabia, Switzerland and Sweden. For Japan only about 6–7 per cent of her total imports come from the EC. Only 2.4 per cent of the EC's exports went to Japan, which constituted the EC's eighth largest market in 1979 whereas 10 per cent of Japan's exports went to the EC.[6]

The EC's deficit with Japan has also to be seen in proper perspective. The EC has always enjoyed big surpluses with other countries such as Switzerland (ECU 5 billion in 1978), Austria (ECU 3.3 billion) or Yugoslavia (ECU 2.1 billion).[7]

Table 1   EC imports from and exports to Japan ($ million)

	EC imports	EC exports	Balance	Export–import coverage ratio
1963	523,385	514,603	−8,782	98.3
1965	763,841	512,324	−251,517	67.1
1970	1,893,011	1,375,819	−517,192	72.6
1975	6,344,406	2,792,383	−3,355,523	44.0
1980	18,551,996	6,362,083	−12,189,913	34.3

Source: CTCI, UN Geneva. Figures are for the EC of the Ten.

Moreover, the EC has a huge deficit with the USA ($17 billion in 1980), although trade between the two is also greater than with Japan.

The reason for considering Japan's trade surplus more offensive than with other countries, despite Japan's low ranking as an EC trading partner, is to be found in Japan's export and import pattern as well as her market's accessibility for European goods.

(ii) *Japan's export pattern*

Japan's exports to Europe have until now been concentrated on a handful of sectors such as the optical industry, electronic industry, radio and television industry, and particularly automobile and motorcycle industry. The major and extremely quick-paced penetration of these sectors has plunged many competing EC companies into a crisis or even out of business, as has been witnessed with Britain's motor cycle industry and the FRG's camera industry. Moreover, Japan's export drive hit precisely those European industries which were big and occupied an important place in the national economy. Automobiles and electronic products share almost half of Japan's manufactured exports to the EC and accounted until recently also for the highest growth rates.

We cannot analyse the reasons for Japan's success in producing such competitive products and flooding them on to the European market, but the following list of strong points of the Japanese economy certainly accounts for it to a large extent:

(a) high level of competitiveness and productivity which is secured in the cut-throat struggle on the Japanese home market;
(b) social cohesion and absence of labour unrest;
(c) coexistence of highly efficient big enterprises which depend to a very high degree on subcontracting with an overwhelming number of small and medium-sized companies (dual structure);
(d) advantageous financing system;
(e) close cooperation between big business, government and bureaucracy.

(iii) *Japan's import pattern*

Although Japan's exports consist overwhelmingly of manufactured products, her imports of manufactured products from all her trading partners have remained very low in absolute terms. Forty-four per cent of the EC's imports (from outside the EC) were manufactured products in 1980, as against only 22 per cent in the case of Japan and 55 per cent in the case of the USA. Whereas Japan imported manufactured products in 1980 valued at $27.2 billion, or $233 per capita, the corresponding figures for the EC were $215 billion and $796 billion, and for the USA $124 billion and $547 billion. Japan's imports of manufactured goods are thus about the size of Switzerland's, and in per capita terms Japan is next to last among the member states of the OECD. Imports from developing countries by Japan are well under half the level of those of the EC.[8]

Table 2   Japanese exports and imports

	Exports		Imports	
	Total exports ($ billion)	Of which manufactured goods ($ billion)	Total imports ($billion)	Of which manufactured goods ($ billion)
1960	4.0	3.0	3.5	0.77
1965	8.4	3.7	6.4	1.5
1970	19.3	18.1	15.0	4.5
1975	54.7	52.1	49.7	9.9
1980	126.7	121.3	124.6	27.2
1981	149.4	136.4	129.3	28.2

Source: Japan Ministry of Finance. Figures are on a FOB/FOB basis. Manufactured products are products under SITC 5–8 calculated as a percentage of trade figures on a customs clearance basis.

One reason for this extreme lopsidedness lies with Japan's poor endowment in natural resources, which obliges the country to minimize imports in order to get primary products, raw materials and fuels. Until the end of the 1960s Japan could not earn sufficient from exports to pay for her imports. This prompted the Government to substitute imports of manufactured goods by self-production.[9] Another reason is Japan's geo-political situation since she has in the past not been surrounded by equally industrialized countries allowing close horizontal integration and thus an exchange of manufactured goods. Although trade with the USA occupied at the time one-third of Japan's total trade, nearly two-thirds of American exports to Japan in 1975 consisted of primary products (37.8 per cent in the case of American exports to the EC).[10] In addition, Japan has a huge domestic market of over 100 million people which it could develop. All these factors encouraged or even necessitated in the past a more autarkic development of Japan's economy.

On the other hand, EC member states maintain preferential trading relations not only among themselves but also with EFTA countries, ACP countries and many Mediterranean countries which discouraged European exporters to look for more complicated markets and to make the same efforts as the Japanese made to break into the European market.[11] In addition, major West European export items to Japan are mostly luxury or intermediate products, machines or machinery for industrial or office use which contrast unfavourably with Japan's mass-consumption consumer durables with a high income elasticity of demand.[12]

(iv) *Accessibility of the Japanese market*

Since the above structural conditions are very difficult to change within a short span of time, discussion on the side of the EC has been focusing on the accessibility of the Japanese market for European products. On 15 December 1976 the European Parliament (EP) requested the EC Commission to 'identify those legal, economic and political difficulties which continue to hinder the efforts of Community exporters seeking to penetrate the Japanese market.'[13]

In discussing the accessibility of the Japanese market one has to differentiate between quantitative (import quotas, tariffs) and qualitative restrictions (non-tariff barriers) on foreign exports to Japan. On the first sort of restrictions, the Japanese side claims that Japan's average tariff rates are already lower than those of the EC, and that the EC, in addition to retaining residual import restrictions on sixty-two items, has discriminatory import restrictions on fifty-seven items from Japan.[14] However, the EC does not accept this as an excuse for Japan's twenty-seven residual import restrictions of which five belong to the agricultural sector, since there are also still very high tariffs on some products which are of particular interest to Europe. The rate of duty and, where available, the Japanese proposal for the rate after eight years within the Multilateral Trade Negotiations (MTNs) is given in parentheses for the key products which are: natural cheese (35 per cent), cocoa powder (25 per cent, 21.5 per cent), chocolate confectionery (33.8 per cent, 30 per cent), and biscuits (35.5 per cent, 34 per cent). Other high rates concern alcoholic beverages such as whisky and wine.[15]

As a result of continuous pressure from the EC as well as from the USA, the Japanese Government proposed in December 1981 to advance implementation of massive tariff reductions on 1,653 items by two years which had been agreed upon during the Tokyo Round. For these products tariffs will go down from an average of 8 per cent to an average of 6.75 per cent. This means that since 1 April 1982 import tariffs for all products will be only on an average of 3.2 per cent. In May 1982 Japan announced the reduction or elimination of tariffs on a further 215 items for 1 April 1983. Further similar measures are to follow.[16]

However, the effects of these tariff cuts will be felt, if at all, only after some time. In addition, these cuts do not concern so much those products (for example, agricultural products) which the EC wants to sell to Japan. A bottle of whisky now costing between 7,000 and 10,000 yen will be reduced in price by only 8–11 yen.[17]

Most of the attention is therefore given to qualitative restrictions which have become famous as Non-Tariff Barriers (NTBs). They concern practical administration of standards, customs, procedures and investment approvals, but also intangible national cultural attitudes towards foreign imports. In February 1972, a parallel understanding was already reached between the USA and Japan, and between the USA and the EC, to the effect that tariff reductions and the removal of NTBs should be promoted within the framework of the MTNs of the GATT. Some easing took place after the mission of the Japanese Federation of Economic Organizations (Keidanren), headed by Mr Toshio Doko, visited Europe in October 1976. As a result, type-approval for imported vehicles was simplified and preclinical test data on pharmaceuticals were accepted by the Japanese.

The existence of NTBs was finally officially recognized only in January 1982 when the Japanese Government announced the elimination or easing of sixty-seven NTBs chosen out of ninety-nine cases of foreign complaints. In addition, a new headquarters (so-called ombudsman) was established to resolve further grievances pertaining to the opening of the Japanese market.[18]

Further similar measures have been announced particularly in view of the summit meeting in Versailles in June 1982. However, in all cases it has to be said that many listed products are not of interest to EC exporters. Moreover, a close look at the proposed measures shows that in most cases the Government only promises to 'make efforts' or to 'notify the respective authorities'. Only time will tell whether the promised measures by the Japanese Government will really facilitate the entrance to the Japanese market. One major NTB, the complicated and expensive distribution system, will not be affected. Moreover, quantitative and qualitative restrictions in the past have left European exporters with the deep-rooted feeling that they never had a chance to build up a market share in Japan.

The political dimension of the relationship

For reasons mentioned above, Japan did not loom large on the political horizon of the EC member states, nor was Japan initially very interested in a political relationship with Europe. In the 1960s, Japan finally turned to Europe in order to obtain most-favoured nation treatment and to prevent isolation in the course of European integration and increasing Atlantic ties.

From 1968, when Japan started to have a continuously growing trade surplus with the EC, the latter could no longer ignore Japan, at least not on an economic level. The announcement of a new American economic policy in August 1971, the concomitant collapse of the IMF framework and the oil crisis with its ensuing recession gave impetus to European leaders to make an issue of growing Japanese trade surpluses.[19]

It was the EC Commission in particular which played a leading role in demonstrating the political dimensions of the EC–Japan relationship. The main reason for the politicization of the trade conflict by the Commission was, and still is, its desire to become the only negotiating partner in matters of external trade as stipulated in Article 113 of the Rome Treaty. However, the main goal of this endeavour, the conclusion of an EC–Japan trade agreement, has constantly been frustrated by the insistence of some member states to include safeguard measures against Japanese imports to replace those in their bilateral trade agreements with Japan.

Instead the Commission could only establish in May 1973 regular high-level consultations between Brussels and Tokyo which have subsequently taken place twice a year. They are similar to those organized with the USA and cover bilateral problems as well as the main multilateral problems. In addition, sectoral consultations have been held on various sectors affected by the Japanese export drive such as automobiles, pharmaceutical products, shipbuilding, etc. From mid-1972 some self-restricting measures were also introduced by Japanese exporters on specific products.

In 1974 an agreement was reached between Brussels and Tokyo on the establishment of an EC delegation in Japan which was officially inaugurated in Tokyo in 1975. In 1976 a Japanese delegation to the EC was established in Brussels.

The EC saw a highly useful opportunity to influence the Japanese side to make some concessions and to politicize the trade dispute when the Doko mission arrived in Europe in 1976. The Japanese were told that the European economies were afflicted with unemployment, inflation, stagnant growth and external trade deficits. Against this background the rapid growth of Japanese exports in some sectors gave rise not only to social problems, but also to political problems. This could easily give way to protectionism, the ultimate enemy of free world trade. Only Japanese self-restrictions, the further opening of the Japanese market and more imports of manufactured goods could solve the problems. These arguments for explaining the inherent political character of the trade conflict are still used today, and now all the more when the EC has over ten million people unemployed. In addition, it is pointed out that some features of Japan give her an 'unfair advantage' over the other industrialized countries. In this context, it is mentioned that Japan spends less on welfare systems, defence (only 0.9 per cent of her GNP or $12 billion in 1981) or aid to the Third World (ODA quota as a percentage of GNP was only 0.34 per cent or 941.8 billion yen in 1982).

Lack of unity among the EC member states

It is the multitude of actors which is adding to the difficulty in finding a coherent approach to solve the EC–Japan trade conflict on an economic as well as political level. This situation is due to a lack of mutual trust among the EC member states. Appeals for solidarity have been belied by the pursuit of purely national and bilateral approaches to their relations with Japan.[20] In addition, some member states argue that the Commission should not handle the issue but leave it to the industrialists who could then work out a solution, whereas others opt for direct bilateral negotiations with Japan, arguing that the Commission is not strong enough. This diversity has paralysed the Commission which has, therefore, never been given a clear mandate to find a comprehensive approach. Furthermore, the absence of an EC industrial policy on which to base discussions with the Japanese makes a multilateral approach even more difficult.[21] The Japanese side has profited greatly from the EC's disunity and has so far skilfully played one member state against the other, although it is realized increasingly in Japan that this approach leads in the long run to only more national restrictions on Japanese exports.

As a result, the Commission has been limited to a role which reflects the lowest common denominator of the member states. In February 1978, the Council noted nevertheless that a common strategy was an essential condition for any worthwhile dialogue with Japan. The substance of this strategy found its expression in the Council's declaration of 25 November 1980 which was extremely vague on the central issue of how the Commission should proceed. In February 1981, when the situation had not improved, the Council decided to institute EC-wide surveillance on imports from Japan of passenger cars, colour television sets, tubes and certain machine tools. In addition, the Commission was called upon to pursue work and contacts with the Japanese on Japanese exports in the automobile and other endangered sectors, to pursue studies on the concentration of Japanese exports to the EC, to continue pressure on Japan to open her market further, and to raise the question of trade with Japan with other major industrialized trading countries on 'every possible occasion'.[22]

It was the issue of Japanese self-restrictions on automobile exports to the EC which demonstrated in 1981 most bluntly the disunity of the EC member states. On 19 May, the Commission was mandated by the Council to negotiate with Tokyo an agreement on Japanese self-restrictions on car exports to the EC which should be analogous to the previously concluded Japanese–American agreement on Japanese self-restrictions to the American market. It was not expressed clearly what the term 'analogous' meant since the German side opposed any quota on the grounds of the principle of free trade.[23] However, on 10 June, the German Minister of Economics suddenly announced in Tokyo that Japan had agreed to limit her car exports to the FRG in 1981 to 10 per cent in comparison to 1980, and two days later a similar agreement was announced by the Benelux countries. This incident proved extremely humiliating to the Commission.[24]

A strategy developed by the Commission and proposed without success to the Council in order to find a comprehensive approach to the trade problem has been to submit to the Japanese side a package deal whereby both sides would revoke their national restrictions in a parallel move as well as the strengthening of industrial and scientific cooperation.[25] Later the Commission added the start of proceedings against Japan under Article 23 of the GATT. A complaint under Article 23 is possible if any GATT member believes that international trade rules are being nullified or impaired, opening in such a case the possibility to the complainant to revoke certain previously granted benefits. However, the Commission could not gain acceptance of this threefold approach in the Council. Italy and France first refused to invoke Article 23 and argued that such a procedure would be too long, whereas other member states opposed it on the grounds that it would bring the trade conflict too much into the open. Some member states were vehemently opposed to the renunciation of national restrictions even as part of a package deal. France argued also against industrial and scientific cooperation with Japan since such action might give Japan the technology of those few sectors where the EC still has an edge over Japan.[26] On 22 March the Council finally decided only to 'explore the possibilities of scientific and technological cooperation between the Community and Japan', and to initiate the procedures of Article 23 with Japan.[27]

As a result, the Commission submitted on 7 April 1982 a letter to the Japanese side which argued that the GATT objective of 'reciprocal and mutually advantageous arrangements' had not been adequately achieved between the EC and Japan. As reasons the Commission mentioned Japan's low imports of manufactured goods, NTBs and some features of the Japanese economy such as the small number of extremely large business groupings, sectoral oligopolies, the distribution system and the low international profile of the Japanese currency.[28]

The importance of these procedures for the EC are twofold. First, it gives the Commission finally a mandate to take some actions which go beyond the regular high-level talks between Brussels and Tokyo. Second, it increases the political pressure on Japan at a time when the USA is increasingly growing impatient with Japan's trade surplus and low-key international role. It is these points which matter, although the arguments put forward in the EC's letter were not new and the procedure under Article 23 is extremely long. However, the Japanese move to lower tariffs and remove some NTBs within recent months has to be seen against this background.

Outlook

This chapter has analysed the economic and political dimensions of the EC–Japan relationship on an issue and actor level. The trade imbalance between the two will change only gradually because of the structural conditions of Japan's economy. The emergence of newly industrializing countries (NICs) and rising labour costs in Japan will, however, deepen the degree of horizontal international division of labour in the field of labour-intensive consumer goods and intermediate industrial materials also in Japan. This will gradually change the closed character of the Japanese economy.

The European exporters, on the other hand, will have to strengthen their competitiveness through adequate investment, modernization and restructuring of industrial sectors, as well as better marketing strategies. The Council and particularly the Commission have repeatedly drawn attention to this in their statements in recent years. In order to assist EC exporters with these necessary efforts, the member states have to agree on a common policy for trade and industry although the chances are not very promising. It has to be understood that the Japanese market is not only important as a further outlet for European products, but also as a testing ground for third country markets. Self-restrictive measures by the Japanese in certain sectors are only then beneficial if Europe's industry uses this breathing space to become more competitive. If these self-restrictive measures serve only as an intermediate step to protectionism the EC will lose world markets and the European consumer will face more expensive, but also qualitatively inferior, products. A further help for European industry lies, as the Commission has repeatedly pointed out, in the promotion of direct investment by Japan in Europe, European investment in Japan, technological exchanges and cooperation in third country markets.[29]

A solution to the EC–Japan trade problem can, however, only be found if the complicated political dimension of the relationship is handled properly. Both parties cannot demand a change of the other's social or economic structure for the sake of a balanced trade. There is also no need for it since both the EC and Japan have not yet fully utilized their potential to find solutions. In the EC's case it is notably the development of a common industrial policy. Mutual accusations have recently poisoned the already tense climate. While some Europeans are losing patience with the 'unfair', 'inscrutable' Japanese, some of the latter become upset about the Europeans who try to put the blame for their own 'ineffectiveness' on the Japanese or who refer to Japanese houses as 'rabbit hutches' or to the Japanese as 'workaholics'. One extreme public statement by an official of the Japanese Ministry of Industry and International Trade should, however, not be over-valued where it was hinted that Japan would be forced to bolster transactions with communist countries and might start to export weapons around the globe.[30]

However, one can expect that Japan will do more international burden-sharing and not only profit from the international system. While a greater international role for the yen or more Japanese aid to the Third World will not raise any objections, it is less advisable simply to ask the Japanese for increased military expenditures without first clarifying the nature and extent of Japan's defence role. In addition, more burden-sharing and international responsibilities by Japan will also necessitate more consultations of the Japanese by her other Western partners.

There is a last aspect of the EC–Japan relationship which should also encourage more consultations between the two. Both sides must realize that they have many economic and political interests in common where they cannot agree with the USA. Examples are the so-called 'reciprocity trade legislation' in the USA or the trilateral trade talks which were started in January 1982 in Key Biscayne.[31] Other issues are Western sanctions against communist countries and the solution of the Middle East problem. Common positions of the EC and Japan would not only give more weight to both, but would also put the trade conflict into proper perspective.

Notes

1. Hanabusa, M., *Trade Problems between Japan and Western Europe* (Farnborough, Saxon House, 1979), p. 2.
2. Ibid., p. 5.
3. Wilkinson, E., *Misunderstanding: Europe versus Japan* (Tokyo, Chuokoronsha, 1980), p. 189.
4. Hanabusa, op. cit., p. 9.
5. Ibid., p. 51.
6. Wilkinson, op. cit., p. 193.
7. Mission of Japan, 'Thirty-Six Questions and Answers on the EEC–Japan Economic Relations', October 1979.
8. *Le Monde*, 23 April 1982; *Neue Zürcher Zeitung*, 8 April 1982.

9.   Hanabusa, op. cit., p. 27.
10. Ibid., p. 61.
11. Ibid., p. 80.
12. Ibid., p. 64.
13. Ibid., p. 58.
14. *Asahi shimbun*, 24 March 1982.
15. Commission of the European Communities, 'Requests by the European Communities', Brussels, 8 December 1981.
16. *Neue Zürcher Zeitung*, 30 January 1982; *International Herald Tribune*, 28 May 1982.
17. *Neue Zürcher Zeitung*, 30 January 1982.
18. *Japan Times*, 2 February 1982.
19. Hosoya, C., 'Relations between the European Communities and Japan', *Journal of Common Market Studies*, 18 (1979), 162.
20. Economic and Social Committee of the European Communities, *The EEC's External Relations—Stocktaking and Consistency of Action*, Brussels, January 1982, p. 33.
21. Ibid.
22. Commission of the European Communities, *The Community's Trade Relations with the United States and Japan*, Communication from the Commission to the European Council, Maastricht, 23 and 24 March 1981, Brussels, 12 March 1981 (COM 123 Final).
23. *Le Monde*, 20 May 1981.
24. *Le Monde*, 15 June 1981.
25. Commission des Communautés européennes, *Réexamen de la politique commerciale de la Communauté à l'égard du Japon*, Brussels, 15 July 1980 (COM (80) 444 Final).
26. *Agence Europe*, 22–3 February 1982 and 4 March 1982.
27. Foreign Affairs Council, 'A strategy towards Japan', supplement to *Communauté Européenne*, 6 March 1982 (Lettre d'information du Bureau de Genève).
28. *Le Monde*, 23 April 1982; *Neue Zürcher Zeitung*, 8 April 1982.
29. *Réexamen de la politique commerciale de la Communauté à l'égard du Japon*, op. cit. Note particularly the trade promotion scheme which comprises the organization of seminars in Europe, concerned with specific sectors, the organization of sales missions to Japan, and the establishment of a scholarship programme for young European businessmen.
30. *International Herald Tribune*, 25 March 1982.
31. *International Herald Tribune*, 2 March 1982; *Neue Zürcher Zeitung*, 19 January 1982.

21 The European Community and China

T. V. SATHYAMURTHY

The importance attached by the Chinese Government to its political relations with European governments has varied over the last three decades; but there is a thread of consistency running through the ideological rationale underlying China's shifts of attitude towards Western Europe. West European governments have, for their part, by and large, taken the view that the People's Republic of China is potentially a vital force in international political and economic relations and that no diplomatic opportunity should be lost for forging trade and other links with it. In this, European countries have been, on balance, more far-sighted than their American superpower ally. The only factor limiting or inhibiting the freedom with which a critically important European power such as the FRG was prepared, during the 1960s and 1970s, to enter into a close relationship with China was its apprehension of how its policy might go down with the Soviet Government which turned against China at about the time when China needed its help most. Even so, undeterred by the Hallstein doctrine,[1] the FRG more than amply made up for lack of diplomatic relations by becoming one of China's strongest partners in trade, second only to Japan in importance.[2]

Under de Gaulle, China assumed considerable political importance in a strategy designed to increase France's capacity to forge independent links with all major centres of power in the world by projecting a new idea of Europe stretching from the Atlantic to the Urals.[3] In general, however, relations between China and West European countries prior to the mid-1970s, when China appeared to have become unequivocally committed to a policy of modernization, were particularly susceptible to the rather dramatic political changes to which domestic Chinese politics were prone.[4] In this essay the most recent chapter in its European policy, which began with the 1977 Trade Treaty between China and the EC, is considered against a background of Sino–European relations since 1949.

In order to appreciate the nuances of the Chinese view of foreign relations as it affects Europe, it is essential to grasp not only the Chinese Communist Party's (CCP) clearly stated position on imperialism since its inception, but also the historical orientation of China to distant foreign countries. Traditionally, China's main concern was with its immediate periphery. Until imperialism penetrated China during the nineteenth century and reduced it to the status of a semi-colony, China had had no *political* contact with any part of the world (that is, no foreign policy for Europe, West Asia, America South and North, Africa, the Pacific region, etc.) beyond the immediate Chinese sphere of influence which was confined to the Far East and South East Asia.[5]

During the course of its revolutionary struggle, CCP adopted the position that the main enemy of the Chinese people (that is, the revolution) was imperialism in general and American imperialism in particular. This general orientation was not altered even during the most serious phase of the party's struggle against Japanese imperialism. Of course, this did not mean that, after the revolution, China was predisposed to be less hostile to West European countries than to the USA or Japan. During its first decade in power, the Chinese Revolutionary Government was very much a part of the socialist camp, and its ideological position towards the West was shaped by its identification with the anti-imperialist and anti-colonial forces in the world as well as with the forces of socialist revolution and national liberation.

In its general orientation to the outside world, the Chinese Government and the CCP were not simply actuated by a desire to follow the Soviet Union. In fact, whilst taking care not to offend the Soviet Union's susceptibilities unnecessarily, China took a number of new initiatives which marked it off as anything but an uncritical camp follower of the Soviet Union.[6]

It is interesting to note that, prior to the eruption of Sino–Soviet differences to the surface for the first time, China and the Soviet Union differed amongst themselves over the question of imperialism. The latter adopted the view that the nuclear question should be given overriding importance in the relations between the imperialist camp and the socialist camp, and a *modus vivendi* should be worked out between the two camps along the lines of peaceful coexistence and peaceful competition leading to *détente*. The Chinese standpoint on this issue was in sharp contrast to that of the Soviet Union. China propounded the view that imperialism was a paper tiger and the tide of revolution was strong enough to drive the USA and its European allies into a defensive position.[7] In this context, China's evaluation of the international role of West European countries was predicated upon the view that they, together with the USA, constituted a united imperialist power bloc in contradiction with socialism and national liberation throughout the world. China thus saw the newly created EC as an instrument of imperialism designed to extend and deepen Western economic penetration and domination of the world, and as yet another device to weaken socialist countries.[8] As such, China was hostile to the EC during the first few years of its existence.

With the development of the Sino–Soviet conflict, and as a consequence of the severe international economic isolation which it had to suffer, China was compelled to re-orientate its domestic politics in the direction of self-reliant development which often tended towards some form of economic autarky.[9] During the early 1960s, China gave exaggerated importance to Soviet–American *rapprochement*.[10] At the height of the Cultural Revolution, and especially at the time of the Soviet armed intervention in Czechoslovakia, China's understanding of the world situation revolved round the possibility that structural contradictions within each of the two superpower camps might be increasingly manifested in the form of allies (for example, Romania, France, EC, etc.) striking independent attitudes in foreign policy matters. This perception of the world imparted a new appearance to China's international role. Its general policy towards Europe became more sophisticated and differentiated though the aim did not extend beyond relations at a state-to-state level, and especially bilateral relations with different European countries in the short and medium run.[11] Thus, within a decade, China's policy towards Western Europe was transformed from relentless hostility to one of regarding the latter as the key zone[12] that needed to be disengaged from both the Soviet Union and the USA.

The views of European countries regarding the international significance of China were (and even now continue to be) governed by two broad considerations. It is true that less powerful and economically less successful countries of Europe (for example, Britain) view the Soviet Union with considerable apprehension and hostility. But Western Europe in general (and France and the FRG in particular) attach great importance to soothing rather than irritating the Soviet Union, sometimes even at the risk of displeasing the USA. West European desire to forge links with China has been tempered by constant awareness of the prime importance of the Soviet factor in the Western Europe–Soviet Union–USA power triangle.[13] China's main political aim in forging close relations with Western Europe has always been to compromise the position of the Soviet Union in the Euro-Atlantic power triangle. During Hua Guofeng's much publicized 1979 European tour this view found expression in the Chinese Chairman's call to Europeans to 'put missiles before Détente'.[14] This, of course, the Western Europeans would never do.

The second main consideration is economic. As the recession deepened during the late 1960s and the 1970s, West European countries came to attach great attention to external trade, and China was seen as one of the as yet relatively untapped avenues of commerce. In fact, there is a symmetrical relationship between the unrealistic character of the Chinese political objective of weaning Western European countries away from a policy of a generally conciliatory diplomatic relationship with the Soviet Union, on the one hand, and, on the other hand, Western Europe's initial expectation (until 1978, and especially during 1977) that trade with China might fill an important gap in its export market. These two strands in Sino-European relations of the post-Cultural Revolution phase constitute a necessary basis for an understanding of the dynamics of present-day trade between China and the EC.

The essential feature of China's relations with the EC is economic, though its bilateral relations with each West European country has a political content in consonance with the CCP's world view. We shall summarize China's view of Europe's place in the world in the wake of what it regards as the increasing power and aggressive character of Soviet 'social imperialism'.[15] During the mid-1960s, China attached a great deal of importance to the major world contradiction between imperialism and national liberation, and even believed that the Indo-China wars of liberation could lead to major war involving the Soviet Union, the USA and China that might well spread to the Chinese mainland. By 1970, however, the main emphasis in China's interpretation of international relations was placed on the scramble between the two superpowers for world hegemony which could eventually engulf the Soviet Union, the USA, and Western Europe in a major war to be fought in Europe. According to the 'Three Worlds' theory originally adumbrated by Mao Zedong and unveiled before the world at the UN by Deng Xiaoping in 1974, China favoured a union between Western Europe and the Third World against the superpowers in general and the Soviet Union in particular.[16] By 1975, when China decided to send a fully-fledged ambassador to the EC and Deng Xiaoping visited France, emphasis in China's policy continued to be placed on the belief that the main threat to peace lay in Soviet expansionism in Europe.

But the crucial material factor in the expansion and intensification of contact with Western Europe lay in the economic needs of China during the epoch following the Cultural Revolution. With the demise of Zhou and Mao, and the ensuing readjustment of the conflict between the 'mass' line and the 'revisionist' line in the sphere of domestic policy, China embarked upon a strategy of 'Four Modernizations'. This involved a modification of the earlier policy of 'walking on two legs', with much greater importance attached to 'learning from the experience of advanced capitalist countries to modernize production by developing technology'.[17]

China's overtures to the EC during the second half of the 1970s should be seen in the light of the overriding importance attached by the dominant faction of the new Chinese leadership to the task of constructing a great modern Chinese society.[18] In order to foster its new policy of raising the technological level of its economy (both in agriculture and in industry) and developing the skills of its work-force, China turned to Western Europe in 1977 in a much bigger way than before. In the remainder of this essay we shall trace the course of the most recent phase of China's relations with the countries of Western Europe in the sphere of foreign trade.

China's foreign trade policy emphasized the importance of modern imports from Western Europe as early as 1955.[19] Even though the importance initially attached to European trade rapidly disappeared from China's foreign economic policy as a result of domestic arguments between pro-Stalin and anti-Stalin elements within the leadership of CCP, by 1962 China seemed to have reached a stage where it acknowledged, objectively speaking, that Western European and Japanese trade would be indispensable to its economic development and modernization. During the early 1960s, however, China was compelled to use a sizeable proportion of its foreign exchange holdings for purchasing essential items such as foodgrains, wool, and other raw materials; it was only after 1965 that the import of machinery, equipment (including aircraft and complete industrial plants), industrial goods of various descriptions, and fertilizers was once again increased.[20]

During the early 1970s, even before the effects of the Cultural Revolution had begun to recede, Deng Xiaoping, during his first rehabilitation, had given the foreign trade policy of China a big boost. In this he seemed to have the full cooperation of the foreign trade bureaucracy of the Government even although, by 1972, powerful ideological criticism within the leadership of CCP, as well as the rank and file, over domestic development goals militated against the level of Chinese foreign trade rising fast, and forced a temporary eclipse of the redoubtable Deng.[21] It was not until 1976 that new trade initiatives could again be confidently launched by the Chinese First Vice-Premier during a period of resurgence in power following his second rehabilitation.[22] The responses of Western European countries were initially rather more enthusiastic than they were to be in subsequent years, even though European observers have been somewhat divided over the real significance of Chinese trade for Western European economies.[23]

China formally recognized the EC on 8 May 1975. Its decision to exchange ambassadorial representatives was preceded by an announcement of China's readiness to begin negotiations for an official trade pact with the EC. This, as has already been pointed out, was a far cry from China's earlier stand (publicly ventilated even as late as 1972) on the EC as 'a centre of imperialist contradictions'. China justified its new policy towards the EC as part of a strategy of 'united' action against the Soviet 'social imperialist' hegemony that had gained the offensive in world politics.[24] China's main economic aim in opening the door of its foreign trade to Western Europe was to import capital goods and technical expertise on a large scale.

The rhetoric of Sino-European relations should not, however, be allowed to obscure the rather more modest level of China's foreign trade (see Tables 1 and 2). In 1976, China's imports and exports represented only 5 to 7 per cent of its national income.[25] Some writers[26] attribute, in a rather unconvincing fashion, China's weaker position as an exporter, and its tendency to import in an unpredictable and haphazard manner (both *what* it imported and *how much* it imported), to its economic backwardness and waywardness. But, it would appear that in spite of all the apparent inconsistencies in its foreign trade policy—open trading during the 1950s at a fast pace, contraction of trade during the 1960s in the wake of the intensification of internal and external contradictions within the socialist world,

Table 1   Trade between the EC and China ($ million)
(At 5-year intervals 1958–73 and annually during 1975–9)

	1958	1963	1968	1973	1975	1976	1977	1978	1979
Imports from China	200	203	259	345	345	1,187	1,191	1,297	1,827
Exports to China	284	186	307	369	369	1,637	1,181	2,455	2,899

Source: Compiled from data contained in EC official documentation.

NB Figures for the years 1958–75 represent the sum of the figures for individual members of the EC because trade was conducted during the period on a bilateral basis with individual West European countries.

A note: Two major points may be noted:

(a)   There is a big shift in quantitative terms in the trade figures prior to and after 1976 (which is also the year in which both Mao and Zhou died).

(b)   Whilst it is true that the % gap between the figures for imports from China and exports to China is much wider during the years 1977 and 1978, the % trade gap for the year 1979 is much less, though still manifesting a positive balance so far as the EC is concerned. European governments, however, have increasingly tended to take the view that China's enthusiasm for promoting exports is somewhat overshadowed by its vacillation over importing large quantities of mechanical and industrial fabrications from the EC.

and expansion of trade during the 1970s especially to Western Europe—China has adamantly adhered to the principle of self-financing all external trade.

The first big increase in China's European trade followed the Sino-Soviet rupture involving a dramatic and crippling reduction of the Soviet trade which persisted throughout the period 1960–8. The FRG, along with Japan, replaced the Soviet bloc as China's trading partners.[27] Broadbent, for example, has calculated that between 1960 and 1972 China's trade with Western Europe steadily expanded as its trade with the Soviet Union declined, with the former outstripping the latter as early as 1963. Agriculture, oil and industry constitute the cornerstone of China's external trade policy. Its agricultural exports, which dramatically expanded during the 1970s, include foodstuffs and raw materials as well as finished products. These, together with textiles, make up the bulk of its agricultural trade with the EC.[28] It is estimated that over 50 per cent of China's total trade in 1976 was concerned with the future development of the farm sector.

Rising oil production represents another source of development for China's economy. European industrialists naturally continue to be impressed by the possibility that in future China could well emerge as a valuable source of oil-related raw materials,[29] especially in view of their diminishing availability at cheap prices under present world conditions. At the same time, China's potential as a world trading power is greatly augmented by the fact that it has 25–30 per cent of the total world supply of rich mineral ore deposits. In the field of oil exploration, China has developed some international contacts, especially with Britain, in relation to offshore drilling. With the development of oil, the demand for shipping in particular, and means of transportation in general, have sharply, it not exponentially, increased over the years, and China has become, over the last decade or so, a regular importer of second-hand vessels from Europe with a view to building up a fleet of oil tankers. With the help of France and Italy, China has also sought to develop an interest in the establishment of catalytic petrochemical facilities and in submarine pipeline construction. China appears to have decided to expand its oil export

Table 2   Main items of trade between China and the EC (1976–)

Chinese exports to the EC	EC exports to China
1. Live animals and animal products (especially meat and edible meat offals, fish, crustaceans and molluscs).	1. Live animals and animal products—especially live animals and dairy products.
2. Vegetable products (especially edible vegetables; coffee, tea, maté and spices; and lacs, gums, resins, etc.).	2. Vegetable products, especially products of milling industry.
3. Edible fats—animal and vegetable.	3. Animal and vegetable fats.
4. Prepared foodstuffs—especially preparations of vegetables, fruit or other parts of plants; prepared animal fodder; tobacco.	4. Processed foodstuffs—especially sugars and sugar confectionery.
5. Mineral products—especially metallic ores, slag and ash; sulphur, lime, cement, etc.	5. Mineral products—especially mineral fuels.
6. Products of chemical and allied industries—especially organic chemicals; soaps, candles and allied products; explosives, pyrotechnics, etc.; inorganic chemicals and organo-metallic compounds of rare earth metals, and radioactive isotopes, etc.; and miscellaneous chemical products.	6. Chemical products—especially pharmaceutical products, tannins, essential oils, etc.
7. Raw hides and skins, furs, etc. and artificial resins, etc.—especially fur skins, leather and raw hides and skins.	7. Artificial resins and plastic materials.

8. Wood and articles of wood—especially basketware, etc.

9. Paper and paper-making material.

10. Textile and textile articles—especially silk, cotton, animal hair, etc.

11. Footwear, headgear, articles of stone, plaster, etc.

12. Pearls, precious and semi-precious stones, etc.

13. Base metals and articles thereof—especially tin, iron, steel, zinc, etc.

14. Machinery and mechanical appliances—e.g., boilers, electrical machinery.

15. Vehicles, aircraft, and parts thereof—e.g., vehicles other than railways.

16. Precision instruments, arms and ammunition, miscellaneous manufactures.

17. Works of art, etc.

Source: EC Information Bulletins.

8. Raw hides and skins, etc., wood and wood articles, paper making material—especially books, pictures, newspapers, etc.

9. Textiles and textile industries—especially continuous man-made fabrics and discontinuous man-made fibres.

10. Footwear and headgear, articles of stone, cement, etc., and especially pearls, precious stones, precious metals, etc.

11. Base metals and articles of base metal—predominantly iron and steel and articles thereof; and aluminium.

12. Machinery and electrical equipment.

13. Vehicles, aircraft, vessels, etc.

14. Optical, photographic, cinematographic equipment, precision instruments, etc.

15. Arms and ammunition and miscellaneous manufactures.

16. Works of art, etc.

market whilst concentrating the use of coal-derived energy for developing its domestic economy.[30]

During the early 1970s, China's exports to Western Europe increased faster than its imports,[31] though this main trend was subsequently reversed. The FRG accounted for the best part of this trade, with Britain lagging rather far behind.[32] China's import of heavy equipment and electronic goods from France[33] exceeded its export of raw materials. As China's interest in Western military hardware increases, France and Britain[34] will stand to gain even more than in the past.[35] It is clear that the development of the civil aviation industry is being increasingly linked to China's European trade. In gross terms, the trade figures for 1974 and 1975 would appear to show that, while the total volume of trade increased by one-third from £954 million to £1,280 million, the FRG, France and the United Kingdom in that order were the three main partners accounting for 68 per cent of the total trade in both years.[36] In the sphere of steel plant fabrication, a West German contract (with Demag), originally negotiated in 1964,[37] and subsequently put in cold storage during the Cultural Revolution, has been revived more recently, with due allowance being made to changed conditions. France has been playing an important role in China's efforts to build import substitution in the motor-car industry.

The estimates for 1975 indicate that 30 per cent of China's external trade was with the EC; in the same year, the enlarged EC (with nine members instead of the original six) was China's third largest trading partner (after the USA, Japan, and Hong Kong), with the FRG accounting for a sufficient proportion of the trade to mark it off as its fourth largest trading partner. During the most acute phase of the Sino-Soviet conflict, China's total trade suffered stagnation if not a decline in real terms at a time when world trade was expanding. But with the oil crisis and the consequent sudden increase in world inflation since 1973, China's imports began to cost more and the gap between them and its exports narrowed.[38] The general picture, on the eve of China's treaty with the EC, was one of cautious advance and a gradual broadening of the range and depth of the trading relationship between two partners.

On 3 September 1978, a comprehensive trade agreement between the People's Republic of China and the EC was signed, thus marking an important stage in the relations between China and Europe. On 18 July 1979, a textile agreement was successfully negotiated. Bilateral trade agreements between EC member states embarked upon a joint trade policy towards third countries. This provided the background to China's decision to establish official relations with the EC and to replace the various bilateral agreements with individual member states with a single agreement between the EC and China. The process of negotiating such an agreement was facilitated by the appointment of a Chinese ambassador to the EC.[39]

The 1978 agreement, valid for five years, is of a non-preferential nature and sets out several rules for the promotion of trade. The most favoured nation clause applies to tariffs. Under Article 3 of the Treaty, each party contributes (according to its means) towards achieving a balance in their trade and jointly remedies situations arising out of serious imbalances. China undertook to give favoured treatment to imports from the EC and, for its part, the EC committed itself to a policy of increased liberalization of imports from China.[40] Both parties agreed that trade in goods and services would be effected 'at market related prices'. A joint committee[41] was set up in 1980 to review the working of the agreement.[42] The two sides agreed to foster exchange of visits 'by individuals, groups, and delegations for the economic, commercial and industrial spheres, facilitating exchanges and contacts and encouraging the organization of fairs and exhibitions'.

The visit to European countries of Premier Hua Guofeng in November 1979, to which reference has already been made, added political significance to the trade treaty between the two sides. But already, with the trial of the 'Gang of Four' in preparation, if not well under way, divisions had begun to appear within the ruling hierarchy of CCP in which Premier Hua and the First Vice-Premier Deng were soon to find themselves on opposite sides.[43] Hua's visit was meant to consolidate the new relationship between Western Europe and China and to establish close understanding at the leadership level between European statespersons and the Chinese Premier.

Although Hua was sensitive to the susceptibilities of the different European powers that he visited, he could not help but attach great importance to China's preoccupation with Soviet 'hegemonism' and 'social imperialism' wherever he went. Nor could he restrain himself when it came to issuing calls to his hosts to unify and join together in order to strengthen their defence so that world war might at least be delayed if not averted.[44] In China's evaluation of the world situation on the eve of the 1980s, the USSR seemed to occupy a place identical with that occupied by the USA during the 1950s and the 1960s. Before *détente* became a commonplace in the diplomatic intercourse between the two superpowers, China insisted on arguing that 'America's offensive posture would only be changed once it had been effectively opposed'.[45] To the Europeans who, by 1979, had begun to wake up to the fact that the prospects of the Chinese market during the 1980s were by no means likely to be as alluring as had been imagined only two or three years before, Premier Hua's almost exclusive concentration (unlike Deng in France in 1975) on international politics must have come as a slight disappointment.

Between 1975 and 1979, trade in both directions doubled.[46] Since 1979, however, the gusto with which the 'Four Modernizations' policy was implemented has had to be tempered by attention to the social impact of foreign economic influences and to new aspects of economic behaviour among certain sections of the population.[47] This has resulted in the Chinese Government's readjustment of its economic policies. Consequently, the rate of growth of foreign trade of China has tended to level off (see Table 1). In order to give a publicity boost to trade with China during the 1980s, the two sides agreed to organize an EC–China Business Week (see Table 2) to 'allow traders on both sides to take advantage of the possibilities offered under China's new policies of stimulating foreign trade'.[48] This event took place between 30 March and 10 April 1981 and was the first of its kind organized by the EC with a third country. It was regarded as a milestone in the relations between the two sides. But it must be seen as an administrative measure to maintain an even flow of trade at a time when the political repercussions of the 'Four Modernizations' policy are beginning to be felt rather more deeply than had been thought possible even three years ago.

In conclusion, it would be appropriate to draw attention to the fact that China's positive overtures to Western Europe were directly linked to its political analysis of the international situation, and, in particular, the role of the superpowers in seeking to exert their combined and mutually conflictive hegemony on the world as a whole. At the same time, the prospects of expansion of China's external trade were dependent upon the shifts in emphasis in the major political controversy of which the Cultural Revolution was a culmination. In other words, the inconclusive debate as to whether socialist construction should aim at fashioning a great modern China (as a necessary prelude to the creation of conditions under which socialist relations of production could eventually be developed), or whether the two tasks should be undertaken simultaneously (with precedence being given to the development of egalitarian, democratic and proletarian social relations over the requirements of modernization and industrialization whenever the two conflicted with each other) held the key to China's external economic policy. However, the adherents of one of these two mutually contradictory lines appeared to take the initiative in calling for an expansion of trade with Western Europe.[49] Since the Cultural Revolution, this line has been generally on the ascendent, but it would appear that it is also under overt and covert attack at various levels within Chinese society. Under these circumstances, the long-term importance of the EC as a trading partner is bound to continue more as a weapon in China's anti-Soviet propaganda than necessarily as a partner in a steady and uninterrupted expansion of mutual trade on a scale sufficient to add confidence to European heavy industry and capital.

Notes

1. The state of war between Germany and China was officially terminated in 1955. The Hallstein Doctrine, however, rendered formal West German recognition of the People's Republic of China an impossibility. During the period 1955–64, trade between the two sides did develop, although subsequent to 1964 there was a phase of difficult relations due to the *Ostpolitik* of West Germany and developments in China leading up to the Cultural Revolution. See, e.g., Grossmann, B., 'Peking—Bonn: Substantial non-relations', *Pacific Community*, 2 (October 1970), 224–36.

2. Even without a trade mission in Peking, the FRG was able to import strategic raw materials from China and to give China some help in rocket technology.

3. Diplomatic relations between China and France were established in January 1964 amid expectations of a new *entente* between the two countries. De Gaulle's dramatic gesture was widely interpreted as a new and dynamic overture to the Third World as a whole, a repudiation of the spirit of the Yalta agreement, and as an expression of French opposition to Soviet and American nuclear hegemony. In the event, however, the actual achievements of the new Sino-French diplomacy were rather limited, especially in view of the fact that the May 1968 upheaval in France and China's Cultural Revolution severely interrupted normal relations between the two countries. See, e.g., Adie, W. A. C., 'China's Foreign Policy. II. The Developed World', *The World Today*, 24 (1968), 257–68; see also Maurer, P. D., 'A Study in Trade: Paris-Peking Relations: 1949–1976', *Issues and Studies*, 13 (1977), 26–55.

4. For a British view of these changes, see Boardman, R., *Britain and the People's Republic of China* (London, 1976), *passim*. See also Fitzgerald, C. P., 'The Chinese View of Foreign Relations', *The World Today*, 19 (1963), 9–17.

5. See Fitzgerald, C. P., op. cit.

6. These include its bold intervention in the Korean war in 1951, its consistent stand on the Indo-China wars of national liberation (especially during the period 1961–1971), and its role in the non-aligned world especially during the period subsequent to Bandung and until about 1972.

7. See Sathyamurthy, T. V., 'China's Role in International Relations', *The Economic and Political Weekly*, 13, Nos. 45–47 (11, 18, 25 November 1978), 1851–8, 1899–1909, 1941–55.

8. See Bouc, A., 'Peking Now Wants a United Europe', *Atlantic Community Quarterly*, 10 (1972), 167–73; Bräker, H., *Die Sowjetunion, China und die EWG* (Köln, 1973); and Yahuda, M. B., 'China's New Foreign Policy', *The World Today*, 28 (1972), 14–22.

9. Although since the Cultural Revolution, China has participated in contractual procedures, accepted in principle foreign deposits, and contracted in principle medium-term quasi-loans, it is still uneasy about involving itself too deeply in such transactions. Foreign trade is even now no more than a small appendage to the economy of China. See, e.g., Denny, D. L., 'Recent Developments in International Financial Policies of the People's Republic of China', *Stanford Journal of International Studies*, 10 (1975), 163–86.

10. See, e.g., Ojha, I. C., 'A Comparison of China's policies towards Western and Eastern Europe covering the period after the Czechoslovakian "invasion" ', *Asia Quarterly*, 2 (1975), 111–25.

11. This, of course, did not rule out defence and security aid in the distant future when China might well develop real strategic capability to provide other countries with a counterweight to Soviet strategic power. See Michel, J., 'L'Europe dans la stratégique Chinoise', *Défense Nationale*, 34 (1978), 89–98.

12. See Hervouet, Gérard, 'La Chine et la CEE: le sens d'un rapprochement prémédité', *Revue d'Intégration Européenne*, 1 (1977), 77–86; Wilson, D., 'China and the European Community', *China Quarterly*, 56 (1973), 647–66; Yahuda, M. B., 'China's Conceptions of their Role in the World', *Political Quarterly*, 45 (1974), 75–94; Gittings, J., 'China's Foreign Policy: Continuity or Change', *Journal of Contemporary Asia*, 2 (1972), 17–35.

13. China's aim has been to weaken the position of the Soviet Union in the Euro-Atlantic triangle of power accommodation and confrontation while, at the same time, preventing it from becoming a factor in the Western Europe–Japan–United States triangle of power. China, for its part, is also very keen to utilize its position in the US–USSR–China triangle to prevent the US and the USSR from reconciling their contradiction of interests particularly in the Pacific. See, e.g., Pfaltzgraff Jr, R. L., 'Multipolarity Alliances and United States–Soviet Union–China Relations', *Orbis*, 17 (1973), 720–36.

14. Reisky de Dubnic, V., 'Germany and China: The Intermediate Zone Theory and the Moscow Treaty', *Asia Quarterly*, 4 (1971), 343–59; Yahuda, M. B., 'Premier Hua Guofeng's Grand Tour' (Note of the Month), in *The World Today*, 35 (1979), 471–3.

15. This particular characterization of the USSR dates back to 1968 with the Soviet armed intervention in Czechoslovakia. Not long after, China propagated the view that in the light of Soviet aggression a 'socialist camp' as such could no longer be said to be in existence. See Sathyamurthy, T. V., op. cit.

16. See Yahuda, M., 'Modernization and Foreign Policy in China', *The World Today*, 36 (1980), 445–52.

17. See, e.g., *Peking Review*, 3 January 1964.

18. See, e.g., for a typical Western view, Terrill, Ross, 'China and the World: Self-Reliance or Interdependence?', *Foreign Affairs*, 55 (1977), 295–305; 'China in the 1980s', ibid., 58 (1980), 920–35. See also the Special Issue on *China's Quest for Independence*, Stanford *Journal of International Studies*, 15 (1979), *passim*.

19. See Remer, C. F., 'Appraising the external economic relations of Communist China', in Szczepanik, E. (ed.), *Symposium on Economic and Social Problems of the Far East* (Hong Kong, 1962).

20. A typical justification for this was given, for example, by the propaganda chief (Chou Yang) in October 1963 who 'outlined the "fighting task" of Chinese social scientists and philosophers in an important speech. In order to know and change the world . . . they must study the situation in foreign countries and quickly evaluate their academic advance', Adie, W. A. C., op. cit., pp. 261–2.

21. See, e.g., Findoff, W. B., 'China and the European Community', *The Round Table*, 251 (1973), 341–50; 'China und die Europäische Gemeinschaft', *Aussenpolitik*, 23 (1972), 656–62; Opitz, P. J., 'Die Chinesische Aussenpolitik seit dem Tode Mao Tse-tungs', *Politik und Zeitgeschichte*, 4 (1979), 3–20; Opitz, P. J. (ed.), *China zwischen Welt Revolution und Realpolitik* (München, 1979), *passim*.; Terrill, Ross, *The Future of China After Mao* (New York, 1978), *passim*.

22. See Fingar, T., 'The Quest for Independence', in Special Issue on *China's Quest for Independence*, op. cit., pp. 1–23.

23. See Millar, T. B., 'The Triumph of Pragmatism: China's Links with the West', *International Affairs*, 55 (1979), 195–205; Senese, D. J., 'Western Aid to Mainland China: The Crucial Factors', *Journal of Social and Political Studies*, 5 (1980), 119–31; Claes, W., 'La Chine et l'Europe', *Studia Diplomatica*, 33 (1980), 361–81; Special Issue on *China's Changing Role in the World Economy*, Stanford *Journal of International Studies*, 10 (1975); Trivière, L., 'La Chine et la sécurité européenne', *Etudes* (1975), 323–40; Yahuda, M. B., 'Towards a New Chinese Political Order: Aftermath of the Death of Chairman Mao', *The Round Table*, 266 (1977), 135–45; Goodman, D. S. G., 'China after Chou', *The World Today*, 32 (1976), 203–13; Guillermaz, J., *La Chine après Mao* (Geneva, 1978); Broadbent, K. P., 'China and the EEC: The Politics of a New Trade Relationship', *The World Today*, 32 (1976), 190–8 (especially p. 190).

24. *Peking Review*, 1975, No. 18, p. 39.

25. Broadbent, K. P., op. cit., p. 191. In 1973, China's external trade was over £4 billion (highest ever); and yet the total turnover was relatively low (cf. Taiwan and other Asian countries). The annual per capita export earnings in that year was less than £3 which made China one of the weakest of the world's exporters.

26. See, e.g., Donnithorne, A., 'China's Foreign Trade System Changes Gear', *US–China Business Review*, I (1974), 17 ff.; Eckstein, A., 'China's Trade Policy and Sino-American Relations', *Foreign Affairs* (1975), 137 ff.
27. China also deeply resented the unfavourable terms of its Soviet trade.
28. China's imports of agriculture-related products from Europe mainly included fertilizers, farm chemicals, farm machinery, tractors, breeding stock, etc., in large quantities.
29. See, e.g., several issues of *Petroleum Economist* 1974 and 1975 (especially November 1974 and April 1975).
30. China's coal deposits are very massive indeed and provide it with 85 per cent of its total current needs in energy consumption.
31. Broadbent (op. cit., p. 195) points out that China's trade with Western Europe as a whole increased by 17 per cent in 1972 (£550 million); its imports rose by only 11 per cent. China's exports, on the other hand, grew by 25 per cent. In 1974, this trade increased substantially (i.e., by over 25 per cent), with China's imports rising by 30 per cent and exports rising by nearly the same amount.
32. In 1974, China's trade deficit with the EC had increased by about 40 per cent over the 1972 figure. The FRG took a big share of this trade. China's exports to the FRG expanded by 27 per cent over the total for 1973, while its imports rose by 33 per cent; China's trade deficit was in this process increased to the figure of £155 million. By contrast, China's imports from Britain fell in 1974 by 19 per cent (to under £100 million), while China's exports increased by 33 per cent over 1973, thus giving an overall trade deficit of under £30 million (a figure significantly less than that for 1973).
33. To an amount of under £20 million.
34. With British Harrier jets and the French Mirage and missiles recently shown to be effective in the South Atlantic, Chinese interest in defence purchases from both countries might well be expected to increase during the 1980s.
35. In 1975, China ordered fifteen Lupor Hornet-type helicopters from France and purchased a similar number of Rolls Royce engines from Britain. China concluded contracts worth £100 million each with France and Britain during that year.
36. The total trade between China and France in 1974 and 1975 amounted respectively to £173 million and £300 million against figures for Sino-British trade of £165 million and £173 million respectively.
37. Broadbent (op. cit., p. 196) has noted that, in order to meet its shortage of variety of steel manufactures and to normalize the unevenness of its domestic capacity in steel production, China entered into negotiations with Demag of the FRG for building a new steel mill complex at Wuhan before the Cultural Revolution. During the Cultural Revolution, which was particularly strong in the Wuhan area, this contract had to be abandoned. Subsequently a contract was signed with the Japanese at a cost of £275 million.
38. See Robinson, J., 'Europe's Links with China', *European Community*, No. 7 (1975), 7 ff.
39. Li Lian Bi was the first Chinese ambassador to the EC.
40. This (Article 4 of the Treaty) was the first time that such a clause was written into an EC agreement.
41. It has been meeting from time to time, since 1979, to review the working of the agreement and to report on the development of trade relations. In 1980, it reported that trade in both directions had increased by 41 per cent during the previous year (reaching a total level of £2,130 million). During the first half of 1980, Chinese exports had continued to increase whereas its imports from the EC had decreased.
42. The text of the agreement is contained in *Europe Information External Relations* 42/81 (March 1981), 8–10.
43. It must be noted that Premier Hua's visit was the first of its kind by a Chinese leader of the highest rank.
44. While this went down well in Britain where Mrs Thatcher was noted for her Soviet-baiting, his West German hosts made it quite clear that they would not take kindly to overt anti-Soviet speeches by the visiting Chinese Premier.
45. Yahuda, M. B., 'Premier Hua Guofeng's Grand Tour', op. cit., p. 472.
46. *Europe Information External Relations*, op. cit., p. 7.
47. See, e.g., David Bonavia's report entitled 'Mandarins on the make', *Far Eastern Economic Review* (18–24 June 1982), 23–5.
48. *Europe Information External Relations*, op. cit., p. 7.
49. In the context of the development of China's external trade, the following periodization of the decade following the Cultural Revolution (1966–76) might be useful:

(1) *1966-9*: Although this was politically the most intense phase of the Cultural Revolution, its economic effects were not yet manifested to a full extent. In fact during this period a continuity in economic policy existed with the pre-Cultural Revolution phase.

(2) *1969-72*: The impact of the Cultural Revolution was clearly felt in the domestic and external spheres of China's economic and trade policy. The impact registered was largely one of contraction.

(3) *1972-6*: A boost was given to foreign trade and economic production, mainly as a consequence of the policies which are generally identified with Deng Xiaoping during this period when he was partially rehabilitated.

See also the essay on 'The European Community and China' in *The European Community: Bibliographical Excursions* (London, Frances Pinter, 1983).

22 The European Community and International Institutions

FRANK GREGORY and FREIDA STACK

In essence, the EC has relations with other international institutions because it has to, because it can do and because it chooses to do so. It has to because it is necessary, in both specific and general instances, for the proper functioning of the EC. It can do so because as an international institution itself it possesses the legal capacity to enter into relations with other institutions. It can in a political sense also have relations with international institutions as well as non-member states because international relations are actually composed of the interactions between states, international institutions and non-governmental organizations such as multinational companies. Lastly, the EC has specifically and publicly chosen to make contacts with other international institutions as part of its external relations.

Because one important relationship between the EC and an international entity is with GATT which is not, formally, an international institution[1] but a form of permanent international conference, this analysis is adopting a broad definition of its terms of reference. The analysis will focus upon the EC's relations with non-state actors which are recognized as international institutions or organizations (the terms are synonymous) and with inter-state activities, like trade regulation, which have become institutionalized as, for example, in GATT. This also allows the analysis to consider the EC's relationship with the ongoing Conference on Security and Cooperation in Europe (CSCE) and with the various forums in which the North–South dialogue has been conducted, for example, the Conference on International Economic Cooperation (CIEC).

The general background to this analysis is to be found partly in theoretical and empirical studies of international relations and regional integration. These studies offer explanations of the place of the EC in international relations and help to suggest why the EC has to have relations with international institutions and why the EC has been developing the scope of its external activities.

It is now generally accepted that the state-centric model of international relations does not explain all the observable forms of international interaction. Space in texts on international relations is increasingly being devoted to the activities of intergovernmental institutions and non-governmental entities such as multinational corporations.[2]

In part, the background is also to be found in writings on international law which aid our understanding of the international legal status and capacity of international organizations. After discussing these background matters, the analysis will proceed to consider how the EC conducts its relations with international institutions, with which institutions it has relations and what general conclusions can be drawn in this area.

There is a considerable debate about the exact description that can be applied to the EC's relations with the member states and to the EC as an institution. In a carefully reasoned argument, Paul Taylor concludes that the relations between the member states and the EC certainly do not exhibit the characteristics of a federal model of political relations.[3] Moreover, complaints have recently surfaced in the EC about member states placing national interests over EC obligations in employing non-tariff barriers to hinder intra-EC trade, and thus going against some of the original objectives in the founding of the EC.[4] Clearly, the evolution of an EC policy is still very much subject to the exercise of formal or informal national vetoes. This is particularly true when some members seek to develop new areas of EC activity and would certainly apply to any ideas formally to link the EC with NATO. For example, Britain has encountered the opposition of other states in its recent efforts to develop an EC response to common security problems and to produce a general form of EC foreign policy.[5]

A number of authors have attempted to tackle the issue of how to describe the EC as an international actor.[6] Alting von Geusau argues that uncertainty about the external relations of the EC can be explained by 'the transitional character of the international system', particularly the fact that the issues raised by economic interdependence cannot be tackled by national governments alone.[7] A similar point is made by Allen, who argues that the increasing occurrence of negotiations between blocs of states, as opposed to bilateral dealings, 'put pressure on the European states to organise themselves in order to act effectively within this new environment'.[8] Because of the dynamic nature of the international system and the debate within the EC and among writers on the EC about whether the EC's external links are divisible into two neat categories—economic links equalling low politics *EC external relations*, and political links equalling high politics *member state*-dominated foreign policy—it is useful to find Sjöstedt arguing that 'It is . . . possible that the capacity of being an actor is most appropriately conceived of as a variable property which the Community may possess to a greater or lesser extent'.[9] This comment is supported by Goodwin's analysis which notes that even on what might be considered obvious EC matters there are differences as to how the EC should be represented externally. He notes that the Commission takes a 'maximalist' line that it should be the EC's negotiating agent on a broad front, whereas the member states take a 'minimalist' line on the Commission's external role. The EC member states particularly feel that industrial policy is not a Commission area in negotiations.[10]

The comments above are illustrated, in the context of EC relations with international institutions, by the case of the International Energy Agency (IEA). In 1973–4, the EC found it difficult to develop an EC response to the energy crisis, which arose from the massive increase in oil prices in 1973, because of differing national needs and policies. As part of an effort to produce a coordinated Western response, the USA promoted, in the Organization for Economic Cooperation and Development (OECD), the formation of the IEA. However, the EC as a single entity was unable to join the IEA because of objections raised by France. Britain also wanted to operate separately because of her interests as an oil-producer. Thus the member states had to make individual links with the IEA and the Commission could only participate with observer status and attempt to act in a coordinating role between the EC and the IEA. Since the founding of the IEA, Britain and the FRG have played leading roles in its activities but France has kept its links at the level of observer status.[11]

By contrast to the writers on international relations, the international lawyers face less difficulties when considering relations between international institutions. In writings on international law there is a consensus that international institutions can possess either the explicit or implicit international personality necessary to enter into relations with states or other non-state entities. However, there does exist the problem of classifying international institutions by type and competence. Schwarzenberger classifies the EC as a hybrid institution in that it is a combination and variation 'of more basic forms of institutional cooperation'.[12] Specifically, he describes the EC as a regional, functional, supranational institution.[13] Bowett describes the EC more simply as a regional institution of limited competence.[14] Schermers notes that whilst the constitution of an international institution may specifically permit relations with other international institutions, as does Article 229 of the Rome Treaty, the relations between institutions can also be governed by their practice in negotiating inter-institutional agreements.[15]

The history of the EC's relations with international institutions can be traced back to the founding of the first of the constituent communities of the EC, the European Coal and Steel Community (ECSC) in 1952. As Schwarzenberger notes, 'The Parties to the ECSC Treaty envisaged distinct "international relationships" of the Coal and Steel Community with non-member states and other international institutions. They, therefore, did all they could to provide the Community with the requisite legal capacity to treat on this level.'[16] The combined Community (ECSC, EEC and EURATOM) has also had relations with international institutions since the foundation of the two later communities, the EEC and EURATOM in 1957.

EC sources provide succinct accounts of the formal bases and forms of EC relations with international institutions,[17] and there are also some useful secondary source commentaries including one by A. Maes who, in 1977, was the Chief of Division concerned with EC relations with international institutions in the EC Commission's Directorate-General for External Relations.[18] The EC has legal personality by virtue of Article 210 of the Rome Treaty and the Court of Justice confirmed (Judgment of 31 March 1971 in Case 22/20) that this meant that 'in its external relations the Community enjoys the capacity to establish contractual links with third countries over the whole field of objectives defined in Part One of the Treaty.' Moreover, in order to attain such EC objectives as the Customs Union, certain powers were given to the EC by the member states and these powers can be used for conducting external relations as well as intra-EC relations and are noted in Articles 113, 235 and 238 of the Rome Treaty. These articles also include provision (Article 235) for the EC, by unanimous decision of the Council, to develop external relations which are not explicitly provided for in the Rome Treaty. Furthermore, the Court of Justice (Opinion 1/76 of 26 April 1977) held that the Rome Treaty also contained implicit general provisions so that, 'whenever Community Law has created for the institutions of the Community powers within its internal system for the purpose of attaining a specific objective, the Community has authority to enter into the international commitments necessary for the attainment of that objective even in the absence of an express provision in that connection.'

Under Article 228 of the Rome Treaty and pursuant to the provisions of Articles 113, 235 and 238, external agreements are to be negotiated by the Commission and concluded by the Council. The procedure is slightly different for EURATOM. Under the EURATOM Treaty it is the Commission which negotiates *and* concludes such agreements, following directives given by the Council. If the issues are not strictly within the terms of the Rome Treaty, Article 116 permits common action if the Council decides so to act on a Commission proposal. In addition, Article 229 of the Rome Treaty makes the Commission responsible, for the EC, for developing relations with international institutions. Article 230 relates specifically to EC cooperation with the Council of Europe and Article 231 similarly to the OECD.

Although, as Allen notes, in 'strictly institutional terms the European Community has two distinct sets of machinery for framing its policies and responses to the outside world.'[19] The two sets of machinery are now less distinct. The first and older one, the 'Community method', covers the formal provisions of the Rome Treaty, as described above. The second, developed since 1970, is known as the 'Davignon or political cooperation procedure (EPC)',[20] which involves intergovernmental contacts between member states for foreign policy cooperation in areas outside the scope of the Rome Treaty. Moreover, by the 1973 Copenhagen 'Declaration on the European Identity', the EC resolved 'to contribute to international progress, both through their relations with third countries and by adopting common positions wherever possible in international organizations, notably the United Nations and the specialized agencies.'

An example of the workings of the formal provisions of the Rome Treaty is in the relations between the EC and GATT. Here the Council of Ministers lay down general negotiating guidelines for GATT tariff reduction rounds which are followed by the Commission in day-to-day talks. An additional Council–Commission link is provided by the Commission cooperating with the Article 113 Committee of Permanent Representatives (COREPER). A good example of the EPC procedure is provided by the EC preparations for the CSCE talks and the approach also shows the blurring of the distinction between the two sets of procedures.[21] The 'Cooperation' part of the conference was handled from the official level by an 'Ad Hoc Group' of members of Foreign Ministries and the Commission, reporting to the Political Directors (British Deputy Under Secretary level plus a Commission representative) and ultimately responsible to the Foreign Ministers sitting with the Commission President or his representative. However, the 'political, humanitarian and cultural' aspects of the CSCE were prepared by a 'Sub-Committee' at 'Ad Hoc Group' level but without the Commission and which reported via the Political Directors to the Foreign Ministers. In order not to complicate a conference of states by introducing an international organization, it was agreed that, in the actual conference, 'the representatives of the Commission should form part of the national delegation of the country exercising the Presidency of the Community, but should speak as members of the Commission when questions of Community competence arose.'[22] Furthermore, the Italian Prime Minister signed the Final Act in his dual capacity as his own country's representative and also as President-in-Office of the EC Council.[23]

As a non-state actor the EC as an international institution is confined in its relations with other international institutions to having mainly 'observer' or 'consultative' status or intersecretariat-level cooperation. 'Observer' or 'consultative' status usually means that the EC may participate but not vote, as an entity, in the work of an international institution's full sessions, committees and working groups. The EC has relations with the following groups of international institutions:

UN (Principal Organs)—General Assembly, Economic and Social Council (ECOSOC) and Secretariat.
UN (Technical Organs)—with ten technical organs including, for example, United Nations Conference on Trade and Development (UNCTAD) and United Nations Environment Programme (UNEP).
UN (Regional Commissions)—with five.
UN (Specialized Agencies)—with fourteen including the International Labour Organization (ILO), the World Bank (IBRD), the International Monetary Fund (IMF) and the International Atomic Energy Agency (IAEA).

GATT (the General Agreement on Tariffs and Trade—Regional Intergovernmental Organizations)—with twelve, mostly to do with European affairs (for example, Western European Union (WEU), Council of Europe and the Central Commission for the Navigation of the Rhine (CCR)) but including OECD, the Association of South East Asian Nations (ASEAN) and the Organization of American States (OAS).

If all parts of the UN system are counted separately, this produces a total of *circa* forty-five EC-international institution links.[24] Sjöstedt shows how EC participation in the work of international institutions grew rapidly from links with ten institutions in 1958 to links with over thirty-five by 1964 and with over forty by 1966.[25]

Sjöstedt has also carried out a detailed analysis of the various forms of EC relations with international institutions and notes that:

Expressed in general terms the interaction between the EC and other international organizations involves the performance of four different functions: (1) exchange of documentation; (2) consultations; (3) participation in the sessions of the general assemblies; and (4) participation in committees and working groups. The four functions are mentioned here in an order which roughly represents an increasing degree of active engagement in the activities of an international organization on the part of the EC.[26]

He has further found that the EC's interaction with twenty-five international institutions covers all four of the above functions and that 'It is indeed not uncommon that the EC practice is related to these organizations as if it were a full member of them, even if it formally only has the status of observer.'[27] The EC's relations with, for example, UNCTAD, IAEA, ILO, GATT and OECD would fall into this 'quasi-member' category.

Having looked at a number of the general aspects of the EC's relations with international institutions, the analysis will now consider in more detail some of the actual inter-institutional relationships. The body of literature most specifically related to the topic of this chapter deals with the EC's relations with the UN system. The literature focuses on how the EC interacts with the UN system and the degree of integration shown by EC member states in their voting behaviour at the UN. In the latter context it must be remembered that the FRG did not become a member of the UN until 1973. Moreover, it is evident that relations with the UN, like other areas of the EC's external relations, are sometimes bedevilled by arguments over whether a particular link belongs only to the competence of the member states or may be shared with the EC as a whole. Lindemann particularly notes the problem of Britain and France being permanent members of the Security Council which may mean that in certain areas their interests do not necessarily coincide with those of the majority of EC countries.[28]

De Gara has an interesting discussion of the granting of observer status to the EC at the General Assembly in 1974. The EC already participated widely in UN activities but 'the request for observer status for the EEC in the General Assembly was the culmination of several years internal debate in the Community concerning the desirability of such an action.'[29] In practice, the EC has 'dual representation' in the General Assembly as the UN list, 'Delegations to the General Assembly', shows both the Permanent Representative to the UN of the EC Council Presidency country and the Chief of the EC Commission delegation. This situation is 'unique among intergovernmental organizations enjoying observer status in the General

Assembly',[30] and gives the EC greater scope for participation as the Council Presidency country can make interactions for the EC in the capacity of a UN member state whereas the Commission representative can only play a more limited role. However, by contrast, in ECOSOC the Commission can intervene in both the committees and the plenary sessions.

De Gara analyses the cooperative efforts of the EC at the UN under the categories of policy coordination and voting cohesion.[31] Under policy coordination he notes that meetings of representatives of the EC have grown from 173 during the 30th Session to 242 at the 32nd Session and the scope of the meetings has also increased to cover twelve different areas of UN activity in the 32nd Session. A single 'voice' for the EC can be produced by the EC Presidency country submitting an agreed EC proposal, by that country speaking for the EC in a general debate or by that country making written or oral statements for the EC and between the 29th–32nd Sessions there was a 'fourfold increase in the number of such oral statements'.[32]

De Gara's analysis of EC voting cohesion in General Assembly plenary sessions will be considered together with the other studies of EC voting cohesion at the UN. He points out that 'it can be assumed that as the nine Governments move toward closer coordination and harmonization of their foreign policies, the more their votes on United Nations resolutions will be identical.'[33] This is borne out by de Gara's data which shows the proportion of identical votes rising from 45.9 per cent in 1973 to 60.6 per cent in 1977. In more detail his figures show high policy coordination on such issues as the Middle East, administration and budgetary issues, human rights; medium-level policy coordination on peace and security issues (excluding the Middle East), arms control and disarmament and economic questions; and low policy coordination on Southern African problems and the broad problems of decolonization.

Hurwitz's 1975 article covering a longer time-period (1948–73) concludes that the voting behaviour of the EC member states up to 1973 was actually not significantly affected by their becoming members of the EC.[34] However, his later article on EC voting and decolonization does have findings in line with de Gara's. Hurwitz found that whilst the EC of the Six managed to achieve a voting cohesiveness of 85.5 per cent on decolonization issues, the three new members' cohesiveness with the rest of the EC was only 79.9 per cent. This was accounted for by Ireland and Denmark being much more 'progressive' on decolonization issues.[35]

Foot's article seeks to test the comment of a Third World diplomat that 'The EEC states vote together on unimportant issues and apart on important ones'.[36] She tests this by analysing the voting record of the EC at the 1975, 1976 and 1977 plenary sessions of the General Assembly. The findings are similar to de Gara's with, for example, a voting cohesion of 62.5 per cent for 1977 (cf. de Gara's 60.6 per cent cohesion). Foot notes also that this degree of unanimity requires considerable preparatory work by the EC states. This preparatory work is the responsibility, primarily, of the EPC machinery. The preparatory work commences at the level of a group of UN specialists from the EC states' foreign ministries, which reports to the Political Committee of senior foreign ministry officials which in turn reports to the EC Foreign Ministers.

In more detail Foot's findings are similar to de Gara's and Hurwitz's.[37] For example, she found that France was usually in a minority voting group on issues of nuclear weaponry and that Denmark, Ireland, plus quite often Italy and the Netherlands, tend to vote apart from the rest of the EC on some decolonization and Third World issues and could be termed a sort of 'progressive' minority voting bloc. Foot concludes that her findings, 'do tend to reduce the credibility of the claim that the Community has become recognised as a limited political force— [and that]—the kind of issues that they disagree upon are the major ones.'[38]

At present the conclusions that may be drawn from the EC's voting record and other activities at the UN seem to be borne out by two other more general studies of the EC's external relations. The specific UN studies show at best limited evidence of developing cooperation among the states. Werner Feld has argued that the coordination of EC activities in the UN and other multilateral forums would not necessarily enhance the cohesion of the EC or produce any measurable 'pro-integration' effects.[39] Philip Taylor, using Schmitter's externalization hypotheses[40] and commenting on Feld, agrees that his own data do not prove that a greater need for coordination of external policy will lead to more internal EC integration. However, Taylor does feel that his findings are not quite as negative as Feld's and that there is some evidence of an integrative influence.[41] The Falkland Islands crisis and its effects on the EC and its member states do, however, seem more in line with Feld's views. The EC is facing difficulties in maintaining a unanimous policy of supporting Britain at the UN and Britain has not yet softened her attitude over disputed EC issues.

The EC must necessarily strive for greater cohesion in its relations and policies towards institutions concerned with economic issues because, for example, tariff harmonization is an EC matter. It is impossible to discuss the EC's external economic relations without considering the EC's relations with the developing countries. These can legitimately be considered in this chapter because, in part, EC-developing country links involve the EC in relations with other international institutions. For example, Allen has shown that the 'Euro-Arab Dialogue' has involved the EC in relations at various levels with the Arab League.[42] Gruhn has also noted that in the negotiations for the Lomé Convention the EC had to negotiate with the OAU on the African side: 'it was made very clear to the Europeans that African states, at least, were intending to negotiate "jointly" with the EEC.'[43]

Moreover, Allen's analysis raises again the crucial question of just how separate the 'Community method' machinery can be kept from the EPC machinery. In the 'Euro-Arab Dialogue' the EC tried to adopt a low key political approach but used the 'EPC' machinery presumably because it expected important political questions to be raised. Thus the EC Commission played a more subordinate role except where clear EC matters were involved; for example, the Commission chaired the joint EC–Arab League working group on agricultural and trade problems.[44] The fact that economic issues can clearly no longer be treated as low-politics issues raises, as Allen notes, a number of important problems for the EC. Firstly, the country holding the EC Presidency has an increasing burden of work when the EPC machinery is used.[45] Secondly, being used for external affairs, the EC states have 'found themselves with an institutional framework, designed essentially to resolve internal disagreements about the nature and future of the European experiment'.[46] There has also been opposition, especially from France, to developing any form of permanent EC foreign affairs secretariat.

The EC's external economic affairs institutional links can be roughly divided into two categories.[47] Firstly, there are links fairly specifically related to the traditional economic interests of the EC's states as advanced industrialized countries, especially the EC links with the OECD, IMF and GATT. As was noted in the case of EC links with the UN, the EC states may not all have equal status in relations with an international institution. France and Britain have permanent seats on the UN Security Council and in the OECD Britain, France and the FRG are members of the 'Big Five'. Secondly, there are the links with developing countries aimed at producing mutually beneficial economic relations. These take place in a number of forums, UNCTAD, GATT, CIEC and the institutions associated with negotiating and operating the Lomé Convention because, as Twitchett has pointed out, 'The Lomé Convention institutionalised the notion of partnership between the EEC states and the ACP states in several ways.'[48]

In GATT the Commission represents the EC states and negotiates on the basis of a package of common policies previously agreed by the Council of Ministers. Even here differences can arise over the precise scope of EC competence as opposed to national competence. At the 1976-7 'North–South Dialogue' in Paris (the CIEC), the EC was also represented by one single delegation comprising the President of the Council and the President of the Commission which dealt with all aspects of the wide agenda. Of particular importance, during the long-running 'Tokyo round' of GATT negotiations, were the contacts between the USA and the EC. As there had been some opposition in the USA to aspects of international trade policy, the series of talks between the US trade representative Mr Strauss and the EC Commission in the summer and autumn of 1977 were of considerable help in providing common negotiating postures which helped towards the final agreement.[49]

However, despite some success in developing a Community approach to international trade, in such forums as GATT it has been found that the EC has been much less successful in acting together on international monetary issues. Coffey has noted that, 'one of the more difficult areas of Community economic policy is the monetary one',[50] and Wellenstein has also stressed, 'that in one essential field, the monetary, the EEC has not yet reached the stage of being an interlocutor at the world level.'[51] Despite the difficulties efforts have been made to produce a common EC international monetary policy. At the April 1967 EC meeting in Munich, France suggested that, 'European Economic Community should start to present a common personality in international monetary relations',[52] and the EC did support the creation of Special Drawing Rights at the IMF meeting in Rio de Janeiro in September 1967. Moreover, the EC has sought to exercise some form of collective pressure within the IMF although this is obviously hampered by the differences between EC members over reform of the international monetary system.

One of the most interesting features of the EC's external economic relations is how some of these relations become institutionalized with quite sophisticated institutional structures. With regard to the Lomé Conventions, Twitchett has stated that both sides found a 'minimum institutional framework' to be useful.[53] This consists of a Consultative Assembly of European Parliament representatives and various ACP states' delegates, a Committee of Ambassadors and a joint Council of Ministers. There are also a number of secondary institutions like the EC–ACP Customs Cooperation Committee and the Centre for Industrial Cooperation and the Industrial Cooperation Board. Moreover, the fulfilment of a complex Convention such as Lomé depends upon a range of supporting activities which can only be carried out on a joint EC–ACP basis. For example, there is a joint ACP–EEC working party of experts to study the implementation of rules on the origin of fishery products, and the Commission's delegates and their counterparts, the Chief Authorizing Officers of the ACP states, play 'a key role in the implementation of financial and technical cooperation'.[54]

It is very evident that the EC does have internal differences on matters affecting economic relations and clearly the current recession does not produce a climate that is specially conducive to cooperative international economic relations. However, Twitchett has commented fairly that the economic importance of the EC and its institutional framework which aids cooperative action has led to 'the member states collectively emerging as one of the most effective negotiating groups within such international bodies as the GATT, OECD and UNCTAD.'[55]

The sparsest area of EC relations with other international institutions is, not surprisingly, in its relations with the Soviet Union and Eastern Europe.[56] One of the institutional problems is that the CMEA (Council for Mutual Economic Assistance) or 'COMECON' is not strictly comparable, as an institution, with the EC. Wellenstein has pointed out that the CMEA is more comparable to the OECD than to the EC and that it has 'no powers or competence comparable to the Community's "common commercial policy", which would enable it to deal with external policies in the same way as the Community does.'[57] However, after initial CMEA overtures to the EC in 1973 and various levels of talks there was an agreement in 1978 to consider areas of possible EC–CMEA cooperation. So far, with the current poor state of East–West relations in Europe, nothing has come of these ideas.

This, therefore, leaves the CSCE forum as the only 'institutionalized' forum which brings the EC into contact with the Soviet Union and the Eastern European States. The efforts of the EC states and the EC as an entity at the CSCE are quite well documented and some of the accounts are by members of national delegations or the Commission.[58] Walschap has argued that the special position of the EC, 'their experience of mutual consultations leading to consent, their common expertise and administrative know-how, brought them into a position of leadership that gained the European Community *de facto* recognition by all participants, including the East,' and further that for the EC the CSCE has been 'an unprecedented test of political harmonisation, the more interesting since it covered diplomatic "virgin" ground, a sort of "New Frontier" both in tactics and on issues. . . .'[59] Von Groll is in agreement with these views noting that a 'large proportion of the CSCE texts are based on common drafts elaborated by the Nine'.[60]

The principal problems for the EC at the CSCE have been, as already noted, the burden placed upon the Presidency country because of the EPC machinery and the fact that the Commission could not participate in all aspects of the CSCE as they were outside the scope of the EC's formal areas of interest. In addition, of course, in a conference of states the Commission could only actually participate by being part of the delegation of the Presidency country and as Wellenstein describes it this meant that the Commission representative started the Conference 'as a "Dane" and finished the conference as an "Italian" '.[61] However, the CSCE is clearly a forum beset with such inherent political difficulties that whilst the EC's experience of cooperative policy-formulation meant, as Tickell suggests, that 'it was increasingly the Nine who not only provided the motor but sat at the steering wheel', the steering wheel 'was usually but not always attached to the front wheels'.[62] For developing EC institutional links perhaps one of the more important functions of the EC's experience at the CSCE is that it produced valuable experience for the future such as in the Euro-Arab dialogue which Allen has argued has replaced the CSCE 'as one of the principal foreign policy activities at the European level'.[63]

Clearly, the EC is very active in both the scope and content of its relations with other international institutions and in 'institutionalized' inter-state forums. Therefore one can agree with Twitchett's comment that 'The future could well witness a larger role of the EEC in international organization generally as the Nine are committed to acting together on matters either directly related to the Community or coming within its authority'.[64] However, this view must be balanced by such considerations as whether the state of international relations is conducive to co-operative ventures; the possible effects on external links of internal differences between the EC states; the difficulties caused by having two forms of EC machinery for external relations, 'EPC' and 'Community', and the effects of the EC's increasing membership on the EC's ability to form common policy lines.

Notes

1. Dam, K. W., *The GATT—Law and International Economic Organization* (Chicago, Chicago University Press, 1970), pp. 335–6.
2. See, e.g., Feld, W. J., *International Relations: A Transnational Approach* (California, Alfred Publishing Co., 1979) and Frankel, J., *International Relations in a Changing World* (Oxford, Oxford University Press, 1979).
3. Taylor, P., 'The European Communities and the Obligations of Membership: Claims and Counter-Claims', *International Affairs*, 57 (1981), 236–53.
4. See the reports in *The Times*, 4 March 1982 and 6 March 1982.
5. There is a general discussion of these issues in Gregory, F. E. C., 'The European Community and Defence', *ADIU Report*, 3 (1981), 5–9.
6. See, e.g., Alting von Geusau, F. A. M. (ed.), *The External Relations of the European Community* (Farnborough, Saxon House, 1974); Cosgrove, C. A. and Twitchett, K. J. (eds), *The New International Actors* (London, Macmillan, 1970); Sjöstedt, G., *The External Role of the European Community* (Farnborough, Saxon House, 1977); Taylor, P., *When Europe Speaks with One Voice* (London, Aldwych, 1979); Twitchett, K. J. (ed.), *Europe and the World* (London, Europa, 1976); and Allen, D., 'Foreign Policy at the European Level: Beyond the Nation State?' in Wallace, W. and Paterson, W. E. (eds), *Foreign Policy-Making in Western Europe* (Farnborough, Saxon House, 1978).
7. Alting von Geusau, op. cit., pp. 126–7.
8. Allen in Wallace and Paterson, op. cit., p. 143.
9. Sjöstedt, op. cit., p. 14.
10. Goodwin, G., 'The External Relations of the European Community: Shadow and Substance', *British Journal of International Studies*, 3 (1977), 39–54.
11. EC responses to the energy crisis in this context are well covered in: Coffey, P., *The External Economic Relations of the EEC* (London, Macmillan, 1976), pp. 46–63; Ehrhardt, C. A., 'Europe and Energy Policy at Top Level', *Aussenpolitik*, 26 (1975), 3–18; Turner, L., 'The EEC—Factors of Disintegration: Politics of the Energy Crisis', *International Affairs*, 50 (1974), 404–15; Keohane, R. O., 'The International Energy Agency: State Influence and Transgovernmental Politics', *International Organization*, 32 (1978), 924–51; Walton, A. M., 'Atlantic Relations: Policy Coordination and Conflict— Atlantic Bargaining Over Energy', *International Affairs*, 52 (1976), 180–207; and Commission of the European Communities, 'The European Community and the Energy Problem' (Luxembourg, EC Office for Offical Publications, 1978).
12. Schwarzenberger, G., *A Manual of International Law*, 5th edition (London, Stevens, 1967), p. 324.
13. Ibid., p. 332 ff.
14. Bowett, D. W., *The Law of International Institutions* (London, Methuen, 1963), Chapter 6, pp. 139–82.
15. Schermers, H. G., *International Institutional Law*, Vol. 2, Chapter 12, 'External Relations' (Leiden, Sijthoff, 1972).
16. Schwarzenberger, op. cit., p. 370.
17. See Commission of the European Communities, *The European Community, International Organizations and Multilateral Agreements* (Brussels, 1980), pp. 4–8; Commission of the European Communities, *When the Community Speaks as One—The Role of the EEC in International Negotiations* (London, EC Information Office, 1978); Wellenstein, E., *25 Years of European Community External Relations* (Brussels, Office for Official Publications of the EC, 1979); and Commission of the European Communities, *European Political Cooperation (EPC)—The Evolution of Common Attitudes* (London, EC Information Office, 1980).
18. Maes, A., 'La Communauté Européenne. Les Organisations Intergouvernementales et les accords Multilateraux', *Revue du Marché Commun*, No. 210 (1977), 395–400.
19. See, particularly, Allen in Wallace and Paterson, op. cit., p. 146 ff.; Jacque, J. P., 'La participation de la Communauté Economique Européenne aux organisations internationales universelles', *Annuaire Français de Droit International* (1975), 903–23; Maes,

op. cit., pp. 395–400; Sjöstedt, op. cit., pp. 20–58 and Twitchett, K. J. (ed), op. cit., pp. 29–34.

20. Allen in Wallace and Paterson, op. cit., p. 144.
21. The details of EC–CSCE relations are taken from Tickell, C., 'Enlarged Community and Security Conference', *Aussenpolitik*, 25 (1974), 13–22.
22. Ibid., p. 18.
23. Von Groll, G., 'The Final Act of the CSCE', *Aussenpolitik*, 26 (1975), 269.
24. This information was derived from the tables in the EC publication, *The European Community, International Organizations and Multilateral Agreements*, op. cit.
25. Sjöstedt, op. cit., p. 47.
26. Ibid., p. 49.
27. Ibid., p. 50.
28. The principle sources are: Foot, R., 'The European Community's Voting Behaviour at the United Nations General Assembly', *Journal of Common Market Studies*, 17 (1979), 350–60; De Gara, J., 'The European Economic Community and the United Nations' in Andemicael, B. (ed.), *Regionalism and the United Nations* (New York, Oceana, 1979), pp. 543–84; Lindemann, B., 'Europe and the World: The Nine at the United Nations', *The World Today*, 32 (1976), 260–7; Hamer, N., 'Die Europäische Politische Zusammenarbeit bei den Vereinten Nationen', *Europa Archiv*, 15 (1975), 493–500; Hurwitz, L., 'The EEC in the United Nations: The Voting Behaviour of Eight Countries 1948–1973', *Journal of Common Market Studies*, 13 (1975), 224–43; Hurwitz, L., 'The EEC and Decolonization: The Voting Behaviour of the Nine in the UN General Assembly', *Political Studies*, 24 (1976), 435–47; Maes, A., 'The European Community and the United Nations General Assembly', *Journal of European Integration*, 3 (1979), 73–83; and for general background see Twitchett, K. J. (ed.), op. cit., pp. 29–34.
29. De Gara, op. cit., p. 553.
30. Ibid., p. 555.
31. Ibid., pp. 567–75.
32. Ibid., p. 570.
33. Ibid.
34. Hurwitz, *Journal of Common Market Studies*, op. cit., p. 238.
35. Hurwitz, *Political Studies*, op. cit., pp. 446–7.
36. Foot, op. cit., p. 351.
37. Ibid., pp. 356–7.
38. Ibid., pp. 359–60.
39. Feld, W. J., *The European Community in World Affairs* (New York, Alfred Publishing Co., 1976). ·
40. Schmitter, P. G., 'Three Neo-Functional Hypotheses about International Integration', *International Organization*, 23 (1969), 161–6.
41. Taylor, op. cit., p. 204, and see also pp. 87 ff.
42. Allen, D., 'The Euro-Arab Dialogue', *Journal of Common Market Studies*, 16 (1978), 323–42.
43. Gruhn, I. V., 'The Lomé Convention: Inching towards Interdependence', *International Organization*, 30 (1976), 252.
44. Allen, *Journal of Common Market Studies*, op. cit., pp. 337–9.
45. Ibid., p. 332 and cf. Tickell, op. cit., p. 20.
46. Allen, *Journal of Common Market Studies*, op. cit., p. 339.
47. The following are useful sources for this topic: Coffey, P., *The External Economic Relations of the EEC* (London, Macmillan, 1976); Everts, Ph. P., *The European Community in the World* (Rotterdam, Rotterdam University Press, 1972); Tomsa, B., 'La CEE et le Tokyo-Round', *Studia Diplomatica*, 31 (1978), 281–304; Twitchett, C. C., 'The European Community and Development Cooperation', *International Relations*, 6 (1978), 257–71; Twitchett, K. J. (ed.), *Europe and the World* (London, Europa, 1976); and Focke, K., 'From Lomé I towards Lomé II' (Texts of the report and resolution adopted on 26 September 1980 by the ACP–EEC Consultative Assembly) (Luxembourg, Office for Official Publications of the EC, 1980).
48. Twitchett, C. C., op. cit., p. 265.
49. See, in particular, Tomsa, op. cit.
50. Coffey, op. cit., p. xii.
51. Wellenstein, op. cit., p. 24.
52. Coffey, op. cit., pp. 30–4.
53. Twitchett, C. C., op. cit., p. 265.

54. Focke, op. cit., pp. 61, 65.
55. Twitchett, K. J., op. cit., p. 33.
56. For a general study, see John, I. (ed.), *EEC Policy towards Eastern Europe* (Farnborough, Saxon House, 1975).
57. Wellenstein, op. cit., p. 27.
58. See, in particular, Tickell, op. cit. and Tickell, C., 'The Enlarged Community and the European Security Conference' in John, I. (ed.), op. cit., pp. 115–24; Graf Schwerin, O., 'Die Solidarität der EG-Staaten in der KSZE', *Europa Archiv*, 15 (1975), 483–92; Von Groll, op. cit. and Walschap, H., 'The Great European Jamboree', *Res Publica*, 18 (1976), 33–57.
59. Walschap, op. cit., p. 41.
60. Von Groll, op. cit., p. 269.
61. Wellenstein, op. cit., p. 19.
62. Tickell, *Aussenpolitik*, op. cit., p. 21.
63. Allen, *Journal of Common Market Studies*, op. cit., p. 324.
64. Twitchett, K. J. (ed.), op. cit., p. 33.

List of Contributors

ROBERT BOARDMAN is a Professor of Political Science and Director of the Centre for Foreign Policy Studies at Dalhousie University, Nova Scotia, Canada. He was formerly a Lecturer in Politics at the University of Leicester. His most recent books are *International Organization and the Conservation of Nature* (1981) and *Nuclear Exports and World Politics: Policy and Regime* (1983, edited with J. F. Keeley).

ALAN BUTT PHILIP is a Lecturer in the Centre for European Industrial Studies at the University of Bath. He is a Special Adviser to the House of Lords Select Committee on the European Communities. He is the author of *The Welsh Question* (1975) and co-author of *Capital Markets and Industrial Investment in Germany and France: Lessons for the United Kingdom* (1980).

DOREEN COLLINS is a specialist on the social policy of the EC and a Senior Lecturer in the Department of Social Policy and Administration at the University of Leeds. She has acted as Special Adviser on the European Social Fund to the House of Lords Select Committee on the European Communities. She has written extensively on EC social policy and is currently editing, and contributing to, a book on comparative social policies in selected countries.

SCOTT DAVIDSON is a Lecturer in the Faculty of Law at the University of Hull. He has written previously in the field of Public International Law.

REINHARD DRIFTE is a Research Assistant in the Graduate Institute of International Studies at the University of Geneva. He is the author of *Security as a Factor of Japanese Foreign Policy during the American Occupation, 1945–52* (1981). He is currently making a study of Japanese Peace Politics since 1945.

JOHN FITZMAURICE works in Brussels for the Commission of the European Communities. He is the author of *The Party Groups in the European Parliament* (1975), *The European Parliament* (1978) and *Politics in Denmark* (1981); and co-author of *The European Parliament: A Guide to Direct Elections* (1979, with R. Jackson). He has contributed numerous articles on Danish and European politics to scholarly journals. He is currently preparing *Politics in Belgium* for publication in 1983.

ANNA FLEISCH is a research student in the Faculty of Law at the University of Hull.

DAVID FREESTONE is a Lecturer in the Faculty of Law at the University of Hull. He has contributed to a number of legal journals including *Modern Law Review* and *Criminal Law Review*. He has written also on the legal aspects of terrorism in two recent books: 'Legal Responses to Terrorism' in Lodge, J. (ed.), *Terrorism: A Challenge to the State* (1981) and (with Lodge, J.) 'The European Community and Terrorism: Political and Legal Aspects' in Alexander, Y. and Myers, K. (eds), *Terrorism in Europe* (1982).

STEPHEN GEORGE is a Lecturer in the Department of Political Theory and Institutions at the University of Sheffield. He has written several articles on international relations and the EC which have been published in various academic journals. He is preparing a book on *Politics and Policy in the European Community*.

ROY H. GINSBERG is a Lecturer in Political Science at Goucher College, Baltimore, Maryland. He was previously a Visiting Lecturer in Political Science at the College of Notre Dame of Maryland. He was recently awarded a research grant by the Commission of the European Communities to prepare a major study on EC foreign relations.

FRANK GREGORY is a Lecturer in Politics at the University of Southampton. He has written a number of articles and chapters on arms control, defence issues and police studies, and is preparing a basic textbook on the impact of EC membership on the British system of government.

STANLEY HENIG is Professor of European Politics and Head of the School of Social Studies at Preston Polytechnic. He has held lecturing posts at Lancaster and Warwick Universities and at the Civil Service College, London. He was formerly editor of the *Journal of Common Market Studies*. He is the author of *External Relations of the European Community* (1971) and *Power and Decision in Europe* (1980); and editor of *Political Parties in the European Community* (1979).

DAN HIESTER is a Lecturer in Interdisciplinary Studies at the University of Kent. He is a political scientist specializing in international relations, with research interests in international relations theory, European integration and the external relations of the EC, nuclear strategy, and the problems of nuclear proliferation.

T. HITIRIS is a Senior Lecturer in the Department of Economics and Related Studies at the University of York. He was formerly an Economist at the Ministry of Economic Coordination in Athens.

JULIET LODGE is a Lecturer in Politics at the University of Hull. She was formerly a Lecturer in Political Studies at the University of Auckland, New Zealand, Visiting Fellow in the Centre for International Studies at The London School of Economics and Political Science and a Leverhulme Research Fellow. She is the author of *The European Policy of the SPD* (1976) and *The European Community and New Zealand* (1982); co-author of *The New Zealand General Election of 1975* (1976), *The European Parliament and the European Community* (1978) and *Direct Elections to the European Parliament: A Community Perspective* (1982); and editor of *Terrorism: A Challenge to the State* (1981) and *The European Community: Bibliographical Excursions* (1983). She is the author of numerous articles on EC politics and institutions published in journals of international affairs and politics in Europe, North America and Australasia. She is currently preparing a book for publication by The Macmillan Press: *Direct Elections to the European Parliament 1984*.

JOHN MARSH is Professor of Agricultural Economics at the University of Aberdeen and Head of the Economics Division of the North of Scotland College of Agriculture. He was formerly Reader in Economics at the University of Reading. His publications include *Agricultural Policy and the Common Market* (1971, with C. Ritson), *European Agriculture in an Uncertain World* (1975), *United Kingdom Agricultural Policy within the European Community* (1977) and *Agriculture and the European Community* (1980, with P. J. Swanney).

J. D. B. MILLER is Professor of International Relations in the Research School of Pacific Studies at the Australian National University, Canberra. He is the author of numerous books, including *Britain and the Old Dominions* (1966), *The EEC and Australia* (1976) and *The World of States* (1981).

T. V. SATHYAMURTHY is a Lecturer in Politics at the University of York. He is also Visiting Fellow at The Christian Michelsen Institute, Bergen, Norway. His most recent book is *Sociology of Nationalism: Contemporary Perspectives* (1983).

FREIDA STACK has been a Teaching Fellow in the Department of Politics at the University of Southampton since 1978. She has carried out research for the Royal Institute of Public Administration and the Treasury.

CHRISTOPHER STEVENS is a member of the Overseas Development Institute, London and a Research Fellow in the Institute of Development Studies at the University of Sussex. He is currently editor of *EEC and the Third World* and author of *The Soviet Union and Black Africa* and numerous articles.

PAMELA J. SWANNEY is an Agricultural Economist with the North of Scotland College of Agriculture specializing in agricultural policy and marketing. She is the author of *Pricing Policies and Conduct Patterns: Performance of Price Formation of Livestock and Meat Marketing in Selected OECD Member Countries* (1980, with G. van Dijk) and *Agriculture and the European Community* (1980, with J. S. Marsh).

ATHENA ZERVOYIANNI has been researching in the field of international monetary economics in the Department of Economics and Related Studies at the University of York since 1981. She was formerly a Research Assistant in the Graduate School of Economics at the University of Athens, Greece.

Index